Controversies in Constitutional Law

Collections of Documents and Articles on Major Questions of American Law

General Editor

Paul Finkelman
University of Tulsa School of Law

Series Content

Volume 1
THE HISTORY OF MENTAL ILLNESS IN CRIMINAL CASES:
The English Tradition

Volume 2
THE INSANITY DEFENSE:
The American Developments

Volume 3
COMPETENCY TO BE TRIED, IMPRISONED, AND EXECUTED

The Role of Mental Illness in Criminal Trials

Volume 3

Competency to Be Tried, Imprisoned, and Executed

Edited with introductions by

Jane Campbell Moriarty
University of Akron School of Law

Routledge
Taylor & Francis Group
New York London

Published in 2001 by

Routledge
711 Third Avenue
New York, NY 10017

Published in Great Britain by
Routledge
2 Park Square, Milton Park
Abingdon, Oxon, OX14 4RN

Routledge is an imprint of the Taylor & Francis Group, an informa business

Library of Congress Cataloging-in-Publication Data

The role of mental illness in criminal trials / edited with introductions by Jane Campbell Moriarty.
p. cm. -- (Controversies in constitutional law)
Contents: v. 1. The history of mental illness in criminal cases -- v. 2. The insanity defense -- v. 3. Competency to be tried, imprisoned, and executed.
Includes bibliographical references.
ISBN 0-8153-3573-3 (set : alk. paper)
1. Insanity--Jurisprudence--United States. 2. Criminal liability--United States. 3. Competency to stand trial--United States. 4. Forensic psychiatry--United States. I. Moriarty, Jane Campbell. II. Series.

KF9242 .R65 2001
345.73'04--dc21

2001038717

ISBN 0-8153-3573-3 (set)
ISBN 0-8153-4062-1 (v.1)
ISBN 0-8153-4063-X (v.2)
ISBN 0-8153-4064-8 (v.3)

Contents

Series Introduction

This ongoing series, *Controversies in Constitutional Law*, provides teachers, scholars, and students convenient access to the debates and scholarly literature surrounding major questions of constitutional law. Each set of books— from two to four volumes— consists of four elements: an extended introduction to the issue by the editor; reprints of the significant cases and briefs on the subject; congressional testimony, and other primary documents on the issue; and a selection of the best scholarly articles on the subject. By conveniently gathering all this material in one place, each set of volumes allows users to become familiar quite quickly with the arguments and positions surrounding a particular constitutional controversy.

Scholars and students interested in constitutional law and public policy are often overwhelmed by the sheer amount of material published on controversial subjects. The topics in *Controversies in Constitutional Law* are timely, politically significant, and intellectually compelling. They are the issues that bring the legal academy, courts, politicians, and general public together— although not always in harmony.

Many scholars are barely able to keep up with the material in their own fields. Yet there is a need to learn about issues beyond our own specialties. A new course may require an introduction to a problem; our own research may lead us to a new issue. The series *Controversies in Constitutional Law* is designed to meet these needs, enabling scholars and teachers to come up to speed quickly on the topics in each volume.

This series also serves students at all levels of higher education. Students often encounter controversial topics without the background in how the problem developed. These volumes provide such a background. The important cases are reprinted in full; the introductions provide students with a map of the issues; the briefs, congressional testimony, and scholarly articles give convenient access to the arguments and debates.

The volumes bring together in one place a wide variety of sources and materials that are unlikely to be found in any one library. The primary documents include cases, briefs, testimony from legislative committee hearings, and, on occasion, executive branch publications. Few law libraries, university libraries, or public libraries will have all these materials. The secondary literature comes from the scholarly literature of law, history, political science, economics, criminology, and other relevant fields. Some of the articles also may be from serious nonacademic journals.

The related government publications, briefs, and congressional testimony are particularly important. Too often scholars overlook them. There is a tendency to focus on court opinions— what the Supreme Court said. Obviously this is important for understanding doctrine, but briefs, especially amicus briefs, are also an important source of information about the larger constitutional controversy the case represents. The politics of a case are often more apparent in these briefs than in either the oral arguments or the Court's opinion. Similarly, congressional hearings illustrate the social, philosophical, and political dimensions of these questions.

The goal of limiting each collection— two to four focused volumes— and the occasional inability to secure a reasonable copyright permission fee for some important articles often forces hard and judicious choices. Important articles that are not reprinted here are listed in the further reading sections at the end of the introductions.

The ongoing series *Controversies in Constitutional Law* provides in one single place comprehensive introductions to topics that will satisfy most lawyers, scholars, and students. By combining cases, briefs, legislative debates, and testimony from committee hearings with secondary articles, it is hoped to facilitate access to the issue presented in each set of volumes.

Paul Finkelman

General Introduction

Mental illness has always had a substantial role in criminal cases as an excuse or mitigation of a criminal act or as a claim that a defendant is not competent to be tried, to waive rights, or to be executed. By far the most jurisprudentially thorny discussions have involved the insanity defense, which provides a legal excuse for an admitted criminal act. Diminished capacity, which does not generally provide a complete excuse for a criminal act but often mitigates the degree of guilt, has also caused consternation for courts and legal scholars.[1]

During the twentieth century the U.S. Supreme Court developed a body of law governing the question of competence. Without much disagreement, the Court consistently determined that defendants who are not competent should not be tried or executed. The more contentious debates have concerned the appropriateness of forcibly medicating defendants to stand trial[2] or to be executed.[3]

Both the judiciary and the citizenry have debated the appropriateness of putting mentally retarded defendants on trial and punishing them for their acts. Although the Supreme Court in 1989 decided that mentally retarded individuals were not categorically exempt from the death penalty,[4] it revisited this issue in 2001.[5]

---

[1] Diminished capacity is not addressed significantly in these three volumes. For a comprehensive discussion of diminished capacity, *see* Stephen J. Morse, *Undiminished Confusion in Diminished Capacity*, 75 J. Crim. L. 1 (1984); Joshua Dressler, *Reaffirming the Moral Legitimacy of the Doctrine of Diminished Capacity: A Brief Reply to Professor Morse*,75 J. Crim. L. 953 (1984); and Peter Arenella, *The Diminished Capacity and Diminished Responsibility Defenses: Two Children of a Doomed Marriage*, 77 Colum. L. Rev. 827, 828 (1977). For a more general overview, *see* 1 JANE CAMPBELL MORIARTY, PSYCHOLOGICAL AND SCIENTIFIC EVIDENCE IN CRIMINAL TRIALS, §3:16–3:23 (1996, 2000 supp.).

[2] *See* Riggins v. Nevada, 504 U.S. 127 (1992) (holding that forcible medication of a defendant to render him competent to stand trial violated his Sixth and Fourteenth Amendment rights unless the inmate posed a danger to himself or others and unless such treatment was medically necessary).

[3] *See* Singleton v. State, 437 S.E.2d 53 (S.C. 1993) (holding it unconstitutional forcibly to medicate a defendant for the purpose of executing him); and Louisiana v. Perry, 610 So.2d 746 (La. 1992) (same).

[4] Penry v. Lynaugh, 492 U.S. 302, 340 (1989) (holding "we cannot conclude today that the Eighth Amendment precludes the execution of any mentally retarded person of Penry's ability convicted of a capital offense simply by virtue of his or her mental retardation alone"). Penry had an IQ of between 50 and 55 (mild to moderate retardation), a mental age of a six-and-a-half-year-old child, and the social maturity of a nine- or ten-year-old. The *Penry* case was remanded to the lower court on the issue of appropriate jury instructions

The Anglo-American legal relationship to the intersection of mental illness and criminal behavior has always been difficult and fractious, vacillating between a desire to excuse the insane and a desire to prevent a defendant "from getting away with murder." Perhaps we do not fully believe in mental illness; it is an amorphous, unknowable illness, revealed only in the unusual behavior of its victims. We have difficulty finding objective tests to confirm its existence, unlike with cancer and tuberculosis. It is mysterious in its afflictions, causing inexplicable behaviors and often irrational fears. It frightens and intrigues us, and its historical association with evil and demons has led us to mythologize it. Although we may claim a sophisticated view of the universe, we are still beset by historically laden archetypal fears on the subject of mental illness.

Despite plethoric evidence to the contrary, there is a widespread belief that defendants often can and do feign mental illness and that scores of defendants are escaping justice by relying on the insanity defense.[6] Although there is greater acceptance of the role genetics and chemistry play in mental illness, due possibly to the phenomenal success of medical treatment of anxiety, depression, and bipolar disorder at the turn of the twenty-first century, juries and judges frequently remain skeptical of insanity defenses and claims of incompetency.

This three-volume series collects the critical documents that discuss the role of mental illness in criminal cases. Volume 1 is devoted to the English origins of the insanity defense, which animates much of U.S. law on the subject. Starting with the trial of Edward Arnold and including contemporary discussions of early English cases, Volume 1 explores the development of the insanity defense in early English common law, culminating with the famous case of Daniel McNaughton.

Volume 2 discusses the development of the insanity defense in the United States, addressing its historical origins, the development of more liberal tests in the mid-twentieth century, and the rapid regression to a restrictive standard following the trial of John Hinckley, who attempted to assassinate President Ronald Reagan in 1981. Volume 2 also contains material from some of the best contemporary writers about the insanity defense, including excerpts from such highly regarded scholars as Michael J. Perlin and Christopher Slobogin.

Volume 3 addresses U.S. Supreme Court jurisprudence on the issues of competency to be tried, to waive rights, and to be executed. In the last four decades of the twentieth century, Supreme Court decisions produced a substantial body of law on the meaning of incompetence as well as standards governing the appropriate due process considerations to assure that incompetent individuals are neither tried nor executed. Included in this volume is an article by Bruce A. Arrigo and Christopher R. Williams discussing the refusal of treatment for incompetent prisoners awaiting execution. Finally addressed are the issues before the U.S. Supreme Court at the dawn of the twenty-first century.

---

concerning sentencing. In 2000 the U.S. Supreme Court again granted certiorari in this case after defendant was again sentenced to death. *See* Penry v. Johnson, 121 S.Ct. 563 (2000).

[5] *See* McCarver v. North Carolina, 121 S.Ct. 1401 (2001) (granting defendant's petition for certiorari on the issue of the execution of a mentally retarded person).

[6] *See generally*, Michael L. Perlin, *Unpacking the Myths: The Symbolism Mythology of Insanity Defense Jurisprudence*, 40 Case W. Res. L. Rev. 599 (1990).

Volume Introduction

For generations both English and American law has recognized that a civilized justice system cannot permit those who are mentally incompetent to be tried, convicted, or executed for criminal acts.[1] In *Ford* v. *Wainwright,*[2] the U.S. Supreme Court, citing early English common law, began with the proposition that "[t]he bar against executing a prisoner who has lost his sanity bears impressive historical credentials; the practice consistently has been branded 'savage and inhuman.'"[3]

Despite the agreement that the mentally incompetent should not be tried, convicted, or executed, there has been a wealth of Supreme Court decisions over the last half century refining the contours of this basic prohibition. Three Supreme Court cases on the issue of competence to stand trial form the basis for much of the Court's later jurisprudence: *Dusky* v. *United States,*[4] *Pate* v. *Robinson,*[5] and *Drope* v. *Missouri.*[6]

In *Dusky* the Supreme Court resolved the issue of the proper standard to determine competency. The Court articulated the test as "whether [the defendant] has sufficient present ability to consult with his lawyer in a reasonable degree of rational understanding—and whether he has a rational as well as factual understanding of the proceedings against him."[7]

Six years later the Court decided *Pate* v. *Robinson,* in which it held that where the evidence raises a "bona fide doubt" as to the defendant's competence to stand trial, the trial judge should conduct a hearing on the matter.[8] In *Pate* the Supreme Court ruled that the "court's failure to make such inquiry thus deprived Robinson of his constitutional right to a fair trial."[9]

---

[1] *See* Pate v. Robinson, 383 U.S. 375, 378 (1966), holding that "the conviction of an accused person while he is legally incompetent violates due process," citing Bishop v. United States, 350 U.S. 961 (1956). *See also* Ford v. Wainwright, 477 U.S. 399, 406–7 (1986), quoting BLACKSTONE, COMMENTARIES, 24–25, stating, "[I]f a man in his sound memory commits a capital offence, and before arraignment for it, he becomes mad, he ought not to be arraigned for it: because he is not able to plead to it with that advice and caution that he ought. And if, after he has pleaded, the prisoner becomes mad, he shall not be tried: for how can he make his defence?"

[2] Ford v. Wainwright, 477 U.S. 399 (1986).

[3] Id. at 406, citing BLACKSTONE, COMMENTARIES, 24–25.

[4] Dusky v. United States, 362 U.S. 402 (1960) (per curiam); reprinted herein.

[5] Pate v. Robinson, 383 U.S. 375 (1966).

[6] Drope v. Missouri, 420 U.S. 162 (1975).

[7] Dusky v. United States, 362 U.S. at 402.

[8] Pate v. Robinson, 383 U.S. at 842.

[9] Id. at 842.

In *Drope* v. *Missouri* the Court again affirmed that the failure of the trial court to observe procedures to ensure that the defendant is not tried or convicted while incompetent deprives him of the due process right to a fair trial.[10] The Supreme Court held that the defendant's constitutional rights to a fair trial were violated when the trial judge failed to make sufficient inquiry into the defendant's competence to stand trial. The trial court failed to give sufficient weight to witnesses' testimony about the defendant's irrational behavior and to the fact that the defendant had shot himself in the stomach during the trial. The Court stated that "evidence of a defendant's irrational behavior, his demeanor at trial, and any prior medical opinion on competence to stand trial are all relevant in determining whether further inquiry is required, but any one of these factors standing alone may, in some circumstances, be sufficient."[11]

Since the enactment of the Insanity Defense Reform Act in the mid-1980s, the U.S. Supreme Court has decided a number of controversial cases involving a defendant's competency. The issues addressed include whether it is constitutionally permissible to execute an insane defendant;[12] whether the Eighth Amendment categorically prohibits the execution of a mentally retarded defendant;[13] and whether a defendant or convict may be forced to take antipsychotic medication.[14]

In another case the Supreme Court considered what the appropriate burden of proof should be in proving competency and whether the defendant may constitutionally bear the burden of proving his lack of competence.[15] The Supreme Court also addressed whether there was a different standard of competence for a defendant to stand trial as there was for competence to waive rights.[16]

In *Ford* v. *Wainwright*,[17] the Supreme Court held that the execution of an insane defendant violates the Eight Amendment prohibition against cruel and unusual punishment. Concluding that historical commentary from early English common law supported this view, as did every state's law, the Court observed:

> No state in the Union permits the execution of the insane. It is clear that the ancient and humane limitation upon the State's ability to execute its sentences has as firm a hold upon the jurisprudence of today as it had centuries ago. The various reasons put forth in support of the common-law restriction have no less logical, moral, and practical force than they did when first voiced. For today, no less than before, we may seriously question the retributive value of executing a person who has no comprehension of why he has been singled out and stripped of his fundamental right to life.[18]

---

[10] Drope v. Missouri, 420 U.S. 162, 172 (1975).
[11] Id. at 180.
[12] Ford v. Wainwright, 477 U.S. 399 (1986).
[13] Penry v. Lynaugh, 492 U.S. 302 (1989).
[14] Riggins v. Nevada, 504 U.S. 127 (1992), and Washington v. Harper, 494 U.S. 210 (1990).
[15] Medina v. California, 505 U.S. 437 (1992), and Cooper v. Oklahoma.
[16] Godinez v. Moran, 509 U.S. 389 (1993).
[17] Ford v. Wainwright, 477 U.S. 399 (1986).
[18] Id. at 409.

Ford v. *Wainwright,* however, was a plurality decision in which the justices did not agree on what constituted insanity or what were the proper procedures necessary to making such a determination. Thus the procedures for a "*Ford* hearing" currently differ among jurisdictions, although the state procedure must provide, at a minimum, "basic fairness" under the Due Process Clause.[19]

Generally, there are two approaches to determining whether an individual is competent for purposes of execution. Many courts look to Justice Lewis Franklin Powell's concurring opinion in *Ford* as defining competency for purposes of execution: "[T]he Eighth Amendment forbids the execution only of those who are unaware of the punishment they are about to suffer and why they are to suffer it."[20] This test is known as the cognitive test.

The other approach is broader, combining the cognitive test with the "able to assist" test. This latter test considers both the cognitive abilities of the defendant and whether he is able to assist his counsel in the proceeding.[21]

In 1995 one court approved of the American Bar Association Standard of Competency to Be Executed, which provides:

> A. Convicts who have been sentenced to death should not be executed if they are currently mentally incompetent. If it is determined that the condemned convict is currently mentally incompetent, execution should be stayed.
>
> B. A convict is incompetent, to be executed if, as a result of mental illness or mental retardation, the convict cannot understand the nature of the pending proceeding, what he or she was tried for, the reason for the punishment or the nature of the punishment. A convict is also incompetent if, as a result of mental illness or retardation, the convict lacks sufficient capacity to recognize or

---

[19] Ford v. Wainwright, 477 U.S. 399, 424 (Powell, J., concurring).

[20] Id. at 422. Some courts and state legislatures have adopted this rule, which is a narrower and more limited grounds for determining competence to be executed. *See,* e.g., Coe v. Bell, 209 F.3d 815 (6th Cir. 2000); In re Heidnick, 720 A.2d 1016, 1017–18 (Pa. 1998); Ex parte Jordan, 758 S.W.2d 250, 254 n. 7 (Tex. Crim. App. 1988); Garrett v. Collins, 951 F.2d 57, 59 (5th Cir.) (per curiam), *cert. denied,* 502 U.S. 1083 (1992); Rector v. Clark, 923 F.3d 570 (8th Cir. 1991); and Van Tran v. State, 6 S.W.3d 257, 266 (Tenn. 1999), *cert. denied,* 120 S.Ct. 1728 (2000). *See also* §Ariz. Rev. Stat. Ann. §13-4021(B) (West Supp. 1998); Fla. R. Crim. P. 3.811(b) (West Supp. 1999); Ga. Code Ann. § 17-10-60 (1997); Ky. Rev. Stat. Ann. § 431.213 (Michie Supp. 1998); Mo. Rev. Stat. § 552.060(1) (Supp. 1999); N.Y. Correct. Law § 656(a) (McKinney Supp. 1999); Tex. Crim. P. Code Ann. art. 46.04(h) (West Supp. 1999); and Wyo. Stat. § 7-13-901(a)(v) (Michie 1999).

[21] *See* State v. Harris, 789 P.2d 60, 66 (Wash. 1990) (en banc); and Singleton v. State, 437 S.E.2d 53 (S.C. 1993). *See also* Miss. Code Ann. § 99-19-57(2)(b) (1994).

> understand any fact which may exist which would make the punishment unjust or unlawful, or lacks the ability to convey such information to counsel or the court. (Standard 7.5–6, American Bar Association Criminal Justice Mental Health Standards)[22]

Although a defendant found insane cannot be executed without violating the Eighth Amendment, the Court did not decide until 1989 whether the Eighth Amendment prohibits the execution of a mentally retarded defendant. This issue was decided in *Penry* v. *Lynaugh*.[23]

In the *Penry* case the U.S. Supreme Court agreed that the "common law prohibition against punishing 'idiots' for their crimes suggests that it may indeed be 'cruel and unusual' punishment to execute persons who are profoundly or severely retarded and wholly lacking the capacity to appreciate the wrongfulness of their actions."[24] Writing for the majority, Justice Sandra Day O'Connor continued, claiming that "[b]ecause of the protections afforded by the insanity defense today, such a person is not likely to be convicted or face the probability of punishment." Nevertheless, the Court declined to impose a ban on the execution of all mentally retarded convicts sentenced to death, reasoning that "[i]n light of the diverse capacities and life experiences of mentally retarded persons, it cannot be said on the record before us today that all mentally retarded people, by definition, can never act with the level of culpability associated with the death penalty."[25] Thus the Court held, "We cannot conclude today that the Eighth Amendment precludes the execution of any mentally retarded person of Penry's ability convicted of a capital offense simply by virtue of his or her mental retardation alone."[26]

In 2001 the U.S. Supreme Court agreed to revisit the issue of executing mentally retarded defendants in *McCarver* v. *North Carolina*.[27]

In 1990 the U.S. Supreme Court issued the first of two major decisions governing the forcible medication of defendants in the criminal justice system. In *Washington* v. *Harper*,[28] Walter Harper, after conviction and while an inmate, objected to the administration of antipsychotic medication for treatment of his mental illness. The Court agreed that Harper possessed "a significant liberty

---

[22] *See* Weeks v. Jones, 52 F.3d 1559, 1562 (11th Cir.), *cert. denied*, 513 U.S. 1104 (1995). But *see* Rector v. Bryant, 923 F.2d 570 (8th Cir.), *cert. denied*, 501 U.S. 1239 (1991), noting that though the ABA standard is "interesting," it is not required.

[23] Penry v. Lynaugh, 492 U.S. 302 (1989).

[24] Id. at 333.

[25] Id. at 338–39.

[26] Id. at 340. The *Penry* case was remanded to the lower court on the issue of appropriate jury instructions concerning sentencing. In 2000 the U.S. Supreme Court again granted certiorari in this case after the defendant was again sentenced to death. *See* Penry v. Johnson, 121 S.Ct. 563 (2000).

[27] McCarver v. North Carolina, 121 S.Ct. 1401 (2001).

[28] Washington v. Harper, 494 U.S. 210 (1990).

interest in avoiding the unwanted administration of antipsychotic drugs under the Due Process Clause of the Fourteenth Amendment."[29]

The Court decided that this liberty interest was not without limitation and had to be defined in the context of confinement. It stated:

> The Policy under review requires the State to establish, by a medical finding, that a mental disorder exists which is likely to cause harm if not treated. Moreover, the fact that the medication must first be prescribed by a psychiatrist, and then approved by a reviewing psychiatrist, ensures that the treatment in question will be ordered only if it is in the prisoner's medical interests, given the legitimate needs of his institutional confinement. These standards, which recognize both the prisoner's medical interests and the State's interests, meet the demands of the Due Process Clause.[30]

The Supreme Court held that "given the requirements of the prison environment, the Due Process Clause permits the State to treat a prison inmate who has a serious mental illness with antipsychotic drugs against his will if he is dangerous to himself or others *and* the treatment is in the inmate's best medical interest."[31]

Two years after *Washington* v. *Harper* the Supreme Court decided *Riggins* v. *Nevada,* holding that on the facts of that case, the forced administration of antipsychotic medication violated the defendant's Sixth and Fourteenth Amendment rights.[32] In *Riggins* the defendant had argued unsuccessfully to the trial court that forcibly medicating him interfered with his right to show jurors his true mental state. The Supreme Court agreed and, echoing its holding in *Washington* v. *Harper,* stated that the "forcible injection of medication into a nonconsenting person's body...represents a substantial interference with that person's liberty."[33] Moreover, the Court noted, the defendant in *Riggins* was only on trial and had not yet been convicted when his request was denied. The Court reasoned that under *Harper,* "forcing antipsychotic drugs on a convicted prisoner is impermissible absent a finding of overriding justification and a determination of medical appropriateness. The Fourteenth Amendment affords at least as much protection to persons the State detains for trial."[34] Again, however, the Supreme Court cabined this right by noting that due process would have been satisfied "if the prosecution had demonstrated, and the District Court had found, that treatment with antipsychotic medication was medically appropriate and, considering less intrusive alternatives, essential for the sake of Riggins' own safety or the safety of others."[35]

Although the U.S. Supreme Court has yet to answer the question directly, two state supreme courts have addressed the issue directly, holding under their

---

[29] Id. at 221.
[30] Id. at 223.
[31] Id. at 227 (emphasis supplied).
[32] Riggins v. Nevada, 504 U.S. 127 (1992).
[33] Id. at 134.
[34] Id. at 135.
[35] Id.

state constitutions that the state could not forcibly medicate an individual to render him competent for execution.[36]

In the last several years many have recognized that mentally impaired defendants may not be competent to waive certain constitutional rights, such as the right to remain silent, the right to waive a trial, and the right to forgo continuing appeals in death-penalty cases. In 1993 the U.S. Supreme Court addressed the issue of what the appropriate standard of competency should be for individuals who seek to waive such rights.

Justice Clarence Thomas wrote for the Court in *Godinez* v. *Moran*,[37] holding that the standard for competency to waive rights should be the same standard as competency to be tried. The Court stated:

> Requiring that a criminal defendant be competent has a modest aim: It seeks to ensure that he has the capacity to understand the proceedings and to assist counsel. While psychiatrists and scholars may find it useful to classify the various kinds and degrees of competence, and while States are free to adopt competency standards that are more elaborate than the Dusky formulation, the Due Process Clause does not impose these additional requirements.[38]

Justice Harry Blackmun, joined by Justice John Paul Stevens, dissented, troubled by the majority's blithe acceptance that a defendant minimally able to assist his attorney in preparing the case was equally qualified to proceed alone: "[T]he majority cannot isolate the term 'competent' and apply it in a vacuum, divorced from its specific context. A person who is 'competent' to play basketball is not thereby 'competent' to play the violin. The majority's monolithic approach to competency is true to neither life nor the law. Competency for one purpose does not necessarily translate to competency for another purpose."[39]

In 1996, in *Cooper* v. *Oklahoma,* the Supreme Court addressed the question of the proper burden of proof to establish a lack of competence to be tried.[40] In 1992, in *Medina* v. *California,* the Court had upheld a California statute that required the defendant to prove his competence by a preponderance of the evidence.[41] By relying in part on early English and American law, the *Cooper* Court decided that the heightened standard of proof "offends a principle of justice that is deeply 'rooted in the traditions and conscience of our people.'"[42] Moreover, it reasoned that the clear and convincing standard "imposes a significant risk on an erroneous determination

---

[36] *See* Louisiana v. Perry, 610 So.2d 746 (La. 1992), reprinted herein, and Singleton v. State, 437 S.E.2d 53 (S.C. 1993). For an interesting discussion of forcible medication of prisoners awaiting execution, *see* Bruce Arrigo and Christopher R. Williams, *Law, Ideology, and Critical Inquiry: The Case of Treatment Refusal for Incompetent Prisoners Awaiting Execution,* 25 New England Journal on Criminal and Civil Confinement 367 (1999); reprinted herein.

[37] Godinez v. Moran, 509 U.S. 389 (1993).

[38] Id. at 402.

[39] Id. at 413 (Blackmun, J., dissenting).

[40] Cooper v. Oklahoma, 517 U.S. 348 (1996).

[41] Medina v. California, 505 U.S. 437, 449 (1992).

[42] Cooper, 517 U.S. at 362, quoting Medina, 505 U.S. at 445.

that the defendant is competent."[43] Thus once the defendant produces sufficient evidence that it is "more likely than not" that he is incompetent, he has met his burden and nothing more should be required of him on this issue.

One of the more interesting trends in mental health issues has been the development of the therapeutic jurisprudence movement. Professors David B. Wexler and Bruce J. Winick originated this approach and define it as "interdisciplinary, empirical, and international in its orientation."[44] They explain that the purpose of this construct is to "sensitize legal policy makers to a frequently ignored aspect of mental health law policy analysis—the therapeutic impact of legal rules and procedures."[45]

In this thoughtful and interesting approach, the authors suggest that the consideration of treatment for offenders needs to be factored into legal decision making. Subjects discussed include whether incompetent death-row inmates should have a right to refuse treatment, and the provision of treatment to defendants found incompetent to stand trial.

---

[43] Cooper, 517 U.S. at 363.

[44] David B. Wexler and Bruce J. Winick, *Therapeutic Jurisprudence and Criminal Justice Mental Health Issues,* 16 Mental & Physical Disability L. Rep. 225 (1992); reprinted herein. *See also* DAVID B. WEXLER AND BRUCE J. WINICK, ESSAYS IN THERAPEUTIC JURISPRUDENCE (Carolina Academic Press, 1991).

[45] Id.

The Role of Mental Illness in Criminal Trials

Volume 3

Competency to Be Tried, Imprisoned, and Executed

DUSKY v. UNITED STATES.

ON PETITION FOR WRIT OF CERTIORARI TO THE UNITED STATES COURT OF APPEALS FOR THE EIGHTH CIRCUIT.

No. 504, Misc. Decided April 18, 1960.

Certiorari granted.

Since the record in this case does not sufficiently support the findings of petitioner's competency to stand trial, the judgment affirming his conviction is reversed and the case is remanded to the District Court for a hearing to determine his present competency to stand trial, and for a new trial if he is found competent. Pp. 402–403.

271 F. 2d 385, reversed.

James W. Benjamin for petitioner.

Solicitor General Rankin for the United States.

PER CURIAM.

The motion for leave to proceed *in forma pauperis* and the petition for a writ of certiorari are granted. Upon consideration of the entire record we agree with the Solicitor General that "the record in this case does not sufficiently support the findings of competency to stand trial," for to support those findings under 18 U. S. C. § 4244 the district judge "would need more information than this record presents." We also agree with the suggestion of the Solicitor General that it is not enough for the district judge to find that "the defendant [is] oriented to time and place and [has] some recollection of events," but that the "test must be whether he has sufficient present ability to consult with his lawyer with a reasonable degree of rational understanding—and whether he has a rational as well as factual understanding of the proceedings against him."

In view of the doubts and ambiguities regarding the legal significance of the psychiatric testimony in this case and the resulting difficulties of retrospectively determining the petitioner's competency as of more than a year ago, we reverse the judgment of the Court of Appeals affirming the judgment of conviction, and remand the case to the District Court for a new hearing to ascertain petitioner's present competency to stand trial, and for a new trial if petitioner is found competent.

It is so ordered.

IZZO *v.* ILLINOIS.

APPEAL FROM THE SUPREME COURT OF ILLINOIS.

No. 772, Misc. Decided April 18, 1960.

Appeal dismissed and certiorari denied.

PER CURIAM.

The appeal is dismissed. Treating the papers whereon the appeal was taken as a petition for writ of certiorari, certiorari is denied.

Syllabus.

PATE, WARDEN v. ROBINSON.

CERTIORARI TO THE UNITED STATES COURT OF APPEALS FOR THE SEVENTH CIRCUIT.

No. 382. Argued January 26, 1966.—Decided March 7, 1966.

Respondent was convicted in 1959 of murdering his common-law wife and given a life sentence. It was conceded at trial that he had shot and killed her but counsel claimed that respondent was insane at the time of the incident and also not competent to stand trial. It was uncontradicted that respondent had a long history of disturbed behavior, had been confined as a psychopathic patient, and had committed acts of violence including the killing of his infant son and an attempted suicide. Four defense witnesses testified that respondent was insane. The trial court declined rebuttal medical testimony as to respondent's sanity, deeming sufficient a stipulation that a doctor would testify that when respondent was examined a few months before trial he knew the nature of the charges and could cooperate with his counsel. The trial court's rejection of contentions as to respondent's sanity was challenged on appeal as a deprivation of due process of law under the Fourteenth Amendment. The State Supreme Court affirmed the conviction on the grounds that no hearing on mental capacity to stand trial had been requested and that the evidence was insufficient to require the trial court to conduct a sanity hearing *sua sponte* or to raise a "reasonable doubt" as to respondent's sanity at the time of the homicide. This Court denied certiorari. The District Court denied respondent's subsequently filed petition for writ of habeas corpus. The Court of Appeals reversed, holding that the unduly hurried trial did not provide a fair opportunity for development of facts on the insanity issues and remanded the case to the District Court for a limited hearing as to the sanity of respondent at the time of the homicide and as to whether he was constitutionally entitled to a hearing upon his competence to stand trial. *Held:*

1. The evidence raised a sufficient doubt as to respondent's competence to stand trial so that respondent was deprived of due process of law under the Fourteenth Amendment by the trial court's failure to afford him a hearing on that issue. Pp. 378–386.

(a) The conviction of a legally incompetent defendant violates due process. *Bishop* v. *United States,* 350 U. S. 961. P. 378.

(b) The record shows that respondent did not waive the defense of incompetence to stand trial. P. 384.

(c) In view of evidence raising a doubt on the competence issue, the court was required to impanel a jury and conduct a sanity hearing and could not rely in lieu thereof on respondent's demeanor at trial or on the stipulated medical testimony. Pp. 385–386.

2. In view of the difficulty of retrospectively determining the issue of an accused's competence to stand trial (particularly where, as here, the time lapse is over six years), a hearing limited to that issue will not suffice; respondent must therefore be discharged unless the State gives him a new trial within a reasonable time. P. 387.

345 F. 2d 691, affirmed in part and remanded.

Richard A. Michael, Assistant Attorney General of Illinois, argued the cause for petitioner. With him on the brief were *William G. Clark*, Attorney General, and *Philip J. Rock*, Assistant Attorney General.

John C. Tucker argued the cause for respondent. With him on the brief was *Albert E. Jenner, Jr.*

MR. JUSTICE CLARK delivered the opinion of the Court.

In 1959 respondent Robinson was convicted of the murder of his common-law wife, Flossie May Ward, and was sentenced to imprisonment for life. Being an indigent he was defended by court-appointed counsel. It was conceded at trial that Robinson shot and killed Flossie May, but his counsel claimed that he was insane at the time of the shooting and raised the issue of his incompetence to stand trial. On writ of error to the Supreme Court of Illinois it was asserted that the trial court's rejection of these contentions deprived Robinson of due process of law under the Fourteenth Amendment. His conviction was affirmed, the court finding that no hearing on mental capacity to stand trial had been requested, that the evidence failed to raise sufficient doubt as to his competence to require the trial court to conduct a hearing on its own motion, and further that the evidence did not raise a "reasonable doubt" as to his sanity at the time of the offense. 22 Ill. 2d 162, 174 N. E. 2d 820 (1961). We denied certiorari. 368 U. S. 995 (1962). Thereupon, Robinson filed this petition for habeas corpus, which was denied without a hearing by the United States District Court for the Northern District of Illinois. The Court of Appeals reversed, 345 F. 2d 691 (1965), on the ground that Robinson was convicted in an unduly hurried trial without a fair opportunity to obtain expert psychiatric testimony, and without sufficient development of the facts on the issues of Robinson's insanity when he committed the homicide and his present incompetence. It remanded the case to the District Court with directions to appoint counsel for Robinson; to hold a hearing as to his sanity when he committed the alleged offense; and, if it found him to have been insane at that time, to order his release, subject to an examination into his present mental condition. The Court of Appeals directed that the District Court should also determine upon the hearing whether Robinson was denied due process by the state court's failure to conduct a hearing upon his competence to stand trial; and, if it were found his rights had been violated in this respect, that Robinson "should be ordered released, but such release may be delayed for a reasonable time . . . to permit the State of Illinois to grant Robinson a new trial." 345 F. 2d, at 698. We granted certiorari to resolve the difficult questions of state-federal relations posed by these rulings. 382 U. S. 890 (1965). We have concluded that Robinson was constitutionally entitled to a hearing on the issue of his competence to stand trial. Since we do not think there could be a meaningful hearing on that issue at this late date, we direct that the District Court, after affording the State another opportunity to put Robinson to trial on its charges within a reasonable time, order him discharged. Accordingly, we affirm the decision of the Court of Appeals in this respect, except insofar as it contemplated a hearing in the District Court on Robinson's competence. Our disposition makes it unnecessary to reach the other reasons given by the Court of Appeals for reversal.[1]

I.

The State concedes that the conviction of an accused person while he is legally incompetent violates due process, *Bishop* v. *United States,* 350 U. S. 961 (1956), and that state procedures must be adequate to protect this right. It insists, however, that Robinson intelligently waived this issue by his failure to request a hearing on his competence at the trial; and, further, that on the basis of the evidence before the trial judge no duty rested upon him to order a hearing *sua sponte.* A determination of these claims necessitates a detailed discussion of the conduct of the trial and the evidence touching upon the question of Robinson's competence at that time.

The uncontradicted testimony of four witnesses[2] called by the defense revealed that Robinson had a long history of disturbed behavior. His mother testified that when he was between seven and eight years of age a brick dropped from a third floor hit Robinson on the head. "He blacked out and the blood run from his head like a faucet." Thereafter "he acted a little peculiar." The blow knocked him "cockeyed" and his mother took him to a specialist "to correct the crossness of his eyes." He also suffered headaches during his childhood, apparently stemming from the same event. His conduct became

---

[1] Nor do we pass on the contention that Robinson was denied his Sixth Amendment rights by the trial judge's refusal to issue summonses for material witnesses.

[2] These witnesses were Miss Willie Ceola Peterson, Robinson's mother; Mr. William H. Langham, his grandfather; Mrs. Helen Calhoun, his aunt; and Mrs. Alice Moore, a family friend.

noticeably erratic about 1946 or 1947 when he was visiting his mother on a furlough from the Army. While Robinson was sitting and talking with a guest, "he jumped up and run to a bar and kicked a hole in the bar and he run up in the front." His mother asked "what on earth was wrong with him and he just stared at [her], and paced the floor with both hands in his pockets." On other occasions he appeared in a daze, with a "glare in his eyes," and would not speak or respond to questions. In 1951, a few years after his discharge from the service, he "lost his mind and was pacing the floor saying something was after him." This incident occurred at the home of his aunt, Helen Calhoun. Disturbed by Robinson's conduct, Mrs. Calhoun called his mother about six o'clock in the morning, and she "went to see about him." Robinson tried to prevent Mrs. Calhoun from opening the door, saying "that someone was going to shoot him or someone was going to come in after him." His mother testified that, after gaining admittance, "I went to him and hugged him to ask him what was wrong and he went to pushing me back, telling me to get back, somebody was going to shoot him, somebody was going to shoot him." Upon being questioned as to Robinson's facial expression at the time, the mother stated that he "had that starey look and seemed to be just a little foamy at the mouth." A policeman was finally called. He put Robinson, his mother and aunt in a cab which drove them to Hines Hospital. On the way Robinson tried to jump from the cab, and upon arrival at the hospital he was so violent that he had to be strapped in a wheel chair. He then was taken in an ambulance to the County Psychopathic Hospital, from which he was transferred to the Kankakee State Hospital. The medical records there recited:

> "The reason for admission: The patient was admitted to this hospital on the 5th day of June, 1952,

from the Hines Hospital. Patient began presenting symptoms of mental illness about a year ago at which time he came to his mother's house. He requested money and when it was refused, he suddenly kicked a hole in her bar.

. . . . .

"Was drinking and went to the Psychopathic Hospital. He imagined he heard voices, voices of men and women and he also saw things. He saw a little bit of everything. He saw animals, snakes and elephants and this lasted for about two days. He went to Hines. They sent him to the Psychopathic Hospital. The voices threatened him. He imagined someone was outside with a pistol aimed at him. He was very, very scared and he tried to call the police and his aunt then called the police. He thought he was going to be harmed. And he says this all seems very foolish to him now. Patient is friendly and tries to cooperate.

. . . . .

"He went through an acute toxic episode from which he has some insight. He had been drinking heavily. I am wondering possibly he isn't schizophrenic. I think he has recovered from this condition. I have seen the wife and she is in a pathetic state. I have no objection to giving him a try."

After his release from the state hospital Robinson's irrational episodes became more serious. His grandfather testified that while Robinson was working with him as a painter's assistant, "all at once, he would come down [from the ladder] and walk on out and never say where he is going and whatnot and he would be out two or three hours, and at times he would be in a daze and when he comes out, he comes back just as fresh. He just says he didn't do anything. I noticed that he wasn't at all himself." The grandfather also related that one night when Robinson was staying at his house Robinson and his wife had a "ruckus," which caused his wife to flee to the grandfather's bedroom. Robinson first tried to kick down the door. He then grabbed all of his wife's clothes from their room and threw them out in the yard, intending to set them on fire. Robinson got so unruly that the grandfather called the police to lock him up.

In 1953 Robinson, then separated from his wife, brought their 18-month-old son to Mrs. Calhoun's home and asked permission to stay there for a couple of days. She observed that he was highly nervous, prancing about and staring wildly. While she was at work the next day Robinson shot and killed his son and attempted suicide by shooting himself in the head. It appeared that after Robinson shot his son, he went to a nearby park and tried to take his life again by jumping into a lagoon. By his mother's description, he "was wandering around" the park, and walked up to a policeman and "asked him for a cigarette." It was stipulated that he went to the South Park Station on March 10, 1953, and said that he wanted to confess to a crime. When he removed his hat the police saw that he had shot himself in the head. They took him to the hospital for treatment of his wound.

Robinson served almost four years in prison for killing his son, being released in September 1956. A few months thereafter he began to live with Flossie May Ward at her home. In the summer of 1957 or 1958 Robinson "jumped on" his mother's brother-in-law and "beat him up terrible." She went to the police station and swore out a warrant for his arrest. She described his abnormalities and told the officers that Robinson "seemed to have a disturbed mind." She asked the police "to pick him up so I can have him put away." Later she went back to see why they had not taken him into custody because of "the way he was fighting around in the streets, people were beating him up." She made another complaint a month or so before Robinson killed Flossie May Ward. However, no warrant was ever served on him.

The killing occurred about 10:30 p. m. at a small barbecue house where Flossie May Ward worked. At that time there were 10 customers in the restaurant, six of them sitting at the counter. It appears from the record that Robinson entered the restaurant with a gun in his hand. As he approached the counter, Flossie May said, "Don't start nothing tonight." After staring at her for about a minute, he walked to the rear of the room and, with the use of his hand, leaped over the counter. He then rushed back toward the front of the restaurant, past two other employees working behind the counter, and fired once or twice at Flossie May. She jumped over the counter and ran out the front door with Robinson in pursuit. She was found dead on the sidewalk.[3] Robinson never spoke a word during the three-to-four-minute episode.

Subsequently Robinson went to the apartment of a friend, Mr. Moore, who summoned the police. When three officers, two in uniform, arrived, Robinson was standing in the hall approximately half way between the elevator and the apartment. Unaware of his identity, the officers walked past him and went to the door of the apartment. Mrs. Moore answered the door and told them that Robinson had left a short time earlier. As the officers turned around they saw Robinson still standing where they had first observed him. Robinson made no attempt to avoid being arrested. When asked his address

[3] The Reverend Elmer Clemons was also shot and killed in the fracas. The indictment covering that offense was dismissed at the close of the trial in question.

he gave several evasive answers. He also denied knowing anything about the killing.[4]

Four defense witnesses expressed the opinion that Robinson was insane.[5] In rebuttal the State introduced only a stipulation that Dr. William H. Haines, Director of the Behavior Clinic of the Criminal Court of Cook County would, if present, testify that in his opinion Robinson knew the nature of the charges against him and was able to cooperate with counsel when he examined him two or three months before trial. However, since the stipulation did not include a finding of sanity the prosecutor advised the court that "we should have

---

[4] According to the testimony of an arresting officer the following exchange took place:

"I asked him what his name was and he said, 'My name is Ted.' I said, 'What is your real name?' And he said, 'Theodore Robinson.' Then I asked him—I told him he was under arrest and he said, 'For what?' I said, 'Well, you are supposed to be wanted for killing two people on the south side.' I asked him did he know anything about it. He said, 'No, I don't know what you are talking about.' So then I asked him where he lived and he said, 'I don't live no place.'

"I said, 'What do you mean you don't live no place?' He said, 'That's what I said.'

"So then pretty soon asked him again and he said, 'Sometimes I stay with my mother.' And I said, 'Where does she live?' He said, 'Some address on East 44th Street.'

"So then we took him on to the 27th District and while we were making the arrest slip, asked him again his address and he said he lived at 7320 South Parkway. That's about all he said. He didn't know anything about any killing or anything."

[5] His mother stated: "I think he is insane." Mrs. Calhoun testified as follows:

"Q. Do you have an opinion as to whether or not presently he is sane or insane?

"A. He is sick. He is insane.

"Q. First of all, do you have an opinion?

"A. Yes.

"Q. What is your opinion as to his present sanity? . . .

"A. He is mentally sick."

Dr. Haines' testimony as to his opinion whether this man is sane or insane. It is possible that the man might be insane and know the nature of the charge or be able to cooperate with his counsel. I think it should be in evidence, your Honor, that Dr. Haines' opinion is that this defendant was sane when he was examined." However, the court told the prosecutor, "You have enough in the record now. I don't think you need Dr. Haines." In his summation defense counsel emphasized "our defense is clear . . . . It is as to the sanity of the defendant at the time of the crime and also as to the present time." The court, after closing argument by the defense, found Robinson guilty and sentenced him to prison for his natural life.

II.

The State insists that Robinson deliberately waived the defense of his competence to stand trial by failing to demand a sanity hearing as provided by Illinois law. But it is contradictory to argue that a defendant may be incompetent, and yet knowingly or intelligently "waive" his right to have the court determine his capacity to stand trial. See *Taylor* v. *United States*, 282 F. 2d 16, 23 (C. A. 8th Cir. 1960). In any event, the record shows that counsel throughout the proceedings insisted that Robinson's present sanity was very much in issue. He made a point to elicit Mrs. Robinson's opinion of Robinson's "present sanity." And in his argument to the judge, he asserted that Robinson "should be found not guilty and presently insane on the basis of the testimony that we have heard." Moreover, the prosecutor himself suggested at trial that "we should have Dr. Haines' testimony as to his opinion whether this man is sane or insane." With this record we cannot say that Robinson waived the defense of incompetence to stand trial.[6]

[6] Although defense counsel phrased his questions and argument in terms of Robinson's present insanity, we interpret his language as

We believe that the evidence introduced on Robinson's behalf entitled him to a hearing on this issue. The court's failure to make such inquiry thus deprived Robinson of his constitutional right to a fair trial.[7] See *Thomas* v. *Cunningham,* 313 F. 2d 934 (C. A. 4th Cir. 1963). Illinois jealously guards this right. Where the evidence raises a "*bona fide* doubt" as to a defendant's competence to stand trial, the judge on his own motion must impanel a jury and conduct a sanity hearing pursuant to Ill. Rev. Stat., c. 38, § 104–2 (1963). *People* v. *Shrake,* 25 Ill. 2d 141, 182 N. E. 2d 754 (1962). The Supreme Court of Illinois held that the evidence here was not sufficient to require a hearing in light of the mental alertness and understanding displayed in Robinson's "colloquies" with the trial judge. 22 Ill. 2d, at 168, 174 N. E. 2d, at 823. But this reasoning offers no justification for ignoring the uncontradicted testimony

---

necessarily placing in issue the question of Robinson's mental competence to stand trial. Counsel was simply borrowing the terminology of the relevant Illinois statutes and decisions. The state law in effect at the time of Robinson's trial differentiated between lack of criminal responsibility and competence to stand trial, but used "insanity" to describe both concepts. Ill. Rev. Stat., c. 38, §§ 592, 593 (1963). The judges likewise phrased their decisions only in terms of sanity and insanity. See, *e. g.*, *People* v. *Baker,* 26 Ill. 2d 484, 187 N. E. 2d 227 (1962). The statutory provisions and terminology in this field have now been clarified by the enactment of an article dealing with the "competency of accused." Ill. Rev. Stat., c. 38, §§ 104–1 to 104–3 (1963), as amended by the Code of Criminal Procedure of 1963. Even if counsel may also have meant to refer to the statutory provisions dealing with commitment for present insanity, Ill. Rev. Stat., c. 38, § 592 (1963), this fact would not affect the determination that counsel's words raised a question as to competence that the trial judge should have considered.

[7] Moreover, as the Court of Appeals stressed, the trial judge did not give Robinson an opportunity to introduce expert testimony on the question of his sanity. The judge denied counsel's request for a continuance of several hours in order to secure the appearance of a psychiatrist from the Illinois Psychiatric Institute

of Robinson's history of pronounced irrational behavior. While Robinson's demeanor at trial might be relevant to the ultimate decision as to his sanity, it cannot be relied upon to dispense with a hearing on that very issue. Cf. *Bishop* v. *United States*, 350 U. S. 961 (1956), reversing 96 U. S. App. D. C. 117, 120, 223 F. 2d 582, 585 (1955). Likewise, the stipulation of Dr. Haines' testimony was some evidence of Robinson's ability to assist in his defense. But, as the state prosecutor seemingly admitted, on the facts presented to the trial court it could not properly have been deemed dispositive on the issue of Robinson's competence.[8]

III.

Having determined that Robinson's constitutional rights were abridged by his failure to receive an adequate hearing on his competence to stand trial, we direct that the writ of habeas corpus must issue and Robinson be discharged, unless the State gives him a new trial within a reasonable time. This disposition accords with the procedure adopted in *Rogers* v. *Richmond*, 365 U. S. 534 (1961). We there determined that since the state court had applied an erroneous standard to judge the admissibility of a confession, the "defendant should have the opportunity to have all issues which may be determinative of his guilt tried by a state judge or a state jury under appropriate state procedures which conform to the requirements of the Fourteenth Amendment." At 547–

[8] As defense counsel insisted in his closing argument:

"In this case, which is a very serious case, the defendant has been able to cooperate with counsel with some reservations. . . . However, I do not feel that this present . . . lucidity bears on the issue of his sanity at the time of the crime and his sanity at the present time. I think the words sanity and insanity, the words are legal terms. I think that presently Mr. Theodore Robinson is in a lucid interval. I believe that from the witness stand you have heard testimony to indicate and prove that Mr. Theodore Robinson is presently insane. . . ."

548. It has been pressed upon us that it would be sufficient for the state court to hold a limited hearing as to Robinson's mental competence at the time he was tried in 1959. If he were found competent, the judgment against him would stand. But we have previously emphasized the difficulty of retrospectively determining an accused's competence to stand trial. *Dusky* v. *United States*, 362 U. S. 402 (1960). The jury would not be able to observe the subject of their inquiry, and expert witnesses would have to testify solely from information contained in the printed record. That Robinson's hearing would be held six years after the fact aggravates these difficulties. This need for concurrent determination distinguishes the present case from *Jackson* v. *Denno*, 378 U. S. 368 (1964), where we held that on remand the State could discharge its constitutional obligation by giving the accused a separate hearing on the voluntariness of his confession.

If the State elects to retry Robinson, it will of course be open to him to raise the question of his competence to stand trial at that time and to request a special hearing thereon. In the event a sufficient doubt exists as to his present competence such a hearing must be held. If found competent to stand trial, Robinson would have the usual defenses available to an accused.

The case is remanded to the District Court for action consistent with this opinion.

It is so ordered.

MR. JUSTICE HARLAN, whom MR. JUSTICE BLACK joins, dissenting.

The facts now canvassed by this Court to support its constitutional holding were fully sifted by the Illinois Supreme Court. I cannot agree that the state court's unanimous appraisal was erroneous and still less that it was error of constitutional proportions.

The Court appears to hold that a defendant's present incompetence may become sufficiently manifest during a trial that it denies him due process for the trial court to fail to conduct a hearing on that question on its own initiative. I do not dissent from this very general proposition, and I agree also that such an error is not "waived" by failure to raise it and that it may entitle the defendant to a new trial without further proof. Waiver is not an apposite concept where we premise a defendant so deranged that he cannot oversee his lawyers. Since our further premise is that the trial judge should and could have avoided the error, a new trial seems not too drastic an exaction in view of the proof problems arising after a significant lapse of time.[1] However, I do not believe the facts known to the trial judge in this case suggested Robinson's incompetence at time of trial with anything like the force necessary to make out a violation of due process in the failure to pursue the question.

Before turning to the facts, it is pertinent to consider the quality of the incompetence they are supposed to indicate. In federal courts—and I assume no more is asked of state courts—the test of incompetence that warrants postponing the trial is reasonably well settled. In language this Court adopted on the one occasion it faced the issue, "the 'test must be whether . . . [the defendant] has sufficient present ability to consult with his lawyer with a reasonable degree of rational understanding—and whether he has a rational as well as factual understanding of the proceedings against him.'" *Dusky* v. *United States*, 362 U. S. 402. In short, emphasis is on capacity to consult with counsel and to comprehend the proceed-

[1] The constitutional violation alleged is the failure to make an inquiry. In the more usual case, the simple claim that a defendant was convicted while incompetent during the trial, there is of course no proof of a constitutional violation until that incompetence is established in appropriate proceedings.

ings, and lower courts have recognized that this is by no means the same test as those which determine criminal responsibility at the time of the crime.[2] The question, then, is not whether the facts before the trial judge suggested that Robinson's crime was an insane act but whether they suggested he was incompetent to stand trial.

The Court's affirmative answer seemingly rests on two kinds of evidence, principally adduced by Robinson to prove an insanity defense after the State rested its main case. First, there was evidence of a number of episodes of severe irrationality in Robinson's past. Among them were the slaying of his infant son, his attempted suicide, his efforts to burn his wife's clothing, his fits of temper and of abstraction, and his seven-week incarceration in a state hospital eight years before the trial. This evidence may be tempered by the State's counterarguments, for example, that Robinson was found guilty of his son's killing and that alcoholism may explain his hospitalization, but it cannot be written off entirely. The difficulty remains that while this testimony may suggest that Flossie May Ward's killing was just one more irrational act, I cannot say as a matter of common knowledge that it evidences incapacity during the trial. Indeed, the pattern revealed may best indicate that Robinson did function adequately during most of his life interrupted by periods of severe derangement that would have been quite apparent had they occurred at trial. The second class of data pertinent to the Court's theory, remarks by witnesses and counsel that Robinson was "presently insane," deserves little comment. I think it apparent that these statements were addressed to Robinson's re-

[2] See *James* v. *Boles*, 339 F. 2d 431; *United States* v. *Kendrick*, 331 F. 2d 110; *Lyles* v. *United States*, 103 U. S. App. D. C. 22, 254 F. 2d 725.

sponsibility for the killing, that is, his ability to do insane acts, and not to his general competency to stand trial.[3]

Whatever mild doubts this evidence may stir are surely allayed by positive indications of Robinson's competence at the trial. Foremost is his own behavior in the courtroom. The record reveals colloquies between Robinson and the trial judge which undoubtedly permitted a reasonable inference that Robinson was quite cognizant of the proceedings and able to assist counsel in his defense.[4] Turning from lay impressions to those of an expert, it was stipulated at trial that a Dr. Haines, Director of the Behavior Clinic of the Criminal Court of Cook County, had examined Robinson several months earlier and, if called, would testify that Robinson "knows

[3] At the time Robinson's mother and Mrs. Calhoun made the statements noted in the Court's opinion, p. 383, n. 5, *ante*, they also stated Robinson did not know the difference between right and wrong. Counsel's statement, too, quoted by the Court at p. 386, n. 8, *ante*, was directed to acquittal, not postponement. See, n. 5, *infra*. Mrs. Moore, a family friend, responded to the question on Robinson's sanity by saying: "When he is in those moods, I think he is insane; when he is in those moods, because he is terrible."

[4] The Illinois Supreme Court stated in its opinion: "[T]he record reflects several instances where defendant displayed his ability to assist in the conduct of his defense in a reasonable and rational manner. Typical instances of when defendant displayed mental alertness, as well as understanding and knowledge of the proceeding, appear in his remarks to the court as follows: 'Your honor, they were on the State's witness list and the State said they have several witnesses. They produced two. For what reason, I don't know, but I am on trial here and I would like to be given every consideration, and I would like that the court be adjourned until tomorrow morning—to give me time to confer with counsel for the calling of witnesses.' Again, when discussing witnesses with the court, defendant said: 'Well, the police are contending that the clothes they have found in Moore's apartment was mine. That is the reason at the beginning of trial, I asked the attorney to have a pre-trial preliminary to determine the admissibility and validity of the evidence that the State was intending to use against me.' " 22 Ill. 2d, at 168, 174 N. E. 2d, at 823.

the nature of the charge and is able to cooperate with his counsel." The conclusive factor is that Robinson's own lawyers, the two men who apparently had the closest contact with the defendant during the proceedings, never suggested he was incompetent to stand trial and never moved to have him examined on incompetency grounds during trial; [5] indeed, counsel's remarks to the jury seem best read as an affirmation of Robinson's present "lucidity" which would be highly peculiar if Robinson had been unable to assist properly in his defense. See p. 386, n. 8, *ante*, of the Court's opinion.

Thus, I cannot agree with the Court that the requirements of due process were violated by the failure of the trial judge, who had opportunities for personal observation of the defendant that we do not possess, to halt the trial and hold a competency hearing on his own motion.

Several other grounds have been urged as a basis for habeas corpus relief for Robinson. These other grounds are understandably not discussed in the Court's opinion, and I think it is sufficient for me to say I do not believe that they warrant further proceedings. In my view, the Court of Appeals should be reversed and the District Court's dismissal of the petition reinstated.

---

[5] The record in my view does not bear out any suggestion that Robinson's counsel apprised the trial judge that he believed Robinson incompetent to stand trial, even granting that "insane" was a synonym for "incompetent" under then-existing state law (pp. 384–385, n. 6, *ante*). Under Illinois law, as one would naturally expect, incompetence at the time of trial has been a ground not for acquitting the defendant but for postponing his trial; and nowhere in the record does Robinson's counsel even hint to the judge that he believes the trial should be deferred or abated because his client is not fit to continue. The ready explanation for counsel's references to "present insanity," apart from emphasizing Robinson's general lack of criminal responsibility, is that Illinois law provided that one acquitted on grounds of insanity at the time of the crime shall by the same verdict be found cured of or still afflicted with "such insanity" and committed in the latter instance. Ill. Rev. Stat., c. 38, § 592 (1959).

DROPE *v.* MISSOURI

CERTIORARI TO THE COURT OF APPEALS OF MISSOURI FOR THE ST. LOUIS DISTRICT

No. 73-6038. Argued November 13, 1974—Decided February 19, 1975

In 1969 petitioner was indicted, with two others, for rape of petitioner's wife. Following severance of petitioner's case, he filed a motion for a continuance so that he might be further examined and receive psychiatric treatment, attaching thereto the report of a psychiatrist who had examined him at his counsel's request and had suggested such treatment. The motion was denied and the case proceeded to trial. Petitioner's wife testified, repeating and confirming information concerning petitioner's "strange behavior" which was contained in the report and stating that she had changed her mind about not wanting to prosecute petitioner because he had tried to kill her on the Sunday prior to trial. On the second day of the trial petitioner shot himself in a suicide attempt and was hospitalized, but despite his absence the trial court denied a motion for a mistrial on the ground that his absence was voluntary, and the trial continued. The jury returned a guilty verdict and petitioner was sentenced to life imprisonment. His motion for a new trial, asserting that the trial court had erred in proceeding with the trial when no evidence was produced that his absence was voluntary, was denied, the trial court finding again that his absence was voluntary. The Missouri Supreme Court affirmed, sustaining that finding and also holding that the trial court's denial of the continuance motion was not an abuse of discretion. Subsequently, petitioner's motion to vacate the conviction and sentence, alleging, *inter alia,* that his constitutional rights had been violated by the failure to order a pretrial psychiatric examination and by completing the trial in his absence, was denied. The Missouri Court of Appeals affirmed, holding that neither the psychiatric report attached to petitioner's motion for a continuance nor his wife's testimony raised a reasonable doubt of his fitness to proceed, that petitioner's suicide attempt did not create a reasonable doubt of his competence as a matter of law, and that he had failed to demonstrate the inadequacy of the procedures employed for protecting his rights. The court also held that the trial court's finding as to voluntary absence was not clearly erroneous. *Held:*

1. The Missouri courts failed to accord proper weight to the evidence suggesting petitioner's incompetence. When considered together with the information available prior to trial and the testimony of petitioner's wife at trial, the information concerning petitioner's suicide attempt created a sufficient doubt of his competence to stand trial to require further inquiry. Pp. 178–181.

2. Whatever the relationship between mental illness and incompetence to stand trial, in this case the bearing of the former on the latter was sufficiently likely that, in light of the evidence of petitioner's behavior including his suicide attempt, and there being no opportunity without his presence to evaluate that bearing in fact, the correct course was to suspend the trial until such an evaluation could be made. Pp. 181–182.

3. Assuming petitioner's right to be present at the trial was one that could be waived, there was an insufficient inquiry to afford a basis for deciding the issue of waiver. P. 182.

4. Petitioner's due process rights would not be adequately protected by remanding the case for a psychiatric examination to determine whether he was in fact competent to stand trial in 1969, but the State is free to retry him, assuming that at the time of such trial he is competent to be tried. P. 183.

498 S. W. 2d 838, reversed and remanded.

BURGER, C. J., delivered the opinion for a unanimous Court.

Thomas C. Walsh argued the cause for petitioner. With him on the briefs was *Charles A. Weiss*.

Neil MacFarlane, Assistant Attorney General of Missouri, argued the cause for respondent. With him on the brief were *John C. Danforth*, Attorney General, and *David Robards*, Assistant Attorney General.

MR. CHIEF JUSTICE BURGER delivered the opinion of the Court.

We granted certiorari in this case to consider petitioner's claims that he was deprived of due process of law by the failure of the trial court to order a psychiatric examination with respect to his competence to stand trial and by the conduct in his absence of a portion of his trial on an indictment charging a capital offense.

I

In February 1969 an indictment was returned in the Circuit Court of St. Louis, Mo., charging petitioner and two others with the forcible rape of petitioner's wife. Following severance of petitioner's case from those of the other defendants and a continuance, on May 27 his counsel filed a motion for a continuance until September, in order that petitioner might be examined and receive psychiatric treatment. Treatment had been suggested by a psychiatrist who had examined petitioner at his counsel's request and whose report was attached to the motion.[1] On the same date respondent, through the

[1] The motion recites: "Comes now the Defendant, JAMES E. DROPE, and states to the court that he has had a psychiatric examination made by Dr. Joseph F. Shuman, M. D., a copy of which report is attached hereto.

"Defendant moves the court to continue his case until September, 1969 in order that he might receive an Examination, Evaluation and psychiatric treatment, as suggested by Dr. Shuman, at the Malcomb Bliss Hospital in the City of St. Louis, Missouri." App. 7.

The report, in the form of a letter to petitioner's attorney, states that the psychiatrist examined petitioner on February 20, 1969. In a section entitled "Past Medical History" it describes petitioner as "markedly agitated and upset," noting that he "appeared to be cooperative in this examination, but he had difficulty in participating well." The report continues: "The patient had a difficult time relating. He was markedly circumstantial and irrelevant in his speech. . . . There was no sign as to the presence of any delusions, illusions, hallucinations, obsessions, ideas of reference, compulsions or phobias at this time.

"In a simple IQ exam Mr. Drope was able to achieve a score in the low normal range . . . . Mr. Drope was well oriented in all spheres. With much difficulty he was able to

Assistant Circuit Attorney, filed a document stating that the State did not oppose the motion for a psychiatric examination. Apparently no action was taken on the motion, and petitioner's case was continued until June 23, at which time his counsel objected to proceeding with the trial on the ground that he had understood the case would be continued until September and consequently was not prepared. He objected further "for the reason that the defendant is not a person of sound mind and should have a further psychiatric examination before the case should be forced to trial." App. 19. The trial judge noted that the motion for a continuance was not in proper form and that, although petitioner's counsel had agreed to file another, he had failed to do so, and he overruled his objections and directed that the case proceed to trial.

On June 24 a jury was empaneled, and the prosecution called petitioner's wife as its first witness. She testified that petitioner participated with four of his acquaintances in forcibly raping her and subjecting her to other bizarre abuse and indignities, but that she had resumed living

---

explain a few abstractions. . . . He was able, without trouble, to answer questions testing judgement. He had much difficulty even doing the simple counting and calculation problems." The report then recounts the details of a conversation between the psychiatrist and petitioner's wife. The latter admitted that she had left petitioner on a number of occasions because of his sexual perversions and described the "strange behavior" of petitioner, including falling down flights of stairs, as an attempt to gain sympathy from her. In a section entitled "Impression," the report states that petitioner had "always led a marginal existence," that he had a "history of anti-social conduct," but that there were no "strong signs of psychosis at this time." It concludes that petitioner "certainly needs the aid of a psychiatrist," and that he "is a very neurotic individual who is also depressed and perhaps he is depressed for most of the time," and it offers as diagnoses: "(1) Sociopathic personality disorder, sexual perversion. (2) Borderline mental deficiency. (3) Chronic Anxiety reaction with depression." *Id.*, at 11–12.

with him after the incident on the advice of petitioner's psychiatrist and so that their children would be taken care of. On cross-examination, she testified that she had told petitioner's attorney of her belief that her husband was sick and needed psychiatric care and that for these reasons she had signed a statement disavowing a desire to prosecute. She related that on several occasions when petitioner did not "get his way or [was] worried about something," he would roll down the stairs. She could explain such behavior only by relating "what they told him many times at City Hospital, that is something he does upon hisself [*sic*]." *Id.*, at 47. However, she also stated that she was not convinced petitioner was sick after talking to his psychiatrist, and that she had changed her mind about not wanting to prosecute petitioner because, as she testified, he had "tried to choke me, tried to kill me" on the Sunday evening prior to trial. *Id.*, at 52.

The prosecution called three more witnesses, but did not conclude its case, before adjournment on June 24. The following morning, petitioner did not appear. When the trial judge directed counsel to proceed, petitioner's attorney moved for a mistrial "in view of the fact that the defendant, I am informed, shot himself this morning." App. 63. The trial judge denied the motion, stating that he had already decided the matter would proceed for trial, and when petitioner's counsel complained of the difficulty of proceeding without a client, the trial judge replied that the difficulty was brought about by petitioner, who was on bond and had a responsibility to be present. The prosecution then called four more witnesses and, after producing proof of a prior conviction,[2] rested its case. Petitioner's "Motion for Verdict of Acquittal," including

[2] Petitioner was tried as a second offender under Mo. Rev. Stat. § 556.280 (1969), having been convicted in 1958 of second-degree burglary and "stealing."

in effect a renewal of the motion for a mistrial, was denied, and his counsel stated that he had "no evidence to produce at this time under the circumstances." *Id.*, at 64. The jury returned a verdict of guilty, and on July 21, 1969, petitioner, who had been in the hospital for three weeks recovering from a bullet wound in the abdomen, appeared, and the trial court fixed the penalty at life imprisonment.

Petitioner filed a motion for a new trial, the burden of which was that the trial court had erred in proceeding with the trial when no evidence had been produced that his absence from the trial was voluntary. A hearing was held before the judge who had presided at trial. Petitioner testified that on June 25 he had gone to his brother's house and that he remembered nothing concerning the shooting except that he felt a burning pain in his stomach and later woke up in the hospital. He testified he did not remember talking to anyone at the hospital. The State presented evidence that upon admission to the hospital petitioner stated that he had shot himself because of " 'some problem with the law,' " *id.*, at 90, and that he had told a policeman he had shot himself because "he was supposed to go to court for rape, and he didn't do it; he rather be [*sic*] dead than to go to trial for something he didn't do." *Id.*, at 97. The trial judge denied the motion. Stating that on the morning of petitioner's failure to appear he had received information on the telephone which was checked with the hospital, the judge concluded that petitioner had the burden of showing that his absence was not voluntary and found on the basis of the evidence that his absence " 'was due to his own voluntary act in shooting himself; done for the very purpose of avoiding trial.' " *Id.*, at 103.

The Missouri Supreme Court affirmed, accepting the trial court's finding, in ruling on petitioner's motion for a new trial, that his absence was voluntary,[3] and holding that there was "no logical basis" for positing a different rule with respect to waiver of the right to be present in capital cases[4] than that which applies in felony cases generally. 462 S. W. 2d 677, 683–684. The Missouri Supreme Court also held that the denial of petitioner's motion for a continuance of the trial in order to procure further psychiatric evaluation was not an abuse of discretion, noting that petitioner did not contend that he lacked the mental capacity to proceed with the trial.

In April 1971 petitioner filed a motion to vacate the judgment of conviction and sentence in the court where sentence had been imposed, pursuant to Missouri Supreme Court Rule 27.26.[5] He alleged that his rights under Mo. Rev. Stat. § 552.020 (2) (1969)[6] and his

[3] As to the situation at trial, the Missouri Supreme Court stated: "We disagree with defendant's contention that there is 'no evidence upon the record' that he voluntarily absented himself. The court made such a determination before proceeding with the trial, although the basis for that determination is not fully disclosed. However, when defendant is free on bond, and he does not appear at the appointed time, it is presumed that the absence is voluntary until established otherwise." 462 S. W. 2d 677, 681 (1971).

[4] At the time of petitioner's trial, rape was punishable by death under Mo. Rev. Stat. § 559.260 (1969), and respondent had not waived the death penalty.

[5] A petition for a writ of habeas corpus previously filed in the United States District Court for the Eastern District of Missouri had been dismissed without prejudice on April 1, 1971, for failure to exhaust available state remedies. See 28 U. S. C. §§ 2254 (b), (c).

[6] Subdivision 2 of § 552.020 provides in pertinent part: "Whenever any judge or magistrate has reasonable cause to believe that the accused has a mental disease or defect excluding fitness to proceed he shall, upon his own motion or upon motion filed by the state or by or on behalf of the accused, by order of record, appoint one or more private physicians to make a psychiatric examination of the accused or shall direct the superintendent of a facility of the division of mental diseases to have the accused so examined by one or more physi-

constitutional rights had been violated by the failure to order a psychiatric examination prior to trial and by conducting the trial to conclusion in his absence. Petitioner also asserted that he had been denied the effective assistance of counsel, a claim which is not before us.

In July 1971 a hearing was held on the motion; petitioner called two psychiatrists as witnesses. The psychiatrist who had examined petitioner prior to his trial testified that in his opinion there was reasonable cause to believe that a person who attempted to commit suicide in the midst of a trial might not be mentally competent to understand the proceedings against him. Another psychiatrist, whose duties included the examination of accused persons under Mo. Rev. Stat. c. 552, testified that in his opinion a man who was charged with raping his wife and attempted suicide during his trial was in need of a psychiatric evaluation to find out his mental condition, and that there should be an evaluation to determine whether the person was competent to assist in his own defense and whether he was "malingering or did it intentionally or if it was due to a true psychiatric disorder." App. 156. The same psychiatrist stated that he had examined petitioner at City Hospital in 1965 and had found that he had psychiatric problems and was in need of care. Petitioner took the stand, repeating his previous testimony with respect to the shooting.

In June 1972 the sentencing judge denied petitioner's Rule 27.26 motion, and the Missouri Court of Appeals affirmed. The Court of Appeals concluded that the provisions for psychiatric examinations and hearings under Mo. Rev. Stat. § 552.020 (1969) comported with the re-

---

cians whom the superintendent shall designate." Subdivision 3 delineates the requirements for reports of psychiatric examinations, and subdivision 6 requires the court to hold a hearing if the opinion relative to fitness to proceed which is required to be included in the report is contested.

quirements of *Pate* v. *Robinson,* 383 U. S. 375 (1966), and that the test of incompetence to stand trial was that stated in *Dusky* v. *United States,* 362 U. S. 402 (1960).[7] It reasoned that it was necessary to examine the indicia of petitioner's incompetence "at three different times—before the trial, during the trial after the suicide attempt, and at the time of the motion for new trial." 498 S. W. 2d 838, 842.

As to the situation before trial, the court held that the psychiatric report attached to petitioner's motion for a continuance did not raise a reasonable doubt of his fitness to proceed. Turning to the second time period, "during the trial after the suicide attempt," the court held that *Pate* v. *Robinson, supra,* which involved a competence hearing rather than a competence examination followed by a hearing, did not require that the examination and hearing be held during the trial rather than immediately thereafter. With regard to the period after trial, and accepting petitioner's contention that his was a "bona fide attempt at suicide," the court was of the view that the legal significance of the attempt under *Robinson* should be evaluated without resort to the psychiatric testimony presented at the Rule 27.26 hearing, which was not before the trial judge. It held that petitioner's suicide attempt did not create a reasonable doubt of his competence as a matter of law, that petitioner had failed to demonstrate the inadequacy of the procedures employed for protecting his rights, and that the finding of the trial court was not clearly erroneous.[8]

[7] "[T]he 'test must be whether he has sufficient present ability to consult with his lawyer with a reasonable degree of rational understanding—and whether he has a rational as well as factual understanding of the proceedings against him.'" See also Mo. Rev. Stat. § 552.020 (1) (1969).

[8] Under Missouri Supreme Court Rule 27.26 (f) (1969), the "prisoner has the burden of establishing his grounds for relief by a

Finally, the Missouri Court of Appeals rejected petitioner's claim that he was deprived of due process of law by the conduct of a portion of his trial in his absence; it noted that the State Supreme Court had upheld a finding of voluntary absence on petitioner's direct appeal and concluded that the psychiatrists' testimony at the Rule 27.26 hearing did not meet the burden of proof placed on petitioner. "Again we cannot hold the trial court's finding to be clearly erroneous." 498 S. W. 2d, at 843. We granted certiorari, and we now reverse.

II

It has long been accepted that a person whose mental condition is such that he lacks the capacity to understand the nature and object of the proceedings against him, to consult with counsel, and to assist in preparing his defense may not be subjected to a trial. Thus, Blackstone wrote that one who became "mad" after the commission of an offense should not be arraigned for it "because he is not able to plead to it with that advice and caution that he ought." Similarly, if he became "mad" after pleading, he should not be tried, "for how can he make his defense?" 4 W. Blackstone, Commentaries *24. See *Youtsey* v. *United States*, 97 F. 937, 940–946 (CA6 1899). Some have viewed the common-law prohibition "as a by-product of the ban against trials *in absentia;* the mentally incompetent defendant, though physically present in the courtroom, is in reality afforded no opportunity to defend himself." Foote, A Comment on Pre-Trial Commitment of Criminal Defendants, 108 U. Pa. L. Rev. 832, 834 (1960). See *Thomas* v. *Cunningham*, 313 F. 2d 934, 938 (CA4 1963). For our purposes, it suffices

---

preponderance of the evidence." Appellate review is limited under Rule 27.26 (j) "to a determination of whether the findings, conclusions and judgment of the trial court are clearly erroneous."

to note that the prohibition is fundamental to an adversary system of justice. See generally Note, Incompetency to Stand Trial, 81 Harv. L. Rev. 455, 457–459 (1967). Accordingly, as to federal cases, we have approved a test of incompetence which seeks to ascertain whether a criminal defendant " 'has sufficient present ability to consult with his lawyer with a reasonable degree of rational understanding—and whether he has a rational as well as factual understanding of the proceedings against him.' " *Dusky* v. *United States,* 362 U. S., at 402.

In *Pate* v. *Robinson,* 383 U. S. 375 (1966), we held that the failure to observe procedures adequate to protect a defendant's right not to be tried or convicted while incompetent to stand trial deprives him of his due process right to a fair trial. Although in *Robinson* we noted that Illinois "jealously guard[ed] this right," *id.,* at 385, we held that the failure of the state courts to invoke the statutory procedures deprived Robinson of the inquiry into the issue of his competence to stand trial to which, on the facts of the case, we concluded he was constitutionally entitled. The Court did not hold that the procedure prescribed by Ill. Rev. Stat., c. 38, § 104–2 (1963), was constitutionally mandated, although central to its discussion was the conclusion that the statutory procedure, if followed, was constitutionally adequate. See, *e. g., United States* v. *Knohl,* 379 F. 2d 427, 434–435 (CA2), cert. denied, 389 U. S. 973 (1967); *United States ex rel. Evans* v. *LaVallee,* 446 F. 2d 782, 785–786 (CA2 1971), cert. denied, 404 U. S. 1020 (1972). Nor did the Court prescribe a general standard with respect to the nature or quantum of evidence necessary to require resort to an adequate procedure.[9] Rather, it noted that

[9] In discussing the evidence adduced at Robinson's trial, the Court did, however, indicate that a history of irrational behavior is a rele-

under the Illinois statute a hearing was required where the evidence raised a " '*bona fide* doubt' " as to a defendant's competence, and the Court concluded "that the evidence introduced on Robinson's behalf entitled him to a hearing on this issue." 383 U. S., at 385. See *United States* v. *Marshall*, 458 F. 2d 446, 450 (CA2 1972).

As was true of Illinois in *Robinson*, Missouri's statutory scheme "jealously guards" a defendant's right to a fair trial. Missouri Rev. Stat. § 552.020 (1) (1969) provides: "No person who as a result of mental disease or defect lacks capacity to understand the proceedings against him or to assist in his own defense shall be tried, convicted or sentenced for the commission of an offense so long as the incapacity endures." Section 552.020 (2), see n. 6, provides that a judge or magistrate shall, "upon his own motion or upon motion filed by the state or by or on behalf of the accused," order a psychiatric examination whenever he "has reasonable cause to believe that the accused has a mental disease or defect excluding fitness to proceed." Section 552.020 (3) prescribes the contents of a report of the psychiatric examination, and § 552.030 (6) requires the court to hold a hearing if the opinion relative to fitness to proceed which is required to be included in the report is contested. In addition, the trial court may conduct a hearing on its own motion. Such a procedure is, on its face, constitutionally adequate to protect a defendant's right not to be tried while legally incompetent. Our task is to determine whether the proceedings in this case were consistent with petitioner's right to a fair trial.

---

vant factor which, on the record before it, was sufficient to require further inquiry notwithstanding Robinson's demeanor at trial and the stipulated opinion of a psychiatrist that Robinson knew the nature of the charges against him and could cooperate with counsel when the psychiatrist examined him two or three months before. See *infra*, at 180–181.

At the outset we are met by respondent's argument that the Court is bound by "limitations placed on proceedings under" Missouri Supreme Court Rule 27.26. Brief for Respondent 23. Specifically, respondent notes that under Rule 27.26 (f) petitioner had "the burden of establishing his grounds for relief by a preponderance of the evidence," and that the appellate-review function of the Missouri Court of Appeals was limited by Rule 27.26 (j) "to a determination of whether the findings, conclusions and judgment of the trial court [were] clearly erroneous." It urges that the Rule was "designed . . . to provide a valuable post-conviction remedy and not to provide another direct appeal . . . ," and expresses concern that "the state-federal relationship . . . remain in proper balance." Brief for Respondent 22.

We share respondent's concern for this necessary balance, and we do not question the State's power, in post-conviction proceedings, to reallocate the respective burdens of the individual and the State and to delimit the scope of state appellate review. Cf. *Hawk* v. *Olson,* 326 U. S. 271, 279 (1945); *Conner* v. *Wingo,* 429 F. 2d 630, 637–639 (CA6 1970). At the same time we note that while proceedings under the Rule "ordinarily cannot be used as a substitute for direct appeal involving mere trial errors or as a substitute for a second appeal," nevertheless "trial errors affecting constitutional rights may be raised even though the error could have been raised on appeal." Mo. Sup. Ct. Rule 27.26 (b)(3).

In the present case there is no dispute as to the evidence possibly relevant to petitioner's mental condition that was before the trial court prior to trial and thereafter. Rather, the dispute concerns the inferences that were to be drawn from the undisputed evidence and whether, in light of what was then known, the failure to make further inquiry into petitioner's competence to stand trial, denied him a fair trial. In such circumstances we believe it is "incumbent upon us to analyze the facts in order that the appropriate enforcement of the federal right may be assured." *Norris* v. *Alabama,* 294 U. S. 587, 590 (1935).[10] "When the corrective process is provided by the state but error, in relation to the federal question of constitutional violation, creeps into the record, we have the responsibility to review the state proceedings." *Hawk* v. *Olson, supra,* at 276.

III

The sentencing judge and the Missouri Court of Appeals concluded that the psychiatric evaluation of petitioner attached to his pretrial motion for a continuance did not contain sufficient indicia of incompetence to stand trial to require further inquiry. Both courts mentioned aspects of the report suggesting competence, such as the impressions that petitioner did not have "any delusions, illusions, hallucinations . . . ," was "well oriented in all spheres," and "was able, without trouble, to answer questions testing judgement," but neither court mentioned the contrary data. The report also showed that petitioner, although cooperative in the examination, "had difficulty in participating well," "had a difficult

---

[10] "But 'issue of fact' is a coat of many colors. It does not cover a conclusion drawn from uncontroverted happenings, when that conclusion incorporates standards of conduct or criteria for judgment which in themselves are decisive of constitutional rights. Such standards and criteria, measured against the requirements drawn from constitutional provisions, and their proper applications, are issues for this Court's adjudication. . . . Especially in cases arising under the Due Process Clause is it important to distinguish between issues of fact that are here foreclosed and issues which, though cast in the form of determinations of fact, are the very issues to review which this Court sits." *Watts* v. *Indiana,* 338 U. S. 49, 51 (1949) (opinion of Frankfurter, J.). See also *Culombe* v. *Connecticut,* 367 U. S. 568, 605 (1961) (opinion of Frankfurter, J.).

time relating," and that he "was markedly circumstantial and irrelevant in his speech." In addition, neither court felt that petitioner's episodic irrational acts described in the report or the psychiatrist's diagnoses of "[b]orderline mental deficiency" and "[c]hronic [a]nxiety reaction with depression" created a sufficient doubt of competence to require further inquiry.[11]

It does not appear that the examining psychiatrist was asked to address himself to medical facts bearing specifically on the issue of petitioner's competence to stand trial, as distinguished from his mental and emotional condition generally. Thus, it is not surprising that before this Court the dispute centers on the inferences that could or should properly have been drawn from the report. Even where the issue is in focus we have recognized "the uncertainty of diagnosis in this field and the tentativeness of professional judgment." *Greenwood* v. *United States,* 350 U. S. 366, 375 (1956). Here the inquiry is rendered more difficult by the fact that a defendant's mental condition may be relevant to more than one legal issue, each governed by distinct rules reflecting quite different policies. See *Jackson* v. *Indiana,* 406 U. S. 715, 739 (1972); *Pate* v. *Robinson,* 383 U. S., at 388–389 (Harlan, J., dissenting); Weihofen, The Definition of Mental Illness, 21 Ohio St. L. J. 1 (1960).

Like the report itself, the motion for a continuance did not clearly suggest that petitioner's competence to stand trial was the question sought to be resolved. While we have expressed doubt that the right to further inquiry upon the question can be waived, see *Pate* v. *Robinson,* 383 U. S., at 384, it is nevertheless true that judges must

[11] See n. 1, *supra.* The Court of Appeals determined that the other diagnosis offered, "[s]ociopathic personality disorder, sexual perversion," was excluded as a "mental disease or defect" under Missouri law. See Mo. Rev. Stat. § 552.010 (1969).

depend to some extent on counsel to bring issues into focus. Petitioner's somewhat inartfully drawn motion for a continuance probably fell short of appropriate assistance to the trial court in that regard. However, we are constrained to disagree with the sentencing judge that counsel's pretrial contention that "the defendant is not a person of sound mind and should have a further psychiatric examination before the case should be forced to trial," did not raise the issue of petitioner's competence to stand trial.[12] This statement also may have tended to blur the aspect of petitioner's mental condition which would bear on his criminal responsibility and that which would bear on his competence to stand trial. However, at that stage, and with the obvious advantages of hindsight, it seems to us that it would have been, at the very least, the better practice to order an immediate examination under Mo. Rev. Code § 552.020 (2) (1969).[13] It

[12] In a colloquy with the trial judge, petitioner's counsel noted that the examination and evaluation "could be done during the summer months and be ready for trial *or else the examination would eliminate trial by September*." App. 17. (Emphasis added.)

[13] The sentencing judge observed that "motions for psychiatric examinations have often been made merely for the purpose of delay," and "estimated that almost seventy-five percent of those sent for psychiatric examinations are returned mentally competent." App. 202. Although we do not, of course, suggest that courts must accept without question a lawyer's representations concerning the competence of his client, see *United States ex rel. Rizzi* v. *Follette*, 367 F. 2d 559, 561 (CA2 1966), an expressed doubt in that regard by one with "the closest contact with the defendant," *Pate* v. *Robinson*, 383 U. S. 375, 391 (1966) (Harlan, J., dissenting), is unquestionably a factor which should be considered. Moreover, resolution of the issue of competence to stand trial at an early date best serves both the interests of fairness, see *Peyton* v. *Rowe*, 391 U. S. 54, 62 (1968), and of sound judicial administration. See Panel on Recognizing and Determining Mental Competency to Stand Trial—Insanity as a Defense, in Institutes on Sentencing, 37 F. R. D. 111, 155, 161 (1964). Realization of those facts may have prompted the practice, noted by the sentencing

is unnecessary for us to decide whether such examination was constitutionally required on the basis of what was then known to the trial court since in our view the question was settled by later events.

IV

Turning to the situation at petitioner's trial, the state courts viewed the evidence as failing to show that during trial petitioner had acted in a manner that would cause the trial court to doubt his competence. The testimony of petitioner's wife, some of which repeated and confirmed information contained in the psychiatric evaluation attached to petitioner's motion for a continuance, was given little weight.[14] Finally, the sentencing judge, relying on his finding on petitioner's motion for a new trial and although stating "that it does not take a psychiatrist to know that such a man has a problem and indicates poor judgment," App. 203, concluded that the "fact that Mr. Drope shot himself to avoid trial suggests very

court, "of the Circuit Attorney at the time to consent in all cases to a psychiatric examination whether with or without merit and without looking into the matter further." App. 206.

[14] See n. 1, *supra*. The sentencing court noted: "She did testify in answer to the question 'And at that time didn't you tell me that you felt your husband was sick and needed psychiatric care?' The answer 'Yes.' There was also some evidence of disputes and trouble accompanied by some physical force between husband and wife but not to the extent to indicate inability to understand the proceedings. There was no recitation of facts upon which a layman could base the opinion that the defendant was insane except the testimony perhaps that he rolled down the steps but this occurred only two or three times over a period of eight or nine or ten years." App. 201. The Court of Appeals dealt with her testimony only insofar as it repeated information in the psychiatric evaluation. It concluded that her feelings that petitioner had mental problems "bore on his sexual perversions—not his competency," and that the stairs episodes "demonstrate[d] pique more than anything." 498 S. W. 2d, at 842.

strongly an awareness of what was going on." *Id.*, at 208. The Missouri Court of Appeals, accepting *arguendo* petitioner's contention that his was "a bona fide attempt at suicide," refused to conclude "that as a matter of law an attempt at suicide creates a reasonable doubt as to the movant's competency to stand trial." *Id.*, at 222.

Notwithstanding the difficulty of making evaluations of the kind required in these circumstances, we conclude that the record reveals a failure to give proper weight to the information suggesting incompetence which came to light during trial. This is particularly so when viewed in the context of the events surrounding petitioner's suicide attempt and against the background of the pretrial showing. Although a defendant's demeanor during trial may be such as to obviate "the need for extensive reliance on psychiatric prediction concerning his capabilities," Note, 81 Harv. L. Rev., at 469, we concluded in *Pate* v. *Robinson,* 383 U. S., at 385–386, that "this reasoning offers no justification for ignoring the uncontradicted testimony of . . . [a] history of pronounced irrational behavior." We do not mean to suggest that the indicia of such behavior in this case approximated those in *Robinson,* but we believe the Missouri courts failed to consider and give proper weight to the record evidence. Too little weight was given to the testimony of petitioner's wife that on the Sunday prior to trial he tried to choke her to death. For a man whose fate depended in large measure on the indulgence of his wife, who had hesitated about pressing the prosecution, this hardly could be regarded as rational conduct.[15] Moreover, in considering the indicia of petitioner's

[15] It appears that under Mo. Rev. Stat. § 546.260 (1969) petitioner's wife could not be compelled to testify against him. See *State* v. *Dunbar,* 360 Mo. 788, 230 S. W. 2d 845 (1950). Similarly, neither court mentioned Mrs. Drope's testimony concerning petitioner's consultations at City Hospital. At the Rule 27.26 hearing, it will be recalled, a psychiatrist testified that he had examined peti-

incompetence separately, the state courts gave insufficient attention to the aggregate of those indicia in applying the objective standard of Mo. Rev. Stat. § 552.020 (2). We need not address the Court of Appeals' conclusion that an attempt to commit suicide does not create a reasonable doubt of competence to stand trial as a matter of law. As was true of the psychiatric evaluation, petitioner's attempt to commit suicide "did not stand alone." *Moore* v. *United States*, 464 F. 2d 663, 666 (CA9 1972). We conclude that when considered together with the information available prior to trial and the testimony of petitioner's wife at trial, the information concerning petitioner's suicide attempt created a sufficient doubt of his competence to stand trial to require further inquiry on the question.

The import of our decision in *Pate* v. *Robinson* is that evidence of a defendant's irrational behavior, his demeanor at trial, and any prior medical opinion on competence to stand trial are all relevant in determining whether further inquiry is required, but that even one of these factors standing alone may, in some circumstances, be sufficient. There are, of course, no fixed or immutable signs which invariably indicate the need for further inquiry to determine fitness to proceed; the question is often a difficult one in which a wide range of manifestations and subtle nuances are implicated. That they are difficult to evaluate is suggested by the varying opinions trained psychiatrists can entertain on the same facts.

Here, the evidence of irrational behavior prior to trial was weaker than in *Robinson,* but there was no opinion evidence as to petitioner's competence to stand trial. See n. 9, *supra.* Moreover, Robinson was present throughout his trial; petitioner was absent for a crucial portion of his

---

tioner at City Hospital in 1965 and had determined that he was in need of psychiatric care.

trial. Petitioner's absence bears on the analysis in two ways: first, it was due to an act which suggests a rather substantial degree of mental instability contemporaneous with the trial, see *Pate* v. *Robinson,* 383 U. S., at 389 (Harlan, J., dissenting);[16] second, as a result of petitioner's absence the trial judge and defense counsel were no longer able to observe him in the context of the trial and to gauge from his demeanor whether he was able to cooperate with his attorney and to understand the nature and object of the proceedings against him.

Even when a defendant is competent at the commencement of his trial, a trial court must always be alert to circumstances suggesting a change that would render the accused unable to meet the standards of competence to stand trial. Whatever the relationship between mental illness and incompetence to stand trial, in this case the bearing of the former on the latter was sufficiently likely that, in light of the evidence of petitioner's behavior including his suicide attempt, and there being no opportunity without his presence to evaluate that bearing in fact, the correct course was to suspend the trial until such an evaluation could be made.[17] That this might have

[16] We assume, as did the Missouri Court of Appeals, that petitioner's was a "bona fide" suicide attempt, rather than, as respondent contends, malingering. In that regard, the hearsay information in the possession of the trial judge when he denied the motion for a mistrial suggested an intent on the part of petitioner to kill himself, and a self-inflicted wound near vital organs does not suggest malingering. Of course we also recognize that "the empirical relationship between mental illness and suicide" or suicide attempts is uncertain and that a suicide attempt need not always signal "an inability to perceive reality accurately, to reason logically and to make plans and carry them out in an organized fashion." Greenberg, Involuntary Psychiatric Commitments to Prevent Suicide, 49 N. Y. U. L. Rev. 227, 234, 236 (1974). See also Pokorny, Myths about Suicide, in Suicidal Behaviors 64–65 (H. Resnik ed. 1968).

[17] In reaching this conclusion we have not relied on the testimony of the psychiatrists at the Rule 27.26 hearing, which, we agree with

aborted the trial is a hard reality, but we cannot fail to note that such a result might have been avoided by prompt psychiatric examination before trial, when it was sought by petitioner.

V

Our resolution of the first issue raised by petitioner makes it unnecessary to decide whether, as he contends, it was constitutionally impermissible to conduct the remainder of his trial on a capital offense in his enforced absence from a self-inflicted wound. See *Diaz* v. *United States*, 223 U. S. 442, 445 (1912). However, even assuming the right to be present was one that could be waived, what we have already said makes it clear that there was an insufficient inquiry to afford a basis for deciding the issue of waiver. Cf. *Westbrook* v. *Arizona*, 384 U. S. 150 (1966); *United States* v. *Silva*, 418 F. 2d 328 (CA2 1969).

The Missouri Court of Appeals concluded that, had further inquiry into petitioner's competence to stand trial been constitutionally mandated in this case, it would have been permissible to defer it until the trial had been completed. Such a procedure may have advantages, at least where the defendant is present at the trial and the appropriate inquiry is implemented with dispatch. See Note, 81 Harv. L. Rev., at 469; *Hansford* v. *United States*, 127 U. S. App. D. C. 359, 360, 384 F. 2d 311, 312 (1966) (rehearing en banc denied) (statement of Leventhal, J.); *Jackson* v. *Indiana*, 406 U. S., at 741. However, because of petitioner's absence during a critical stage of his trial, neither the judge nor counsel was able to observe him, and the hearing on his motion for a new trial, held approximately three months after the trial, was not informed by an inquiry into either his competence to stand

---

the Missouri Court of Appeals, is not relevant to the question before us.

trial or his capacity effectively to waive his right to be present.

The question remains whether petitioner's due process rights would be adequately protected by remanding the case now for a psychiatric examination aimed at establishing whether petitioner was in fact competent to stand trial in 1969. Given the inherent difficulties of such a *nunc pro tunc* determination under the most favorable circumstances, see *Pate* v. *Robinson,* 383 U. S., at 386–387; *Dusky* v. *United States,* 362 U. S., at 403, we cannot conclude that such a procedure would be adequate here. Cf. *Conner* v. *Wingo,* 429 F. 2d, at 639–640. The State is free to retry petitioner, assuming, of course, that at the time of such trial he is competent to be tried.

The judgment is reversed, and the cause is remanded for proceedings not inconsistent with this opinion.

Reversed and remanded.

Syllabus

FORD *v.* WAINWRIGHT, SECRETARY, FLORIDA DEPARTMENT OF CORRECTIONS

CERTIORARI TO THE UNITED STATES COURT OF APPEALS FOR THE ELEVENTH CIRCUIT

No. 85-5542. Argued April 22, 1986—Decided June 26, 1986

In 1974, petitioner was convicted of murder in a Florida state court and sentenced to death. There is no suggestion that he was incompetent at the time of the offense, at trial, or at sentencing. But subsequently he began to manifest changes in behavior, indicating a mental disorder. This led to extensive separate examinations by two psychiatrists at his counsel's request, one of whom concluded that petitioner was not competent to suffer execution. Counsel then invoked a Florida statute governing the determination of a condemned prisoner's competency. Following the statutory procedures, the Governor appointed three psychiatrists, who together interviewed petitioner for 30 minutes in the presence of eight other people, including petitioner's counsel, the State's attorneys, and correctional officials. The Governor's order directed that the attorneys should not participate in the examination in any adversarial manner. Each psychiatrist filed a separate report with the Governor, to whom the statute delegates the final decision. The reports reached conflicting diagnoses but were in accord on the question of petitioner's competency. Petitioner's counsel then attempted to submit to the Governor other written materials, including the reports of the two psychiatrists who had previously examined petitioner, but the Governor's office refused to inform counsel whether the submission would be considered. The Governor subsequently signed a death warrant without explanation or statement. After unsuccessfully seeking a hearing in state court to determine anew petitioner's competency, his counsel filed a habeas corpus proceeding in Federal District Court, seeking an evidentiary hearing, but the court denied the petition without a hearing, and the Court of Appeals affirmed.

Held: The judgment is reversed, and the case is remanded.

752 F. 2d 526, reversed and remanded.

JUSTICE MARSHALL delivered the opinion of the Court with respect to Parts I and II, concluding that the Eighth Amendment prohibits the State from inflicting the death penalty upon a prisoner who is insane. The reasons at common law for not condoning the execution of the insane—that such an execution has questionable retributive value, presents no example to others and thus has no deterrence value, and simply offends humanity—have no less logical, moral, and practical force at present. Whether the aim is to protect the condemned from fear and pain without comfort of understanding, or to protect the dignity of society itself from the barbarity of exacting mindless vengeance, the restriction finds enforcement in the Eighth Amendment. Pp. 405–410.

JUSTICE MARSHALL, joined by JUSTICE BRENNAN, JUSTICE BLACKMUN, and JUSTICE STEVENS, concluded in Parts III, IV, and V, that Florida's statutory procedures for determining a condemned prisoner's sanity provide inadequate assurance of accuracy to satisfy the requirement of *Townsend* v. *Sain*, 372 U. S. 293, and that, having been denied a factfinding procedure "adequate to afford a full and fair hearing" on the critical issue as required by 28 U. S. C. § 2254(d)(2), petitioner is entitled to a *de novo* evidentiary hearing in the District Court on the question of his competence to be executed. Pp. 410–418.

(a) No state court has issued any determination to which the presumption of correctness under § 2254(d) could attach, and indeed no state court played any role in the rejection of petitioner's claim of insanity. P. 410.

(b) The first defect in Florida's procedures is the failure to include the prisoner in the truth-seeking process. Any procedure that precludes the prisoner or his counsel from presenting material relevant to his sanity or bars consideration of that material by the factfinder is necessarily inadequate. A related flaw in the procedures is the denial of any opportunity to challenge or impeach the state-appointed psychiatrists' opinions, thus creating a significant possibility that the ultimate decision made in reliance on those experts will be distorted. And perhaps the most striking defect in the procedures is the placement of the ultimate decision wholly within the Executive Branch. The Governor, who appoints the experts and ultimately decides whether the State will be able to carry out the death sentence and whose subordinates have been responsible for initiating every stage of the prosecution, cannot be said to have the neutrality that is necessary for reliability in the factfinding proceedings. Pp. 413–416.

JUSTICE POWELL concluded that the test for whether a prisoner is insane for Eighth Amendment purposes is whether the prisoner is aware of his impending execution and of the reason for it. He further concluded that petitioner's claim falls within this definition, and that because petitioner's claim was not adjudicated fairly within the meaning of due process or of 28 U. S. C. § 2254(d), petitioner is entitled to have his claim adjudicated on remand by the District Court. Finally, he concluded that the States could satisfy due process by providing an impartial officer or board that can receive evidence and argument from the prisoner's counsel, including expert psychiatric evidence. Beyond these requirements, the States retain substantial discretion to create appropriate procedures. Pp. 419–427.

MARSHALL, J., announced the judgment of the Court and delivered an opinion of the Court with respect to Parts I and II, in which BRENNAN, BLACKMUN, POWELL, and STEVENS, JJ., joined, and an opinion with respect to Parts III, IV, and V, in which BRENNAN, BLACKMUN, and STEVENS, JJ., joined. POWELL, J., filed an opinion concurring in part and concurring in the judgment, *post*, p. 418. O'CONNOR, J., filed an opinion concurring in the result in part and dissenting in part, in which WHITE, J., joined, *post*, p. 427. REHNQUIST, J., filed a dissenting opinion, in which BURGER, C. J., joined, *post*, p. 431.

Richard H. Burr III argued the cause for petitioner. With him on the briefs were *Richard L. Jorandby*, *Craig S. Barnard*, and *Laurin A. Wollan, Jr.*

Joy B. Shearer, Assistant Attorney General of Florida, argued the cause for respondent. With her on the brief was *Jim Smith*, Attorney General.*

JUSTICE MARSHALL announced the judgment of the Court and delivered the opinion of the Court with respect to Parts I and II and an opinion with respect to Parts III, IV, and V, in which JUSTICE BRENNAN, JUSTICE BLACKMUN, and JUSTICE STEVENS join.

For centuries no jurisdiction has countenanced the execution of the insane, yet this Court has never decided whether the Constitution forbids the practice. Today we keep faith with our common-law heritage in holding that it does.

I

Alvin Bernard Ford was convicted of murder in 1974 and sentenced to death. There is no suggestion that he was incompetent at the time of his offense, at trial, or at sentenc-

*Briefs of *amici curiae* urging reversal were filed for the American Psychiatric Association by *Joel I. Klein* and *Robert D. Luskin;* for the American Psychological Association et al. by *Donald N. Bersoff* and *Bruce J. Ennis, Jr.;* and for the Capital Collateral Representative et al. by *Sanford L. Bohrer.*

ing. In early 1982, however, Ford began to manifest gradual changes in behavior. They began as an occasional peculiar idea or confused perception, but became more serious over time. After reading in the newspaper that the Ku Klux Klan had held a rally in nearby Jacksonville, Florida, Ford developed an obsession focused upon the Klan. His letters to various people reveal endless brooding about his "Klan work," and an increasingly pervasive delusion that he had become the target of a complex conspiracy, involving the Klan and assorted others, designed to force him to commit suicide. He believed that the prison guards, part of the conspiracy, had been killing people and putting the bodies in the concrete enclosures used for beds. Later, he began to believe that his women relatives were being tortured and sexually abused somewhere in the prison. This notion developed into a delusion that the people who were tormenting him at the prison had taken members of Ford's family hostage. The hostage delusion took firm hold and expanded, until Ford was reporting that 135 of his friends and family were being held hostage in the prison, and that only he could help them. By "day 287" of the "hostage crisis," the list of hostages had expanded to include "senators, Senator Kennedy, and many other leaders." App. 53. In a letter to the Attorney General of Florida, written in 1983, Ford appeared to assume authority for ending the "crisis," claiming to have fired a number of prison officials. He began to refer to himself as "Pope John Paul, III," and reported having appointed nine new justices to the Florida Supreme Court. *Id.*, at 59.

Counsel for Ford asked a psychiatrist who had examined Ford earlier, Dr. Jamal Amin, to continue seeing him and to recommend appropriate treatment. On the basis of roughly 14 months of evaluation, taped conversations between Ford and his attorneys, letters written by Ford, interviews with Ford's acquaintances, and various medical records, Dr. Amin concluded in 1983 that Ford suffered from "a severe, uncontrollable, mental disease which closely resembles 'Paranoid

Schizophrenia With Suicide Potential'"—a "major mental disorder . . . severe enough to substantially affect Mr. Ford's present ability to assist in the defense of his life." *Id.*, at 91.

Ford subsequently refused to see Dr. Amin again, believing him to have joined the conspiracy against him, and Ford's counsel sought assistance from Dr. Harold Kaufman, who interviewed Ford in November 1983. Ford told Dr. Kaufman that "I know there is some sort of death penalty, but I'm free to go whenever I want because it would be illegal and the executioner would be executed." *Id.*, at 65. When asked if he would be executed, Ford replied: "I can't be executed because of the landmark case. I won. Ford v. State will prevent executions all over." *Id.*, at 66. These statements appeared amidst long streams of seemingly unrelated thoughts in rapid succession. Dr. Kaufman concluded that Ford had no understanding of why he was being executed, made no connection between the homicide of which he had been convicted and the death penalty, and indeed sincerely believed that he would not be executed because he owned the prisons and could control the Governor through mind waves. *Id.*, at 67. Dr. Kaufman found that there was "no reasonable possibility that Mr. Ford was dissembling, malingering or otherwise putting on a performance . . . ." *Id.*, at 65. The following month, in an interview with his attorneys, Ford regressed further into nearly complete incomprehensibility, speaking only in a code characterized by intermittent use of the word "one," making statements such as "Hands one, face one. Mafia one. God one, father one, Pope one. Pope one. Leader one." *Id.*, at 72.

Counsel for Ford invoked the procedures of Florida law governing the determination of competency of a condemned inmate, Fla. Stat. § 922.07 (1985). Following the procedures set forth in the statute, the Governor of Florida appointed a panel of three psychiatrists to evaluate whether, under § 922.07(2), Ford had "the mental capacity to understand the nature of the death penalty and the reasons why it was imposed upon him." At a single meeting, the three psychiatrists together interviewed Ford for approximately 30 minutes. Each doctor then filed a separate two- or three-page report with the Governor, to whom the statute delegates the final decision. One doctor concluded that Ford suffered from "psychosis with paranoia" but had "enough cognitive functioning to understand the nature and the effects of the death penalty, and why it is to be imposed on him." App. 103. Another found that, although Ford was "psychotic," he did "know fully what can happen to him." *Id.*, at 105–106. The third concluded that Ford had a "severe adaptational disorder," but did "comprehend his total situation including being sentenced to death, and all of the implications of that penalty." *Id.*, at 99–100. He believed that Ford's disorder, "although severe, seem[ed] contrived and recently learned." *Id.*, at 100. Thus, the interview produced three different diagnoses, but accord on the question of sanity as defined by state law.

The Governor's decision was announced on April 30, 1984, when, without explanation or statement, he signed a death warrant for Ford's execution. Ford's attorneys unsuccessfully sought a hearing in state court to determine anew Ford's competency to suffer execution. *Ford* v. *Wainwright*, 451 So. 2d 471, 475 (Fla. 1984). Counsel then filed a petition for habeas corpus in the United States District Court for the Southern District of Florida, seeking an evidentiary hearing on the question of Ford's sanity, proffering the conflicting findings of the Governor-appointed commission and subsequent challenges to their methods by other psychiatrists. The District Court denied the petition without a hearing. The Court of Appeals granted a certificate of probable cause and stayed Ford's execution, *Ford* v. *Strickland*, 734 F. 2d 538 (CA11 1984), and we rejected the State's effort to vacate the stay of execution. *Wainwright* v. *Ford*, 467 U. S. 1220 (1984). The Court of Appeals then addressed the merits of Ford's claim and a divided panel affirmed the District Court's denial of the writ. 752 F. 2d 526 (CA11 1985). This Court granted Ford's petition for certiorari in order to resolve the important issue whether the Eighth Amendment prohibits the execution of the insane and, if so, whether the District Court should have held a hearing on petitioner's claim. 474 U. S. 1019 (1985).

II

Since this Court last had occasion to consider the infliction of the death penalty upon the insane, our interpretations of the Due Process Clause and the Eighth Amendment have evolved substantially. In *Solesbee* v. *Balkcom,* 339 U. S. 9 (1950), a condemned prisoner claimed a due process right to a judicial determination of his sanity, yet the Court did not consider the possible existence of a right under the Eighth Amendment, which had not yet been applied to the States. The sole question the Court addressed was whether Georgia's procedure for ascertaining sanity adequately effectuated that State's own policy of sparing the insane from execution. See also *Caritativo* v. *California,* 357 U. S. 549 (1958); *United States ex rel. Smith* v. *Baldi,* 344 U. S. 561 (1953); *Phyle* v. *Duffy,* 334 U. S. 431 (1948); *Nobles* v. *Georgia,* 168 U. S. 398 (1897). Now that the Eighth Amendment has been recognized to affect significantly both the procedural and the substantive aspects of the death penalty, the question of executing the insane takes on a wholly different complexion. The adequacy of the procedures chosen by a State to determine sanity, therefore, will depend upon an issue that this Court has never addressed: whether the Constitution places a substantive restriction on the State's power to take the life of an insane prisoner.

There is now little room for doubt that the Eighth Amendment's ban on cruel and unusual punishment embraces, at a minimum, those modes or acts of punishment that had been considered cruel and unusual at the time that the Bill of Rights was adopted. See *Solem* v. *Helm,* 463 U. S. 277, 285–286 (1983); *id.,* at 312–313 (BURGER, C. J., joined by

WHITE, REHNQUIST, and O'CONNOR, JJ., dissenting); *Furman* v. *Georgia*, 408 U. S. 238, 264 (1972) (BRENNAN, J., concurring); *McGautha* v. *California*, 402 U. S. 183, 226 (1971) (Black, J., concurring). "Although the Framers may have intended the Eighth Amendment to go beyond the scope of its English counterpart, their use of the language of the English Bill of Rights is convincing proof that they intended to provide at least the same protection . . . ." *Solem* v. *Helm*, *supra*, at 286.

Moreover, the Eighth Amendment's proscriptions are not limited to those practices condemned by the common law in 1789. See *Gregg* v. *Georgia*, 428 U. S. 153, 171 (1976) (opinion of Stewart, POWELL, and STEVENS, JJ.). Not bound by the sparing humanitarian concessions of our forebears, the Amendment also recognizes the "evolving standards of decency that mark the progress of a maturing society." *Trop* v. *Dulles*, 356 U. S. 86, 101 (1958) (plurality opinion). In addition to considering the barbarous methods generally outlawed in the 18th century, therefore, this Court takes into account objective evidence of contemporary values before determining whether a particular punishment comports with the fundamental human dignity that the Amendment protects. See *Coker* v. *Georgia*, 433 U. S. 584, 597 (1977) (plurality opinion).

A

We begin, then, with the common law. The bar against executing a prisoner who has lost his sanity bears impressive historical credentials; the practice consistently has been branded "savage and inhuman." 4 W. Blackstone, Commentaries *24–*25 (hereinafter Blackstone). Blackstone explained:

> "[I]diots and lunatics are not chargeable for their own acts, if committed when under these incapacities: no, not even for treason itself. Also, if a man in his sound memory commits a capital offence, and before arraignment for it, he becomes mad, he ought not to be arraigned for

> it: because he is not able to plead to it with that advice and caution that he ought. And if, after he has pleaded, the prisoner becomes mad, he shall not be tried: for how can he make his defence? If, after he be tried and found guilty, he loses his senses before judgment, judgment shall not be pronounced; and if, after judgment, he becomes of nonsane memory, execution shall be stayed: for peradventure, says the humanity of the English law, had the prisoner been of sound memory, he might have alleged something in stay of judgment or execution." *Ibid.* (footnotes omitted).

Sir Edward Coke had earlier expressed the same view of the common law of England: "[B]y intendment of Law the execution of the offender is for example, . . . but so it is not when a mad man is executed, but should be a miserable spectacle, both against Law, and of extream inhumanity and cruelty, and can be no example to others." 3 E. Coke, Institutes 6 (6th ed. 1680) (hereinafter Coke). Other recorders of the common law concurred. See 1 M. Hale, Pleas of the Crown 35 (1736) (hereinafter Hale); 1 W. Hawkins, Pleas of the Crown 2 (7th ed. 1795) (hereinafter Hawkins); Hawles, Remarks on the Trial of Mr. Charles Bateman, 11 How. St. Tr. 474, 477 (1685) (hereinafter Hawles).

As is often true of common-law principles, see O. Holmes, The Common Law 5 (1881), the reasons for the rule are less sure and less uniform than the rule itself. One explanation is that the execution of an insane person simply offends humanity, Coke 6; another, that it provides no example to others and thus contributes nothing to whatever deterrence value is intended to be served by capital punishment. *Ibid.* Other commentators postulate religious underpinnings: that it is uncharitable to dispatch an offender "into another world, when he is not of a capacity to fit himself for it," Hawles 477. It is also said that execution serves no purpose in these cases because madness is its own punishment: *furiosus* *solo furore punitur.* Blackstone *395. More recent commentators opine that the community's quest for "retribution"—the need to offset a criminal act by a punishment of equivalent "moral quality"—is not served by execution of an insane person, which has a "lesser value" than that of the crime for which he is to be punished. Hazard & Louisell, Death, the State, and the Insane: Stay of Execution, 9 UCLA L. Rev. 381, 387 (1962). Unanimity of rationale, therefore, we do not find. "But whatever the reason of the law is, it is plain the law is so." Hawles 477. We know of virtually no authority condoning the execution of the insane at English common law.[1]

Further indications suggest that this solid proscription was carried to America, where it was early observed that "the judge is bound" to stay the execution upon insanity of the prisoner. 1 J. Chitty, A Practical Treatise on the Criminal Law *761; see 1 F. Wharton, A Treatise on Criminal Law § 59 (8th ed. 1880).

B

This ancestral legacy has not outlived its time. Today, no State in the Union permits the execution of the insane.[2] It

---

[1] At one point, Henry VIII enacted a law requiring that if a man convicted of treason fell mad, he should nevertheless be executed. 33 Hen. VIII, ch. 20. This law was uniformly condemned. See Blackstone *25; 1 Hale 35; 1 Hawkins 2. The "cruel and inhumane Law lived not long, but was repealed, for in that point also it was against the Common Law . . . ." Coke 6.

[2] Of the 50 States, 41 have a death penalty or statutes governing execution procedures. Of those, 26 have statutes explicitly requiring the suspension of the execution of a prisoner who meets the legal test for incompetence. See Ala. Code § 15-16-23 (1982); Ariz. Rev. Stat. Ann. § 13-4023 (1978); Ark. Stat. Ann. § 43-2622 (1977); Cal. Penal Code Ann. § 3703 (West 1982); Colo. Rev. Stat. § 16-8-112(2) (Supp. 1985); Conn. Gen. Stat. § 54-101 (1985); Fla. Stat. § 922.07 (1985 and Supp. 1986); Ga. Code Ann. § 17-10-62 (1982); Ill. Rev. Stat., ch. 38, ¶ 1005-2-3 (1982); Kan. Stat. Ann. § 22-4006(3) (1981); Ky. Rev. Stat § 431.240(2) (1985); Md. Ann. Code, Art. 27, § 75(c) (Supp. 1985); Miss. Code Ann. § 99-19-57(2) (Supp. 1985);

is clear that the ancient and humane limitation upon the State's ability to execute its sentences has as firm a hold upon the jurisprudence of today as it had centuries ago in England. The various reasons put forth in support of the common-law restriction have no less logical, moral, and practical force than they did when first voiced. For today, no less than before, we may seriously question the retributive value of executing a person who has no comprehension of why he has been singled out and stripped of his fundamental right to life. See Note, The Eighth Amendment and the Execution of the Presently Incompetent, 32 Stan. L. Rev. 765, 777, n. 58 (1980). Similarly, the natural abhorrence civilized societies feel at killing one who has no capacity to come to grips with his own conscience or deity is still vivid today. And the intuition that such an execution simply offends humanity is evidently shared across this Nation. Faced with such widespread evidence of a restriction upon sovereign power, this Court is compelled to conclude that the Eighth Amendment

---

Mo. Rev. Stat § 552.060 (1978); Mont. Code Ann. § 46–14–221 (1984); Neb. Rev. Stat. § 29–2537 (1979); Nev. Rev. Stat. § 176.445 (1985); N. J. Stat. Ann. § 30:4–82 (West 1981); N. M. Stat. Ann. § 31–14–6 (1984); N. Y. Correc. Law § 656 (McKinney Supp. 1986); N. C. Gen. Stat. § 15A–1001 (1983); Ohio Rev. Code Ann. § 2949.29 (1982); Okla. Stat., Tit. 22, § 1008 (1986); S. D. Codified Laws § 23A–27A–24 (1979); Utah Code Ann. § 77–19–13 (1982); Wyo. Stat. § 7–13–901 (Supp. 1986). Others have adopted the common-law rule by judicial decision. See *State* v. *Allen*, 204 La. 513, 515, 15 So. 2d 870, 871 (1943); *Commonwealth* v. *Moon*, 383 Pa. 18, 22–23, 117 A. 2d 96, 99 (1955); *Jordan* v. *State*, 124 Tenn. 81, 89–90 135 S. W. 327, 329 (1911); *State* v. *Davis*, 6 Wash. 2d 696, 717, 108 P. 2d 641, 651 (1940). Still others have more discretionary statutory procedures providing for the suspension of sentence and transfer to mental facilities for convicted prisoners who have developed mental illness. See Del. Code Ann., Tit. 11, § 406 (1979); Ind. Code § 11–10–4–2 (1982); Mass. Gen. Laws, ch. 279, § 62 (1984); R. I. Gen. Laws § 40.1–5.3–7 (1984); S. C. Code § 44–23–220 (1985); Tex. Code Crim. Proc. Ann., Art. 46.01 (1979); Va. Code § 19.2–177 (1983). The remaining four States having a death penalty have no specific procedure governing insanity, but have not repudiated the common-law rule.

prohibits a State from carrying out a sentence of death upon a prisoner who is insane. Whether its aim be to protect the condemned from fear and pain without comfort of understanding, or to protect the dignity of society itself from the barbarity of exacting mindless vengeance, the restriction finds enforcement in the Eighth Amendment.

III

The Eighth Amendment prohibits the State from inflicting the penalty of death upon a prisoner who is insane. Petitioner's allegation of insanity in his habeas corpus petition, if proved, therefore, would bar his execution. The question before us is whether the District Court was under an obligation to hold an evidentiary hearing on the question of Ford's sanity. In answering that question, we bear in mind that, while the underlying social values encompassed by the Eighth Amendment are rooted in historical traditions, the manner in which our judicial system protects those values is purely a matter of contemporary law. Once a substantive right or restriction is recognized in the Constitution, therefore, its enforcement is in no way confined to the rudimentary process deemed adequate in ages past.

A

In a habeas corpus proceeding, "a federal evidentiary hearing is required unless the state-court trier of fact has after a full hearing reliably found the relevant facts." *Townsend* v. *Sain*, 372 U. S. 293, 312–313 (1963). The habeas corpus statute, following this Court's decision in *Townsend*, provides that, in general, "a determination after a hearing on the merits of a factual issue, made by a State court of competent jurisdiction . . . , shall be presumed to be correct," and an evidentiary hearing not required. 28 U. S. C. § 2254(d). In this case, it is clear that no state court has issued any determination to which that presumption of correctness could be said to attach; indeed, no court played any role in the rejection of petitioner's claim of insanity. Thus, quite simply,

Townsend and § 2254 require the District Court to grant a hearing *de novo* on that question.

But our examination does not stop there. For even when a state court has rendered judgment, a federal court is obliged to hold an evidentiary hearing on habeas corpus if, among other factors, "the factfinding procedure employed by the State court was not adequate to afford a full and fair hearing," § 2254(d)(2); or "the material facts were not adequately developed at the State court hearing," § 2254(d)(3); or "the applicant did not receive a full, fair, and adequate hearing in the State court proceeding." § 2254(d)(6). If federal factfinding is to be avoided, then, in addition to providing a court judgment on the constitutional question, the State must also ensure that its procedures are adequate for the purpose of finding the facts.

B

The adequacy of a state-court procedure under *Townsend* is largely a function of the circumstances and the interests at stake. In capital proceedings generally, this Court has demanded that factfinding procedures aspire to a heightened standard of reliability. See, *e. g.*, *Spaziano* v. *Florida*, 468 U. S. 447, 456 (1984). This especial concern is a natural consequence of the knowledge that execution is the most irremediable and unfathomable of penalties; that death is different. See *Woodson* v. *North Carolina*, 428 U. S. 280, 305 (1976) (opinion of Stewart, POWELL, and STEVENS, JJ.).

Although the condemned prisoner does not enjoy the same presumptions accorded a defendant who has yet to be convicted or sentenced, he has not lost the protection of the Constitution altogether; if the Constitution renders the fact or timing of his execution contingent upon establishment of a further fact, then that fact must be determined with the high regard for truth that befits a decision affecting the life or death of a human being. Thus, the ascertainment of a prisoner's sanity as a predicate to lawful execution calls for no less stringent standards than those demanded in any other aspect of a capital proceeding. Indeed, a particularly acute need for guarding against error inheres in a determination that "in the present state of the mental sciences is at best a hazardous guess however conscientious." *Solesbee* v. *Balkcom*, 339 U. S., at 23 (Frankfurter, J., dissenting). That need is greater still because the ultimate decision will turn on the finding of a single fact, not on a range of equitable considerations. Cf. *Woodson* v. *North Carolina*, *supra*, at 304. In light of these concerns, the procedures employed in petitioner's case do not fare well.

C

Florida law directs the Governor, when informed that a person under sentence of death may be insane, to stay the execution and appoint a commission of three psychiatrists to examine the prisoner. Fla. Stat. § 922.07 (1985 and Supp. 1986). "The examination of the convicted person shall take place with all three psychiatrists present at the same time." *Ibid.* After receiving the report of the commission, the Governor must determine whether "the convicted person has the mental capacity to understand the nature of the death penalty and the reasons why it was imposed on him." *Ibid.* If the Governor finds that the prisoner has that capacity, then a death warrant is issued; if not, then the prisoner is committed to a mental health facility. The procedure is conducted wholly within the executive branch, *ex parte*, and provides the exclusive means for determining sanity. *Ford* v. *Wainwright*, 451 So. 2d, at 475.

Petitioner received the statutory process. The Governor selected three psychiatrists, who together interviewed Ford for a total of 30 minutes, in the presence of eight other people, including Ford's counsel, the State's attorneys, and correctional officials. The Governor's order specifically directed that the attorneys should not participate in the examination in any adversarial manner. This order was consistent with the present Governor's "publicly announced policy of excluding all advocacy on the part of the condemned from the process of determining whether a person under a sentence of death is insane." *Goode* v. *Wainwright*, 448 So. 2d 999, 1001 (Fla. 1984).

After submission of the reports of the three examining psychiatrists, reaching conflicting diagnoses but agreeing on the ultimate issue of competency, Ford's counsel attempted to submit to the Governor some other written materials, including the reports of the two other psychiatrists who had examined Ford at greater length, one of whom had concluded that the prisoner was not competent to suffer execution. The Governor's office refused to inform counsel whether the submission would be considered. The Governor subsequently issued his decision in the form of a death warrant. That this most cursory form of procedural review fails to achieve even the minimal degree of reliability required for the protection of any constitutional interest, and thus falls short of adequacy under *Townsend*, is self-evident.

IV

A

The first deficiency in Florida's procedure lies in its failure to include the prisoner in the truth-seeking process. Notwithstanding this Court's longstanding pronouncement that "[t]he fundamental requisite of due process of law is the opportunity to be heard," *Grannis* v. *Ordean*, 234 U. S. 385, 394 (1914), state practice does not permit any material relevant to the ultimate decision to be submitted on behalf of the prisoner facing execution. In all other proceedings leading to the execution of an accused, we have said that the factfinder must "have before it all possible relevant information about the individual defendant whose fate it must determine." *Jurek* v. *Texas*, 428 U. S. 262, 276 (1976) (plurality opinion). And we have forbidden States to limit the capital defendant's submission of relevant evidence in mitigation of the sentence. *Skipper* v. *South Carolina*, 476 U. S. 1, 8

(1986); *Lockett* v. *Ohio*, 438 U. S. 586, 604 (1978) (joint opinion). It would be odd were we now to abandon our insistence upon unfettered presentation of relevant information, before the final fact antecedent to execution has been found.

Rather, consistent with the heightened concern for fairness and accuracy that has characterized our review of the process requisite to the taking of a human life, we believe that any procedure that precludes the prisoner or his counsel from presenting material relevant to his sanity or bars consideration of that material by the factfinder is necessarily inadequate. "[T]he minimum assurance that the life-and-death guess will be a truly informed guess requires respect for the basic ingredient of due process, namely, an opportunity to be allowed to substantiate a claim before it is rejected." *Solesbee* v. *Balkcom*, *supra*, at 23 (Frankfurter, J., dissenting).

We recently had occasion to underscore the value to be derived from a factfinder's consideration of differing psychiatric opinions when resolving contested issues of mental state. In *Ake* v. *Oklahoma*, 470 U. S. 68 (1985), we recognized that, because "psychiatrists disagree widely and frequently on what constitutes mental illness [and] on the appropriate diagnosis to be attached to given behavior and symptoms," the factfinder must resolve differences in opinion within the psychiatric profession "on the basis of the evidence offered by each party" when a defendant's sanity is at issue in a criminal trial. *Id.*, at 81. The same holds true after conviction; without any adversarial assistance from the prisoner's representative—especially when the psychiatric opinion he proffers is based on much more extensive evaluation than that of the state-appointed commission—the factfinder loses the substantial benefit of potentially probative information. The result is a much greater likelihood of an erroneous decision.

B

A related flaw in the Florida procedure is the denial of any opportunity to challenge or impeach the state-appointed psychiatrists' opinions. "[C]ross-examination . . . is beyond any doubt the greatest legal engine ever invented for the discovery of truth." 5 J. Wigmore, Evidence § 1367 (J. Chadbourn rev. 1974). Cross-examination of the psychiatrists, or perhaps a less formal equivalent, would contribute markedly to the process of seeking truth in sanity disputes by bringing to light the bases for each expert's beliefs, the precise factors underlying those beliefs, any history of error or caprice of the examiner, any personal bias with respect to the issue of capital punishment, the expert's degree of certainty about his or her own conclusions, and the precise meaning of ambiguous words used in the report. Without some questioning of the experts concerning their technical conclusions, a factfinder simply cannot be expected to evaluate the various opinions, particularly when they are themselves inconsistent. See *Barefoot* v. *Estelle*, 463 U. S. 880, 899 (1983). The failure of the Florida procedure to afford the prisoner's representative any opportunity to clarify or challenge the state experts' opinions or methods creates a significant possibility that the ultimate decision made in reliance on those experts will be distorted.[3]

[3] The adequacy of the factfinding procedures is further called into question by the cursory nature of the underlying psychiatric examination itself. While this Court does not purport to set substantive guidelines for the development of expert psychiatric opinion, cf. *Barefoot* v. *Estelle*, 463 U. S. 880, 903 (1983), we can say that the goal of reliability is unlikely to be served by a single group interview, with no provision for the exercise of the psychiatrists' professional judgment regarding the possible need for different or more comprehensive evaluative techniques. The inconsistency and vagueness of the conclusions reached by the three examining psychiatrists in this case attest to the dubious value of such an examination.

C

Perhaps the most striking defect in the procedures of Fla. Stat. § 922.07 (1985 and Supp. 1986), as noted earlier, is the State's placement of the decision wholly within the executive branch. Under this procedure, the person who appoints the experts and ultimately decides whether the State will be able to carry out the sentence that it has long sought is the Governor, whose subordinates have been responsible for initiating every stage of the prosecution of the condemned from arrest through sentencing. The commander of the State's corps of prosecutors cannot be said to have the neutrality that is necessary for reliability in the factfinding proceeding.

Historically, delay of execution on account of insanity was not a matter of executive clemency *(ex mandato regis)* or judicial discretion *(ex arbitrio judicis);* rather, it was required by law *(ex necessitate legis).* 1 N. Walker, Crime and Insanity in England 196 (1968). Thus, history affords no better basis than does logic for placing the final determination of a fact, critical to the trigger of a constitutional limitation upon the State's power, in the hands of the State's own chief executive. In no other circumstance of which we are aware is the vindication of a constitutional right entrusted to the unreviewable discretion of an administrative tribunal.

V

A

Having identified various failings of the Florida scheme, we must conclude that the State's procedures for determining sanity are inadequate to preclude federal redetermination of the constitutional issue. We do not here suggest that only a full trial on the issue of sanity will suffice to protect the federal interests; we leave to the State the task of developing appropriate ways to enforce the constitutional restriction upon its execution of sentences.[4] It may be that some high threshold showing on behalf of the prisoner will be found a necessary means to control the number of nonmeritorious or repetitive claims of insanity. Cf. *Pate* v. *Robinson*, 383 U. S. 375, 387 (1966) (hearing on competency to stand trial required if "sufficient doubt" of competency exists). Other legitimate pragmatic considerations may also supply the boundaries of the procedural safeguards that feasibly can be provided.

Yet the lodestar of any effort to devise a procedure must be the overriding dual imperative of providing redress for those with substantial claims and of encouraging accuracy in the factfinding determination. The stakes are high, and the "evidence" will always be imprecise. It is all the more important that the adversary presentation of relevant information be as unrestricted as possible. Also essential is that the manner of selecting and using the experts responsible for producing that "evidence" be conducive to the formation of neutral, sound, and professional judgments as to the prisoner's ability to comprehend the nature of the penalty. Fidelity to these principles is the solemn obligation of a civilized society.

B

Today we have explicitly recognized in our law a principle that has long resided there. It is no less abhorrent today than it has been for centuries to exact in penance the life of one whose mental illness prevents him from comprehending the reasons for the penalty or its implications. In light of the

---

[4] Instructive analogies may be found in the State's own procedures for determining whether a defendant is competent to stand trial, Fla. Stat. §§ 916.11–916.12 (1985 and Supp. 1986), or in the comprehensive safeguards that Florida ensures to those subjected to involuntary commitment proceedings, Fla. Stat. § 394.467 (1986). The parties' interests are of course somewhat different in those contexts; nevertheless, all such inquests share the common goal of reaching a fair assessment of the subject's mental state.

clear need for trustworthiness in any factual finding that will prevent or permit the carrying out of an execution, we hold that Fla. Stat. § 922.07 (1985 and Supp. 1986) provides inadequate assurances of accuracy to satisfy the requirements of *Townsend* v. *Sain*, 372 U. S. 293 (1963). Having been denied a factfinding procedure "adequate to afford a full and fair hearing" on the critical issue, 28 U. S. C. § 2254(d)(2), petitioner is entitled to an evidentiary hearing in the District Court, *de novo*, on the question of his competence to be executed. *Townsend* v. *Sain*, *supra*, at 312.

The judgment of the Court of Appeals is reversed, and the case is remanded for further proceedings consistent with this opinion.

It is so ordered.

JUSTICE POWELL, concurring in part and concurring in the judgment.

I join Parts I and II of the Court's opinion. As JUSTICE MARSHALL ably demonstrates, execution of the insane was barred at common law precisely because it was considered cruel and unusual. In *Solem* v. *Helm*, 463 U. S. 277 (1983), we explained that while the Framers "may have intended the Eighth Amendment to go beyond the scope of its English counterpart, their use of the language of the English Bill of Rights is convincing proof that they intended to provide at least the same protection." *Id.*, at 286. It follows that the practice of executing the insane is barred by our own Constitution.

That conclusion leaves two issues for our determination: (i) the meaning of insanity in this context, and (ii) the procedures States must follow in order to avoid the necessity of *de novo* review in federal courts under 28 U. S. C. § 2254(d). The Court's opinion does not address the first of these issues, and as to the second, my views differ substantially from JUSTICE MARSHALL's. I therefore write separately.

I

The Court holds today that the Eighth Amendment bars execution of a category of defendants defined by their mental state. The bounds of that category are necessarily governed by federal constitutional law. I therefore turn to the same sources that give rise to the substantive right to determine its precise definition: chiefly, our common-law heritage and the modern practices of the States, which are indicative of our "evolving standards of decency." *Trop* v. *Dulles*, 356 U. S. 86, 101 (1958) (plurality opinion). See *Solem* v. *Helm*, *supra*, at 284–286; *Gregg* v. *Georgia*, 428 U. S. 153, 175–176 (1976) (opinion of Stewart, POWELL, and STEVENS, JJ.).

A

As the Court recognizes, *ante*, at 407–408, the ancient prohibition on execution of the insane rested on differing theories. Those theories do not provide a common answer when it comes to defining the mental awareness required by the Eighth Amendment as a prerequisite to a defendant's execution. On the one hand, some authorities contended that the prohibition against executing the insane was justified as a way of preserving the defendant's ability to make arguments on his own behalf. See 1 M. Hale, Pleas of the Crown 35 (1736) ("if after judgment he become of *non sane memory*, his execution shall be spared; for were he of sound memory he might allege somewhat in stay of judgment or execution"); accord 4 W. Blackstone, Commentaries *388–*389. Other authorities suggest, however, that the prohibition derives from more straightforward humanitarian concerns. Coke expressed the view that execution was intended to be an "example" to the living, but that the execution of "a mad man" was such "a miserable spectacle . . . of extream inhumanity and cruelty" that it "can be no example to others." 3 E. Coke, Institutes 6 (1794). Hawles added that it is "against christian charity to send a great offender quick . . . into another world, when he is not of a capacity to fit himself for it."

Hawles, Remarks on the Trial of Mr. Charles Bateman, 11 How. St. Tr. 474, 477 (1685).

The first of these justifications has slight merit today. Modern practice provides far more extensive review of convictions and sentences than did the common law, including not only direct appeal but ordinarily both state and federal collateral review.[1] Throughout this process, the defendant has access to counsel, by constitutional right at trial, and by employment or appointment at other stages of the process whenever the defendant raises substantial claims. Nor does the defendant merely have the right to counsel's assistance; he also has the right to the *effective* assistance of counsel at trial and on appeal. *Evitts* v. *Lucey*, 469 U. S. 387 (1985); *Strickland* v. *Washington*, 466 U. S. 668 (1984). See *Kimmelman* v. *Morrison*, *ante*, at 392–393 (POWELL, J., concurring in judgment). These guarantees are far broader than those enjoyed by criminal defendants at common law. It is thus unlikely indeed that a defendant today could go to his death with knowledge of undiscovered trial error that might set him free.

In addition, in cases tried at common law execution often followed fairly quickly after trial, so that incompetence at the

[1] Petitioner offers a good example. Petitioner was convicted of first-degree murder in 1974. On direct appeal, his conviction and sentence were affirmed, *Ford* v. *State*, 374 So. 2d 496 (Fla. 1979), and this Court denied certiorari. 445 U. S. 972 (1980). Petitioner then joined 122 other death row inmates in seeking extraordinary relief from the Florida Supreme Court, based on that court's allegedly improper procedure for review of capital cases. This petition for relief was denied, *Brown* v. *Wainwright*, 392 So. 2d 1327 (Fla. 1981), and this Court again denied certiorari. 454 U. S. 1000 (1981). Petitioner filed a motion for postconviction relief in state court, and relief was again denied. *Ford* v. *State*, 407 So. 2d 907 (Fla. 1981). Following these unsuccessful attempts to obtain relief from his conviction or execution in state court, petitioner filed a petition for habeas corpus in federal court. Relief was again denied, *Ford* v. *Strickland*, 696 F. 2d 804 (CA11) (en banc), cert. denied, 464 U. S. 865 (1983). Only after all of these challenges had been resolved against him did petitioner challenge his impending execution on the ground of insanity.

time of execution was linked as a practical matter with incompetence at the trial itself. Our decisions already recognize, however, that a defendant must be competent to stand trial, and thus the notion that a defendant must be able to assist in his defense is largely provided for. See *Drope* v. *Missouri*, 420 U. S. 162 (1975).[2]

B

The more general concern of the common law—that executions of the insane are simply cruel—retains its vitality. It is as true today as when Coke lived that most men and women value the opportunity to prepare, mentally and spiritually, for their death. Moreover, today as at common law, one of the death penalty's critical justifications, its retributive force, depends on the defendant's awareness of the penalty's existence and purpose. Thus, it remains true that executions of the insane both impose a uniquely cruel penalty and are inconsistent with one of the chief purposes of executions generally. For precisely these reasons, Florida requires the Governor to stay executions of those who "d[o] not have the mental capacity to understand the nature of the death penalty and why it was imposed" on them. Fla. Stat. § 922.07 (1985 and Supp. 1986). See also Ill. Rev. Stat., ch. 38, ¶ 1005-2-3(a) (1985) ("A person is unfit to be executed if because of a mental condition he is unable to understand the nature and purpose of such sentence"); *State* v. *Pastet*, 169 Conn. 13, 28, 363 A. 2d 41, 49 (question is "whether the defendant was able to understand the nature of the sentencing proceedings, i. e., why he was being punished and the nature of his punishment"), cert. denied, 423 U. S. 937 (1975). A number of

[2] Moreover, a standard that focused on the defendant's ability to assist in his defense would give too little weight to the State's interest in finality, since it implies a constitutional right to raise new challenges to one's criminal conviction until sentence has run its course. Such an implication is false: we have made clear that States have a strong and legitimate interest in avoiding repetitive collateral review through procedural bars. See *Kuhlmann* v. *Wilson*, *post*, at 452-454 (plurality opinion).

States have more rigorous standards,[3] but none disputes the need to require that those who are executed know the fact of their impending execution and the reason for it.

Such a standard appropriately defines the kind of mental deficiency that should trigger the Eighth Amendment prohibition. If the defendant perceives the connection between his crime and his punishment, the retributive goal of the criminal law is satisfied. And only if the defendant is aware that his death is approaching can he prepare himself for his passing. Accordingly, I would hold that the Eighth Amendment forbids the execution only of those who are unaware of the punishment they are about to suffer and why they are to suffer it.

Petitioner's claim of insanity plainly fits within this standard. According to petitioner's proffered psychiatric examination, petitioner does not know that he is to be executed, but rather believes that the death penalty has been invalidated. App. 65–67. If this assessment is correct, petitioner

---

[3] A number of States have remained faithful to Blackstone's view that a defendant cannot be executed unless he is able to assist in his own defense. *E. g.*, Miss. Code Ann. § 99–19–57(2)(b) (Supp. 1985); Mo. Rev. Stat. § 552.060(1) (1978); Utah Code Ann. § 77–15–2 (1982). The majority of States appear not to have addressed the issue in their statutes. Modern case authority on this question is sparse, and while some older cases favor the Blackstone view, see 24 C. J. S., Criminal Law § 1619 (1961), those cases largely antedate the recent expansion of both the right to counsel and the availability of federal and state collateral review. Moreover, other cases suggest that the prevailing test is "whether the condemned man was aware of his conviction and the nature of his impending fate"—essentially the same test stated by Florida's statute. Note, Insanity of the Condemned, 88 Yale L. J. 533, 540 (1979); see Hazard & Louisell, Death, the State, and the Insane: Stay of Execution, 9 UCLA L. Rev. 381, 394, and n. 44 (1962) (discussing cases). Under these circumstances, I find no sound basis for constitutionalizing the broader definition of insanity, with its requirement that the defendant be able to assist in his own defense. States are obviously free to adopt a more expansive view of sanity in this context than the one the Eighth Amendment imposes as a constitutional minimum.

cannot connect his execution to the crime for which he was convicted. Thus, the question is whether petitioner's evidence entitles him to a hearing in Federal District Court on his claim.

II

Petitioner concedes that the Governor of Florida has determined that he is not insane under the standard prescribed by Florida's statute, which is the same as the standard just described. Petitioner further concedes that there is expert evidence that supports the Governor's finding. Thus, if that finding is entitled to a presumption of correctness under 28 U. S. C. § 2254(d), there is no ground for holding a hearing on petitioner's federal habeas corpus petition.

I agree with JUSTICE MARSHALL that the Governor's finding is not entitled to a presumption of correctness under § 2254(d). I reach this conclusion for two independent reasons. First, § 2254(d) requires deference to the factual findings of "a State court of competent jurisdiction." The term "State court" may have a certain amount of flexibility,[4] but no amount of stretching can extend it to include the Governor. The essence of a "court" is independence from the prosecutorial arm of government and, as JUSTICE MARSHALL correctly notes, the Governor is "[t]he commander of the State's corps of prosecutors." *Ante*, at 416. Unless the relevant language is to be read out of the statute, I see no basis for affording any deference to the Governor's determination.

Second, the presumption of correctness does not attach to the Governor's implicit finding of sanity because the State did not give petitioner's claim "a full and fair hearing," 28 U. S. C. § 2254(d)(2). This statutory phrase apparently was drawn from the Court's opinion in *Townsend* v. *Sain*, 372 U. S. 293, 313 (1963). There, the Court concluded that where the state court's "fact-finding procedure . . . was not

[4] Although we need not decide the issue in this case, the term "State court" may well encompass an independent panel of psychiatric experts who might both examine the defendant and determine his legal sanity.

adequate for reaching reasonably correct results," or where the process "appear[ed] to be seriously inadequate for the ascertainment of the truth," no presumption of correctness would attach to the state court's findings when those findings were challenged on federal habeas corpus. *Id.*, at 316.

At least in the context of competency determinations prior to execution, this standard is no different from the protection afforded by procedural due process. It is clear that an insane defendant's Eighth Amendment interest in forestalling his execution unless or until he recovers his sanity cannot be deprived without a "fair hearing." Indeed, fundamental fairness is the hallmark of the procedural protections afforded by the Due Process Clause. See *Lassiter* v. *Department of Social Services of Durham County*, 452 U. S. 18, 24–25 (1981). Thus, the question in this case is whether Florida's procedures for determining petitioner's sanity comport with the requirements of due process.

Together with JUSTICE MARSHALL and JUSTICE O'CONNOR, I would hold that they do not. As JUSTICE O'CONNOR states, "[i]f there is one 'fundamental requisite' of due process, it is that an individual is entitled to an 'opportunity to be heard.'" *Post*, at 430 (quoting *Grannis* v. *Ordean*, 234 U. S. 385, 394 (1914)). In this case, petitioner was deprived of that opportunity. The Florida statute does not require the Governor to consider materials submitted by the prisoner, and the present Governor has a "publicly announced policy of excluding" such materials from his consideration. *Goode* v. *Wainwright*, 448 So. 2d 999, 1001 (Fla. 1984). Thus, the determination of petitioner's sanity appears to have been made *solely* on the basis of the examinations performed by state-appointed psychiatrists. Such a procedure invites arbitrariness and error by preventing the affected parties from offering contrary medical evidence or even from explaining the inadequacies of the State's examinations. It does not, therefore, comport with due process. It follows that the State's procedure was not "fair," and that the District Court on remand must consider the question of petitioner's competency to be executed.

III

While the procedures followed by Florida in this case do not comport with basic fairness, I would not require the kind of full-scale "sanity trial" that JUSTICE MARSHALL appears to find necessary. See *ante*, at 413–416, 418. Due process is a flexible concept, requiring only "such procedural protections as the particular situation demands." *Mathews* v. *Eldridge*, 424 U. S. 319, 334 (1976); *Morrissey* v. *Brewer*, 408 U. S. 471, 481 (1972). See also *post*, at 429 (O'CONNOR, J., concurring in result in part and dissenting in part). In this instance, a number of considerations support the conclusion that the requirements of due process are not as elaborate as JUSTICE MARSHALL suggests.

First, the Eighth Amendment claim at issue can arise only after the prisoner has been validly convicted of a capital crime and sentenced to death. Thus, in this case the State has a substantial and legitimate interest in taking petitioner's life as punishment for his crime. That interest is not called into question by petitioner's claim. Rather, the only question raised is not *whether*, but *when*, his execution may take place.[5] This question is important, but it is not comparable to the antecedent question whether petitioner should be executed at all. It follows that this Court's decisions imposing heightened procedural requirements on capital trials and sentencing proceedings—*e. g.*, *Lockett* v. *Ohio*, 438 U. S. 586 (1978) (plurality opinion); *Turner* v. *Murray*, 476 U. S. 28 (1986)—do not apply in this context.

Second, petitioner does not make his claim of insanity against a neutral background. On the contrary, in order to

[5] It is of course true that some defendants may lose their mental faculties and never regain them, and thus avoid execution altogether. My point is only that if petitioner is cured of his disease, the State is free to execute him.

have been convicted and sentenced, petitioner must have been judged competent to stand trial, or his competency must have been sufficiently clear as not to raise a serious question for the trial court. The State therefore may properly presume that petitioner remains sane at the time sentence is to be carried out,[6] and may require a substantial threshold showing of insanity merely to trigger the hearing process. Cf. *Ake* v. *Oklahoma*, 470 U. S. 68, 82–83 (1985).

Finally, the sanity issue in this type of case does not resemble the basic issues at trial or sentencing. Unlike issues of historical fact, the question of petitioner's sanity calls for a basically subjective judgment. See *Addington* v. *Texas*, 441 U. S. 418, 429–430 (1979); cf. *Barefoot* v. *Estelle*, 463 U. S. 880, 898–901 (1983). And unlike the determination of whether the death penalty is appropriate in a particular case, the competency determination depends substantially on expert analysis in a discipline fraught with "subtleties and nuances." *Addington*, *supra*, at 430. This combination of factors means that ordinary adversarial procedures—complete with live testimony, cross-examination, and oral argument by counsel—are not necessarily the best means of arriving at sound, consistent judgments as to a defendant's sanity. Cf. *Parham* v. *J. R.*, 442 U. S. 584, 609 (1979) ("Common human experience and scholarly opinions suggest that the supposed protections of an adversary proceeding to determine the appropriateness of medical decisions for the commitment and treatment of mental and emotional illness may well be more illusory than real").

---

[6] Cf. *Addington* v. *Texas*, 441 U. S. 418 (1979). In *Addington*, the Court held that States must require proof by clear and convincing evidence in order to involuntarily commit an individual to a mental hospital for treatment. In this context, it is the defendant and not the State who seeks to overcome the presumption that he is sane; moreover, he does so following a trial and sentencing at which his sanity was either conceded or determined by the court.

We need not determine the precise limits that due process imposes in this area. In general, however, my view is that a constitutionally acceptable procedure may be far less formal than a trial. The State should provide an impartial officer or board that can receive evidence and argument from the prisoner's counsel, including expert psychiatric evidence that may differ from the State's own psychiatric examination. Beyond these basic requirements, the States should have substantial leeway to determine what process best balances the various interests at stake. As long as basic fairness is observed, I would find due process satisfied, and would apply the presumption of correctness of § 2254(d) on federal habeas corpus.

IV

Because petitioner has raised a viable claim under the Eighth Amendment, and because that claim was not adjudicated fairly within the meaning of due process or of § 2254(d), petitioner is entitled to have his claim adjudicated by the District Court on federal habeas corpus. I therefore join the Court's judgment.

JUSTICE O'CONNOR, with whom JUSTICE WHITE joins, concurring in the result in part and dissenting in part.

I am in full agreement with JUSTICE REHNQUIST's conclusion that the Eighth Amendment does not create a substantive right not to be executed while insane. Accordingly, I do not join the Court's reasoning or opinion. Because, however, the conclusion is for me inescapable that Florida positive law has created a protected liberty interest in avoiding execution while incompetent, and because Florida does not provide even those minimal procedural protections required by due process in this area, I would vacate the judgment and remand to the Court of Appeals with directions that the case be returned to the Florida system so that a hearing can be held in a manner consistent with the requirements of the Due Process Clause. I cannot agree, however, that the federal courts should have any role whatever in the substantive determination of a defendant's competency to be executed.

As we explained in *Hewitt* v. *Helms*, 459 U. S. 460, 466 (1983), "[l]iberty interests protected by the Fourteenth Amendment may arise from two sources—the Due Process Clause itself and the laws of the States." See also *Meachum* v. *Fano*, 427 U. S. 215, 223–227 (1976). With JUSTICE REHNQUIST, I agree that the Due Process Clause does not independently create a protected interest in avoiding the execution of a death sentence during incompetency. See also *Solesbee* v. *Balkcom*, 339 U. S. 9 (1950). The relevant provision of the Florida statute, however, provides that the Governor "*shall*" have the prisoner committed to a "Department of Corrections mental health treatment facility" if the prisoner "does not have the mental capacity to understand the nature of the death penalty and why it was imposed on him." Fla. Stat. § 922.07(3) (1985 and Supp. 1986). Our cases leave no doubt that where a statute indicates with "language of an unmistakable mandatory character," that state conduct injurious to an individual will not occur "absent specified substantive predicates," the statute creates an expectation protected by the Due Process Clause. *Hewitt* v. *Helms*, *supra*, at 471–472. See also *Vitek* v. *Jones*, 445 U. S. 480, 488–491 (1980); *Greenholtz* v. *Nebraska Penal Inmates*, 442 U. S. 1, 10 (1979) (entitlement created where under state law "there is [a] set of facts which, if shown, mandate a decision favorable to the individual"). That test is easily met here. Nor is it relevant that the statute creating the interest also specifies the procedures to be followed when the State seeks to deprive the individual of that interest. As we reaffirmed last Term, "[t]he categories of substance and procedure are distinct." *Cleveland Board of Education* v. *Loudermill*, 470 U. S. 532, 541 (1985). Thus, regardless of the procedures the State deems adequate for determining the preconditions to adverse official action, federal law defines the kind of process a State must afford prior to depriving an individual of a protected liberty or property interest. *Id.*, at 541.

Although the state-created entitlement to avoid execution while insane unquestionably triggers the demands of the Due Process Clause, in my judgment those demands are minimal in this context. "It is axiomatic that due process 'is flexible and calls for such procedural protections as the particular situation [requires].'" *Greenholtz* v. *Nebraska Penal Inmates, supra,* at 12, quoting *Morrissey* v. *Brewer*, 408 U. S. 471, 481 (1972). And there are any number of reasons for concluding that this "particular situation" warrants substantial caution before reading the Due Process Clause to mandate anything like the full panoply of trial-type procedures. The prisoner's interest in avoiding an erroneous determination is, of course, very great. But I consider it self-evident that once society has validly convicted an individual of a crime and therefore established its right to punish, the demands of due process are reduced accordingly. *Meachum* v. *Fano, supra,* at 224. Moreover, the potential for false claims and deliberate delay in this context is obviously enormous. *Nobles* v. *Georgia*, 168 U. S. 398, 405–406 (1897). This potential is exacerbated by a unique feature of the prisoner's protected interest in suspending the execution of a death sentence during incompetency. By definition, this interest can *never* be conclusively and finally determined: Regardless of the number of prior adjudications of the issue, until the very moment of execution the prisoner can claim that he has become insane sometime after the previous determination to the contrary. Hazard & Louisell, Death, the State and the Insane: Stay of Execution, 9 UCLA L. Rev. 381, 399–400 (1962). These difficulties, together with the fact that the issue arises only after conviction and sentencing, convince me that the Due Process Clause imposes few requirements on the States in this context.

Even given the broad latitude I would leave to the States in this area, however, I believe that one aspect of the Florida procedure for determining competency to be executed renders that procedure constitutionally deficient. If there is one "fundamental requisite" of due process, it is that an individual is entitled to an "opportunity to be heard." *Grannis* v. *Ordean*, 234 U. S. 385, 394 (1914). As currently implemented, the Florida procedure for determining competency violates this bedrock principle. By Executive Order, the present Governor has provided that "[c]ounsel for the inmate and the State Attorney may be present [at the competency hearing] but shall not participate in the examination in any adversarial manner." Exec. Order No. 83–137 (Dec. 9, 1983). See also *Goode* v. *Wainwright*, 448 So. 2d 999, 1001 (Fla. 1984) (describing the Governor's "publicly announced policy of excluding all advocacy on the part of the condemned from the process of determining whether a person under a sentence of death is insane"). Indeed, respondent does not dispute that the Governor's office has steadfastly refused to acknowledge whether it would even review the extensive psychiatric materials submitted by petitioner concerning his present mental state. While I would not invariably require oral advocacy or even cross-examination, due process at the very least requires that the decisionmaker consider the prisoner's written submissions.

I conclude therefore that Florida law has created a protected expectation that no execution will be carried out while the prisoner lacks the "mental capacity to understand the nature of the death penalty and why it was imposed on him." Fla. Stat. § 922.07(3) (1985). Because Florida's procedures are inadequate to satisfy even the minimal requirements of due process in this context, I would vacate the judgment below with instructions that the case be returned to Florida so that it might assess petitioner's competency in a manner that accords with the command of the Fourteenth Amendment. In my view, however, the only federal question presented in cases such as this is whether the State's positive law has created a liberty interest and whether its procedures are adequate to protect that interest from arbitrary deprivation. Once satisfied that the procedures were adequate, a federal court has no authority to second-guess a State's substantive competency determination.

JUSTICE REHNQUIST, with whom THE CHIEF JUSTICE joins, dissenting.

The Court today holds that the Eighth Amendment prohibits a State from carrying out a lawfully imposed sentence of death upon a person who is currently insane. This holding is based almost entirely on two unremarkable observations. First, the Court states that it "know[s] of virtually no authority condoning the execution of the insane at English common law." *Ante*, at 408. Second, it notes that "[t]oday, no State in the Union permits the execution of the insane." *Ibid.* Armed with these facts, and shielded by the claim that it is simply "keep[ing] faith with our common-law heritage," *ante*, at 401, the Court proceeds to cast aside settled precedent and to significantly alter both the common-law and current practice of not executing the insane. It manages this feat by carefully ignoring the fact that the Florida scheme it finds unconstitutional, in which the Governor is assigned the ultimate responsibility of deciding whether a condemned prisoner is currently insane, is fully consistent with the "common-law heritage" and current practice on which the Court purports to rely.

The Court places great weight on the "impressive historical credentials" of the common-law bar against executing a prisoner who has lost his sanity. *Ante*, at 406–408. What it fails to mention, however, is the equally important and unchallenged fact that at common law it was the *executive* who passed upon the sanity of the condemned. See 1 N. Walker, Crime and Insanity in England 194–203 (1968). So when the Court today creates a constitutional right to a determination of sanity outside of the executive branch, it does so not in keeping with but at the expense of "our common-law heritage."

In *Solesbee* v. *Balkcom*, 339 U. S. 9 (1950), a condemned prisoner claimed that he had a constitutional right to a judicial determination of his sanity. There, as here, the State did not approve the execution of insane persons and vested in the Governor the responsibility for determining, with the aid of experts, the sanity *vel non* of persons sentenced to death. In rejecting the prisoner's claim, this Court stated:

> "Postponement of execution because of insanity bears a close affinity not to trial for a crime but rather to reprieves of sentences in general. The power to reprieve has usually sprung from the same source as the power to pardon. Power of executive clemency in this country undoubtedly derived from the practice as it had existed in England. Such power has traditionally rested in governors or the President, although some of that power is often delegated to agencies such as pardon or parole boards. Seldom, if ever, has this power of executive clemency been subjected to review by the courts." *Id.*, at 11–12.

Despite references to "evolving standards of decency," *ante*, at 406, and "the jurisprudence of today," *ante*, at 409, the Court points to no change since *Solesbee* in the States' approach to determining the sanity of a condemned prisoner. Current statutes quite often provide that initiation of inquiry into and/or final determination of postsentencing insanity is a matter for the executive or the prisoner's custodian.* The Court's profession of "faith to our common-law heritage" and

---

*See Ariz. Rev. Stat. Ann. § 13–4021 (1978); Ark. Stat. Ann. § 43–2622 (1977); Cal. Penal Code Ann. § 3701 (West 1982); Conn. Gen. Stat. § 54–101 (1985); Ga. Code Ann. § 17–10–61 (1982); Kan. Stat. Ann. § 22–4006 (1981); Md. Ann. Code, Art. 27, § 75(c) (Supp. 1985); Mass. Gen Laws § 279:62 (1984); Miss. Code Ann. § 99–19–57 (Supp. 1985); Neb. Rev. Stat. § 29–2537 (1979); Nev. Rev. Stat. § 176.425 (1985); N. M. Stat. Ann. § 31–14–4 (1984); N. Y. Correc. Law § 655 (McKinney Supp. 1986); Ohio Rev. Code Ann. § 2949.28 (1982); Okla Stat., Tit. 22, § 1005 (1986); Utah Code Ann. § 77–19–13(1) (1982); Wyo. Stat. § 7–13–901 (Supp. 1986).

"evolving standards of decency" is thus at best a half-truth. It is Florida's scheme—which combines a prohibition against execution of the insane with executive-branch procedures for evaluating claims of insanity—that is more faithful to both traditional and modern practice. And no matter how long-standing and universal, laws providing that the State should not execute persons the executive finds insane are not themselves sufficient to create an Eighth Amendment right that sweeps away as inadequate the procedures for determining sanity crafted by those very laws.

Petitioner makes the alternative argument, not reached by the Court, that even if the Eighth Amendment does not prohibit execution of the insane, Florida's decision to bar such executions creates a right in condemned persons to trial-type procedures to determine sanity. Here, too, *Solesbee* is instructive:

> "Recently we have pointed out the necessary and inherent differences between trial procedures and post-conviction procedures such as sentencing. *Williams* v. *New York*, 337 U. S. 241. In that case we emphasized that certain trial procedure safeguards are not applicable to the process of sentencing. This principle applies even more forcefully to an effort to transplant every trial safeguard to a determination of sanity after conviction. As was pointed out in [*Nobles* v. *Georgia*, 168 U. S. 398 (1897)], to require judicial review every time a convicted defendant suggested insanity would make the possibility of carrying out a sentence depend upon 'fecundity in making suggestion after suggestion of insanity.' *Nobles* v. *Georgia*, *supra*, at 405–406. See also *Phyle* v. *Duffy*, [334 U. S. 431 (1948)]. To protect itself society must have power to try, convict, and execute sentences. Our legal system demands that this governmental duty be performed with scrupulous fairness to the accused. We cannot say that it offends due process to leave the question of a convicted person's sanity to the solemn respon-

> sibility of a state's highest executive with authority to invoke the aid of the most skillful class of experts on the crucial questions involved." 339 U. S., at 12–13.

Even the sole dissenter in *Solesbee*, Justice Frankfurter, agreed that if the Constitution afforded condemned prisoners no substantive right not to be executed when insane, then the State would be free to place on the Governor the responsibility for determining sanity. *Id.*, at 15.

Petitioner argues that *Solesbee* is no longer controlling because it was decided "at a time when due process analysis still turned on the right-privilege distinction." Brief for Petitioner 8. But as petitioner concedes, his due process claim turns on a showing that the Florida statute at issue here created an individual right not to be executed while insane. Even a cursory reading of the statute reveals that the only right it creates in a condemned prisoner is to inform the Governor that the prisoner may be insane. Fla. Stat. § 922.07(1) (1985). The only legitimate expectation it creates is that "*[i]f the Governor decides* that the convicted person does not have the mental capacity to understand the nature of the death penalty and why it was imposed on him, he shall have him committed to a Department of Corrections mental health treatment facility." § 922.07(3) (Supp. 1986) (emphasis added). Our recent cases in this area of the law may not be wholly consistent with one another. See *Olim* v. *Wakinekona*, 461 U. S. 238 (1983); *Hewitt* v. *Helms*, 459 U. S. 460 (1983); *Vitek* v. *Jones*, 445 U. S. 480 (1980); *Greenholtz* v. *Nebraska Penal Inmates*, 442 U. S. 1 (1979); *Meachum* v. *Fano*, 427 U. S. 215 (1976). I do not think this state of the law requires the conclusion that Florida has granted petitioner the sort of entitlement that gives rise to the procedural protections for which he contends.

In any event, I see no reason to reject the *Solesbee* Court's conclusion that wholly executive procedures can satisfy due process in the context of a post-trial, postappeal, post-collateral-attack challenge to a State's effort to carry out a lawfully imposed sentence. Creating a constitutional right to a judicial determination of sanity before that sentence may be carried out, whether through the Eighth Amendment or the Due Process Clause, needlessly complicates and postpones still further any finality in this area of the law. The defendant has already had a full trial on the issue of guilt, and a trial on the issue of penalty; the requirement of still a third adjudication offers an invitation to those who have nothing to lose by accepting it to advance entirely spurious claims of insanity. A claim of insanity may be made at any time before sentence and, once rejected, may be raised again; a prisoner found sane two days before execution might claim to have lost his sanity the next day, thus necessitating another judicial determination of his sanity and presumably another stay of his execution. See *Nobles* v. *Georgia*, 168 U. S. 398, 405–406 (1897).

Since no State sanctions execution of the insane, the real battle being fought in this case is over what procedures must accompany the inquiry into sanity. The Court reaches the result it does by examining the common law, creating a constitutional right that no State seeks to violate, and then concluding that the common-law procedures are inadequate to protect the newly created but common-law based right. I find it unnecessary to "constitutionalize" the already uniform view that the insane should not be executed, and inappropriate to "selectively incorporate" the common-law practice. I therefore dissent.

PENRY *v.* LYNAUGH, DIRECTOR, TEXAS DEPARTMENT OF CORRECTIONS

CERTIORARI TO THE UNITED STATES COURT OF APPEALS FOR THE FIFTH CIRCUIT

No. 87–6177. Argued January 11, 1989—Decided June 26, 1989

Petitioner was charged with capital murder in Texas state court. He was found competent to stand trial, although a psychologist testified that he was mildly to moderately retarded and had the mental age of a 6½-year-old. At the guilt-innocence phase of the trial, petitioner raised an insanity defense and presented psychiatric testimony that he suffered from a combination of organic brain damage and moderate retardation which resulted in poor impulse control and an inability to learn from experience. His evidence also indicated that he had been abused as a child. The State introduced testimony that petitioner was legally sane but had an antisocial personality. The jury rejected petitioner's insanity defense and found him guilty of capital murder. At the penalty phase of the trial, the sentencing jury was instructed to consider all the evidence introduced at trial in answering the following "special issues": (1) whether petitioner's conduct was committed deliberately and with the reasonable expectation that death would result; (2) whether there was a probability that he would be a continuing threat to society; and (3) whether the killing was unreasonable in response to any provocation by the victim. The trial court rejected petitioner's request for jury instructions defining the terms in the special issues and authorizing a grant of mercy based upon the existence of mitigating circumstances. The jury answered "yes" to each special issue, and, as required by Texas law, the court therefore sentenced petitioner to death. A "no" answer to any of the special issues would have required a sentence of life imprisonment. The Texas Court of Criminal Appeals affirmed, rejecting petitioner's contentions that his death sentence violated the Eighth Amendment first, because the jury was not adequately instructed to consider all of his mitigating evidence and because the special issues' terms were not defined in such a way that the jury could consider and give effect to that evidence in answering them; and, second, because it is cruel and unusual punishment to execute a mentally retarded person with petitioner's mental ability. After this Court denied certiorari on direct review, the Federal District Court and the Court of Appeals upheld petitioner's death sentence in habeas corpus proceedings. Although it denied him relief, the Court of Appeals nevertheless found considerable merit in petitioner's claim that his mitigating evidence of mental retardation and childhood abuse could not be given effect by the jury, under the instructions given, in answering the special issues.

Held: The judgment is affirmed in part and reversed in part, and the case is remanded.

832 F. 2d 915, affirmed in part, reversed in part, and remanded.

JUSTICE O'CONNOR delivered the opinion of the Court with respect to Parts I, II–A, II–B, III, IV–A, and IV–B, concluding that:

1. Granting petitioner relief on his claim that when mitigating evidence of mental retardation and an abused childhood is presented, Texas juries must, upon request, be given instructions that allow them to give effect to that mitigating evidence in determining whether to impose the death penalty, would not create a "new rule" which, under *Teague* v. *Lane*, 489 U. S. 288, 301, may not generally be applied or announced in cases on collateral review. Pp. 313–319.

(a) The *Teague* rule of nonretroactivity and its two exceptions are applicable in the capital sentencing context. A criminal judgment includes the sentence imposed, and collateral challenges to sentences foster delay and undermine the finality concerns underlying *Teague*'s rule of nonretroactivity. Pp. 313–314.

(b) Under *Teague*, a case announces a "new rule" when it breaks new ground or imposes a new obligation on the States or the Federal Government, or if the result is not dictated by precedent which existed at the time the defendant's conviction became final. 489 U. S., at 301. Here, since *Lockett* v. *Ohio*, 438 U. S. 586, and *Eddings* v. *Oklahoma*, 455 U. S. 104, were decided before petitioner's conviction became final when this Court denied his certiorari petition on direct review, he is entitled to the benefit of those decisions under *Griffith* v. *Kentucky*, 479 U. S. 314. The rule that petitioner seeks does not impose a new obligation on Texas because *Jurek* v. *Texas*, 428 U. S. 262, upheld the Texas death penalty statute on the basis of assurances that the special issues would be interpreted broadly enough to permit the jury to consider all of the relevant mitigating evidence a defendant might present in imposing sentence. Moreover, the rule that petitioner seeks in this case is dictated by *Eddings* and *Lockett*, which established that a State cannot, consistent with the Eighth and Fourteenth Amendments, prevent the sentencer from considering and giving effect to evidence relevant to the defendant's background or character or to the circumstances of the offense that mitigates against imposing the death penalty. Pp. 314–319.

2. The absence of instructions informing the jury that it could consider and give effect to petitioner's mitigating evidence of mental retardation and abused background by declining to impose the death penalty

compels the conclusion that the jury was not provided with a vehicle for expressing its "reasoned moral response" to that evidence in rendering its sentencing decision, as is required by the Eighth and Fourteenth Amendments under *Lockett, Eddings*, and subsequent decisions. Those decisions are based on the principle that punishment must be directly related to the defendant's personal culpability, and that a defendant who commits crimes attributable to a disadvantaged background or emotional and mental problems may be less culpable than one who has no such excuse. Here, although petitioner was permitted to introduce and argue the significance of his mitigating evidence to the jury, the jury instructions did not permit the jury to give effect to that evidence in answering the three special issues. As to the first such issue, without a special instruction defining "deliberately" in a way that would clearly direct the jury to fully consider petitioner's mitigating evidence as it bears on his moral culpability, a juror who believed that that evidence made imposition of the death penalty unwarranted would be unable to give effect to that conclusion if the juror also believed that petitioner committed the crime "deliberately." Nor did the second special issue provide a vehicle for the jury to give mitigating effect to petitioner's evidence of mental retardation and childhood abuse; to the contrary, the evidence concerning his inability to learn from his mistakes by virtue of his mental retardation actually suggests that he will be dangerous in the future. Although such evidence may lessen his blameworthiness, it made an affirmative answer to the second issue more likely. Furthermore, a juror who believed that petitioner lacked the moral culpability to be sentenced to death could not express that view in answering the third special issue if the juror also believed that his conduct was not a reasonable response to provocation by the victim. There is no merit to the State's contention that to instruct the jury that it could decline to impose the death penalty based on petitioner's mitigating evidence would allow it the sort of unbridled discretion prohibited by *Furman* v. *Georgia*, 408 U. S. 238. As *Gregg* v. *Georgia*, 428 U. S. 153, made clear, so long as the class of murderers subject to capital punishment is narrowed, there is no constitutional infirmity in a procedure that allows a jury to recommend mercy based on the mitigating evidence introduced by a defendant. Furthermore, because the punishment imposed should be directly related to the personal culpability of the defendant, the sentencer must be allowed to consider and give effect to mitigating evidence relevant to a defendant's background, character, and crime. Full consideration of such mitigating evidence enhances the reliability of the jury's sentencing decision. Pp. 319–328.

3. The Eighth Amendment does not categorically prohibit the execution of mentally retarded capital murderers of petitioner's reasoning ability. Pp. 328–335.

(a) Although granting petitioner relief on this issue would create a "new rule" within the meaning of *Teague*, *supra*, that rule would fall within the first exception to *Teague*'s general rule of nonretroactivity. That exception applies not only to new rules that place certain kinds of primary, private individual conduct beyond the power of the criminal law-making authority to proscribe. It also applies to new rules prohibiting a certain category of punishment for a class of defendants because of their status or offense. Cf., *e. g.*, *Ford* v. *Wainwright*, 477 U. S. 399, 410. Pp. 329–330.

(b) The Eighth Amendment's categorical prohibition upon the infliction of cruel and unusual punishment applies to practices condemned by the common law at the time the Bill of Rights was adopted, as well as to punishments which offend our society's evolving standards of decency as expressed in objective evidence of legislative enactments and the conduct of sentencing juries. Since the common law prohibited the punishment of "idiots"—which term was generally used to describe persons totally lacking in reason, understanding, or the ability to distinguish between good and evil—it may indeed be "cruel and unusual punishment" to execute persons who are profoundly or severely retarded and wholly lacking in the capacity to appreciate the wrongfulness of their actions. Such persons, however, are not likely to be convicted or face the prospect of punishment today, since the modern insanity defense generally includes "mental defect" as part of the legal definition of insanity, and since *Ford* v. *Wainwright*, *supra*, prohibits the execution of persons who are unaware of their punishment and why they must suffer it. Moreover, petitioner is not such a person, since the jury (1) found him competent to stand trial and therefore to have a rational as well as factual understanding of the proceedings; and (2) rejected his insanity defense, thereby reflecting the conclusion that he knew his conduct was wrong and was capable of conforming it to the requirements of law. Nor is there sufficient objective evidence today of a national consensus against executing mentally retarded capital murderers, since petitioner has cited only one state statute that explicitly bans that practice and has offered no evidence of the general behavior of juries in this regard. Opinion surveys indicating strong public opposition to such executions do not establish a societal consensus, absent some legislative reflection of the sentiment expressed therein. Pp. 330–335.

JUSTICE O'CONNOR concluded in Part IV–C that, on the present record, it cannot be said that executing capital murderers who are mentally retarded violates the Eighth Amendment's proportionality requirement.

To be sure, retardation has long been regarded as a factor that may diminish culpability, and, in its most severe form, may result in complete exculpation. Moreover, most States with death penalty statutes that list mitigating factors include reduced mental capacity as a mitigating circumstance, and this Court holds today that the sentencing body must be allowed to consider retardation in making the individualized determination whether the death penalty is appropriate. Mentally retarded persons, however, are individuals whose abilities and behavioral deficits can vary greatly depending on the degree of their retardation, their life experience, and the ameliorative effects of education and habilitation. On the present record, it cannot be said that all mentally retarded people of petitioner's ability—by virtue of their mental retardation alone, and apart from any individualized consideration of their personal responsibility—inevitably lack the cognitive, volitional, and moral capacity to act with the degree of culpability associated with the death penalty. Moreover, the concept of "mental age" is an insufficient basis for a categorical Eighth Amendment rule, since it is imprecise, does not adequately account for individuals' varying experiences and abilities, ceases to change after a person reaches the chronological age of 15 or 16, and could have a disempowering effect if applied to retarded persons in other areas of the law, such as the opportunity to enter contracts or to marry. Pp. 335–340.

O'CONNOR, J., announced the judgment of the Court and delivered the opinion for a unanimous Court with respect to Parts I and IV–A, the opinion of the Court with respect to Parts II–B and III, in which BRENNAN, MARSHALL, BLACKMUN, and STEVENS, JJ., joined, the opinion of the Court with respect to Parts II–A and IV–B, in which REHNQUIST, C. J., and WHITE, SCALIA, and KENNEDY, JJ., joined, and an opinion with respect to Part IV–C. BRENNAN, J., filed an opinion concurring in part and dissenting in part, in which MARSHALL, J., joined, *post*, p. 341. STEVENS, J., filed an opinion concurring in part and dissenting in part, in which BLACKMUN, J., joined, *post*, p. 349. SCALIA, J., filed an opinion concurring in part and dissenting in part, in which REHNQUIST, C. J., and WHITE and KENNEDY, JJ., joined, *post*, p. 350.

Curtis C. Mason argued the cause and filed briefs for petitioner.

Charles A. Palmer, Assistant Attorney General of Texas, argued the cause for respondent. With him on the briefs were *Jim Mattox*, Attorney General, *Mary F. Keller*, First Assistant Attorney General, *Lou McCreary*, Executive Assistant Attorney General, and *Michael P. Hodge* and *William C. Zapalac*, Assistant Attorneys General.*

JUSTICE O'CONNOR delivered the opinion of the Court, except as to Part IV–C.

In this case, we must decide whether petitioner, Johnny Paul Penry, was sentenced to death in violation of the Eighth Amendment because the jury was not instructed that it could consider and give effect to his mitigating evidence in imposing its sentence. We must also decide whether the Eighth Amendment categorically prohibits Penry's execution because he is mentally retarded.

I

On the morning of October 25, 1979, Pamela Carpenter was brutally raped, beaten, and stabbed with a pair of scissors in her home in Livingston, Texas. She died a few hours later in the course of emergency treatment. Before she died, she described her assailant. Her description led two local sheriff's deputies to suspect Penry, who had recently been released on parole after conviction on another rape charge. Penry subsequently gave two statements confessing to the crime and was charged with capital murder.

At a competency hearing held before trial, a clinical psychologist, Dr. Jerome Brown, testified that Penry was mentally retarded. As a child, Penry was diagnosed as having organic brain damage, which was probably caused by trauma to the brain at birth. App. 34–35. Penry was tested over the years as having an IQ between 50 and 63, which indicates

---

*Briefs of *amici curiae* urging reversal were filed for the American Association on Mental Retardation et al. by *James W. Ellis*, *Ruth Luckasson*, *Barbara Bergman*, and *Donald N. Bersoff*; for the Texas Criminal Defense Lawyers Association by *David Botsford*, *Mark Stevens*, and *Carolyn Garcia*; and for Billy Conn Gardner by *Eugene O. Duffy* and *Christine M. Wiseman*.

Stanley G. Schneider filed a brief for the Harris County Criminal Lawyers Association as *amicus curiae*.

mild to moderate retardation.[1] *Id.*, at 36–38, 55. Dr. Brown's own testing before the trial indicated that Penry had an IQ of 54. Dr. Brown's evaluation also revealed that Penry, who was 22 years old at the time of the crime, had the mental age of a 6½-year-old, which means that "he has the ability to learn and the learning or the knowledge of the average 6½ year old kid." *Id.*, at 41. Penry's social maturity, or ability to function in the world, was that of a 9- or 10-year-old. Dr. Brown testified that "there's a point at which anyone with [Penry's] IQ is always incompetent, but, you know, this man is more in the borderline range." *Id.*, at 47.

The jury found Penry competent to stand trial. *Id.*, at 20–24. The guilt-innocence phase of the trial began on March 24, 1980. The trial court determined that Penry's confessions were voluntary, and they were introduced into evidence. At trial, Penry raised an insanity defense and presented the testimony of a psychiatrist, Dr. Jose Garcia. Dr. Garcia testified that Penry suffered from organic brain damage and moderate retardation, which resulted in poor impulse control and an inability to learn from experience. *Id.*, at 18, 19, 87–90. Dr. Garcia indicated that Penry's brain damage was probably caused at birth, *id.*, at 106, but may have been caused by beatings and multiple injuries to the

---

[1] Persons who are mentally retarded are described as having "significantly subaverage general intellectual functioning existing concurrently with deficits in adaptive behavior and manifested during the developmental period." American Association on Mental Deficiency (now Retardation) (AAMR), Classification in Mental Retardation 1 (H. Grossman ed. 1983). To be classified as mentally retarded, a person generally must have an IQ of 70 or below. *Id.*, at 11. Under the AAMR classification system, individuals with IQ scores between 50–55 and 70 have "mild" retardation. Individuals with scores between 35–40 and 50–55 have "moderate" retardation. "Severely" retarded people have IQ scores between 20–25 and 35–40, and "profoundly" retarded people have scores below 20 or 25. *Id.*, at 13. Approximately 89% of retarded persons are "mildly" retarded. Ellis & Luckasson, Mentally Retarded Criminal Defendants, 53 Geo. Wash. L. Rev. 414, 423 (1985).

brain at an early age. *Id.*, at 18, 90. In Dr. Garcia's judgment, Penry was suffering from an organic brain disorder at the time of the offense which made it impossible for him to appreciate the wrongfulness of his conduct or to conform his conduct to the law. *Id.*, at 86–87.

Penry's mother testified at trial that Penry was unable to learn in school and never finished the first grade. Penry's sister testified that their mother had frequently beaten him over the head with a belt when he was a child. Penry was also routinely locked in his room without access to a toilet for long periods of time. *Id.*, at 124, 126, 127. As a youngster, Penry was in and out of a number of state schools and hospitals, until his father removed him from state schools altogether when he was 12. *Id.*, at 120. Penry's aunt subsequently struggled for over a year to teach Penry how to print his name. *Id.*, at 133.

The State introduced the testimony of two psychiatrists to rebut the testimony of Dr. Garcia. Dr. Kenneth Vogtsberger testified that although Penry was a person of limited mental ability, he was not suffering from any mental illness or defect at the time of the crime, and that he knew the difference between right and wrong and had the potential to honor the law. *Id.*, at 144–145. In his view, Penry had characteristics consistent with an antisocial personality, including an inability to learn from experience and a tendency to be impulsive and to violate society's norms. *Id.*, at 149–150. He testified further that Penry's low IQ scores underestimated his alertness and understanding of what went on around him. *Id.*, at 146.

Dr. Felix Peebles also testified for the State that Penry was legally sane at the time of the offense and had a "full-blown anti-social personality." *Id.*, at 171. In addition, Dr. Peebles testified that he personally diagnosed Penry as being mentally retarded in 1973 and again in 1977, and that Penry "had a very bad life generally, bringing up." *Id.*, at 168–169. In Dr. Peebles' view, Penry "had been socially and emotionally deprived and he had not learned to read and write adequately." *Id.*, at 169. Although they disagreed with the defense psychiatrist over the extent and cause of Penry's mental limitations, both psychiatrists for the State acknowledged that Penry was a person of extremely limited mental ability, and that he seemed unable to learn from his mistakes. *Id.*, at 149, 172–173.

The jury rejected Penry's insanity defense and found him guilty of capital murder. Tex. Penal Code Ann. § 19.03 (1974 and Supp. 1989). The following day, at the close of the penalty hearing, the jury decided the sentence to be imposed on Penry by answering three "special issues":

> "(1) whether the conduct of the defendant that caused the death of the deceased was committed deliberately and with the reasonable expectation that the death of the deceased or another would result;
>
> "(2) whether there is a probability that the defendant would commit criminal acts of violence that would constitute a continuing threat to society; and
>
> "(3) if raised by the evidence, whether the conduct of the defendant in killing the deceased was unreasonable in response to the provocation, if any, by the deceased." Tex. Code Crim. Proc. Ann., Art. 37.071(b) (Vernon 1981 and Supp. 1989).

If the jury unanimously answers "yes" to each issue submitted, the trial court must sentence the defendant to death. Arts. 37.071(c)–(e). Otherwise, the defendant is sentenced to life imprisonment. *Ibid.*

Defense counsel raised a number of objections to the proposed charge to the jury. With respect to the first special issue, he objected that the charge failed to define the term "deliberately." App. 210. With respect to the second special issue, he objected that the charge failed to define the terms "probability," "criminal acts of violence," and "continuing threat to society." *Id.*, at 210–211. Defense counsel also objected to the charge because it failed to "authorize a discretionary grant of mercy based upon the existence of mitigating circumstances" and because it "fail[ed] to require as a condition to the assessment of the death penalty that the State show beyond a reasonable doubt that any aggravating circumstances found to exist outweigh any mitigating circumstances." *Id.*, at 211. In addition, the charge failed to instruct the jury that it may take into consideration all of the evidence whether aggravating or mitigating in nature which was submitted in the full trial of the case. *Id.*, at 212. Defense counsel also objected that, in light of Penry's mental retardation, permitting the jury to assess the death penalty in this case amounted to cruel and unusual punishment prohibited by the Eighth Amendment. *Id.*, at 211.

These objections were overruled by the trial court. The jury was then instructed that the State bore the burden of proof on the special issues, and that before any issue could be answered "yes," all 12 jurors must be convinced by the evidence beyond a reasonable doubt that the answer to that issue should be "yes." *Id.*, at 25. The jurors were further instructed that in answering the three special issues, they could consider all the evidence submitted in both the guilt-innocence phase and the penalty phase of the trial. *Id.*, at 26. The jury charge then listed the three questions, with the names of the defendant and the deceased inserted.

The jury answered "yes" to all three special issues, and Penry was sentenced to death. The Texas Court of Criminal Appeals affirmed his conviction and sentence on direct appeal. *Penry* v. *State*, 691 S. W. 2d 636 (1985). That court held that terms such as "deliberately," "probability," and "continuing threat to society" used in the special issues need not be defined in the jury charge because the jury would know their common meaning. *Id.*, at 653–654. The court concluded that Penry was allowed to present all relevant mitigating evidence at the punishment hearing, and that there was no constitutional infirmity in failing to require the jury to find that aggravating circumstances outweighed mitigating ones or in failing to authorize a discretionary grant of mercy based upon the existence of mitigating circumstances. *Id.*, at 654. The court also held that imposition of the death penalty was not prohibited by virtue of Penry's mental retardation. *Id.*, at 654–655. This Court denied certiorari on direct review. *Sub nom. Penry* v. *Texas*, 474 U. S. 1073 (1986).

Penry then filed this federal habeas corpus petition challenging his death sentence. Among other claims, Penry argued that he was sentenced in violation of the Eighth Amendment because the trial court failed to instruct the jury on how to weigh mitigating factors in answering the special issues and failed to define the term "deliberately." Penry also argued that it was cruel and unusual punishment to execute a mentally retarded person. The District Court denied relief, App. 234–273, and Penry appealed to the Court of Appeals for the Fifth Circuit.

The Court of Appeals affirmed the District Court's judgment. 832 F. 2d 915 (1987). The court stressed, however, that it found considerable merit in Penry's claim that the jury was not allowed to consider and apply all of his personal mitigating circumstances in answering the Texas special issues. Although the jury was presented with evidence that might mitigate Penry's personal culpability for the crime, such as his mental retardation, arrested emotional development, and abused background, the jury could not give effect to that evidence by mitigating Penry's sentence to life imprisonment. "Having said that it was a deliberate murder and that Penry will be a continuing threat, the jury can say no more." *Id.*, at 920. In short, the court did not see how Penry's mitigating evidence, under the instructions given, could be fully acted upon by the jury because "[t]here is no place for the jury to say 'no' to the death penalty" based on the mitigating force of those circumstances. *Id.*, at 925. Although the court questioned whether Penry was given the individualized sentencing that the Constitution requires, it ultimately concluded that prior Circuit decisions required it to reject Penry's claims. *Id.*, at 926. The court also rejected Penry's contention that it was cruel and unusual punishment to execute a mentally retarded person such as himself. *Id.*, at 918 (citing *Brogdon* v. *Butler*, 824 F. 2d 338, 341 (CA5 1987)).

We granted certiorari to resolve two questions. 487 U. S. 1233 (1988). First, was Penry sentenced to death in violation of the Eighth Amendment because the jury was not adequately instructed to take into consideration all of his mitigating evidence and because the terms in the Texas special issues were not defined in such a way that the jury could consider and give effect to his mitigating evidence in answering them? Second, is it cruel and unusual punishment under the Eighth Amendment to execute a mentally retarded person with Penry's reasoning ability?

II

A

Penry is currently before the Court on his petition in federal court for a writ of habeas corpus. Because Penry is before us on collateral review, we must determine, as a threshold matter, whether granting him the relief he seeks would create a "new rule." *Teague* v. *Lane*, 489 U. S. 288, 301 (1989). Under *Teague*, new rules will not be applied or announced in cases on collateral review unless they fall into one of two exceptions. *Id.*, at 311–313.

Teague was not a capital case, and the plurality opinion expressed no views regarding how the retroactivity approach adopted in *Teague* would be applied in the capital sentencing context. *Id.*, at 314, n. 2. The plurality noted, however, that a criminal judgment necessarily includes the sentence imposed, and that collateral challenges to sentences "delay the enforcement of the judgment at issue and decrease the possibility that 'there will at some point be the certainty that comes with an end to litigation.'" *Ibid.* (quoting *Sanders* v.

United States, 373 U. S. 1, 25 (1963) (Harlan, J., dissenting)). See also *Mackey* v. *United States*, 401 U. S. 667, 690–695 (1971) (Harlan, J., concurring in judgments in part and dissenting in part). In our view, the finality concerns underlying Justice Harlan's approach to retroactivity are applicable in the capital sentencing context, as are the two exceptions to his general rule of nonretroactivity. See *Teague*, *supra*, at 311–313.

B

As we indicated in *Teague*, "[i]n general . . . a case announces a new rule when it breaks new ground or imposes a new obligation on the States or the Federal Government." 489 U. S., at 301. Or, "[t]o put it differently, a case announces a new rule if the result was not *dictated* by precedent existing at the time the defendant's conviction became final." *Ibid.* (emphasis in original). *Teague* noted that "[i]t is admittedly often difficult to determine when a case announces a new rule." *Ibid.* Justice Harlan recognized "the inevitable difficulties that will arise in attempting 'to determine whether a particular decision has really announced a "new" rule at all or whether it has simply applied a well-established constitutional principle to govern a case which is closely analogous to those which have been previously considered in the prior case law.'" *Mackey*, *supra*, at 695 (opinion concurring in judgments in part and dissenting in part) (quoting *Desist* v. *United States*, 394 U. S. 244, 263 (1969) (Harlan, J., dissenting)). See generally *Yates* v. *Aiken*, 484 U. S. 211, 216–217 (1988) (concluding that *Francis* v. *Franklin*, 471 U. S. 307 (1985), did not announce a new rule but was "merely an application of the principle that governed our decision in *Sandstrom* v. *Montana*, [442 U. S. 510 (1979),] which had been decided before petitioner's trial took place").

Penry's conviction became final on January 13, 1986, when this Court denied his petition for certiorari on direct review of his conviction and sentence. *Sub nom. Penry* v. *Texas*, *supra*. This Court's decisions in *Lockett* v. *Ohio*, 438 U. S.

586 (1978), and *Eddings* v. *Oklahoma*, 455 U. S. 104 (1982), were rendered before his conviction became final. Under the retroactivity principles adopted in *Griffith* v. *Kentucky*, 479 U. S. 314 (1987), Penry is entitled to the benefit of those decisions. Citing *Lockett* and *Eddings*, Penry argues that he was sentenced to death in violation of the Eighth Amendment because, in light of the jury instructions given, the jury was unable to fully consider and give effect to the mitigating evidence of his mental retardation and abused background, which he offered as the basis for a sentence less than death. Penry thus seeks a rule that when such mitigating evidence is presented, Texas juries must, upon request, be given jury instructions that make it possible for them to give effect to that mitigating evidence in determining whether a defendant should be sentenced to death. We conclude, for the reasons discussed below, that the rule Penry seeks is not a "new rule" under *Teague*.

Penry does not challenge the facial validity of the Texas death penalty statute, which was upheld against an Eighth Amendment challenge in *Jurek* v. *Texas*, 428 U. S. 262 (1976). Nor does he dispute that some types of mitigating evidence can be fully considered by the sentencer in the absence of special jury instructions. See *Franklin* v. *Lynaugh*, 487 U. S. 164, 175 (1988) (plurality opinion); *id.*, at 185–186 (O'CONNOR, J., concurring in judgment). Instead, Penry argues that, on the facts of this case, the jury was unable to fully consider and give effect to the mitigating evidence of his mental retardation and abused background in answering the three special issues. In our view, the relief Penry seeks does not "impos[e] a new obligation" on the State of Texas. *Teague*, *supra*, at 301. Rather, Penry simply asks the State to fulfill the assurance upon which *Jurek* was based: namely, that the special issues would be interpreted broadly enough to permit the sentencer to consider all of the relevant mitigating evidence a defendant might present in imposing sentence.

In *Jurek*, the joint opinion of Justices Stewart, Powell, and STEVENS noted that the Texas statute narrowed the circumstances in which the death penalty could be imposed to five categories of murders. 428 U. S., at 268. Thus, although Texas had not adopted a list of statutory aggravating factors that the jury must find before imposing the death penalty, "its action in narrowing the categories of murders for which a death sentence may ever be imposed serves much the same purpose," *id.*, at 270, and effectively "requires the sentencing authority to focus on the particularized nature of the crime." *Id.*, at 271. To provide the individualized sentencing determination required by the Eighth Amendment, however, the sentencer must be allowed to consider mitigating evidence. *Ibid.* Indeed, as *Woodson* v. *North Carolina*, 428 U. S. 280 (1976), made clear, "in capital cases the fundamental respect for humanity underlying the Eighth Amendment . . . requires consideration of the character and record of the individual offender and the circumstances of the particular offense as a constitutionally indispensable part of the process of inflicting the penalty of death." *Id.*, at 304 (plurality opinion).

Because the Texas death penalty statute does not explicitly mention mitigating circumstances, but rather directs the jury to answer three questions, *Jurek* reasoned that the statute's constitutionality "turns on whether the enumerated questions allow consideration of particularized mitigating factors." 428 U. S., at 272. Although the various terms in the special questions had yet to be defined, the joint opinion concluded that the sentencing scheme satisfied the Eighth Amendment on the assurance that the Texas Court of Criminal Appeals would interpret the question concerning future dangerousness so as to allow the jury to consider whatever mitigating circumstances a defendant may be able to show, including a defendant's prior criminal record, age, and mental or emotional state. *Id.*, at 272–273.

Our decisions subsequent to *Jurek* have reaffirmed that the Eighth Amendment mandates an individualized assessment of the appropriateness of the death penalty. In *Lockett* v. *Ohio*, 438 U. S. 586 (1978), a plurality of this Court held that the Eighth and Fourteenth Amendments require that the sentencer "not be precluded from considering, *as a mitigating factor*, any aspect of a defendant's character or record and any of the circumstances of the offense that the defendant proffers as a basis for a sentence less than death." *Id.*, at 604 (emphasis in original). Thus, the Court held unconstitutional the Ohio death penalty statute which mandated capital punishment upon a finding of one aggravating circumstance unless one of three statutory mitigating factors were present.

Lockett underscored *Jurek*'s recognition that the constitutionality of the Texas scheme "turns on whether the enumerated questions allow consideration of particularized mitigating factors." *Jurek*, *supra*, at 272. The plurality opinion in *Lockett* indicated that the Texas death penalty statute had "survived the petitioner's Eighth and Fourteenth Amendment attack [in *Jurek*] because three Justices concluded that the Texas Court of Criminal Appeals had broadly interpreted the second question—despite its facial narrowness—so as to permit the sentencer to consider 'whatever mitigating circumstances' the defendant might be able to show." 438 U. S., at 607. Thus, the *Lockett* plurality noted that neither the Texas statute upheld in 1976 nor the statutes that had survived facial challenges in *Gregg* v. *Georgia*, 428 U. S. 153 (1976), and *Proffitt* v. *Florida*, 428 U. S. 242 (1976), "clearly operated at that time to prevent the sentencer from considering any aspect of the defendant's character and record or any circumstances of his offense as an independently mitigating factor." *Lockett*, *supra*, at 607. Cf. *Hitchcock* v. *Dugger*, 481 U. S. 393 (1987) (sustaining "as applied" challenge to Florida death penalty statute); *Godfrey*

v. *Georgia*, 446 U. S. 420 (1980) (sustaining "as applied" challenge to Georgia death penalty statute).

In *Eddings* v. *Oklahoma*, 455 U. S. 104 (1982), a majority of the Court reaffirmed that a sentencer may not be precluded from considering, and may not refuse to consider, any relevant mitigating evidence offered by the defendant as the basis for a sentence less than death. In *Eddings*, the Oklahoma death penalty statute permitted the defendant to introduce evidence of any mitigating circumstance, but the sentencing judge concluded, as a matter of law, that he was unable to consider mitigating evidence of the youthful defendant's troubled family history, beatings by a harsh father, and emotional disturbance. Applying *Lockett*, we held that "[j]ust as the State may not by statute preclude the sentencer from considering any mitigating factor, neither may the sentencer refuse to consider, *as a matter of law*, any relevant mitigating evidence." 455 U. S., at 113–114 (emphasis in original). In that case, "it was as if the trial judge had instructed a jury to disregard the mitigating evidence [the defendant] proffered on his behalf." *Id.*, at 114.

Thus, at the time Penry's conviction became final, it was clear from *Lockett* and *Eddings* that a State could not, consistent with the Eighth and Fourteenth Amendments, prevent the sentencer from considering and giving effect to evidence relevant to the defendant's background or character or to the circumstances of the offense that mitigate against imposing the death penalty. Moreover, the facial validity of the Texas death penalty statute had been upheld in *Jurek* on the basis of assurances that the special issues would be interpreted broadly enough to enable sentencing juries to consider all of the relevant mitigating evidence a defendant might present. Penry argues that those assurances were not fulfilled *in his particular case* because, without appropriate instructions, the jury could not fully consider and give effect to the mitigating evidence of his mental retardation and abused childhood in rendering its sentencing decision. The rule

Penry seeks—that when such mitigating evidence is presented, Texas juries must, upon request, be given jury instructions that make it possible for them to give effect to that mitigating evidence in determining whether the death penalty should be imposed— is not a "new rule" under *Teague* because it is dictated by *Eddings* and *Lockett*. Moreover, in light of the assurances upon which *Jurek* was based, we conclude that the relief Penry seeks does not "impos[e] a new obligation" on the State of Texas. *Teague*, 489 U. S., at 301.

III

Underlying *Lockett* and *Eddings* is the principle that punishment should be directly related to the personal culpability of the criminal defendant. If the sentencer is to make an individualized assessment of the appropriateness of the death penalty, "evidence about the defendant's background and character is relevant because of the belief, long held by this society, that defendants who commit criminal acts that are attributable to a disadvantaged background, or to emotional and mental problems, may be less culpable than defendants who have no such excuse." *California* v. *Brown*, 479 U. S. 538, 545 (1987) (O'CONNOR, J., concurring). Moreover, *Eddings* makes clear that it is not enough simply to allow the defendant to present mitigating evidence to the sentencer. The sentencer must also be able to consider and give effect to that evidence in imposing sentence. *Hitchcock* v. *Dugger*, *supra*. Only then can we be sure that the sentencer has treated the defendant as a "uniquely individual human bein[g]" and has made a reliable determination that death is the appropriate sentence. *Woodson*, 428 U. S., at 304, 305. "Thus, the sentence imposed at the penalty stage should reflect a reasoned *moral* response to the defendant's background, character, and crime." *California* v. *Brown*, *supra*, at 545 (O'CONNOR, J., concurring) (emphasis in original).

Although Penry offered mitigating evidence of his mental retardation and abused childhood as the basis for a sentence of life imprisonment rather than death, the jury that sentenced him was only able to express its views on the appropriate sentence by answering three questions: Did Penry act deliberately when he murdered Pamela Carpenter? Is there a probability that he will be dangerous in the future? Did he act unreasonably in response to provocation? The jury was never instructed that it could consider the evidence offered by Penry as *mitigating* evidence and that it could give mitigating effect to that evidence in imposing sentence.

Like the petitioner in *Franklin* v. *Lynaugh*, Penry contends that in the absence of his requested jury instructions, the Texas death penalty statute was applied in an unconstitutional manner by precluding the jury from acting upon the particular mitigating evidence he introduced. *Franklin* was the first case considered by this Court since *Jurek* to address a claim concerning the treatment of mitigating evidence under the Texas special issues. Like *Jurek* itself, *Franklin* did not produce a majority opinion for the Court. The *Franklin* plurality, and the two concurring Justices, concluded that Franklin was not sentenced to death in violation of the Eighth Amendment because the jury was free to give effect to his mitigating evidence of good behavior in prison by answering "no" to the question on future dangerousness. 487 U. S., at 177 (plurality opinion); *id.*, at 185 (O'CONNOR, J., concurring in judgment). Moreover, a majority agreed that "residual doub[t]" as to Franklin's guilt was not a constitutionally mandated mitigating factor. *Id.*, at 173, and n. 6 (plurality opinion); *id.*, at 187–188 (O'CONNOR, J., concurring in judgment).

In *Franklin*, however, the five concurring and dissenting Justices did not share the plurality's categorical reading of *Jurek*. In the plurality's view, *Jurek* had expressly and unconditionally upheld the manner in which mitigating evidence is considered under the special issues. *Id.*, at 179–180, and

n. 10. In contrast, five Members of the Court read *Jurek* as not precluding a claim that, in a particular case, the jury was unable to fully consider the mitigating evidence introduced by a defendant in answering the special issues. 487 U. S., at 183 (O'CONNOR, J., concurring in judgment); *id.*, at 199–200 (STEVENS, J., dissenting). Indeed, both the concurrence and the dissent understood *Jurek* as resting fundamentally on the express assurance that the special issues would permit the jury to fully consider all the mitigating evidence a defendant introduced that was relevant to the defendant's background and character and to the circumstances of the offense. Moreover, both the concurrence and the dissent stressed that "the right to have the sentencer consider and weigh relevant mitigating evidence would be meaningless unless the sentencer was also permitted to give effect to its consideration" in imposing sentence. 487 U. S., at 185 (O'CONNOR, J., concurring in judgment); *id.*, at 199 (STEVENS, J., dissenting).

The concurrence in *Franklin* concluded that there was no Eighth Amendment violation in that case because Franklin's evidence of his good prison behavior had no clear relevance to his character other than to demonstrate his ability to live in a highly structured prison environment without endangering others. Thus, the jury was able to give effect to the mitigating force of this evidence in answering the second special issue. The concurrence noted, however:

> "If . . . petitioner had introduced mitigating evidence about his background or character or the circumstances of the crime that was not relevant to the special verdict questions, or that had relevance to the defendant's moral culpability beyond the scope of the special verdict questions, the jury instructions would have provided the jury with no vehicle for expressing its 'reasoned moral response' to that evidence. If this were such a case, then we would have to decide whether the jury's inability to give effect to that evidence amounted to an Eighth Amendment violation." *Id.*, at 185.

Penry argues that his mitigating evidence of mental retardation and childhood abuse has relevance to his moral culpability beyond the scope of the special issues, and that the jury was unable to express its "reasoned moral response" to that evidence in determining whether death was the appropriate punishment. We agree. Thus, we reject the State's contrary argument that the jury was able to consider and give effect to all of Penry's mitigating evidence in answering the special issues without any jury instructions on mitigating evidence.

The first special issue asks whether the defendant acted "deliberately and with the reasonable expectation that the death of the deceased . . . would result." Neither the Texas Legislature nor the Texas Court of Criminal Appeals have defined the term "deliberately," and the jury was not instructed on the term, so we do not know precisely what meaning the jury gave to it. Assuming, however, that the jurors in this case understood "deliberately" to mean something more than that Penry was guilty of "intentionally" committing murder, those jurors may still have been unable to give effect to Penry's mitigating evidence in answering the first special issue.

Penry's mental retardation was relevant to the question whether he was capable of acting "deliberately," but it also "had relevance to [his] moral culpability beyond the scope of the special verdict questio[n]." *Franklin*, *supra*, at 185. Personal culpability is not solely a function of a defendant's capacity to act "deliberately." A rational juror at the penalty phase of the trial could have concluded, in light of Penry's confession, that he deliberately killed Pamela Carpenter to escape detection. Because Penry was mentally retarded, however, and thus less able than a normal adult to control his impulses or to evaluate the consequences of his conduct, and because of his history of childhood abuse, that same juror could also conclude that Penry was less morally "culpable than defendants who have no such excuse," but who acted "deliberately" as that term is commonly understood. *California* v. *Brown*, 479 U. S., at 545 (O'CONNOR, J., concurring). See also *Skipper* v. *South Carolina*, 476 U. S. 1, 13–14 (1986) (Powell, J., concurring in judgment) (evidence concerning a defendant's "emotional history . . . bear[s] directly on the fundamental justice of imposing capital punishment").

In the absence of jury instructions defining "deliberately" in a way that would clearly direct the jury to consider fully Penry's mitigating evidence as it bears on his personal culpability, we cannot be sure that the jury was able to give effect to the mitigating evidence of Penry's mental retardation and history of abuse in answering the first special issue. Without such a special instruction, a juror who believed that Penry's retardation and background diminished his moral culpability and made imposition of the death penalty unwarranted would be unable to give effect to that conclusion if the juror also believed that Penry committed the crime "deliberately." Thus, we cannot be sure that the jury's answer to the first special issue reflected a "reasoned moral response" to Penry's mitigating evidence.

The second special issue asks "whether there is a probability that the defendant would commit criminal acts of violence that would constitute a continuing threat to society." The mitigating evidence concerning Penry's mental retardation indicated that one effect of his retardation is his inability to learn from his mistakes. Although this evidence is relevant to the second issue, it is relevant only as an *aggravating* factor because it suggests a "yes" answer to the question of future dangerousness. The prosecutor argued at the penalty hearing that there was "a very strong probability, based on the history of this defendant, his previous criminal record, and the psychiatric testimony that we've had in this case, that the defendant will continue to commit acts of this nature." App. 214. Even in a prison setting, the prosecutor argued, Penry could hurt doctors, nurses, librarians, or teachers who worked in the prison.

Penry's mental retardation and history of abuse is thus a two-edged sword: it may diminish his blameworthiness for his crime even as it indicates that there is a probability that he will be dangerous in the future. As Judge Reavley wrote for the Court of Appeals below:

> "What was the jury to do if it decided that Penry, because of retardation, arrested emotional development and a troubled youth, should not be executed? If anything, the evidence made it more likely, not less likely, that the jury would answer the second question yes. It did not allow the jury to consider a major thrust of Penry's evidence as *mitigating* evidence." 832 F. 2d, at 925 (footnote omitted) (emphasis in original).

The second special issue, therefore, did not provide a vehicle for the jury to give mitigating effect to Penry's evidence of mental retardation and childhood abuse.

The third special issue asks "whether the conduct of the defendant in killing the deceased was unreasonable in response to the provocation, if any, by the deceased." On this issue, the State argued that Penry stabbed Pamela Carpenter with a pair of scissors not in response to provocation, but "for the purpose of avoiding detection." App. 215. Penry's own confession indicated that he did not stab the victim after she wounded him superficially with a scissors during a struggle, but rather killed her after her struggle had ended and she was lying helpless. Even if a juror concluded that Penry's mental retardation and arrested emotional development rendered him less culpable for his crime than a normal adult, that would not necessarily diminish the "unreasonableness" of his conduct in response to "the provocation, if any, by the deceased." Thus, a juror who believed Penry lacked the moral culpability to be sentenced to death could not express that view in answering the third special issue if she also concluded that Penry's action was not a reasonable response to provocation.

The State contends, notwithstanding the three interrogatories, that Penry was free to introduce and argue the significance of his mitigating circumstances to the jury. In fact, defense counsel did argue that if a juror believed that Penry, because of the mitigating evidence of his mental retardation and abused background, did not deserve to be put to death, the juror should vote "no" on one of the special issues even if she believed the State had proved that the answer should be "yes." Thus, Penry's counsel stressed the evidence of Penry's mental retardation and abused background, and asked the jurors, "can you be proud to be a party to putting a man to death with that affliction?" App. 222. He urged the jury to answer the first special issue "no" because "it would be the just answer, and I think it would be a proper answer." *Id.*, at 223. As for the prediction of the prosecution psychiatrist that Penry was likely to continue to get into trouble, the defense argued: "That may be true. But, a boy with this mentality, with this mental affliction, even though you have found that issue against us as to insanity, I don't think that there is any question in a single one of you juror's *[sic]* minds that there is something definitely wrong, basically, with this boy. And I think there is not a single one of you that doesn't believe that this boy had brain damage. . . ." *Id.*, at 223–224. In effect, defense counsel urged the jury to "[t]hink about each of those special issues and see if you don't find that we're inquiring into the mental state of the defendant in each and every one of them." *Id.*, at 221.

In rebuttal, the prosecution countered by stressing that the jurors had taken an oath to follow the law, and that they must follow the instructions they were given in answering the special issues:

> "You've all taken an oath to follow the law and you know what the law is. . . . In answering these questions based on the evidence and following the law, and that's all that

> I asked you to do, is to go out and look at the evidence. The burden of proof is on the State as it has been from the beginning, and we accept that burden. And I honestly believe that we have more than met that burden, and that's the reason that you didn't hear Mr. Newman [defense attorney] argue. He didn't pick out these issues and point out to you where the State had failed to meet this burden. He didn't point out the weaknesses in the State's case because, ladies and gentlemen, I submit to you we've met our burden. . . . [Y]our job as jurors and your duty as jurors is not to act on your emotions, but to act on the law as the Judge has given it to you, and on the evidence that you have heard in this courtroom, then answer those questions accordingly." *Id.*, at 225–226.

In light of the prosecutor's argument, and in the absence of appropriate jury instructions, a reasonable juror could well have believed that there was no vehicle for expressing the view that Penry did not deserve to be sentenced to death based upon his mitigating evidence.

The State conceded at oral argument in this Court that if a juror concluded that Penry acted deliberately and was likely to be dangerous in the future, but also concluded that because of his mental retardation he was not sufficiently culpable to deserve the death penalty, that juror would be unable to give effect to that mitigating evidence under the instructions given in this case. Tr. of Oral Arg. 38. The State contends, however, that to instruct the jury that it could render a discretionary grant of mercy, or say "no" to the death penalty, based on Penry's mitigating evidence, would be to return to the sort of unbridled discretion that led to *Furman* v. *Georgia*, 408 U. S. 238 (1972). We disagree.

To be sure, *Furman* held that "in order to minimize the risk that the death penalty would be imposed on a capriciously selected group of offenders, the decision to impose it had to be guided by standards so that the sentencing authority would focus on the particularized circumstances of the crime and the defendant." *Gregg* v. *Georgia*, 428 U. S. 153, 199 (1976) (joint opinion of Stewart, Powell, and STEVENS, JJ.). But as we made clear in *Gregg*, so long as the class of murderers subject to capital punishment is narrowed, there is no constitutional infirmity in a procedure that allows a jury to recommend mercy based on the mitigating evidence introduced by a defendant. *Id.*, at 197–199, 203. As JUSTICE WHITE wrote in *Gregg:*

> "The Georgia legislature has plainly made an effort to guide the jury in the exercise of its discretion, while at the same time permitting the jury to dispense mercy on the basis of factors too intangible to write into a statute, and I cannot accept the naked assertion that the effort is bound to fail. As the types of murders for which the death penalty may be imposed become more narrowly defined and are limited to those which are particularly serious or for which the death penalty is particularly appropriate as they are in Georgia by reason of the aggravating-circumstance requirement, it becomes reasonable to expect that juries—even given discretion *not* to impose the death penalty—will impose the death penalty in a substantial portion of the cases so defined. If they do, it can no longer be said that the penalty is being imposed wantonly and freakishly or so infrequently that it loses its usefulness as a sentencing device." *Id.*, at 222 (opinion concurring in judgment).

"In contrast to the carefully defined standards that must narrow a sentencer's discretion to *impose* the death sentence, the Constitution limits a State's ability to narrow a sentencer's discretion to consider relevant evidence that might cause it to *decline to impose* the death sentence." *McCleskey* v. *Kemp*, 481 U. S. 279, 304 (1987) (emphasis in original). Indeed, it is precisely because the punishment should be directly related to the personal culpability of the defendant that the jury must be allowed to consider and give effect to mitigating evidence relevant to a defendant's character or record or the circumstances of the offense. Rather than creating the risk of an unguided emotional response, full consideration of evidence that mitigates against the death penalty is essential if the jury is to give a "'reasoned *moral* response to the defendant's background, character, and crime.'" *Franklin*, 487 U. S., at 184 (O'CONNOR, J., concurring in judgment) (quoting *California* v. *Brown*, 479 U. S., at 545 (O'CONNOR, J., concurring)). In order to ensure "reliability in the determination that death is the appropriate punishment in a specific case," *Woodson*, 428 U. S., at 305, the jury must be able to consider and give effect to any mitigating evidence relevant to a defendant's background and character or the circumstances of the crime.

In this case, in the absence of instructions informing the jury that it could consider and give effect to the mitigating evidence of Penry's mental retardation and abused background by declining to impose the death penalty, we conclude that the jury was not provided with a vehicle for expressing its "reasoned moral response" to that evidence in rendering its sentencing decision. Our reasoning in *Lockett* and *Eddings* thus compels a remand for resentencing so that we do not "risk that the death penalty will be imposed in spite of factors which may call for a less severe penalty." *Lockett*, 438 U. S., at 605; *Eddings*, 455 U. S., at 119 (O'CONNOR, J., concurring). "When the choice is between life and death, that risk is unacceptable and incompatible with the commands of the Eighth and Fourteenth Amendments." *Lockett*, *supra*, at 605.

IV

Penry's second claim is that it would be cruel and unusual punishment, prohibited by the Eighth Amendment, to execute a mentally retarded person like himself with the reasoning capacity of a 7-year-old. He argues that because of their mental disabilities, mentally retarded people do not possess the level of moral culpability to justify imposing the death sentence. He also argues that there is an emerging national consensus against executing the mentally retarded. The State responds that there is insufficient evidence of a national consensus against executing the retarded, and that existing procedural safeguards adequately protect the interests of mentally retarded persons such as Penry.

A

Under *Teague*, we address the retroactivity issue as a threshold matter because Penry is before us on collateral review. 489 U. S., at 310. If we were to hold that the Eighth Amendment prohibits the execution of mentally retarded persons such as Penry, we would be announcing a "new rule." *Id.*, at 301. Such a rule is not dictated by precedent existing at the time Penry's conviction became final. Moreover, such a rule would "brea[k] new ground" and would impose a new obligation on the States and the Federal Government. *Ibid.* (citing *Ford* v. *Wainwright*, 477 U. S. 399, 410 (1986), which held that the Eighth Amendment prohibits the execution of insane persons, as a case announcing a new rule).

In *Teague*, we concluded that a new rule will not be applied retroactively to defendants on collateral review unless it falls within one of two exceptions. Under the first exception articulated by Justice Harlan, a new rule will be retroactive if it places "'certain kinds of primary, private individual conduct beyond the power of the criminal law-making authority to proscribe.'" *Teague*, *supra*, at 307 (quoting *Mackey*, 401 U. S., at 692 (Harlan, J., concurring in judgments in part and dissenting in part)). Although *Teague* read this exception as focusing solely on new rules according constitutional protection to an actor's primary conduct, Justice Harlan did speak in terms of substantive categorical guarantees accorded by the Constitution, regardless of the procedures followed. This Court subsequently held that the Eighth Amendment, as a substantive matter, prohibits imposing the death penalty on a certain class of defendants because of their status, *Ford* v. *Wainwright*, *supra*, at 410 (insanity), or because of the nature of their offense, *Coker* v. *Georgia*, 433 U. S. 584 (1977) (rape) (plurality opinion). In our view, a new rule placing a certain class of individuals beyond the State's power to punish by death is analogous to a new rule placing certain conduct beyond the State's power to punish at all. In both cases, the Constitution itself deprives the State of the power to impose a certain penalty, and the finality and comity concerns underlying Justice Harlan's view of retroactivity have little force. As Justice Harlan wrote: "There is little societal interest in permitting the criminal process to rest at a point where it ought properly never to repose." *Mackey*, *supra*, at 693. Therefore, the first exception set forth in *Teague* should be understood to cover not only rules forbidding criminal punishment of certain primary conduct but also rules prohibiting a certain category of punishment for a class of defendants because of their status or offense. Thus, if we held, as a substantive matter, that the Eighth Amendment prohibits the execution of mentally retarded persons such as Penry regardless of the procedures followed, such a rule would fall under the first exception to the general rule of nonretroactivity and would be applicable to defendants on collateral review. Accordingly, we address the merits of Penry's claim.

B

The Eighth Amendment categorically prohibits the infliction of cruel and unusual punishments. At a minimum, the Eighth Amendment prohibits punishment considered cruel and unusual at the time the Bill of Rights was adopted. *Ford* v. *Wainwright*, *supra*, at 405; *Solem* v. *Helm*, 463 U. S. 277, 285–286 (1983). The prohibitions of the Eighth Amendment are not limited, however, to those practices condemned by the common law in 1789. *Ford*, *supra*, at 406; *Gregg* v. *Georgia*, 428 U. S., at 171. The prohibition against cruel and unusual punishments also recognizes the "evolving standards of decency that mark the progress of a maturing society." *Trop* v. *Dulles*, 356 U. S. 86, 101 (1958) (plurality opinion); *Ford, supra*, at 406. In discerning those "evolving standards," we have looked to objective evidence of how our society views a particular punishment today. See *Coker* v. *Georgia, supra*, at 593–597; *Enmund* v. *Florida*, 458 U. S. 782, 788–796 (1982). The clearest and most reliable objective evidence of contemporary values is the legislation enacted by the country's legislatures. We have also looked to data concerning the actions of sentencing juries. *Enmund, supra*, at 794–796; *Thompson* v. *Oklahoma*, 487 U. S. 815, 831 (1988) (plurality opinion).

It was well settled at common law that "idiots," together with "lunatics," were not subject to punishment for criminal acts committed under those incapacities. As Blackstone wrote:

> "The second case of a deficiency in will, which excuses from the guilt of crimes, arises also from a defective or vitiated understanding, viz. in an *idiot* or a *lunatic*. . . . [I]diots and lunatics are not chargeable for their own acts, if committed when under these incapacities: no, not even for treason itself. . . . [A] total idiocy, or absolute insanity, excuses from the guilt, and of course from the punishment, of any criminal action committed under such deprivation of the senses. . . . " 4 W. Blackstone, Commentaries *24—*25 (emphasis in original).

See also 1 W. Hawkins, Pleas of the Crown 1–2 (7th ed. 1795) ("[T]hose who are under a natural disability of distinguishing between good and evil, as . . . ideots, and lunaticks are not punishable by any criminal prosecution whatsoever"). Idiocy was understood as "a defect of understanding from the moment of birth," in contrast to lunacy, which was "a partial derangement of the intellectual faculties, the senses returning at uncertain intervals." *Id.*, at 2, n. 2.

There was no one definition of idiocy at common law, but the term "idiot" was generally used to describe persons who had a total lack of reason or understanding, or an inability to distinguish between good and evil. Hale wrote that a person who is deaf and mute from birth "is in presumption of law an ideot . . . because he hath no possibility to understand what is forbidden by law to be done, or under what penalties: but if it can appear, that he hath the use of understanding, . . . then he may be tried, and suffer judgment and execution." 1 M. Hale, Pleas of the Crown 34 (1736) (footnote omitted). See also *id.*, at 29 (citing A. Fitzherbert, 2 Natura Brevium 233 (7th ed. 1730)); *Trial of Edward Arnold*, 16 How. St. Tr. 695, 765 (Eng. 1724) ("[A] man that is totally deprived of his understanding and memory, and doth not know what he is doing, no more than an infant, than a brute, or a wild beast, such a one is never the object of punishment"); S. Glueck, Mental Disorder and the Criminal Law 128–144 (1925).

The common law prohibition against punishing "idiots" and "lunatics" for criminal acts was the precursor of the insanity defense, which today generally includes "mental defect" as well as "mental disease" as part of the legal definition of insanity. See, *e. g.*, American Law Institute, Model Penal Code § 4.01, p. 61 (1985) ("A person is not responsible for criminal conduct if at the time of such conduct as a result of mental disease or defect he lacks substantial capacity either to appreciate the criminality [wrongfulness] of his conduct or to conform his conduct to the requirements of law"); 18 U. S. C. § 17 (1982 ed., Supp. V) (it is an affirmative defense to federal prosecution if "the defendant, as a result of a severe mental disease or defect, was unable to appreciate the nature and quality or the wrongfulness of his acts" at the time the offense was committed). See generally Ellis & Luckasson, Mentally Retarded Criminal Defendants, 53 Geo. Wash. L. Rev. 414, 432–444 (1985).

In its emphasis on a permanent, congenital mental deficiency, the old common law notion of "idiocy" bears some similarity to the modern definition of mental retardation. Ellis & Luckasson, *supra*, at 417. The common law prohibition against punishing "idiots" generally applied, however, to persons of such severe disability that they lacked the reasoning capacity to form criminal intent or to understand the difference between good and evil. In the 19th and early 20th centuries, the term "idiot" was used to describe the most retarded of persons, corresponding to what is called "profound" and "severe" retardation today. See AAMR, Classification in Mental Retardation 179 (H. Grossman ed. 1983); *id.*, at 9 ("idiots" generally had IQ of 25 or below).

The common law prohibition against punishing "idiots" for their crimes suggests that it may indeed be "cruel and unusual" punishment to execute persons who are profoundly or severely retarded and wholly lacking the capacity to appreciate the wrongfulness of their actions. Because of the protections afforded by the insanity defense today, such a person is not likely to be convicted or face the prospect of punishment. See ABA Standards for Criminal Justice 7–9.1, commentary, p. 460 (2d ed. 1980) (most retarded people who reach the point of sentencing are mildly retarded). Moreover, under *Ford* v. *Wainwright*, 477 U. S. 399 (1986), someone who is "unaware of the punishment they are about to suffer and why they are to suffer it" cannot be executed. *Id.*, at 422 (Powell, J., concurring in part and concurring in judgment).

Such a case is not before us today. Penry was found competent to stand trial. In other words, he was found to have the ability to consult with his lawyer with a reasonable degree of rational understanding, and was found to have a rational as well as factual understanding of the proceedings against him. *Dusky* v. *United States*, 362 U. S. 402 (1960); App. 20–24. In addition, the jury rejected his insanity defense, which reflected their conclusion that Penry knew that his conduct was wrong and was capable of conforming his conduct to the requirements of the law. Tex. Penal Code Ann. § 8.01(a) (1974 and Supp. 1989).

Penry argues, however, that there is objective evidence today of an emerging national consensus against execution of the mentally retarded, reflecting the "evolving standards of decency that mark the progress of a maturing society." *Trop* v. *Dulles*, 356 U. S., at 101. Brief for Petitioner 37–39. The federal Anti-Drug Abuse Act of 1988, Pub. L. 100–690, § 7001(l), 102 Stat. 4390, 21 U. S. C. § 848*(l)* (1988 ed.), prohibits execution of a person who is mentally retarded. Only one State, however, currently bans execution of retarded persons who have been found guilty of a capital offense. Ga. Code Ann. § 17–7–131(j) (Supp. 1988). Maryland has enacted a similar statute which will take effect on July 1, 1989. Md. Ann. Code, Art. 27, § 412(f)(1) (1989).

In contrast, in *Ford* v. *Wainwright*, which held that the Eighth Amendment prohibits execution of the insane, considerably more evidence of a national consensus was available. No State permitted the execution of the insane, and 26 States had statutes explicitly requiring suspension of the execution of a capital defendant who became insane. *Ford*, 477 U. S., at 408, n. 2. Other States had adopted the common law prohibition against executing the insane. *Ibid.* Moreover, in examining the objective evidence of contemporary standards of decency in *Thompson* v. *Oklahoma*, the plurality noted that 18 States expressly established a minimum age in their death penalty statutes, and all of them required that the defendant have attained at least the age of 16 at the time of the offense. 487 U. S., at 829, and n. 30. In our view, the two state statutes prohibiting execution of the mentally retarded, even when added to the 14 States that have rejected capital punishment completely, do not provide sufficient evidence at present of a national consensus.

Penry does not offer any evidence of the general behavior of juries with respect to sentencing mentally retarded defendants, nor of decisions of prosecutors. He points instead to several public opinion surveys that indicate strong public opposition to execution of the retarded. For example, a poll taken in Texas found that 86% of those polled supported the death penalty, but 73% opposed its application to the mentally retarded. Reply Brief for Petitioner 6–7; Austin American Statesman, November 15, 1988, p. B3. A Florida poll found 71% of those surveyed were opposed to the execution of mentally retarded capital defendants, while only 12% were in favor. Brief for Petitioner 38; App. 279. A Georgia poll found 66% of those polled opposed to the death penalty for the retarded, 17% in favor, with 16% responding that it depends how retarded the person is. Brief for Petitioner 38; App. 283. In addition, the AAMR, the country's oldest and largest organization of professionals working with the mentally retarded, opposes the execution of persons who are mentally retarded. AAMR, Resolution on Mental Retardation and the Death Penalty, January 1988, App. to Brief for American Association on Mental Retardation et al. as *Amici Curiae* 1a–2a (hereafter *Amici* Brief for AAMR et al.). The public sentiment expressed in these and other polls and resolutions may ultimately find expression in legislation, which is an objective indicator of contemporary values upon which we can rely. But at present, there is insufficient evidence of a national consensus against executing mentally retarded people convicted of capital offenses for us to conclude that it is categorically prohibited by the Eighth Amendment.

C

Relying largely on objective evidence such as the judgments of legislatures and juries, we have also considered whether application of the death penalty to particular categories of crimes or classes of offenders violates the Eighth Amendment because it "makes no measurable contribution to acceptable goals of punishment and hence is nothing more than the purposeless and needless imposition of pain and suffering" or because it is "grossly out of proportion to the severity of the crime." *Coker* v. *Georgia*, 433 U. S., at 592 (plurality opinion); *Thompson* v. *Oklahoma*, 487 U. S., at 833 (plurality opinion); *Tison* v. *Arizona*, 481 U. S. 137 (1987); *Enmund* v. *Florida*, 458 U. S., at 798–801. *Gregg* noted that "[t]he death penalty is said to serve two principal social purposes: retribution and deterrence of capital crimes by prospective offenders." *Gregg* v. *Georgia*, 428 U. S., at 183 (joint opinion of Stewart, Powell, and STEVENS, JJ.). "The heart of the retribution rationale is that a criminal sentence must be directly related to the personal culpability of the criminal offender." *Tison* v. *Arizona, supra,* at 149. See also *Enmund, supra,* at 825 (O'CONNOR, J., dissenting) (the Eighth Amendment concept of "proportionality requires a nexus between the punishment imposed and the defendant's blameworthiness").

Penry argues that execution of a mentally retarded person like himself with a reasoning capacity of approximately a 7-year-old would be cruel and unusual because it is disproportionate to his degree of personal culpability. Brief for Petitioner 49–50. Just as the plurality in *Thompson* reasoned that a juvenile is less culpable than an adult for the same crime, 487 U. S., at 835, Penry argues that mentally retarded people do not have the judgment, perspective, and self-control of a person of normal intelligence. In essence, Penry argues that because of his diminished ability to control his impulses, to think in long-range terms, and to learn from his mistakes, he "is not capable of acting with the degree of culpability that can justify the ultimate penalty," *id.*, at 823.

The AAMR and other groups working with the mentally retarded agree with Penry. They argue as *amici* that all mentally retarded people, regardless of their degree of retardation, have substantial cognitive and behavioral disabilities that reduce their level of blameworthiness for a capital offense. *Amici* Brief for AAMR et al. 5–9, 13–15. *Amici* do not argue that people with mental retardation cannot be held responsible or punished for criminal acts they commit. Rather, they contend that because of "disability in the areas of cognitive impairment, moral reasoning, control of impulsivity, and the ability to understand basic relationships between cause and effect," mentally retarded people cannot act with the level of moral culpability that would justify imposition of the death sentence. *Id.*, at 4. Thus, in their view, execution of mentally retarded people convicted of capital offenses serves no valid retributive purpose. *Id.*, at 19.

It is clear that mental retardation has long been regarded as a factor that may diminish an individual's culpability for a criminal act. See *supra*, at 331–333; ABA Standards for Criminal Justice 7–9.3, commentary, at 463; *State* v. *Hall*, 176 Neb. 295, 310, 125 N. W. 2d 918, 927 (1964). See generally Ellis & Luckasson, 53 Geo. Wash. L. Rev., at 414. In its most severe forms, mental retardation may result in complete exculpation from criminal responsibility. Moreover, virtually all of the States with death penalty statutes that list statutory mitigating factors include as a mitigating circumstance evidence that "[t]he capacity of the defendant to appreciate the criminality of his conduct or to conform his conduct to the requirements of law was substantially impaired."[2] A number of States explicitly mention "mental defect" in connection with such a mitigating circumstance.[3] Indeed, as the Court holds in Part III of this opinion, the sentencing body must be allowed to consider mental retardation

[2] Ala. Code § 13A–5–51(6) (1982). See also Ariz. Rev. Stat. Ann. § 13–702(E)(2) (Supp. 1988); Colo. Rev. Stat. § 16–11–103(5)(b) (1986 and Supp. 1988); Conn. Gen. Stat. § 53a–46a(g)(2) (1989); Fla. Stat. § 921.141(6)(f) (1987); Miss. Code Ann. § 99–19–101(6)(f) (Supp. 1988); Mo. Rev. Stat. § 565.032(3)(6) (1986); Mont. Code Ann. § 46–18–304(4) (1987); N. H. Rev. Stat. Ann. § 630:5 (II)(b)(4) (1986); N. M. Stat. Ann. § 31–20A–6(C) (1987); N. C. Gen. Stat. § 15A–2000(f)(6) (1988); 42 Pa. Cons. Stat. § 9711(e)(3) (1982); S. C. Code § 16–3–20(C)(b)(6) (1985); Va. Code § 19.2–264.4(B)(iv) (1983); Wyo. Stat. § 6–2–102(j)(vi) (1988).

[3] Ark. Code Ann. § 5–4–605(3) (1987); Cal. Penal Code Ann. § 190.3(h) (West 1988); Ky. Rev. Stat. Ann. § 532.025(2)(b)7 (Baldwin 1984); La. Code Crim. Proc. Ann., Art. 905.5(e) (West 1984); Neb. Rev. Stat. § 29–2523 (2)(g) (1985); N. J. Stat. Ann. § 2C: 11–3(c)(5)(d) (West Supp. 1988); Ohio Rev. Code Ann. § 2929.04(B)(3) (1987); Tenn. Code Ann. § 39–2–203(j)(8) (1982); Wash. Rev. Code § 10.95.070(6) (1987). Other formulations are used in Ind. Code § 35–50–2–9(c)(6) (1988); Md. Ann. Code, Art. 27, § 413 (g)(4) (1988); and Utah Code Ann. § 76–3–207(2)(d) (Supp. 1988).

as a mitigating circumstance in making the individualized determination whether death is the appropriate punishment in a particular case.

On the record before the Court today, however, I cannot conclude that all mentally retarded people of Penry's ability—by virtue of their mental retardation alone, and apart from any individualized consideration of their personal responsibility—inevitably lack the cognitive, volitional, and moral capacity to act with the degree of culpability associated with the death penalty. Mentally retarded persons are individuals whose abilities and experiences can vary greatly. As the AAMR's standard work, Classification in Mental Retardation, points out:

> "The term *mental retardation*, as commonly used today, embraces a heterogeneous population, ranging from totally dependent to nearly independent people. Although all individuals so designated share the common attributes of low intelligence and inadequacies in adaptive behavior, there are marked variations in the degree of deficit manifested and the presence or absence of associated physical handicaps, stigmata, and psychologically disordered states." Classification in Mental Retardation, at 12.

In addition to the varying degrees of mental retardation, the consequences of a retarded person's mental impairment, including the deficits in his or her adaptive behavior, "may be ameliorated through education and habilitation." Ellis & Luckasson, *supra*, at 424, n. 54. Although retarded persons generally have difficulty learning from experience, *Amici* Brief for AAMR et al. 7, some are fully "capable of learning, working, and living in their communities." *Id.*, at 6. See American Association on Mental Deficiency, Monograph 6, Lives in Process: Mildly Retarded Adults in a Large City (R. Edgerton ed. 1984). In light of the diverse capacities and life experiences of mentally retarded persons, it cannot be said on the record before us today that all mentally retarded people, by definition, can never act with the level of culpability associated with the death penalty.

Penry urges us to rely on the concept of "mental age," and to hold that execution of any person with a mental age of seven or below would constitute cruel and unusual punishment. Tr. of Oral Arg. 22–25. Mental age is "calculated as the chronological age of nonretarded children whose average IQ test performance is equivalent to that of the individual with mental retardation." *Amici* Brief for AAMR et al. 14, n. 6. See D. Wechsler, The Measurement and Appraisal of Adult Intelligence 24–25 (4th ed. 1958). Such a rule should not be adopted today. First, there was no finding below by the judge or jury concerning Penry's "mental age." One of Penry's expert witnesses, Dr. Brown, testified that he estimated Penry's "mental age" to be 6½. App. 41. That same expert estimated that Penry's "social maturity" was that of a 9- or 10-year-old. *Ibid.* As a more general matter, the "mental age" concept, irrespective of its intuitive appeal, is problematic in several respects. As the AAMR acknowledges, "[t]he equivalence between nonretarded children and retarded adults is, of course, imprecise." *Amici* Brief for AAMR et al. 14, n. 6. The "mental age" concept may underestimate the life experiences of retarded adults, while it may overestimate the ability of retarded adults to use logic and foresight to solve problems. *Ibid.* The mental age concept has other limitations as well. Beyond the chronological age of 15 or 16, the mean scores on most intelligence tests cease to increase significantly with age. Wechsler 26. As a result, "[t]he average mental age of the average 20 year old is not 20 but 15 years." *Id.*, at 27. See also *In re Ramon M.*, 22 Cal. 3d 419, 429, 584 P. 2d 524, 531 (1978) ("[T]he 'mental age' of the average adult under present norms is approximately 16 years and 8 months").

Not surprisingly, courts have long been reluctant to rely on the concept of mental age as a basis for exculpating a defendant from criminal responsibility. See, *e. g.*, *In re*

Ramon M., *supra*, at 429, 584 P. 2d, at 531; *State* v. *Schilling*, 95 N. J. L. 145, 148, 112 A. 400, 402 (1920); *People* v. *Marquis*, 344 Ill. 261, 267, 176 N. E. 314, 316 (1931); *Chriswell* v. *State*, 171 Ark. 255, 259, 283 S. W. 981, 983 (1926). Cf. *Pickett* v. *State*, 71 So. 2d 102, 107 (Ala. 1954). See generally Ellis & Luckasson, 53 Geo. Wash. L. Rev., at 435. Moreover, reliance on mental age to measure the capabilities of a retarded person for purposes of the Eighth Amendment could have a disempowering effect if applied in other areas of the law. Thus, on that premise, a mildly mentally retarded person could be denied the opportunity to enter into contracts or to marry by virtue of the fact that he had a "mental age" of a young child. In light of the inherent problems with the mental age concept, and in the absence of better evidence of a national consensus against execution of the retarded, mental age should not be adopted as a line-drawing principle in our Eighth Amendment jurisprudence.

In sum, mental retardation is a factor that may well lessen a defendant's culpability for a capital offense. But we cannot conclude today that the Eighth Amendment precludes the execution of any mentally retarded person of Penry's ability convicted of a capital offense simply by virtue of his or her mental retardation alone. So long as sentencers can consider and give effect to mitigating evidence of mental retardation in imposing sentence, an individualized determination whether "death is the appropriate punishment" can be made in each particular case. While a national consensus against execution of the mentally retarded may someday emerge reflecting the "evolving standards of decency that mark the progress of a maturing society," there is insufficient evidence of such a consensus today.

Accordingly, the judgment below is affirmed in part and reversed in part, and the case is remanded for further proceedings consistent with this opinion.

It is so ordered.

JUSTICE BRENNAN, with whom JUSTICE MARSHALL joins, concurring in part and dissenting in part.

I agree that the jury instructions given at sentencing in this case deprived petitioner of his constitutional right to have a jury consider all mitigating evidence that he presented before sentencing him to die. I would also hold, however, that the Eighth Amendment prohibits the execution of offenders who are mentally retarded and who thus lack the full degree of responsibility for their crimes that is a predicate for the constitutional imposition of the death penalty.

I

I dissented in *Teague* v. *Lane*, 489 U. S. 288, 326 (1989), and I continue to believe that the plurality's unprecedented curtailment of the reach of the Great Writ in that case was without foundation. The *Teague* plurality adopted for no adequate reason a novel threshold test for federal review of state criminal convictions that, subject to narrow exceptions, precludes federal courts from considering a vast array of important federal questions on collateral review, and thereby both prevents the vindication of personal constitutional rights and deprives our society of a significant safeguard against future violations. In this case, the Court compounds its error by extending *Teague*'s notion that new rules will not generally be announced on collateral review to cases in which a habeas petitioner challenges the constitutionality of a capital sentencing procedure. This extension means that a person may be killed although he or she has a sound constitutional claim that would have barred his or her execution had this Court only announced the constitutional rule before his or her conviction and sentence became final. It is intolerable that the difference between life and death should turn on such a fortuity of timing, and beyond my comprehension that a majority of this Court will so blithely allow a State to take a human life though the method by which sentence was determined violates our Constitution.

I say the Court takes this step "blithely" advisedly. The Court extends *Teague* without the benefit of briefing or oral argument. *Teague*, indeed, was decided only after we had heard argument in this case. Rather than postponing decision on the important issue whether *Teague* should be extended to capital cases until it is presented in a case in which it may be briefed and argued, the Court rushes to decide *Teague*'s applicability in such circumstances here. It does so in two sentences, *ante*, at 313–314, saying merely that not to apply *Teague* would result in delay in killing the prisoner and in a lack of finality. There is not the least hint that the Court has even considered whether different rules might be called for in capital cases, let alone any sign of reasoning justifying the extension. Such peremptory treatment of the issue is facilitated, of course, by the Court's decision to reach the *Teague* question without allowing counsel to set out the opposing arguments.

Though I believe *Teague* was wrongly decided, and the Court's precipitate decision to extend *Teague* to capital cases an error, nevertheless if these mistakes are to be made law I agree that the Court's discussion of the question whether the jury had an opportunity to consider Penry's mitigating evidence in answering Texas' three "special issues" does not establish a "new rule." I thus join Part II-B of the Court's opinion, and all of Parts I and III. I also agree that there is an exception to *Teague* so that new rules "prohibiting a certain category of punishment for a class of defendants because of their status or offense" may be announced in, and applied to, cases on collateral review. *Ante*, at 330. I thus join Part IV-A of the Court's opinion.

II

A majority of the Court today reaffirms, in this case and in *Stanford* v. *Kentucky*, *post*, at 382 (O'CONNOR, J., concurring in part and concurring in judgment); *post*, at 393 (BRENNAN, J., dissenting), the well-established principle that "application of the death penalty to particular categories of crimes or classes of offenders violates the Eighth Amendment [if] it 'makes no measurable contribution to acceptable goals of punishment and hence is nothing more than the purposeless and needless imposition of pain and suffering' or [if] it is 'grossly out of proportion to the severity of the crime.'" *Ante*, at 335 (opinion of O'CONNOR, J.), quoting *Coker* v. *Georgia*, 433 U. S. 584, 592 (1977). The contours of these two inquiries are clear. We gauge whether a punishment is disproportionate by comparing "the gravity of the offense," understood to include not only the injury caused, but also the defendant's moral culpability, with "the harshness of the penalty." *Solem* v. *Helm*, 463 U. S. 277, 292 (1983). See *ante*, at 336; *Stanford*, *post*, at 382 (O'CONNOR, J., concurring in part and concurring in judgment); *post*, at 393–394 (BRENNAN, J., dissenting); *Thompson* v. *Oklahoma*, 487 U. S. 815, 834 (1988) (plurality opinion); *id.*, at 853 (opinion of O'CONNOR, J.); *Coker*, *supra*, at 598; *Enmund* v. *Florida*, 458 U. S. 782, 798 (1982) (opinion of the Court); *id.*, at 815 (O'CONNOR, J., dissenting). And we require that a punishment further the penal goals of deterrence or retribution. *Ante*, at 335–336; *Stanford*, *post*, at 403 (BRENNAN, J., dissenting); *Thompson*, *supra*, at 836 (plurality opinion); *Enmund*, *supra*, at 798; *Coker*, *supra*, at 592; *Gregg* v. *Georgia*, 428 U. S. 153, 183 (1976) (opinion of Stewart, Powell, and STEVENS, JJ.). In my view, execution of the mentally retarded is unconstitutional under both these strands of Eighth Amendment analysis.

A

I agree with JUSTICE O'CONNOR that one question to be asked in determining whether the execution of mentally retarded offenders is always unconstitutional because disproportionate is whether the mentally retarded as a class "by virtue of their mental retardation alone, . . . inevitably lack the cognitive, volitional, and moral capacity to act with the degree of culpability associated with the death penalty." *Ante*, at 338. JUSTICE O'CONNOR answers that question in the negative, "[i]n light of the diverse capacities and life experiences of mentally retarded persons." *Ibid.* It seems to me that the evidence compels a different conclusion.

For many purposes, legal and otherwise, to treat the mentally retarded as a homogeneous group is inappropriate, bringing the risk of false stereotyping and unwarranted discrimination. See Ellis & Luckasson, Mentally Retarded Criminal Defendants, 53 Geo. Wash. L. Rev. 414, 427 (1985). Nevertheless, there are characteristics as to which there is no danger of spurious generalization because they are a part of the clinical definition of mental retardation. "Mental retardation" is defined by the American Association on Mental Retardation (AAMR) as "significantly subaverage general intellectual functioning existing concurrently with deficits in adaptive behavior and manifested during the developmental period." AAMR, Classification in Mental Retardation 11 (H. Grossman ed. 1983) (hereafter AAMR Classification). To fall within this definition, an individual must be among the approximately two percent of the population with an IQ below 70 on standardized measures of intelligence, see *id.*, at 31, and *in addition* must be subject to "significant limitations in [his or her] effectiveness in meeting the standards of maturation, learning, personal independence, and/or social responsibility that are expected for his or her age level and cultural group," *id.*, at 11; see also *id.*, at 76 (noting "the imperfect correlation of intelligence and adaptive behavior, especially at the upper ends of the intellectual range of retardation"). Thus, while as between the mildly, moderately, severely, and profoundly mentally retarded, with IQs ranging from 70 to below 20, there are indeed "marked variations in the degree of deficit manifested," it is also true that "*all* individuals [designated as mentally retarded] share the common attributes of low intelligence and inadequacies in adaptive behavior." *Id.*, at 12 (emphasis added).[1]

In light of this clinical definition of mental retardation, I cannot agree that the undeniable fact that mentally retarded persons have "diverse capacities and life experiences," *ante*, at 338, is of significance to the Eighth Amendment proportionality analysis we must conduct in this case. "Every individual who has mental retardation"—irrespective of his or her precise capacities or experiences—has "a substantial disability in cognitive ability and adaptive behavior." Brief for the AAMR et al. as *Amici Curiae* 5 (hereafter AAMR Brief). This is true even of the "highest functioning individuals in the 'mild' retardation category," *id.*, at 14, and of course of those like Penry whose cognitive and behavioral disabilities place them on the borderline between mild and moderate retardation. See *ante*, at 307–308, and n. 1. Among the mentally retarded, "reduced ability is found in every dimension of the individual's functioning, including his language, communication, memory, attention, ability to control impulsivity, moral development, self-concept, self-perception, suggestibility, knowledge of basic information, and general motivation." AAMR Brief 6. Though individuals, particularly those who are mildly retarded, may be quite capable of overcoming these limitations to the extent of being able to "main-

[1] It is of course possible to classify those with developmental disabilities in different ways. Indeed, the question on which certiorari was granted in this case—whether it violates the Eighth Amendment "to execute an individual with the reasoning capacity of a seven year old"—concerned classification according to mental age. Petitioner conflates mental age and the AAMR's mental retardation classifications in his brief, and the Court addresses both proposals for Eighth Amendment line drawing. JUSTICE O'CONNOR's opinion does not, however, preclude the possibility that an Eighth Amendment line might be drawn using a classification that encompasses only a more substantially disabled group than all those within the AAMR's clinical definition of the mentally retarded, and that lacks the problems JUSTICE O'CONNOR associates with the concept of mental age. *ante*, at 338–340.

tain themselves independently or semi-independently in the community," AAMR Classification 184; see *id.*, at 207–208, nevertheless, the mentally retarded by definition "have a reduced ability to cope with and function in the everyday world." *Cleburne* v. *Cleburne Living Center, Inc.*, 473 U. S. 432, 442 (1985). The impairment of a mentally retarded offender's reasoning abilities, control over impulsive behavior, and moral development in my view limits his or her culpability so that, whatever other punishment might be appropriate, the ultimate penalty of death is always and necessarily disproportionate to his or her blameworthiness and hence is unconstitutional.[2]

Even if mental retardation alone were not invariably associated with a lack of the degree of culpability upon which death as a proportionate punishment is predicated, I would still hold the execution of the mentally retarded to be unconstitutional. If there are among the mentally retarded exceptional individuals as responsible for their actions as persons who suffer no such disability, the individualized consideration afforded at sentencing fails to ensure that they are the only mentally retarded offenders who will be picked out to receive a death sentence. The consideration of mental retardation as a mitigating factor is inadequate to guarantee, as the Con-

---

[2] Because a person's "mental age" is a factor only of his or her IQ and of the average IQs of nonretarded children, see *ante*, at 339, it is a less sophisticated and reliable guide to an individual's abilities than the accepted standards for diagnosing mental retardation, and must be supplemented with estimates of a person's "social maturity" measured in comparison to that of nonretarded children. In the present case, for example, there was testimony that petitioner had a mental age of 6½ and a social maturity equivalent to that of a 9- or 10-year-old. This evidence surely gives some insight into just what it is that Texas has proposed to do in killing Penry. However, "[t]he equivalence between nonretarded children and retarded adults is . . . imprecise." AAMR Brief 14, n. 6, and it seems on the basis of the information before us to be more appropriate to conduct proportionality analysis by reference to the accepted clinical classification of mental retardation than on the basis of age comparisons.

stitution requires, that an individual who is not fully blameworthy for his or her crime because of a mental disability does not receive the death penalty.

That "sentencers can consider and give effect to mitigating evidence of mental retardation in imposing sentence" provides no assurance that an adequate individualized determination of whether the death penalty is a proportionate punishment will be made at the conclusion of each capital trial. *Ante*, at 340. At sentencing, the judge or jury considers an offender's level of blameworthiness only along with a host of other factors that the sentencer may decide outweigh any want of responsibility. The sentencer is free to weigh a mentally retarded offender's relative lack of culpability against the heinousness of the crime and other aggravating factors and to decide that even the most retarded and irresponsible of offenders should die. Indeed, a sentencer will entirely discount an offender's retardation as a factor mitigating against imposition of a death sentence if it adopts this line of reasoning:

> "It appears to us that there is all the more reason to execute a killer if he is also . . . retarded. Killers often kill again; [a] retarded killer is more to be feared than a . . . normal killer. There is also far less possibility of his ever becoming a useful citizen." Upholding Law and Order, Hartsville Messenger, June 24, 1987, p. 5B, col. 1 (approving death sentence imposed on mentally retarded murderer by a South Carolina court).

Lack of culpability as a result of mental retardation is simply not isolated at the sentencing stage as a factor that determinatively bars a death sentence; for individualized consideration at sentencing is not designed to ensure that mentally retarded offenders are not sentenced to death if they are not culpable to the degree necessary to render execution a proportionate response to their crimes. When Johnny Penry is resentenced, absent a change in Texas law there will be nothing to prevent the jury, acting lawfully, from sentencing him to death once again—even though it finds his culpability significantly reduced by reason of mental retardation. I fail to see how that result is constitutional, in the face of the acknowledged Eighth Amendment requirement of proportionality.

B

There is a second ground upon which I would conclude that the execution of mentally retarded offenders violates the Eighth Amendment: killing mentally retarded offenders does not measurably further the penal goals of either retribution or deterrence. "The heart of the retribution rationale is that a criminal sentence must be directly related to the personal culpability of the criminal offender." *Tison* v. *Arizona*, 481 U. S. 137, 149 (1987); see also *Enmund*, 458 U. S., at 800. Since mentally retarded offenders as a class lack the culpability that is a prerequisite to the proportionate imposition of the death penalty, it follows that execution can never be the "just deserts" of a retarded offender, *id.*, at 801, and that the punishment does not serve the retributive goal, see *Stanford*, *post*, at 404 (BRENNAN, J., dissenting) ("A punishment that fails the Eighth Amendment test of proportionality because disproportionate to the offender's blameworthiness by definition is not justly deserved").

Furthermore, killing mentally retarded offenders does not measurably contribute to the goal of deterrence. It is highly unlikely that the exclusion of the mentally retarded from the class of those eligible to be sentenced to death will lessen any deterrent effect the death penalty may have for nonretarded potential offenders, for they, of course, will under present law remain at risk of execution. And the very factors that make it disproportionate and unjust to execute the mentally retarded also make the death penalty of the most minimal deterrent effect so far as retarded potential offenders are concerned. "[I]ntellectual impairments . . . in logical reasoning, strategic thinking, and foresight," the lack of the intellectual and developmental predicates of an "ability to anticipate consequences," and "impairment in the ability to control impulsivity," AAMR Brief 6–7, mean that the possibility of receiving the death penalty will not in the case of a mentally retarded person figure in some careful assessment of different courses of action. See also *id.*, at 7 ("[A] person who has mental retardation often cannot independently generate in his mind a sufficient range of behaviors from which to select an action appropriate to the situation he faces (particularly a stressful situation)"). In these circumstances, the execution of mentally retarded individuals is "nothing more than the purposeless and needless imposition of pain and suffering," *Coker*, 433 U. S., at 592, and is unconstitutional under the Eighth Amendment.

Because I believe that the Eighth Amendment to the United States Constitution stands in the way of a State killing a mentally retarded person for a crime for which, as a result of his or her disability, he or she is not fully culpable, I would reverse the judgment of the Court of Appeals in its entirety.

JUSTICE STEVENS, with whom JUSTICE BLACKMUN joins, concurring in part and dissenting in part.

As I stated in my separate opinion in *Teague* v. *Lane*, 489 U. S. 288, 318–319, and n. 2 (1989), it is neither logical nor prudent to consider a rule's retroactive application before the rule itself is articulated. Nor am I at all sure that courts should decide the retroactivity issue if it was not raised below. Cf. *Zant* v. *Moore*, 489 U. S. 836, 837 (1989) (BLACKMUN, J., dissenting). Finally, I do not support the Court's assertion, without benefit of argument or briefing on the issue, that *Teague*'s retroactivity principles pertain to capital cases. Cf. *Teague*, 489 U. S., at 321, and n. 3 (STEVENS, J., concurring in part and concurring in judgment). But assuming, *arguendo*, that those principles do apply, it is clear that the Court's discussion of the mitigating evidence question, with which I agree, does not establish a "new rule" as that term is used for retroactivity purposes. I thus join Parts I, II–B, and III.

In Part IV–A the Court decides that a rule that the Eighth Amendment prohibits the execution of a mentally retarded person ought to apply retroactively. Assuming retroactivity is pertinent, I agree that the first exception to Justice Harlan's nonretroactivity doctrine "should be understood to cover not only rules forbidding criminal punishment of certain primary conduct but also rules prohibiting a certain category of punishment for a class of defendants because of their status or offense," *ante*, at 330, and that this claim lies within that exception.*

The remaining sections of Part IV adequately and fairly state the competing arguments respecting capital punishment of mentally retarded persons. In my judgment, however, that explication—particularly the summary of the arguments advanced in the Brief for American Association on Mental Retardation et al. as *Amici Curiae*, *ante*, at 336–337—compels the conclusion that such executions are unconstitutional. I would therefore reverse the judgment of the Court of Appeals in its entirety.

JUSTICE SCALIA, with whom THE CHIEF JUSTICE, JUSTICE WHITE, and JUSTICE KENNEDY join, concurring in part and dissenting in part.

I

I join Part I of the Court's opinion, setting forth the facts and procedural history of this case; Part II–A, holding that *Teague* v. *Lane*, 489 U. S. 288 (1989), which precludes collat-

*Because I believe that retroactivity should not be considered until after a right is established, see *Teague* v. *Lane*, 489 U. S. 288, 318–319, and n. 2 (1989) (STEVENS, J., concurring in part and concurring in judgment), the Court's rejection of this claim ordinarily would preclude me from agreeing even for purposes of argument that the rule Penry seeks may be applied retroactively. I do so here because the Court has fleshed out the merits of Penry's claim sufficiently to allow me to reach a contrary conclusion.

eral relief that would establish a "new rule," applies to capital sentencing; and Part IV–A, holding that the exception to *Teague* for a new rule that places certain matters "'beyond the power of the criminal law-making authority,'" *id.*, at 311, quoting *Mackey* v. *United States*, 401 U. S. 667, 692 (1971) (separate opinion of Harlan, J.), applies to petitioner's contention that the Eighth Amendment forbids the execution of mentally retarded offenders. I also join Part IV–B, rejecting the latter contention on the ground that execution of mentally retarded offenders contravenes neither those practices condemned at the time the Bill of Rights was adopted nor the "evolving standards of decency that mark the progress of a maturing society." *Trop* v. *Dulles*, 356 U. S. 86, 101 (1958) (plurality opinion). Unlike JUSTICE O'CONNOR, however, I think we need go no further to resolve the Eighth Amendment issue. Part IV–C of her opinion goes on to examine whether application of the death penalty to mentally retarded offenders "violates the Eighth Amendment because it 'makes no measurable contribution to acceptable goals of punishment and hence is nothing more than the purposeless and needless imposition of pain and suffering' or because it is 'grossly out of proportion to the severity of the crime.'" *Ante*, at 335 (citations omitted). For the reasons explained by the plurality in *Stanford* v. *Kentucky*, *post*, p. 361, I think this inquiry has no place in our Eighth Amendment jurisprudence. "The punishment is either 'cruel *and* unusual' (*i. e.*, society has set its face against it) or it is not." *Post*, at 378 (emphasis in original). If it is not unusual, that is, if an objective examination of laws and jury determinations fails to demonstrate society's disapproval of it, the punishment is not unconstitutional even if out of accord with the theories of penology favored by the Justices of this Court. See *post*, at 379.

II

I disagree with the holding in Part II–B of the Court's opinion that petitioner's contention, that his sentencing was unconstitutional because the Texas jury was not permitted fully to consider and give effect to the mitigating evidence of his mental retardation and background of abuse, does not seek the application of a "new rule" and is therefore not barred by *Teague*. I also disagree with the disposition of the merits of this contention, in Part III of the Court's opinion.

A

The merits of this mitigation issue, and the question whether, in raising it on habeas, petitioner seeks application of a "new rule" within the meaning of *Teague*, are obviously interrelated. I will say only a few words addressed exclusively to the latter. Our holding in *Teague* rested upon the historic role of habeas corpus in our system of law, which is to provide a "deterrence," "'the threat of [which] serves as a necessary additional incentive for trial and appellate courts throughout the land to conduct their proceedings in a manner consistent with established constitutional standards.'" 489 U. S., at 306, quoting *Desist* v. *United States*, 394 U. S. 244, 262–263 (1969) (Harlan, J., dissenting). "Deterrence" and "threat" are meaningless concepts as applied to a situation in which the law is so uncertain that a judge acting in all good faith and with the greatest of care could reasonably read our precedents as permitting the result the habeas petitioner contends is wrong. Thus, a "new rule," for purposes of *Teague*, must include not only a new rule that replaces an old one, but a new rule that replaces palpable uncertainty as to what the rule might be. We acknowledged as much in *Teague* (in a passage given lip-service by the Court today, see *ante*, at 314) when we said that "a case announces a new rule if the result was not *dictated* by precedent existing at the time the defendant's conviction became final." 489 U. S., at 301.

As my discussion of the merits will make plain, it challenges the imagination to think that today's result is "dictated" by our prior cases. Indeed, if there is any available contention that our prior cases *compelled* a particular result, it is the contention that petitioner's claim was considered and rejected by *Jurek* v. *Texas*, 428 U. S. 262 (1976). Even if that contention is rejected, however, there is *no* basis for finding a compulsion in the opposite direction. It seems to me utterly impossible to say that a judge acting in good faith and with care should have known the rule announced today, and that future fault similar to that of which the Texas courts have been guilty must be deterred by making good on the "threat" of habeas corpus.

In a system based on precedent and *stare decisis*, it is the tradition to find each decision "inherent" in earlier cases (however well-concealed its presence might have been), and rarely to replace a previously announced rule with a new one. If *Teague* does not apply to a claimed "inherency" as vague and debatable as that in the present case, then it applies only to habeas requests for plain overruling—which means that it adds little if anything to the principles already in place concerning the retroactivity of new rules in criminal cases, which provide that "a decision announcing a new standard 'is almost automatically nonretroactive' where the decision 'has explicitly overruled past precedent.'" *Allen* v. *Hardy*, 478 U. S. 255, 258 (1986), quoting *Solem* v. *Stumes*, 465 U. S. 638, 646, 647 (1984). It is rare that a principle of law as significant as that in *Teague* is adopted and gutted in the same Term.

B

I turn next to the merits of petitioner's mitigation claim. In *Furman* v. *Georgia*, 408 U. S. 238 (1972), we invalidated Georgia's capital punishment scheme on the ground that, since there were no standards as to when it would be applied for a particular crime, it created too great a risk that the death penalty would be irrationally imposed. Four years later, however, we struck down the capital sentencing schemes of North Carolina and Louisiana for the opposite vice—because they unduly *constricted* sentencing discretion by failing to allow for individualized consideration of the particular defendant and offense, see *Woodson* v. *North Carolina*, 428 U. S. 280 (1976); *Roberts* v. *Louisiana*, 428 U. S. 325 (1976). On the same day, however, we upheld the schemes of Georgia, Texas, and Florida, because they struck the proper balance, channeling the sentencer's discretion without unduly restricting it. *Gregg* v. *Georgia*, 428 U. S. 153 (1976); *Jurek* v. *Texas*, *supra; Proffitt* v. *Florida*, 428 U. S. 242, 253 (1976). The Texas system upheld in *Jurek* was precisely the same one the Court finds unacceptable today, which structures the jury's discretion through three questions relating to the defendant's personal culpability for the crime, his future dangerousness, and the reasonableness of his response to any provocation by the victim. In holding that this scheme unconstitutionally limits the jury's discretion to consider the mitigating evidence of Penry's mental retardation and abused childhood, the Court today entirely disregards one of the two lines of our concern, requiring individualized consideration to displace the channeling of discretion, and throwing away *Jurek* in the process.

The Court contends that its conclusion is not inconsistent with *Jurek* because that case merely upheld a facial challenge to the Texas Special Issues framework. According to the Court, it did not "preclud[e] a claim that, in a particular case, the jury was unable to fully consider the mitigating evidence introduced by a defendant in answering the special issues." *Ante*, at 321. I disagree. While rejection of a facial challenge to a statute does not preclude all as-applied attacks, surely it precludes one resting upon the same asserted principle of law. And that is the situation here. The joint opinion announcing the judgment in *Jurek* (it is necessary only to describe the joint opinion, since the three Justices subscribing to the opinion of JUSTICE WHITE, 428 U. S., at 277, would have upheld the Texas statute on even broader grounds) said that "the constitutionality of the Texas procedures turns on whether the enumerated questions allow consideration of particularized mitigating factors." *Id.*, at 272. The claim that the Court entertains and vindicates today flatly contradicts that analysis, holding that the constitutionality turns on whether the questions allow mitigating factors not only to be considered (and, of course, given effect in answering the questions), *but also to be given effect in all possible ways, including ways that the questions do not permit.* It is simply not true that, as today's opinion asserts, the *Jurek* Court had before it "the express assurance that the special issues would permit the jury to fully consider all the mitigating evidence a defendant introduced." *Ante*, at 321. What the Court means by "fully consider" (what it *must* mean to distinguish *Jurek*) is to consider *for all purposes, including purposes not specifically permitted by the questions.* But there was no such assurance at all. To the contrary, the portion of the Texas Court of Criminal Appeals' opinion quoted in *Jurek* to evidence the assurance began: "'In determining the likelihood that the defendant would be a continuing threat to society [*i. e.*, in considering the second question under the Texas statute], the jury could consider . . . [,]'" 428 U. S., at 272–273, quoting 522 S. W. 2d 934, 939–940 (1975). The same focus upon the use of mitigating evidence for the limited purpose of answering the enumerated questions, rather than upon the jury's ability to use it for all purposes, is also evident in the joint opinion's statement that "[the] Texas Court of Criminal Appeals has not yet construed the first and third questions . . . ; thus it is as yet undetermined whether or not the jury's *consideration of those questions* would properly include consideration of mitigating circumstances." 428 U. S., at 272, n. 7 (emphasis added).

In short, it could not be clearer that *Jurek* adopted the constitutional rule that the instructions had to render all mitigating circumstances relevant to the jury's verdict, but that the precise manner of their relevance—the precise *effect* of their consideration—could be channeled by law. The joint opinion approved the Texas statute expressly because it "focuses the jury's objective consideration of the particularized circumstances of the individual offense and the individual offender." *Id.*, at 274. Of course there remains available, in an as-applied challenge to the Texas statute, the contention that a particular mitigating circumstance is in fact irrelevant to any of the three questions it poses, and hence could not be considered. But that is not the case here, nor is it the ground upon which the Court relies. Special Issue One required the jury to determine whether "'the conduct of the defendant that caused the death of the deceased was committed deliberately and with the reasonable expectation that the death of the deceased or another would result.'" *Ante*, at 310. As the plurality observed in *Franklin* v. *Lynaugh*, 487 U. S. 164 (1988), "[t]he Texas courts have consistently held that something more must be found in the penalty phase—something beyond the guilt-phase finding of 'intentional' commission of the crime—before the jury can determine that a capital murder is 'deliberate' within the meaning of the first Special Issue." *Id.*, at 171–175 (citing Texas cases). Evidence of Penry's mental retardation and abused childhood was relevant to that point. He was permitted to introduce all that evidence, relied upon it in urging the jury to answer "no" to the Special Issues, and had the benefit of an instruction specifically telling the jury to consider all evidence for that purpose. See App. 26. Thus, the only available contention here, and the basis on which the Court decides the case, is that this evidence "has relevance to . . . moral culpability beyond the scope of the special issues." *Ante*, at 322. That contention was considered and rejected by *Jurek*'s holding that the statute's "focus[ing of] the jury's objective consideration" was constitutional. 428 U. S., at 274.

But even if petitioner's claim is not foreclosed by *Jurek*, the Court clearly errs in asserting that our later precedents "compe[l]" the conclusion that it is valid, *ante*, at 328. While it is true that our cases have held that "a death penalty statute must not preclude consideration of relevant mitigating factors," including "any aspect of a defendant's character or record and any of the circumstances of the offense," *Lockett* v. *Ohio*, 438 U. S. 586, 604, 608, (1978); see also *Eddings* v. *Oklahoma*, 455 U. S. 104, 110–112 (1982), we have never held that "the State has no role in structuring or giving shape to the jury's consideration of these mitigating factors." *Franklin, supra*, at 179. As JUSTICE STEVENS pointed out in *Barclay* v. *Florida*, 463 U. S. 939 (1983), neither *Lockett* nor *Eddings* "establish[ed] the weight which must be given to any particular mitigating evidence, or the manner in which it must be considered; they simply condemn any procedure in which such evidence has no weight at all." 463 U. S., at 961, n. 2 (opinion concurring in judgment). See also *Zant* v. *Stephens*, 462 U. S. 862, 875–876, n. 13 (1983) ("[S]pecific standards for balancing aggravating against mitigating circumstances are not constitutionally required").

We have held that a State may not make the death penalty mandatory, see *Sumner* v. *Shuman*, 483 U. S. 66 (1987); *Woodson*, 428 U. S. 280 (1976); *Roberts*, 428 U. S. 325 (1976), and that it may not affirmatively preclude a sentencer from considering mitigating evidence presented by a defendant, see *Hitchcock* v. *Dugger*, 481 U. S. 393 (1987); *Skipper* v. *South Carolina*, 476 U. S. 1 (1986). The sentences in *Eddings* and *Lockett*, the cases upon which the Court principally relies, ran afoul of the latter rule—*Eddings* because the sentencing judge thought Oklahoma law categorically prevented him from considering certain mitigating evidence, and *Lockett* because Ohio law limited the mitigating factors to three, which on their face would not embrace even such rudimentary elements as lack of intent to kill the victim, the defendant's comparatively minor role in the offense, and age. As we noted in *Jurek* and the Court does not contest today, Texas permits *all* mitigating factors to be considered, though only for purposes of answering the three Special Issues (and there is no question that the specific mitigation offered was relevant to at least one of them). That is why the *Lockett*

Court found the Texas statute "significantly different" from the Ohio scheme. 438 U. S., at 607. And that is why we have continued to say, after *Eddings* and *Lockett*, that the Texas Special Issues "allo[w] the jury to consider the mitigating aspects of the crime and the unique characteristics of the perpetrator, and therefore sufficiently provid[e] for jury discretion." *Lowenfield* v. *Phelps*, 484 U. S. 231, 245 (1988). See also *Pulley* v. *Harris*, 465 U. S. 37, 48–49 (1984); *Zant* v. *Stephens*, *supra*, at 875–876, n. 13; *Adams* v. *Texas*, 448 U. S. 38, 46 (1980). I acknowledge that some statements in *Lockett* and *Eddings*, read in isolation from the facts of the cases, might be thought to establish the principle that the Court today adopts. One must read cases, however, not in a vacuum, but in light of their facts—which, in conjunction with the clear and constant reaffirmation of *Jurek*, leads to the conclusion that all mitigating factors must be able to be considered by the sentencer, but need not be able to be considered for all purposes.

Finally, I turn briefly to the place of today's holding within the broad scheme of our constitutional jurisprudence regarding capital sentencing, as opposed to the immediately applicable precedents. It is out of order there as well. As noted at the outset of this discussion, our law regarding capital sentencing has sought to strike a balance between complete discretion, which produces "wholly arbitary and capricious action," *Gregg*, 428 U. S., at 189, and no discretion at all, which prevents the individuating characteristics of the defendant and of the crime to be taken into account, *Woodson*, *supra*, at 303–304. That is why, in *Jurek*, we did not regard the Texas Special Issues as inherently bad, but to the contrary thought them a desirable means of "focus[ing] the jury's objective consideration of the particularized circumstances," 428 U. S., at 274, or, as the plurality put it in *Franklin*, "channel[ing] jury discretion . . . to achieve a more rational and equitable administration of the death penalty," 487 U. S., at 181. In providing for juries to consider all mitigating circumstances insofar as they bear upon (1) deliberateness, (2) future dangerousness, and (3) provocation, it seems to me Texas had adopted a rational scheme that meets the two concerns of our Eighth Amendment jurisprudence. The Court today demands that it be replaced, however, with a scheme that simply dumps before the jury all sympathetic factors bearing upon the defendant's background and character, and the circumstances of the offense, so that the jury may decide without further guidance whether he "lacked the moral culpability to be sentenced to death," *ante*, at 324, "did not deserve to be sentenced to death," *ante*, at 326, or "was not sufficiently culpable to deserve the death penalty," *ibid.* The Court seeks to dignify this by calling it a process that calls for a "reasoned moral response," *ante*, at 323, 328—but reason has nothing to do with it, the Court having eliminated the structure that required reason. It is an unguided, emotional "moral response" that the Court demands be allowed—an outpouring of personal reaction to all the circumstances of a defendant's life and personality, an unfocused sympathy. Not only have we never before said the Constitution requires this, but the line of cases following *Gregg* sought to eliminate precisely the unpredictability it produces. See, *e. g.*, *Godfrey* v. *Georgia*, 446 U. S. 420, 428 (1980) (States "must channel the [capital] sentencer's discretion by 'clear and objective standards' that provide 'specific and detailed guidance,' and that 'make rationally reviewable the process for imposing a sentence of death'") (citations omitted); *California* v. *Brown*, 479 U. S. 538, 541 (1987) ("[S]entencers may not be given unbridled discretion in determining the fates of those charged with capital offenses"; the "Constitution . . . requires that death penalty statutes be structured so as to prevent the penalty from being administered in an arbitrary and unpredictable fashion").

The Court cannot seriously believe that rationality and predictability can be achieved, and capriciousness avoided, by "'narrow[ing] a sentencer's discretion to *impose* the death sentence,'" but expanding his discretion "'to *decline to impose* the death sentence.'" *ante*, at 327, quoting *McCleskey* v. *Kemp*, 481 U. S. 279, 304 (1987) (emphasis in original). The decision whether to impose the death penalty is a unitary one; unguided discretion not to impose is unguided discretion to impose as well. In holding that the jury had to be free to deem Penry's mental retardation and sad childhood relevant for whatever purpose it wished, the Court has come full circle, not only permitting but requiring what *Furman* once condemned. "Freakishly" and "wantonly," *Furman*, 408 U. S., at 310 (Stewart, J. concurring), have been rebaptized "reasoned moral response." I do not think the Constitution forbids what the Court imposes here, but I am certain it does not require it.

I respectfully dissent.

WASHINGTON ET AL. *v.* HARPER

CERTIORARI TO THE SUPREME COURT OF WASHINGTON

No. 88-599. Argued October 11, 1989—Decided February 27, 1990

Respondent Harper has been a ward of the Washington state penal system since his 1976 robbery conviction. Both as an inmate and while temporarily on parole, he received psychiatric treatment, including the consensual administration of antipsychotic drugs. He has engaged in violent conduct, and his condition has deteriorated when he did not take the drugs. On two occasions, he was transferred to the Special Offender Center (SOC or Center), a state institute for convicted felons with serious mental illness, where he was diagnosed as suffering from a manic-depressive disorder. While at the Center, he was required to take antipsychotic drugs against his will pursuant to an SOC Policy. The Policy provides, *inter alia*, that, if a psychiatrist orders such medication, an inmate may be involuntarily treated only if he (1) suffers from a "mental disorder" and (2) is "gravely disabled" or poses a "likelihood of serious harm" to himself or others; that, after a hearing and upon a finding that the above conditions are met, a special committee consisting of a psychiatrist, a psychologist, and a Center official, none of whom may be currently involved in the inmate's diagnosis or treatment, may order involuntary medication if the psychiatrist is in the majority; and that the inmate has the right to notice of the hearing, the right to attend, present evidence, and cross-examine witnesses, the right to representation by a disinterested lay adviser versed in the psychological issues, the right to appeal to the Center's Superintendent, and the right to periodic review of any involuntary medication ordered. In addition, state law gives him the right to state-court review of the committee's decision. Both of the involuntary treatment proceedings were conducted in accordance with the SOC Policy. During his second stay at the Center, but before his transfer to a state penitentiary, Harper filed suit in state court under 42 U. S. C. § 1983. The trial court rejected his claim that the failure to provide a judicial hearing before the involuntary administration of antipsychotic medication violated the Due Process Clause of the Fourteenth Amendment. The State Supreme Court reversed and remanded, concluding that, under the Clause, the State could administer such medication to a competent, nonconsenting inmate only if, in a judicial hearing at which the inmate had the full panoply of adversarial procedural protections, the State proved by "clear, cogent, and convincing" evidence that the medication was both necessary and effective for furthering a compelling state interest.

Held:

1. The case is not rendered moot by the fact that the State has ceased administering antipsychotic drugs to Harper against his will. A live case or controversy remains, since there is no evidence that Harper has recovered from his mental illness; he continues to serve his sentence in the state prison system; and there is a strong likelihood that he may again be transferred to the Center, where officials would seek to administer antipsychotic medication pursuant to the Policy. Thus, the alleged injury likely would recur but for the decision of the State Supreme Court. Pp. 218–219.

2. The Due Process Clause permits the State to treat a prison inmate who has a serious mental illness with antipsychotic drugs against his will, if he is dangerous to himself or others and the treatment is in his medical interest. Although Harper has a liberty interest under the Clause in being free from the arbitrary administration of such medication, the Policy comports with substantive due process requirements, since it is reasonably related to the State's legitimate interest in combating the danger posed by a violent, mentally ill inmate. The Policy is a rational means of furthering that interest, since it applies exclusively to mentally ill inmates who are gravely disabled or represent a significant danger to themselves or others; the drugs may be administered only for treatment and under the direction of a licensed psychiatrist; and there is little dispute in the psychiatric profession that the proper use of the drugs is an effective means of treating and controlling a mental illness likely to cause violent behavior. Harper's contention that, as a precondition to antipsychotic drug treatment, the State must find him incompetent, and then obtain court approval of the treatment using a "substituted judgment" standard, is rejected, since it does not take account of the State's legitimate interest in treating him where medically appropriate for the purpose of reducing the danger he poses. Similarly, it has not been shown that the alternatives of physical restraints or seclusion would accommodate his rights at *de minimis* cost to valid penological interests. Pp. 219–227.

3. The Policy's administrative hearing procedures comport with procedural due process. Pp. 228–236.

(a) The Due Process Clause does not require a judicial hearing before the State may treat a mentally ill prisoner with antipsychotic drugs against his will. Harper's not insubstantial liberty interest, when considered with the government interests involved and the efficacy of the particular procedural requirements, is adequately protected, and perhaps better served, by allowing the decision to medicate to be made by medical professionals rather than a judge. It cannot be assumed that a mentally disturbed patient's intentions, or a substituted judgment approximating those intentions, can be determined in a single judicial hearing apart from the realities of frequent and ongoing medical observation. Nor can it be ignored that requiring judicial hearings will divert scarce prison resources from the care and treatment of mentally ill inmates. Moreover, the risks associated with antipsychotic drugs are for the most part medical ones, best assessed by medical professionals. The Policy contains adequate procedural safeguards to ensure that the prisoner's interests are taken into account. In particular, the independence of the decisionmaker is adequately addressed, since none of the hearing committee members may be involved in the inmate's current treatment or diagnosis, and the record is devoid of evidence that staff members lack the necessary independence to provide a full and fair hearing. Pp. 228–235.

(b) The Policy's procedures satisfy due process requirements in all other respects. The provisions mandating notice and the specified hearing rights satisfy the requirement of a meaningful opportunity to be heard, and are not vitiated by prehearing meetings between the committee members and staff absent evidence of resulting bias or that the actual decision is made before the hearing. The hearing need not be conducted in accordance with the rules of evidence, and the state court's "clear, cogent, and convincing" standard of proof is neither required nor helpful when medical personnel are making the judgment required by the Policy. An inmate may obtain judicial review of the committee's decision, and the trial court found that the record compiled under the Policy was adequate to allow such a review. Nor is the Policy deficient in not allowing representation by counsel, since the provision of an independent lay adviser who understands the psychiatric issues is sufficient protection given the medical nature of the decision to be made. Pp. 235–236.

110 Wash. 2d 873, 759 P. 2d 358, reversed and remanded.

KENNEDY, J., delivered the opinion for a unanimous Court with respect to Part II, and the opinion of the Court with respect to Parts I, III, IV, and V, in which REHNQUIST, C. J., and WHITE, BLACKMUN, O'CONNOR, and SCALIA, JJ., joined. BLACKMUN, J., filed a concurring opinion, *post*, p. 236. STEVENS, J., filed an opinion concurring in part and dissenting in part, in which BRENNAN and MARSHALL, JJ., joined, *post*, p. 237.

William L. Williams, Senior Assistant Attorney General of Washington, argued the cause for petitioners. With him on the briefs were *Kenneth O. Eikenberry*, Attorney General, and *Glenn L. Harvey*, Assistant Attorney General.

Paul J. Larkin, Jr., argued the cause for the United States as *amicus curiae* urging reversal. With him on the brief was *William C. Bryson*, Acting Solicitor General.

Brian Reed Phillips, by appointment of the Court, 490 U. S. 1002, argued the cause for respondent. With him on the brief was *Leonard Rubenstein*.*

JUSTICE KENNEDY delivered the opinion of the Court.

The central question before us is whether a judicial hearing is required before the State may treat a mentally ill prisoner with antipsychotic drugs against his will. Resolution of the case requires us to discuss the protections afforded the prisoner under the Due Process Clause of the Fourteenth Amendment.

I

Respondent Walter Harper was sentenced to prison in 1976 for robbery. From 1976 to 1980, he was incarcerated at the Washington State Penitentiary. Most of that time, respondent was housed in the prison's mental health unit, where he consented to the administration of antipsychotic drugs.

---

*Briefs of *amici curiae* urging reversal were filed for the State of California by *John K. Van de Kamp*, Attorney General, *Richard B. Iglehart*, Chief Assistant Attorney General, *Kenneth C. Young*, Assistant Attorney General, *Kristofer Jorstad*, Senior Supervising Deputy Attorney General, and *Morris Lenk*, *Karl S. Mayer*, and *Bruce M. Slavin*, Deputy Attorneys General; and for the American Psychiatric Association et al. by *Joel I. Klein* and *Robert D. Luskin*.

Briefs of *amici curiae* urging affirmance were filed for the Mental Health Legal Advisors Committee of the Massachusetts Supreme Judicial Court et al. by *Stan Goldman*, *Robert D. Fleischner*, and *Steven J. Schwartz;* for the National Association of Protection and Advocacy Systems et al. by *Arthur J. Rosenberg;* and for the New Jersey Department of the Public Advocate by *Linda G. Rosenzweig*.

Briefs of *amici curiae* were filed for the American Psychological Association by *Clifford D. Stromberg* and *John G. Roberts, Jr.;* for the Coalition for the Fundamental Rights and Equality of Ex-Patients by *Peter Margulies;* and for the Washington Community Mental Health Council et al. by *Barbara A. Weiner*.

Antipsychotic drugs, sometimes called "neuroleptics" or "psychotropic drugs," are medications commonly used in treating mental disorders such as schizophrenia. Brief for American Psychiatric Association et al. as *Amici Curiae* 2–3, n. 1. As found by the trial court, the effect of these and similar drugs is to alter the chemical balance in the brain, the desired result being that the medication will assist the patient in organizing his or her thought processes and regaining a rational state of mind. See App. to Pet. for Cert. B–7.[1]

Respondent was paroled in 1980 on the condition that he participate in psychiatric treatment. While on parole, he continued to receive treatment at the psychiatric ward at Harborview Medical Center in Seattle, Washington, and was later sent to Western State Hospital pursuant to a civil commitment order. In December 1981, the State revoked respondent's parole after he assaulted two nurses at a hospital in Seattle.

Upon his return to prison, respondent was sent to the Special Offender Center (SOC or Center), a 144-bed correctional institute established by the Washington Department of Corrections to diagnose and treat convicted felons with serious mental disorders. At the Center, psychiatrists first diagnosed respondent as suffering from a manic-depressive disorder.[2] At first, respondent gave voluntary consent to treatment, including the administration of antipsychotic medications. In November 1982, he refused to continue taking the prescribed medications. The treating physician then sought to medicate respondent over his objections, pursuant to SOC Policy 600.30.

---

[1] The drugs administered to respondent included Trialafon, Haldol, Prolixin, Taractan, Loxitane, Mellaril, and Navane. See App. to Pet. for Cert. B–7. Like the Washington Supreme Court, we limit our holding to the category of antipsychotic drugs. See 110 Wash. 2d 873, 876, n. 3, 759 P. 2d 358, 361, n. 3 (1988).

[2] Since that initial diagnosis, respondent has also been thought to have been suffering from schizo-affective disorder, and his current diagnosis is that he is schizophrenic.

Policy 600.30 was developed in partial response to this Court's decision in *Vitek* v. *Jones*, 445 U. S. 480 (1980). The Policy has several substantive and procedural components. First, if a psychiatrist determines that an inmate should be treated with antipsychotic drugs but the inmate does not consent, the inmate may be subjected to involuntary treatment with the drugs only if he (1) suffers from a "mental disorder" and (2) is "gravely disabled" or poses a "likelihood of serious harm" to himself, others, or their property.[3] Only a psychiatrist may order or approve the medication. Second, an inmate who refuses to take the medication voluntarily is entitled to a hearing before a special committee consisting of a psychiatrist, a psychologist, and the Associate Superintendent of the Center, none of whom may be, at the time of the hearing, involved in the inmate's treatment or diagnosis. If the committee determines by a majority vote that the inmate suffers from a mental disorder and is gravely disabled or dan-

[3] The Policy's definitions of the terms "mental disorder," "gravely disabled," and "likelihood of serious harm" are identical to the definitions of the terms as they are used in the state involuntary commitment statute. See App. to Pet. for Cert. B–3. "Mental disorder" means "any organic, mental, or emotional impairment which has substantial adverse effects on an individual's cognitive or volitional functions." Wash. Rev. Code § 71.05.020(2) (1987). "Gravely disabled" means "a condition in which a person, as a result of a mental disorder: (a) [i]s in danger of serious physical harm resulting from a failure to provide for his essential human needs of health or safety, or (b) manifests severe deterioration in routine functioning evidenced by repeated and escalating loss of cognitive or volitional control over his or her actions and is not receiving such care as is essential for his or her health or safety." § 71.05.020(1). "Likelihood of serious harm" means "either: (a) [a] substantial risk that physical harm will be inflicted by an individual upon his own person, as evidenced by threats or attempts to commit suicide or inflict physical harm on one's self, (b) a substantial risk that physical harm will be inflicted by an individual upon another, as evidenced by behavior which has caused such harm or which places another person or persons in reasonable fear of sustaining such harm, or (c) a substantial risk that physical harm will be inflicted by an individual upon the property of others, as evidenced by behavior which has caused substantial loss or damage to the property of others." § 71.05.020(3).

gerous, the inmate may be medicated against his will, provided the psychiatrist is in the majority.

Third, the inmate has certain procedural rights before, during, and after the hearing. He must be given at least 24 hours' notice of the Center's intent to convene an involuntary medication hearing, during which time he may not be medicated. In addition, he must receive notice of the tentative diagnosis, the factual basis for the diagnosis, and why the staff believes medication is necessary. At the hearing, the inmate has the right to attend; to present evidence, including witnesses; to cross-examine staff witnesses; and to the assistance of a lay adviser who has not been involved in his case and who understands the psychiatric issues involved. Minutes of the hearing must be kept, and a copy provided to the inmate. The inmate has the right to appeal the committee's decision to the Superintendent of the Center within 24 hours, and the Superintendent must decide the appeal within 24 hours after its receipt. See App. to Pet. for Cert. B-3. The inmate may seek judicial review of a committee decision in state court by means of a personal restraint petition or extraordinary writ. See Wash. Rules App. Proc. 16.3 to 16.17; App. to Pet. for Cert. B-8.

Fourth, after the initial hearing, involuntary medication can continue only with periodic review. When respondent first refused medication, a committee, again composed of a nontreating psychiatrist, a psychologist, and the Center's Associate Superintendent, was required to review an inmate's case after the first seven days of treatment. If the committee reapproved the treatment, the treating psychiatrist was required to review the case and prepare a report for the Department of Corrections medical director every 14 days while treatment continued.[4]

---

[4] The Policy was later amended to allow treatment for up to 14 days after the first hearing. Further treatment could be authorized only after the same committee conducted a second hearing on the written record. Thereafter, the treating psychiatrist was required to submit biweekly re-

In this case, respondent was absent when members of the Center staff met with the committee before the hearing. The committee then conducted the hearing in accordance with the Policy, with respondent being present and assisted by a nurse practitioner from another institution. The committee found that respondent was a danger to others as a result of a mental disease or disorder, and approved the involuntary administration of antipsychotic drugs. On appeal, the Superintendent upheld the committee's findings. Beginning on November 23, 1982, respondent was involuntarily medicated for about one year. Periodic review occurred in accordance with the Policy.

In November 1983, respondent was transferred from the Center to the Washington State Reformatory. While there, he took no medication, and as a result, his condition deteriorated. He was retransferred to the Center after only one month. Respondent was the subject of another committee hearing in accordance with Policy 600.30, and the committee again approved medication against his will. Respondent continued to receive antipsychotic drugs, subject to the required periodic reviews, until he was transferred to the Washington State Penitentiary in June 1986.

In February 1985, respondent filed suit in state court under 42 U. S. C. § 1983 (1982 ed.) against various individual defendants and the State, claiming that the failure to provide a judicial hearing before the involuntary administration of antipsychotic medication violated the Due Process, Equal Protection, and Free Speech Clauses of both the Federal and State Constitutions, as well as state tort law. He sought both damages and declaratory and injunctive relief. After a bench trial in March 1987, the court held that, although respondent had a liberty interest in not being subjected to the involuntary administration of antipsychotic medication, the

ports to the Department of Corrections medical director. At the end of 180 days, a new hearing was required to consider the need for continued treatment.

procedures contained in the Policy met the requirements of due process as stated in *Vitek*.

On appeal, the Washington Supreme Court reversed and remanded the case to the trial court. 110 Wash. 2d 873, 759 P. 2d 358 (1988). Agreeing with the trial court that respondent had a liberty interest in refusing antipsychotic medications, the court concluded that the "highly intrusive nature" of treatment with antipsychotic medications warranted greater procedural protections than those necessary to protect the liberty interests at stake in *Vitek*. 110 Wash. 2d, at 880–881, 759 P. 2d, at 363. It held that, under the Due Process Clause, the State could administer antipsychotic medication to a competent, nonconsenting inmate only if, in a judicial hearing at which the inmate had the full panoply of adversarial procedural protections, the State proved by "clear, cogent, and convincing" evidence that the administration of antipsychotic medication was both necessary and effective for furthering a compelling state interest.[5] *Id.*, at 883–884, 759 P. 2d, at 364–365.

We granted certiorari, 489 U. S. 1064 (1989), and we reverse.

II

Respondent contends that because the State has ceased administering antipsychotic drugs to him against his will, the case is moot. We disagree.

Even if we confine our attention to those facts found in the record,[6] a live case or controversy between the parties re-

[5] Because it decided the case on due process grounds, the court did not address respondent's equal protection or free speech claims, and they are not before us here. The court also concluded that the individual defendants were entitled to qualified immunity, but remanded the case to the lower court for further consideration of respondent's claims for injunctive and declaratory relief under § 1983, as well as of his claims under state law. See 110 Wash. 2d, at 885–886, 759 P. 2d, at 366.

[6] In response to our questions at oral argument, counsel for the State informed us that respondent was transferred back to the Center in April 1987 and involuntarily medicated pursuant to the Policy from September

mains. There is no evidence that respondent has recovered from his mental illness. Since being sentenced to prison in 1976, he has been diagnosed and treated for a serious mental disorder. Even while on parole, respondent continued to receive treatment, at one point under a civil commitment order, at state mental hospitals. At the time of trial, after his transfer from the Center for a second time, respondent was still diagnosed as suffering from schizophrenia.

Respondent continues to serve his sentence in the Washington state prison system, and is subject to transfer to the Center at any time. Given his medical history, and the fact that he has been transferred not once but twice to the Center from other state penal institutions during the period 1982–1986, it is reasonable to conclude that there is a strong likelihood that respondent may again be transferred to the Center. Once there, given his medical history, it is likely that, absent the holding of the Washington Supreme Court, Center officials would seek to administer antipsychotic medications pursuant to Policy 600.30.

On the record before us, the case is not moot. The alleged injury likely would recur but for the decision of the Washington Supreme Court. This sufficiently overcomes the claim of mootness in the circumstances of the case and under our precedents. See *Vitek*, 445 U. S., at 486–487.

III

The Washington Supreme Court gave its primary attention to the procedural component of the Due Process Clause. It phrased the issue before it as whether "a prisoner [is] entitled to a judicial hearing before antipsychotic drugs can be administered against his will." 110 Wash. 2d, at 874, 759 P. 2d, at 360. The court, however, did more than establish ju-

1987 until May 1988. Counsel also informed us that, at the time of oral argument, respondent was at a state mental hospital for a competency determination on an unrelated criminal charge, and that regardless of the outcome of this criminal charge, respondent will return to the state prison system to serve the remainder of his sentence.

dicial procedures for making the factual determinations called for by Policy 600.30. It required that a different set of determinations than those set forth in the Policy be made as a precondition to medication without the inmate's consent. Instead of having to prove, pursuant to the Policy, only that the mentally ill inmate is "gravely disabled" or that he presents a "serious likelihood of harm" to himself or others, the court required the State to prove that it has a compelling interest in administering the medication and that the administration of the drugs is necessary and effective to further that interest. The decisionmaker was required further to consider and make written findings regarding either the inmate's desires or a "substituted judgment" for the inmate analogous to the medical treatment decision for an incompetent person. *Id.*, at 883–884, 759 P. 2d, at 365.

The Washington Supreme Court's decision, as a result, has both substantive and procedural aspects. It is axiomatic that procedural protections must be examined in terms of the substantive rights at stake. But identifying the contours of the substantive right remains a task distinct from deciding what procedural protections are necessary to protect that right. "[T]he substantive issue involves a definition of th[e] protected constitutional interest, as well as identification of the conditions under which competing state interests might outweigh it. The procedural issue concerns the minimum procedures required by the Constitution for determining that the individual's liberty interest actually is outweighed in a particular instance." *Mills* v. *Rogers*, 457 U. S. 291, 299 (1982) (citations omitted).

Restated in the terms of this case, the substantive issue is what factual circumstances must exist before the State may administer antipsychotic drugs to the prisoner against his will; the procedural issue is whether the State's nonjudicial mechanisms used to determine the facts in a particular case are sufficient. The Washington Supreme Court in effect ruled upon the substance of the inmate's right, as well as the procedural guarantees, and both are encompassed by our grant of certiorari.[7] We address these questions beginning with the substantive one.

As a matter of state law, the Policy itself undoubtedly confers upon respondent a right to be free from the arbitrary administration of antipsychotic medication. In *Hewitt* v. *Helms*, 459 U. S. 460 (1983), we held that Pennsylvania had created a protected liberty interest on the part of prison inmates to avoid administrative segregation by enacting regulations that "used language of an unmistakably mandatory character, requiring that certain procedures 'shall,' 'will,' or 'must' be employed, and that administrative segregation will not occur absent specified substantive predicates—viz., 'the need for control,' or 'the threat of a serious disturbance.'" *Id.*, at 471–472 (citations omitted). Policy 600.30 is similarly mandatory in character. By permitting a psychiatrist to treat an inmate with antipsychotic drugs against his wishes only if he is found to be (1) mentally ill and (2) gravely disabled or dangerous, the Policy creates a justifiable expectation on the part of the inmate that the drugs will not be administered unless those conditions exist. See also *Vitek*, 445 U. S., at 488–491.

We have no doubt that, in addition to the liberty interest created by the State's Policy, respondent possesses a significant liberty interest in avoiding the unwanted administration of antipsychotic drugs under the Due Process Clause of the

[7] The two questions presented by the State in its petition for certiorari mirror the division between the substantive and procedural aspects of this case. In addition to seeking a grant of certiorari on the question whether respondent was entitled to "a judicial hearing and attendant adversarial procedural protections" prior to the involuntary administration of antipsychotic drugs, the State sought certiorari on the question, assuming that respondent "possesses a constitutionally protected liberty interest in refusing medically prescribed antipsychotic medication," whether the State must "prove a compelling state interest . . . or [whether] the 'reasonable relation' standard of *Turner* v. *Safley*, [482 U. S. 78 (1987),] control[s]." Pet. for Cert. i.

Fourteenth Amendment. See *id.*, at 491–494; *Youngberg* v. *Romeo*, 457 U. S. 307, 316 (1982); *Parham* v. *J. R.*, 442 U. S. 584, 600–601 (1979). Upon full consideration of the state administrative scheme, however, we find that the Due Process Clause confers upon respondent no greater right than that recognized under state law.

Respondent contends that the State, under the mandate of the Due Process Clause, may not override his choice to refuse antipsychotic drugs unless he has been found to be incompetent, and then only if the factfinder makes a substituted judgment that he, if competent, would consent to drug treatment. We disagree. The extent of a prisoner's right under the Clause to avoid the unwanted administration of antipsychotic drugs must be defined in the context of the inmate's confinement. The Policy under review requires the State to establish, by a medical finding, that a mental disorder exists which is likely to cause harm if not treated. Moreover, the fact that the medication must first be prescribed by a psychiatrist, and then approved by a reviewing psychiatrist, ensures that the treatment in question will be ordered only if it is in the prisoner's medical interests, given the legitimate needs of his institutional confinement.[*] These standards, which rec-

[*] JUSTICE STEVENS contends that the SOC Policy permits respondent's doctors to treat him with antipsychotic medications against his will without reference to whether the treatment is medically appropriate. See *post*, at 243–245. For various reasons, we disagree. That an inmate is mentally ill and dangerous is a necessary condition to medication, but not a sufficient condition: before the hearing committee determines whether these requirements are met, the inmate's treating physician must first make the decision that medication is appropriate. The SOC is a facility whose purpose is not to warehouse the mentally ill, but to diagnose and treat convicted felons, with the desired goal being that they will recover to the point where they can function in a normal prison environment. App. to Pet. for Cert. B–2. In keeping with this purpose, an SOC psychiatrist must first prescribe the antipsychotic medication for the inmate, and the inmate must refuse it, before the Policy is invoked. Unlike JUSTICE STEVENS, we will not assume that physicians will prescribe these drugs for reasons unrelated to the medical needs of the patients; indeed, the ethics of the medical profession are to

ognize both the prisoner's medical interests and the State's interests, meet the demands of the Due Process Clause.

The legitimacy, and the necessity, of considering the State's interests in prison safety and security are well established by our cases. In *Turner* v. *Safley*, 482 U. S. 78 (1987), and *O'Lone* v. *Estate of Shabazz*, 482 U. S. 342 (1987), we held that the proper standard for determining the validity of a prison regulation claimed to infringe on an inmate's constitutional rights is to ask whether the regulation is "reasonably related to legitimate penological interests." *Turner*, *supra*, at 89. This is true even when the constitutional right claimed to have been infringed is fundamental, and the State under other circumstances would have been required to satisfy a more rigorous standard of review. *Estate of Shabazz*, *supra*, at 349. The Washington Supreme Court declined to apply this standard of review to the Center's Policy, reasoning that the liberty interest present here was distinguishable from the First Amendment rights at issue in both *Turner* and *Estate of Shabazz*. 110 Wash. 2d, at 883, n. 9, 759 P. 2d, at 364, n. 9. The court erred in refusing to apply the standard of reasonableness.

Our earlier determination to adopt this standard of review was based upon the need to reconcile our longstanding adherence to the principle that inmates retain at least some constitutional rights despite incarceration with the recognition that prison authorities are best equipped to make difficult

---

the contrary. See Hippocratic Oath; American Psychiatric Association, Principles of Medical Ethics With Annotations Especially Applicable to Psychiatry, in Codes of Professional Responsibility 129–135 (R. Gorlin ed. 1986). This consideration supports our interpretation of the State's Policy as ensuring that antipsychotic medications will be administered only in those cases where appropriate by medical standards. We therefore agree with the State's representations at oral argument that, under the Policy, antipsychotic medications can be administered only for treatment purposes, with the hearing committee reviewing the doctor's decision to ensure that what has been prescribed is appropriate. See Tr. of Oral Arg. 13, 16.

decisions regarding prison administration. *Turner, supra,* at 84–85; *Jones* v. *North Carolina Prisoners' Labor Union, Inc.*, 433 U. S. 119, 128 (1977). These two principles apply in all cases in which a prisoner asserts that a prison regulation violates the Constitution, not just those in which the prisoner invokes the First Amendment. We made quite clear that the standard of review we adopted in *Turner* applies to all circumstances in which the needs of prison administration implicate constitutional rights. See *Turner*, 482 U. S., at 85 ("Our task . . . is to formulate a standard of review for prisoners' constitutional claims that is responsive both to the 'policy of judicial restraint regarding prisoner complaints and [to] the need to protect constitutional rights'") (citation omitted); *id.*, at 89 ("If *Pell*, *Jones*, and *Bell* have not already resolved the question posed in [*Procunier* v.] *Martinez*, [416 U. S. 396 (1974),] we resolve it now: when a prison regulation impinges on inmates' constitutional rights, the regulation is valid if it is reasonably related to legitimate penological interests"); *Estate of Shabazz, supra*, at 349 ("To ensure that courts afford appropriate deference to prison officials, we have determined that prison regulations alleged to infringe constitutional rights are judged under a 'reasonableness' test less restrictive than that ordinarily applied to alleged infringements of fundamental constitutional rights"). In *Turner* itself we applied the reasonableness standard to a prison regulation that imposed severe restrictions on the inmate's right to marry, a right protected by the Due Process Clause. See *Turner, supra*, at 95–96 (citing *Zablocki* v. *Redhail*, 434 U. S. 374 (1978), and *Loving* v. *Virginia*, 388 U. S. 1 (1967)). Our precedents require application of the standard here.

In *Turner*, we considered various factors to determine the reasonableness of a challenged prison regulation. Three are relevant here. "First, there must be a 'valid, rational connection' between the prison regulation and the legitimate governmental interest put forward to justify it." 482 U. S., at 89 (quoting *Block* v. *Rutherford*, 468 U. S. 576, 586 (1984)). Second, a court must consider "the impact accommodation of the asserted constitutional right will have on guards and other inmates, and on the allocation of prison resources generally." 482 U. S., at 90. Third, "the absence of ready alternatives is evidence of the reasonableness of a prison regulation," but this does not mean that prison officials "have to set up and then shoot down every conceivable alternative method of accommodating the claimant's constitutional complaint." *Id.*, at 90–91; see also *Estate of Shabazz*, *supra*, at 350.

Applying these factors to the regulation before us, we conclude that the Policy comports with constitutional requirements. There can be little doubt as to both the legitimacy and the importance of the governmental interest presented here. There are few cases in which the State's interest in combating the danger posed by a person to both himself and others is greater than in a prison environment, which, "by definition," is made up of persons with "a demonstrated proclivity for antisocial criminal, and often violent, conduct." *Hudson* v. *Palmer*, 468 U. S. 517, 526 (1984); *Jones*, *supra*, at 132; *Wolff* v. *McDonnell*, 418 U. S. 539, 561–562 (1974). We confront here the State's obligations, not just its interests. The State has undertaken the obligation to provide prisoners with medical treatment consistent not only with their own medical interests, but also with the needs of the institution. Prison administrators have not only an interest in ensuring the safety of prison staffs and administrative personnel, see *Hewitt*, 459 U. S., at 473, but also the duty to take reasonable measures for the prisoners' own safety. See *Hudson*, *supra*, at 526–527. These concerns have added weight when a penal institution, like the SOC, is restricted to inmates with mental illnesses. Where an inmate's mental disability is the root cause of the threat he poses to the inmate population, the State's interest in decreasing the danger to others necessarily encompasses an interest in providing him with medical treatment for his illness.

SOC Policy 600.30 is a rational means of furthering the State's legitimate objectives. Its exclusive application is to inmates who are mentally ill and who, as a result of their illness, are gravely disabled or represent a significant danger to themselves or others. The drugs may be administered for no purpose other than treatment, and only under the direction of a licensed psychiatrist. There is considerable debate over the potential side effects of antipsychotic medications, but there is little dispute in the psychiatric profession that proper use of the drugs is one of the most effective means of treating and controlling a mental illness likely to cause violent behavior.[9]

The alternative means proffered by respondent for accommodating his interest in rejecting the forced administration of antipsychotic drugs do not demonstrate the invalidity of the State's policy. Respondent's main contention is that, as a precondition to antipsychotic drug treatment, the State must find him incompetent, and then obtain court approval of the treatment using a "substituted judgment" standard. The suggested rule takes no account of the legitimate governmental interest in treating him where medically appropriate for the purpose of reducing the danger he poses. A rule that is in no way responsive to the State's legitimate interests is not a proper accommodation, and can be rejected out of hand. Nor are physical restraints or seclusion "alternative[s] that fully accommodat[e] the prisoner's rights at *de minimis* cost to valid penological interests." *Turner, supra,* at 91. Physical restraints are effective only in the short term, and can have serious physical side effects when used on a resist-

---

[9] See Brief for American Psychiatric Association et al. as *Amici Curiae* 10–11 ("Psychotropic medication is widely accepted within the psychiatric community as an extraordinarily effective treatment for both acute and chronic psychoses, particularly schizophrenia"); Brief for American Psychological Association as *Amicus Curiae* 6.

ing inmate, see Brief for American Psychiatric Association et al. as *Amici Curiae* 12, as well as leaving the staff at risk of injury while putting the restraints on or tending to the inmate who is in them. Furthermore, respondent has failed to demonstrate that physical restraints or seclusion are acceptable substitutes for antipsychotic drugs, in terms of either their medical effectiveness or their toll on limited prison resources.[10]

We hold that, given the requirements of the prison environment, the Due Process Clause permits the State to treat a prison inmate who has a serious mental illness with antipsychotic drugs against his will, if the inmate is dangerous to himself or others and the treatment is in the inmate's medical interest. Policy 600.30 comports with these requirements; we therefore reject respondent's contention that its substantive standards are deficient under the Constitution.[11]

---

[10] There is substantial evidence to the contrary. See Brief for American Psychiatric Association et al. as *Amici Curiae* 11–12; Soloff, Physical Controls: The Use of Seclusion and Restraint in Modern Psychiatric Practice, in Clinical Treatment of the Violent Person 119–137 (L. Roth ed. 1987) (documenting the risks and costs of using physical restraints and seclusion on violent patients).

[11] Perhaps suggesting that the care given to respondent and the Center's utilization of Policy 600.30 may have been suspect, JUSTICE STEVENS uses random citations from exhibits and documents submitted to the state trial court. By using isolated quotations of a few passages from medical and other records running into the hundreds of pages, JUSTICE STEVENS risks presenting a rather one-sided portrait of what they contain. An overview of these extensive materials reveals that respondent has a long history of serious, assaultive behavior, evidenced by at least 20 reported incidents of serious assaults on fellow inmates and staff. Respondent's doctors attributed these incidents to his severe mental illness and believed that his assaultive tendencies increased when he did not receive medication. See App. to Pet. for Cert. B–5. Respondent's opposition to the involuntary administration of antipsychotic drugs was premised at least in part upon his desire to self-medicate with street drugs, especially cocaine. See Lodging filed by Kenneth O. Eikenberry, Attorney General of Washington, Book 3, July 25, 1984, Progress Report. Finally, the records show without doubt that respondent has been the recipient of painstaking medical

IV

Having determined that state law recognizes a liberty interest, also protected by the Due Process Clause, which permits refusal of antipsychotic drugs unless certain preconditions are met, we address next what procedural protections are necessary to ensure that the decision to medicate an inmate against his will is neither arbitrary nor erroneous under the standards we have discussed above. The Washington Supreme Court held that a full judicial hearing, with the inmate being represented by counsel, was required by the Due Process Clause before the State could administer antipsychotic drugs to him against his will. In addition, the court held that the State must justify the authorization of involuntary administration of antipsychotic drugs by "clear, cogent, and convincing" evidence. We hold that the administrative hearing procedures set by the SOC Policy do comport with procedural due process, and conclude that the Washington Supreme Court erred in requiring a judicial hearing as a prerequisite for the involuntary treatment of prison inmates.

A

The primary point of disagreement between the parties is whether due process requires a judicial decisionmaker. As

---

diagnosis and care while at the SOC. In any event, the trial court did not indicate which portions, if any, of these records, all of which are hearsay, it credited or relied upon in making its findings.

For these reasons, we do not intend to engage in a debate with JUSTICE STEVENS over how respondent's medical and institutional records should be interpreted. We rely upon the findings of the trial court that "at all times relevant to this action, [respondent] suffered from a mental disorder and as a result of that disorder constituted a likelihood of serious harm to others," App. to Pet. for Cert. B–8, and that "the medical treatment provided to [respondent] by defendants, including the administration of anti-psychotic medications, was consistent with the degree of care, skill, and learning expected of a reasonably prudent psychiatrist in the State of Washington, acting in the same or similar circumstances." *Ibid.* Contrary to JUSTICE STEVENS' cramped reading of this last finding, see *post*, at 245, n. 13, the breadth of its meaning equals the breadth of its language.

written, the Policy requires that the decision whether to medicate an inmate against his will be made by a hearing committee composed of a psychiatrist, a psychologist, and the Center's Associate Superintendent. None of the committee members may be involved, at the time of the hearing, in the inmate's treatment or diagnosis; members are not disqualified from sitting on the committee, however, if they have treated or diagnosed the inmate in the past. The committee's decision is subject to review by the Superintendent; if the inmate so desires, he may seek judicial review of the decision in a state court. See *supra*, at 216. Respondent contends that only a court should make the decision to medicate an inmate against his will.

The procedural protections required by the Due Process Clause must be determined with reference to the rights and interests at stake in the particular case. *Morrissey* v. *Brewer*, 408 U. S. 471, 481 (1972); *Hewitt*, 459 U. S., at 472; *Greenholtz* v. *Nebraska Penal Inmates*, 442 U. S. 1, 12 (1979). The factors that guide us are well established. "Under *Mathews* v. *Eldridge*, 424 U. S. 319, 335 (1976), we consider the private interests at stake in a governmental decision, the governmental interests involved, and the value of procedural requirements in determining what process is due under the Fourteenth Amendment." *Hewitt*, *supra*, at 473.

Respondent's interest in avoiding the unwarranted administration of antipsychotic drugs is not insubstantial. The forcible injection of medication into a nonconsenting person's body represents a substantial interference with that person's liberty. Cf. *Winston* v. *Lee*, 470 U. S. 753 (1985); *Schmerber* v. *California*, 384 U. S. 757, 772 (1966). The purpose of the drugs is to alter the chemical balance in a patient's brain, leading to changes, intended to be beneficial, in his or her cognitive processes. See n. 1, *supra*. While the therapeutic benefits of antipsychotic drugs are well documented, it is also true that the drugs can have serious, even fatal, side effects. One such side effect identified by the trial court is acute dystonia, a severe involuntary spasm of the upper body, tongue, throat, or eyes. The trial court found that it may be treated and reversed within a few minutes through use of the medication Cogentin. Other side effects include akathesia (motor restlessness, often characterized by an inability to sit still); neuroleptic malignant syndrome (a relatively rare condition which can lead to death from cardiac dysfunction); and tardive dyskinesia, perhaps the most discussed side effect of antipsychotic drugs. See Finding of Fact 9, App. to Pet. for Cert. B–7; Brief for American Psychological Association as *Amicus Curiae* 6–9. Tardive dyskinesia is a neurological disorder, irreversible in some cases, that is characterized by involuntary, uncontrollable movements of various muscles, especially around the face. See *Mills*, 457 U. S., at 293, n. 1. The State, respondent, and *amici* sharply disagree about the frequency with which tardive dyskinesia occurs, its severity, and the medical profession's ability to treat, arrest, or reverse the condition. A fair reading of the evidence, however, suggests that the proportion of patients treated with antipsychotic drugs who exhibit the symptoms of tardive dyskinesia ranges from 10% to 25%. According to the American Psychiatric Association, studies of the condition indicate that 60% of tardive dyskinesia is mild or minimal in effect, and about 10% may be characterized as severe. Brief for American Psychiatric Association et al. as *Amici Curiae* 14–16, and n. 12; see also Brief for American Psychological Association as *Amicus Curiae* 8.[12]

---

[12] JUSTICE STEVENS is concerned with "discount[ing] the severity of these drugs." See *post*, at 239, n. 5. As our discussion in the text indicates, we are well aware of the side effects and risks presented by these drugs; we also are well aware of the disagreements in the medical profession over the frequency, severity, and permanence of these side effects. We have set forth a fair assessment of the current state of medical knowledge about these drugs.

What JUSTICE STEVENS "discount[s]" are the benefits of these drugs, and the deference that is owed to medical professionals who have the full-

Notwithstanding the risks that are involved, we conclude that an inmate's interests are adequately protected, and perhaps better served, by allowing the decision to medicate to be made by medical professionals rather than a judge. The Due Process Clause "has never been thought to require that the neutral and detached trier of fact be law trained or a judicial or administrative officer." *Parham*, 442 U. S., at 607. Though it cannot be doubted that the decision to medicate has societal and legal implications, the Constitution does not prohibit the State from permitting medical personnel to make the decision under fair procedural mechanisms. See *id.*, at 607–609; cf. *Youngberg*, 457 U. S., at 322–323. Particularly where the patient is mentally disturbed, his own intentions will be difficult to assess and will be changeable in any event. Schwartz, Vingiano, & Perez, Autonomy and the Right to Refuse Treatment: Patients' Attitudes After Involuntary Medication, 39 Hospital & Community Psychiatry 1049 (1988). Respondent's own history of accepting and then refusing drug treatment illustrates the point. We cannot make the facile assumption that the patient's intentions, or a substituted judgment approximating those intentions, can be determined in a single judicial hearing apart from the reali-

---

time responsibility of caring for mentally ill inmates like respondent and who possess, as courts do not, the requisite knowledge and expertise to determine whether the drugs should be used in an individual case. After admitting that the proper administration of antipsychotic drugs is one of the most effective means of treating certain mental illnesses, JUSTICE STEVENS contends that the drugs are not indicated for "all patients," and then questions the appropriateness of the treatment provided to respondent. See *post*, at 248, n. 16. All concede that the drugs are not the approved treatment in all cases. As for whether respondent's medical treatment was appropriate, we are not so sanguine as to believe that on the basis of the limited record before us, we have the medical expertise and knowledge necessary to determine whether, on the basis of isolated parts of respondent's medical records, the care given to him is consistent with good medical practice. Again, we must defer to the finding of the trial court, unchallenged by any party in this case, that the medical care provided to respondent was appropriate under medical standards. See n. 11, *supra*.

ties of frequent and ongoing clinical observation by medical professionals. Our holding in *Parham* that a judicial hearing was not required prior to the voluntary commitment of a child to a mental hospital was based on similar observations:

> ". . . [D]ue process is not violated by use of informal, traditional medical investigative techniques. . . . The mode and procedure of medical diagnostic procedures is not the business of judges. . . .
>
> . . . . .
>
> "Although we acknowledge the fallibility of medical and psychiatric diagnosis, see *O'Connor* v. *Donaldson*, 422 U. S. 563, 584 (1975) (concurring opinion), we do not accept the notion that the shortcomings of specialists can always be avoided by shifting the decision from a trained specialist using the traditional tools of medical science to an untrained judge or administrative hearing officer after a judicial-type hearing. Even after a hearing, the nonspecialist decisionmaker must make a medical-psychiatric decision. Common human experience and scholarly opinions suggest that the supposed protections of an adversary proceeding to determine the appropriateness of medical decisions for the commitment and treatment of mental and emotional illness may well be more illusory than real." *Parham*, 442 U. S., at 607–609.

Nor can we ignore the fact that requiring judicial hearings will divert scarce prison resources, both money and the staff's time, from the care and treatment of mentally ill inmates. See *id.*, at 605–606.

Under Policy 600.30, the decisionmaker is asked to review a medical treatment decision made by a medical professional. That review requires two medical inquiries: first, whether the inmate suffers from a "mental disorder"; and second, whether, as a result of that disorder, he is dangerous to himself, others, or their property. Under the Policy, the hearing committee reviews on a regular basis the staff's choice of both the type and dosage of drug to be administered, and can order appropriate changes. 110 Wash. 2d, at 875, 759 P. 2d, at 360. The risks associated with antipsychotic drugs are for the most part medical ones, best assessed by medical professionals. A State may conclude with good reason that a judicial hearing will not be as effective, as continuous, or as probing as administrative review using medical decisionmakers. We hold that due process requires no more.

A State's attempt to set a high standard for determining when involuntary medication with antipsychotic drugs is permitted cannot withstand challenge if there are no procedural safeguards to ensure the prisoner's interests are taken into account. Adequate procedures exist here. In particular, independence of the decisionmaker is addressed to our satisfaction by these procedures. None of the hearing committee members may be involved in the inmate's current treatment or diagnosis. The record before us, moreover, is limited to the hearings given to respondent. There is no indication that any institutional biases affected or altered the decision to medicate respondent against his will. The trial court made specific findings that respondent has a history of assaultive behavior which his doctors attribute to his mental disease, and that all of the Policy's requirements were met. See App. to Pet. for Cert. B–4 to B–5, B–8. The court found also that the medical treatment provided to respondent, including the administration of antipsychotic drugs, was at all times consistent "with the degree of care, skill, and learning expected of a reasonably prudent psychiatrist in the State of Washington, acting in the same or similar circumstances." *Id.*, at B–8. In the absence of record evidence to the contrary, we are not willing to presume that members of the staff lack the necessary independence to provide an inmate with a full and fair hearing in accordance with the Policy. In previous cases involving medical decisions implicating similar liberty interests, we have approved use of similar internal decisionmakers. See *Vitek*, 445 U. S., at 496; *Parham*, *supra*, at 613–616.[13] Cf. *Wolff*, 418 U. S., at 570–571 (prison

---

[13] In an attempt to prove that internal decisionmakers lack the independence necessary to render impartial decisions, respondent and various *amici* refer us to other cases in which it is alleged that antipsychotic drugs were prescribed not for medical purposes, but to control or discipline mentally ill patients. See Brief for Respondent 28; Brief for American Psychological Association as *Amicus Curiae* 14. We rejected a similar claim in *Parham*, and do so again here, using much the same reasoning. "That such a practice may take place in some institutions in some places affords no basis for a finding as to [Washington's] program," *Parham*, 442 U. S., at 616, particularly in light of the trial court's finding here that the administration of antipsychotic drugs to respondent was consistent with good medical practice.

Moreover, the practical effect of mandating an outside decisionmaker such as an "independent psychiatrist" or judge in these circumstances may be chimerical. Review of the literature indicates that outside decisionmakers concur with the treating physician's decision to treat a patient involuntarily in most, if not all, cases. See Bloom, Faulkner, Holm, & Rawlinson, An Empirical View of Patients Exercising Their Right to Refuse Treatment, 7 Int'l J. Law & Psychiatry 315, 325 (1984) (independent examining physician used in Oregon psychiatric hospital concurred in decision to involuntarily medicate patients in 95% of cases); Hickman, Resnick, & Olson, Right to Refuse Psychotropic Medication: An Interdisciplinary Proposal, 6 Mental Disability Law Reporter 122, 130 (1982) (independent reviewing psychiatrist used in Ohio affirmed the recommendation of internal reviewer in 100% of cases). Review by judges of decisions to override a patient's objections to medication yields similar results. Appelbaum, The Right to Refuse Treatment With Antipsychotic Medications: Retrospect and Prospect, 145 Am. J. Psychiatry 413, 417–418 (1988). In comparison, other studies reveal that review by internal decisionmakers is hardly as lackluster as JUSTICE STEVENS suggests. See Hickman, Resnick, & Olson, *supra*, at 130 (internal reviewer approved of involuntary treatment in 75% of cases); Zito, Lentz, Routt, & Olson, The Treatment Review Panel: A Solution to Treatment Refusal?, 12 Bull. American Academy of Psychiatry and Law 349 (1984) (internal review panel used in Minnesota mental hospital approved of involuntary medication in 67% of cases). See generally Appelbaum & Hoge, The Right to Refuse Treatment: What the Research Reveals, 4 Behavioral Sciences and Law 279, 288–290 (1986) (summarizing results of studies on how various institutions review patients' decisions to refuse antipsychotic medications and noting "the infre-

officials sufficiently impartial to conduct prison disciplinary hearings). As we reasoned in *Vitek*, it is only by permitting persons connected with the institution to make these decisions that courts are able to avoid "unnecessary intrusion into either medical or correctional judgments." *Vitek*, *supra*, at 496; see *Turner*, 482 U. S., at 84–85, 89.

B

The procedures established by the Center are sufficient to meet the requirements of due process in all other respects, and we reject respondent's arguments to the contrary. The Policy provides for notice, the right to be present at an adversary hearing, and the right to present and cross-examine witnesses. See *Vitek*, *supra*, at 494–496. The procedural protections are not vitiated by meetings between the committee members and staff before the hearing. Absent evidence of resulting bias, or evidence that the actual decision is made before the hearing, allowing respondent to contest the staff's position at the hearing satisfies the requirement that the opportunity to be heard "must be granted at a meaningful time and in a meaningful manner." *Armstrong* v. *Manzo*, 380 U. S. 545, 552 (1965). We reject also respondent's contention that the hearing must be conducted in accordance with the rules of evidence or that a "clear, cogent, and convincing" standard of proof is necessary. This standard is neither required nor helpful when medical personnel are making the judgment required by the regulations here. See *Vitek*, *supra*, at 494–495. Cf. *Youngberg*, 457 U. S., at 321–323. Finally, we note that under state law an inmate may obtain judicial review of the hearing committee's decision by way of a personal restraint petition or petition for an extraordinary writ, and that the trial court found that the record compiled under the Policy was adequate to allow such review. See App. to Pet. for Cert. B–8.

---

quency with which refusals are allowed, regardless of the system or the decisionmaker").

Respondent contends that the Policy is nonetheless deficient because it does not allow him to be represented by counsel. We disagree. "[I]t is less than crystal clear why *lawyers* must be available to identify possible errors in *medical* judgment." *Walters* v. *National Association of Radiation Survivors*, 473 U. S. 305, 330 (1985) (emphasis in original). Given the nature of the decision to be made, we conclude that the provision of an independent lay adviser who understands the psychiatric issues involved is sufficient protection. See *Vitek*, *supra*, at 499–500 (Powell, J., concurring).

V

In sum, we hold that the regulation before us is permissible under the Constitution. It is an accommodation between an inmate's liberty interest in avoiding the forced administration of antipsychotic drugs and the State's interests in providing appropriate medical treatment to reduce the danger that an inmate suffering from a serious mental disorder represents to himself or others. The Due Process Clause does require certain essential procedural protections, all of which are provided by the regulation before us. The judgment of the Washington Supreme Court is reversed, and the case is remanded for further proceedings not inconsistent with this opinion.

It is so ordered.

JUSTICE BLACKMUN, concurring.

I join the Court's opinion. The difficult and controversial character of this case is illustrated by the simple fact that the American Psychiatric Association and the American Psychological Association, which are respected, knowledgeable, and informed professional organizations, and which are here as *amici curiae*, pull the Court in opposite directions.

I add a caveat. Much of the difficulty will be lessened if, in any appropriate case, the mentally ill patient is formally committed. This on occasion may seem to be a bother or a nuisance, but it is a move that would be protective for all concerned, the inmate, the institution, its staff, the physician, and the State itself. Cf. *Zinermon* v. *Burch*, *ante*, p. 113. It is a step that should not be avoided or neglected when significant indications of incompetency are present.

JUSTICE STEVENS, with whom JUSTICE BRENNAN and JUSTICE MARSHALL join, concurring in part and dissenting in part.

While I join the Court's explanation of why this case is not moot, I disagree with its evaluation of the merits. The Court has undervalued respondent's liberty interest; has misread the Washington involuntary medication Policy and misapplied our decision in *Turner* v. *Safley*, 482 U. S. 78 (1987); and has concluded that a mock trial before an institutionally biased tribunal constitutes "due process of law." Each of these errors merits separate discussion.

I

The Court acknowledges that under the Fourteenth Amendment "respondent possesses a significant liberty interest in avoiding the unwanted administration of antipsychotic drugs," *ante*, at 221, but then virtually ignores the several dimensions of that liberty. They are both physical and intellectual. Every violation of a person's bodily integrity is an invasion of his or her liberty. The invasion is particularly intrusive if it creates a substantial risk of permanent injury and premature death.[1] Moreover, any such action is degrading if it overrides a competent person's choice to reject a specific form of medical treatment.[2] And when the purpose

[1] Cf., *e. g.*, *Winston* v. *Lee*, 470 U. S. 753 (1985) (surgery); *Youngberg* v. *Romeo*, 457 U. S. 307 (1982) (use of physical "soft" restraints for the arms and "muffs" for hands).

[2] See *Mills* v. *Rogers*, 457 U. S. 291, 294, n. 4, 299, n. 16 (1982) (recognizing common-law battery for unauthorized touchings by a physician and assuming liberty interests are implicated by involuntary administration of psychotropic drugs); *United States* v. *Stanley*, 483 U. S. 669, 710 (1987) (O'CONNOR, J., concurring in part and dissenting in part) (the Constitution's promise of due process of law guarantees at least compensation

or effect of forced drugging is to alter the will and the mind of the subject, it constitutes a deprivation of liberty in the most literal and fundamental sense.

> "The makers of our Constitution undertook to secure conditions favorable to the pursuit of happiness. They recognized the significance of man's spiritual nature, of his feelings and of his intellect. They knew that only a part of the pain, pleasure and satisfactions of life are to be found in material things. They sought to protect Americans in their beliefs, their thoughts, their emotions and their sensations. They conferred, as against the Government, the right to be let alone—the most comprehensive of rights and the right most valued by civilized men." *Olmstead* v. *United States*, 277 U. S. 438, 478 (1928) (Brandeis, J., dissenting).

The liberty of citizens to resist the administration of mind altering drugs arises from our Nation's most basic values.[3]

for violations of the principle stated by the Nuremberg Military Tribunals "that the 'voluntary consent of the human subject is absolutely essential . . . to satisfy moral, ethical and legal concepts' "); *Doe* v. *Bolton*, 410 U. S. 179, 213 (1973) (Douglas, J., concurring) (the Fourteenth Amendment protects the "freedom to care for one's health and person" (emphasis deleted)). Harper was not adjudged insane or incompetent. 110 Wash. 2d 873, 882, 759 P. 2d 358, 364 (1988).

[3] See also *Stanley* v. *Georgia*, 394 U. S. 557, 565 (1969) ("Our whole constitutional heritage rebels at the thought of giving government the power to control men's minds").

"It is obligatory that Helsinki signatory states not manipulate the minds of their citizens; that they not step between a man and his conscience or his God; and that they not prevent his thoughts from finding expression through peaceful action. We are all painfully aware, furthermore, that governments which systematically disregard the rights of their own people are not likely to respect the rights of other nations and other people." Hearings on Abuse of Psychiatry in the Soviet Union before the Subcommittee on Human Rights and International Organizations of the House Committee on Foreign Affairs, 98th Cong., 1st Sess., 106 (1983) (Remarks by Max Kampelman, Chair of the U. S. Delegation, to the Plenary Session of the Commission on Security and Cooperation in Europe).

The record of one of Walter Harper's involuntary medication hearings at the Special Offense Center (SOC) notes: "Inmate Harper stated he would rather die th[a]n take medication."[4] That Harper would be so opposed to taking psychotropic drugs is not surprising: as the Court acknowledges, these drugs both "alter the chemical balance in a patient's brain" and can cause irreversible and fatal side effects.[5]

---

[4] Lodging filed by Kenneth O. Eikenberry, Attorney General of Washington (hereinafter Lodging), Book 8, Jan. 5, 1984, Hearing (Harper testified: "Well all you want to do is medicate me and you've been medicating me. . . . Haldol paral[y]zed my right side of my body. . . . [Y]ou are burning me out of my life . . . [Y]ou are burning me out of my freedom").

The Lodging includes "books" of discovery material that the parties stipulated "could be considered by the [Trial] Court as substantive evidence and the [Trial] Court . . . considered those documents." App. to Pet. for Cert. B–1. They are hereinafter referred to by Book number and the date of the entry, where applicable. I use the Lodging not to "engage in a debate" over the assessment of Harper's treatment, *ante*, at 228, n. 11, but simply to illustrate the boundaries of Policy 600.30 in operation.

[5] *Ante*, at 229. The Court relies heavily on the Brief for American Psychiatric Association et al. as *Amici Curiae* (Psychiatrists' Brief), see *ante*, at 214, 226, and n. 9, 227, and n. 10, 230, to discount the severity of these drugs. However, medical findings discussed in other briefs support the conclusions of the Washington Supreme Court and challenge the reliability of the Psychiatrists' Brief. For example, the Brief for American Psychological Association as *Amicus Curiae* (Psychologists' Brief) points out that the observation of tardive dyskinesia has been increasing "at an alarming rate" since the 1950–1970 data relied on by the Psychiatrists' Brief 14–16, and that "the chance of suffering this potentially devastating disorder is greater than one in four." Psychologists' Brief 8. See also Brief for Coalition for Fundamental Rights and Equality of Ex-Patients as *Amicus Curiae* 16–18 (court findings and recent literature on side effects); Brief for National Association of Protection and Advocacy Systems et al. as *Amici Curiae* 7–16 (same). Psychiatrists also may not be entirely disinterested experts. The psychologists charge: "As a psychiatrist has written, '[l]itigation from patients suffering from TD [tardive dyskinesia] is expected to explode within the next five years. Some psychiatrists and other physicians continue to minimize the seriousness of TD . . . [despite] continual warnings.'" Psychologists' Brief 4 (quoting R. Simon, Clinical Psychiatry and the Law 74 (1987)).

The prolixin injections that Harper was receiving at the time of his statement exemplify the intrusiveness of psychotropic drugs on a person's body and mind. Prolixin acts "at all levels of the central nervous system as well as on multiple organ systems."[6] It can induce catatonic-like states, alter electroencephalographic tracings, and cause swelling of the brain. Adverse reactions include drowsiness, excitement, restlessness, bizarre dreams, hypertension, nausea, vomiting, loss of appetite, salivation, dry mouth, perspiration, headache, constipation, blurred vision, impotency, eczema, jaundice, tremors, and muscle spasms. As with all psychotropic drugs, prolixin may cause tardive dyskinesia, an often irreversible syndrome of uncontrollable movements that can prevent a person from exercising basic functions such as driving an automobile, and neuroleptic malignant syndrome, which is 30% fatal for those who suffer from it.[7] The risk of side effects increases over time.[8]

The Washington Supreme Court properly equated the intrusiveness of this mind-altering drug treatment with electroconvulsive therapy or psychosurgery. It agreed with the Supreme Judicial Court of Massachusetts' determination that the drugs have a "'profound effect'" on a person's "'thought

---

[6] Physician's Desk Reference 1639 (43d ed. 1989).

[7] *Id.*, at 1640; Trial Court Finding 9, App. to Pet. for Cert. B–7 to B–8; Guzé & Baxter, Neuroleptic Malignant Syndrome, 313 New England J. Med. 163, 163–164 (1985).

[8] Physician's Desk Reference, *supra*, at 1639. Harper voluntarily took psychotropic drugs for six years before involuntary medication began in 1982, by which time he had already exhibited dystonia (acute muscle spasms) and akathesia (physical-emotional agitation). *E. g.*, Lodging, Book 2, May 28, 1982, Aug. 4, 1982; see also Trial Court Findings 9–10, App. to Pet. for Cert. B–7 to B–8. Although avoidance of akathesia and the risk of tardive dyskinesia require reduction or discontinuance of psychotropics, *ibid.*, Harper's involuntary medication was continuous from November 1982 to June 1986, except for one month spent at Washington State Reformatory. Lodging, Book 8; Trial Court Findings 4–6, 9, App. to Pet. for Cert. B–4 to B–8.

processes'" and a "'well-established likelihood of severe and irreversible adverse side effects,'" and that they therefore should be treated "'in the same manner we would treat psychosurgery or electroconvulsive therapy.'" 110 Wash. 2d 873, 878, 759 P. 2d 358, 362 (1988) (quoting *In re Guardianship of Roe*, 383 Mass. 415, 436–437, 421 N. E. 2d 40, 53 (1981)). There is no doubt, as the State Supreme Court and other courts that have analyzed the issue have concluded, that a competent individual's right to refuse such medication is a fundamental liberty interest deserving the highest order of protection.[9]

II

Arguably, any of three quite different state interests might be advanced to justify a deprivation of this liberty interest. The State might seek to compel Harper to submit to a mind-altering drug treatment program as punishment for the crime he committed in 1976, as a "cure" for his mental illness, or as a mechanism to maintain order in the prison. The Court today recognizes Harper's liberty interest only as against the first justification.

Forced administration of antipsychotic medication may not be used as a form of punishment. This conclusion follows inexorably from our holding in *Vitek* v. *Jones*, 445 U. S. 480 (1980), that the Constitution provides a convicted felon the protection of due process against an involuntary transfer from the prison population to a mental hospital for psychiatric treatment. We explained:

---

[9] 110 Wash. 2d, at 878, 759 P. 2d, at 362. See, *e. g.*, *Large* v. *Superior Court*, 148 Ariz. 229, 714 P. 2d 399 (1986) (en banc); *Riese* v. *St. Mary's Hospital and Medical Center*, 209 Cal. App. 3d 1303, 243 Cal. Rptr. 241 (1st Dist. 1988), review granted but dism'd, 774 P. 2d 698 (1989); *People* v. *Medina*, 705 P. 2d 961 (Colo. 1985) (en banc); *Rogers* v. *Commissioner of Dept. of Mental Health*, 390 Mass. 489, 458 N. E. 2d 308 (1983); *Rivers* v. *Katz*, 67 N. Y. 2d 485, 495 N. E. 2d 337 (1986); *In re Mental Health of K. K. B.*, 609 P. 2d 747 (Okla. 1980). Cf. *In re Schuoler*, 106 Wash. 2d 500, 723 P. 2d 1103 (1986) (right to refuse electroconvulsive therapy).

"Appellants maintain that the transfer of a prisoner to a mental hospital is within the range of confinement justified by imposition of a prison sentence, at least after certification by a qualified person that a prisoner suffers from a mental disease or defect. We cannot agree. None of our decisions holds that conviction for a crime entitles a State not only to confine the convicted person but also to determine that he has a mental illness and to subject him involuntarily to institutional care in a mental hospital. Such consequences visited on the prisoner are qualitatively different from the punishment characteristically suffered by a person convicted of crime. Our cases recognize as much and reflect an understanding that involuntary commitment to a mental hospital is not within the range of conditions of confinement to which a prison sentence subjects an individual. *Baxstrom* v. *Herold*, 383 U. S. 107 (1966); *Specht* v. *Patterson*, 386 U. S. 605 (1967); *Humphrey* v. *Cady*, 405 U. S. 504 (1972); *Jackson* v. *Indiana*, 406 U. S. 715, 724–725 (1972). A criminal conviction and sentence of imprisonment extinguish an individual's right to freedom from confinement for the term of his sentence, but they do not authorize the State to classify him as mentally ill and to subject him to involuntary psychiatric treatment without affording him additional due process protections." *Id.*, at 493–494.

The Court does not suggest that psychotropic drugs, any more than transfer for medical treatment, may be forced on prisoners as a necesssary condition of their incarceration or as a disciplinary measure. Rather, it holds:

"[G]iven the requirements of the prison environment, the Due Process Clause permits the State to treat a prison inmate who has a serious mental illness with antipsychotic drugs against his will, if the inmate is dangerous to himself or others *and the treatment is in the inmate's medical interest.* Policy 600.30 comports with

> these requirements; we therefore reject respondent's contention that its substantive standards are deficient under the Constitution." *Ante*, at 227 (emphasis added).

Crucial to the Court's exposition of this substantive due process standard is the condition that these drugs "may be administered for no purpose other than treatment," and that "the treatment in question will be ordered only if it is in the prisoner's medical interests, given the legitimate needs of his institutional confinement." *Ante*, at 226, 222. Thus, although the Court does not find, as Harper urges, an absolute liberty interest of a competent person to refuse psychotropic drugs, it does recognize that the substantive protections of the Due Process Clause limit the forced administration of psychotropic drugs to all but those inmates whose medical interests would be advanced by such treatment.

Under this standard the Court upholds SOC Policy 600.30, determining that this administrative scheme confers, as a matter of state law, a substantive liberty interest coextensive with that conferred by the Due Process Clause. *Ante*, at 221–222, 227. Whether or not the State's alleged interest in providing medically beneficial treatment to those in its custody who are mentally ill may alone override the refusal of psychotropic drugs by a presumptively competent person, a plain reading of Policy 600.30 reveals that it does not meet the substantive standard set forth by the Court. Even on the Court's terms, the Policy is constitutionally insufficient.

Policy 600.30 permits forced administration of psychotropic drugs on a mentally ill inmate based purely on the impact that his disorder has on the security of the prison environment. The provisions of the Policy make no reference to any expected benefit to the inmate's medical condition. Policy 600.30 requires:

> "In order for involuntary medication to be approved, it must be demonstrated that the inmate suffers from a mental disorder and as a result of that disorder constitutes a likelihood of serious harm to himself or others

> and/or is gravely disabled." Lodging, Book 9, Policy 600.30, p. 1.

"Likelihood of serious harm," according to the Policy,

> "means either (i) A substantial risk that physical harm will be inflicted by an individual upon his own person, as evidenced by threats or attempts to commit suicide or inflict physical harm on one's self, (ii) a substantial risk that physical harm will be inflicted by an individual upon another as evidenced by behavior which has caused such harm or which places another person or persons in reasonable fear of sustaining such harm, or (iii) a substantial risk that physical harm will be inflicted by an individual upon the property of others as evidenced by behavior which has caused substantial loss or damage to the property of others."[10]

Thus, the Policy authorizes long-term involuntary medication not only of any mentally ill inmate who, as a result of a mental disorder, appears to present a future risk to himself, but also of an inmate who presents a future risk to other people or mere property.

Although any application of Policy 600.30 requires a medical judgment as to a prisoner's mental condition and the cause of his behavior, the Policy does not require a determination that forced medication would advance his medical interest.[11] Use of psychotropic drugs, the State readily admits,

---

[10] Lodging, Book 9, Policy 600.30, p. 1. Revised Policy 620.200, effective February 18, 1985, retained these substantive definitions. Lodging, Book 9, Policy 620.200, p. 1.

[11] The Court's reliance on the Hippocratic Oath to save the constitutionality of Policy 600.30 is unavailing. *Ante*, at 223, n. 8. Whether or not the Oath binds treating physicians with a "medical interest" requirement in prescribing medications, it has no bearing on the SOC review committees, which are governed solely by the administrative criteria of Policy 600.30 in authorizing involuntary medication. Nor can the Court possibly believe that any "treatment" is talismanically in a patient's "medical interest." Treatment of a condition with medication facilitates a specific physiological result, which may or may not be in the overall medical interest of the patient. For example, the patient's medical interest in reducing his own vio-

serves to ease the institutional and administrative burdens of maintaining prison security and provides a means of managing an unruly prison population and preventing property damage.[12] By focusing on the risk that the inmate's mental condition poses to other people and property, the Policy allows the State to exercise either *parens patriae* authority or police authority to override a prisoner's liberty interest in refusing psychotropic drugs. Thus, most unfortunately, there is simply no basis for the Court's assertion that medication under the Policy must be to advance the prisoner's medical interest.[13]

Policy 600.30 sweepingly sacrifices the inmate's substantive liberty interest to refuse psychotropic drugs, regardless of his medical interests, to institutional and administrative

---

lence or in altering his mental condition may be often outweighed by the risk or onset of severe medical side effects. See *supra*, at 239–241. Finally, the qualitative judgment of what is a patient's best interest cannot be made without reference to his own preferences. The Policy does not account for either a physician's determination of medical interest or the inmate's wishes.

[12] See, *e. g.*, Brief for Petitioners 29 ("Harper's history of assaultive behavior requires that the state exercise its police power to appropriately medicate him for the protection of others"); *id.*, at 17 ("The policy assists prison administrators in meeting their 'unquestioned duty to provide reasonable safety for all residents and personnel within the institution'"). See also Brief for United States as *Amicus Curiae* 17 ("The paramount concerns in running a prison or a prison mental health facility are maintaining institutional security, preserving internal order, and establishing a therapeutic environment. . . . [I]t goes without saying that the interest in preventing violence and maintaining order is significantly amplified when an entire ward consists of mentally ill prisoners, as at the SOC").

[13] The trial court did not attempt to separate the medical and institutional objectives of Policy 600.30. Nor did it construe the Policy's terms to require that an inmate's best medical interests be served by medication. The trial court's findings were limited to Harper's case. Findings 11–12, App. to Pet. for Cert. B–8. They shed no light on whether Harper's doctors did—or "a reasonably prudent psychiatrist in the State of Washington, acting in the same or similar circumstances" as a SOC psychiatrist could—order medication for any combination of therapeutic or institutional concerns. Finding 12, App. to Pet. for Cert. B–8.

concerns. The State clearly has a legitimate interest in prison security and administrative convenience that encompasses responding to potential risks to persons and property. However, to the extent that the Court recognizes "both the prisoner's medical interests and the State's interests" as potentially *independent* justifications for involuntary medication of inmates,[14] it seriously misapplies the standard announced in *Turner* v. *Safley*, 482 U. S. 78 (1987). In *Turner*, we held that a prison regulation that impinges on inmates' constitutional rights is valid "if it is reasonably related to legitimate penological interests." *Id.*, at 89. Under this test, we determined that a regulation barring inmate-to-inmate correspondence was adequately supported by the State's institutional security concerns. *Id.*, at 93. We also unanimously concluded that a regulation prohibiting inmate marriage, except with consent of the prison superintendent made upon proof of compelling circumstances, was an "exaggerated response" to the prison's claimed security objectives and was not reasonably related to its articulated rehabilitation goal. *Id.*, at 97–98.

The State advances security concerns as a justification for forced medication in two distinct circumstances. A SOC Policy provision not at issue in this case permits 72 hours of involuntary medication on an emergency basis when "an inmate is suffering from a mental disorder and as a result of that disorder presents an *imminent* likelihood of *serious harm* to himself or others." Lodging, Book 9, Policy 600.30, p. 2 (emphasis added). In contrast to the imminent danger of injury that triggers the emergency medication provisions, a general risk of illness-induced injury or property damage—evidenced by no more than past behavior—allows long-term, involuntary medication of an inmate with psychotropic drugs

---

[14] *Ante*, at 223. The Court further conflates its analysis by suggesting that "[t]he State has undertaken the obligation to provide prisoners with medical treatment consistent not only with their own medical interests, but also with the needs of the institution." *Ante*, at 225.

under Policy 600.30. This ongoing interest in security and management is a penological concern of a constitutionally distinct magnitude from the necessity of responding to emergencies. See *Whitley* v. *Albers*, 475 U. S. 312, 321–322 (1986). It is difficult to imagine what, if any, limits would restrain such a general concern of prison administrators who believe that prison environments are, "'by definition,' . . . made up of persons with 'a demonstrated proclivity for antisocial criminal, and often violent, conduct.'" *Ante*, at 225 (quoting *Hudson* v. *Palmer*, 468 U. S. 517, 526 (1984)). A rule that allows prison administrators to address potential security risks by forcing psychotropic drugs on mentally ill inmates for prolonged periods is unquestionably an "exaggerated response" to that concern.

In *Turner* we concluded on the record before us that the marriage "regulation, as written, [was] not reasonably related to . . . penological interests," and that there were "obvious, easy alternatives" that the State failed to rebut by reference to the record. 482 U. S., at 97–98. Today the Court concludes that alternatives to psychotropic drugs would impose more than *de minimis* costs on the State. However, the record before us does not establish that a more narrowly drawn policy withdrawing psychotropics from only those inmates who actually refuse consent[15] and who do not pose

---

[15] There is no evidence that more than a small fraction of inmates would refuse drugs under a voluntary policy. Harper himself voluntarily took psychotropics for six years, and intermittently consented to them after 1982. Lodging, Books 2 and 8. See, *e. g.*, *Rogers* v. *Okin*, 478 F. Supp. 1342, 1369 (Mass. 1979) (only 12 of 1,000 institutionalized patients refused psychotropic drugs for prolonged periods during the two years that judicial restraining order was in effect), modified, 634 F. 2d 650 (CA1 1980), vacated and remanded *sub nom.* *Mills* v. *Rogers*, 457 U. S. 291 (1982). The efficacy of forced drugging is also marginal; involuntary patients have a poorer prognosis than cooperative patients. See Rogers & Webster, Assessing Treatability in Mentally Disordered Offenders, 13 Law and Human Behavior 19, 20–21 (1989).

an imminent threat of serious harm[16] would increase the marginal costs of SOC administration. Harper's own record reveals that administrative segregation and standard disciplinary sanctions were frequently imposed on him over and above forced medication and thus would add no new costs. Lodging, Book 1. Similarly, intramuscular injections of psychotropics, such as those frequently forced on Harper, *id.*, Book 7, entail no greater risk than administration of less dangerous drugs such as tranquilizers.[17] Use of psychotro-

---

[16] As the Court notes, properly used, these drugs are "one of the most effective means of treating and controlling" certain incurable mental illnesses, *ante*, at 226, but they are not a panacea for long-term care of all patients.

"[T]he maintenance treatment literature . . . shows that many patients (approximately 30%) relapse despite receiving neuroleptic medication, while neuroleptics can be withdrawn from other patients for many months and in some cases for years without relapse. Standard maintenance medication treatment strategies, though they are indisputably effective in group comparisons, may be quite inefficient in addressing the treatment requirements of the individual patient." Lieberman et al., Reply to Ethics of Drug Discontinuation Studies in Schizophrenia, 46 Archives of General Psychiatry 387 (1989) (footnotes omitted).

Indeed, the drugs appear to have produced at most minor "savings" in Harper's case. Dr. Petrich reported that "medications are not satisfactory in containing the worst excesses of his labile and irritable behavior. He is uncooperative when on medication," Lodging, Book 2, Nov. 10, 1982, and a therapy supervisor reported before Harper's involuntary medication began:

"[D]uring the time in which he assaulted the nurse at Cabrini he was on neuroleptic medication yet there is indication that he was psychotic. However, during his stay at SOC he has been off of all neuroleptic medications and at times has shown some preoccupation and appearance of psychosis but has not become assaultive. His problems on medication, such as the paradoxical effect from the neuroleptic medications, may be precipitated by increased doses of neuroleptic medications and may cause an exacerbation of his psychosis. Though Mr. Harper is focused on psychosomatic problems from neuroleptic medications as per the side effects, the real problem may be that the psychosis is exacerbated by neuroleptic medications." *Id.*, Book 3, May 6, 1982, p. 6.

[17] Because most psychotropic drugs do induce lethargy, drowsiness, and fatigue, *e. g.*, Physician's Desk Reference 1126, 1236, 1640, 1755, 1788,

pic drugs simply to suppress an inmate's potential violence, rather than to achieve therapeutic results, may also undermine the efficacy of other available treatment programs that would better address his illness.[18]

The Court's careful differentiation in *Turner* between the State's articulated goals of security and rehabilitation should be emulated in this case. The flaw in Washington's Policy 600.30—and the basic error in the Court's opinion today—is the failure to divorce from each other the two justifications for forced medication and to consider the extent to which the Policy is reasonably related to either interest. The State, and arguably the Court, allows the SOC to blend the state interests in responding to emergencies and in convenient prison administration with the individual's interest in receiving beneficial medical treatment. The result is a muddled rationale that allows the "exaggerated response" of forced psychotropic medication on the basis of purely institutional concerns. So serving institutional convenience eviscerates

---

1883 (43d ed. 1989), this form of "medical treatment" may reduce an inmate's dangerousness, not by improving his mental condition, but simply by sedating him with a medication that is grossly excessive for that purpose.

[18] For example, although psychotropic drugs were of mixed value in treating Harper's condition, *supra*, at 248, n. 16, they became the primary means of dealing with him. *E. g.*, Lodging, Book 8, Nov. 7, 1984, Hearing (Dr. Petrich reports: "The patient is still not able to negotiate with the treatment staff or work collectively with them. We have no idea as to the extent of his psychosis nor do we have any working relationship upon which to build internal and external controls"); *id.*, Book 8, Feb. 26, 1985 (Dr. Loeken reports: "because of his lack of participation in therapy it is recommended that the involuntary medication policy continue in use").

Forcing psychotropics on Harper also provoked counterproductive behavior. *E. g.*, *id.*, Book 8, Dec. 16, 1982 (Report of Dr. Petrich that Harper's assault on a male nurse and damage to a television were "in the context of his complaining about medication side effects. Overall the issue of involuntary medications and side effects is a major issue in his management"); *id.*, Book 8, Oct. 7, 1983 (therapist's report that Harper has indicated "that he is going to destroy unit property until the medications are stopped. He has recently destroyed the inmates['] stereo as an example of this").

the inmate's substantive liberty interest in the integrity of his body and mind.[19]

III

The procedures of Policy 600.30 are also constitutionally deficient. Whether or not the State ever may order involuntary administration of psychotropic drugs to a mentally ill person who has been committed to its custody but has not been declared incompetent, it is at least clear that any decision approving such drugs must be made by an impartial professional concerned not with institutional interests, but only with the individual's best interests. The critical defect in Policy 600.30 is the failure to have the treatment decision made or reviewed by an impartial person or tribunal. See *Vitek*, 445 U. S., at 495.[20]

The psychiatrists who diagnose and provide routine care to SOC inmates may prescribe psychotropic drugs and recommend involuntary medication under Policy 600.30. The Policy provides that a nonemergency decision to medicate for up

---

[19] *Youngberg* v. *Romeo*, 457 U. S. 307 (1982), and *Parham* v. *J. R.*, 442 U. S. 584 (1979), are inapposite. Neither involved care of a presumptively competent individual; Romeo, a profoundly retarded adult with the mental capacity of an 18-month-old child, had been committed by the court to a state hospital for treatment, 457 U. S., at 309, and J. R. and appellees were children, 442 U. S., at 587. In addition, the deprivations of liberty at issue in both cases—use of physical restraints in *Youngberg* and institutionalization in *Parham*—fall far short of Harper's interest in refusing mind-altering drugs with potentially permanent and fatal side effects. Cf. *Bee* v. *Greaves*, 744 F. 2d 1387, 1395–1397 (CA10 1984) (forcible medication with psychotropics is not reasonably related to prison security), cert. denied, 469 U. S. 1214 (1985).

[20] It is not necessary to reach the question whether the decision to force psychotropic drugs on a competent person against his will must be approved by a judge, or by an administrative tribunal of professionals who are not members of the prison staff, in order to conclude that the mechanism of Policy 600.30 violates procedural due process. The choice is not between medical experts on the one hand and judges on the other; the choice is between decisionmakers who are biased and those who are not.

to seven consecutive days must be approved by a special committee after a hearing. The committee consists of the Associate Superintendent of SOC, a psychologist, and a psychiatrist. Neither of the medical professionals may be involved in the current diagnosis or treatment of the inmate. The approval of the psychiatrist and one other committee member is required to sustain a 7-day involuntary medication decision. Lodging, Book 9, Policy 600.30, p. 2, § 3.B. A similarly composed committee is required to authorize "long term" involuntary medication lasting over seven days. Policy 600.30 does not bar current treating professionals or previous committee members from serving on the long-term committee. This committee does *not* conduct a new hearing, but merely reviews the inmate's file and minutes of the 7-day hearing. Long-term approval, if granted, allows medication to continue indefinitely with a review and report by the treating psychiatrist every 14 days. *Id.*, Book 9, Policy 600.30, p. 2, § 3.C.[21]

These decisionmakers have two disqualifying conflicts of interest. First, the panel members must review the work of treating physicians who are their colleagues and who, in turn, regularly review their decisions. Such an in-house system pits the interests of an inmate who objects to forced medication against the judgment not only of his doctor, but often his doctor's colleagues.[22] Furthermore, the Court's

[21] Revised Policy 620.200 authorizes up to 14 consecutive days of involuntary medication before long-term committee approval is required, and adds a committee hearing to review continuing involuntary medication every 180 days thereafter. It also bars current treating personnel from sitting on the long-term committee. Lodging, Book 9, Policy 620.200, pp. 3–4.

[22] As regular SOC staff, 600.30 committee members are

"susceptible to implicit or explicit pressure for cooperation ('If you support my orders, I'll support yours'). It is instructive that month after month, year after year, this 'review' panel *always* voted for more medication—despite the scientific literature showing that periodic respites from drugs are advisable and that prolonged use of antipsychotic drugs is proper only

conclusion that "[n]one of the hearing committee members may be involved in the inmate's current treatment or diagnosis," *ante*, at 233, overlooks the fact that Policy 600.30 allows a treating psychiatrist to participate in all but the initial *7-day* medication approval. This revolving door operated in Harper's case. Dr. Petrich treated Harper through 1982 and recommended involuntary medication on October 27, 1982. Lodging, Book 8, Oct. 27, 1982. Dr. Loeken, staff psychologist Giles, and Assistant Superintendent Stark authorized medication for seven days after a 600.30 hearing on November 23, 1982. Dr. Petrich then replaced Dr. Loeken on the committee, and with Giles and Stark approved long-term involuntary medication on December 8, 1982. Solely under this authority, Dr. Petrich prescribed more psychotropic medication for Harper on December 8, 1982, and throughout the following year.[23]

---

when the medical need is clear and compelling." Psychologists' Brief 26–27 (footnote omitted).

Rates of approval by different review bodies are of limited value, of course, because institutions will presumably adjust their medication practices over time to obtain approval under different standards or by different reviewing bodies. However, New Jersey's review of involuntary psychotropic medication in mental institutions is instructive. In 1980 external review by an "independent psychiatrist" who was not otherwise employed by the Department of Human Services resulted in discontinuation or reduction of 59% of dosages. After the Department moved to an internal peer review system, that percentage dropped to 2.5% of cases. Brief for New Jersey Department of Public Advocate as *Amicus Curiae* 38–54.

[23] All of Harper's prescription entries from November 20, 1982, through December 8, 1982, were made "per Dr. Petrich." Lodging, Book 7, primary encounter reports of Nov. 20, 1982, Dec. 2, 1982, Dec. 8, 1982. After Harper's return to the SOC in December 1983, Dr. Loeken became his primary physician, and committees again approved 7-day, then long-term, involuntary medication. Although Dr. Petrich was not on these committees, he sat on the next three 180-day review committees, voting to authorize forced medication through January 1986. Trial Court Finding 7, App. to Pet. for Cert. B–7.

Second, the panel members, as regular staff of the Center, must be concerned not only with the inmate's best medical interests, but also with the most convenient means of controlling the mentally disturbed inmate. The mere fact that a decision is made by a doctor does not make it "certain that professional judgment in fact was exercised." *Youngberg* v. *Romeo*, 457 U. S. 307, 321 (1982). The structure of the SOC committee virtually ensures that it will not be. While the initial inquiry into the mental bases for an inmate's behavior is medical, the ultimate medication decision under Policy 600.30 turns on an assessment of the risk that an inmate's condition imposes on the institution. The prescribing physician and each member of the review committee must therefore wear two hats. This hybrid function disables the independent exercise of each decisionmaker's *professional* judgment.[24] The

[24] The Court cites *Vitek* v. *Jones*, 445 U. S. 480 (1980), and *Parham* as "previous cases involving medical decisions implicating similar liberty interests [in which] we have approved use of similar internal decisionmakers." *Ante*, at 233–234. Aside from the greater liberty interest implicated by forced psychotropic medication, SOC decisionmakers face different demands than their professional counterparts in *Vitek* and *Parham*. In *Vitek*, the Nebraska state transfer policy at issue affected only prisoners determined to be mentally ill who could not "adequately be treated within the penal complex." 445 U. S., at 489. We found that the determination of the necessity of transfer for treatment, "a question that is essentially medical," could be made fairly by professionals after a meaningful hearing. *Id.*, at 495. Similarly, we understood the civil commitment decision at issue in *Parham* to involve examination of the child, review of medical records, and a diagnosis and determination of "whether the child will likely benefit from institutionalized care," emphasizing that "[w]hat is best for a child is an individual medical decision . . . of what the child requires." 442 U. S., at 614–615, 608. Both of these procedures sought to reach an accurate medical determination of the patient's treatment needs without reference to the institution's separate interests. We concluded that, despite their positions inside the Nebraska prison and Georgia hospital, these medical professionals were capable of exercising the independence of professional judgment required by due process. None of the medical professionals at the SOC, charged with making medication decisions in light

structure of the review committee further confuses the objective of the inquiry; two of the committee members are not trained or licensed to prescribe psychotropic drugs, and one has no medical expertise at all. The trump by institutional interests is dramatized by the fact that appeals of committee decisions under the Policy are made solely to the SOC Superintendent.[25]

The Court asserts that "[t]here is no indication that any institutional biases affected or altered the decision to medicate respondent against his will" and that there is no evidence that "antipsychotic drugs were prescribed not for medical purposes, but to control or discipline mentally ill patients." *Ante*, at 233, and 234, n. 13. A finding of bias in an individual case is unnecessary to determine that the structure of Policy 600.30 fails to meet the due process requirements of the Fourteenth Amendment. In addition, Harper's own record illustrates the potential abuse of psychotropics under Policy 600.30 for institutional ends. For example, Dr. Petrich added Taractan, a psychotropic drug, to Harper's medication around October 27, 1982, noting: "The goal of the increased medication to sedate him at night and relieve the residents and evening *[sic]* alike of the burden of supervising him as intensely."[26] A 1983 examination by non-SOC physicians

---

of the inmate's impact on the institution and its needs, can claim such independence.

[25] Lodging, Book 9, Policy 600.30, p. 4. The Court notes that an inmate may bring a personal restraint petition or seek an extraordinary writ under Wash. Rules App. Proc. 16.3 to 16.17, *ante*, at 216, 235. However, a nonemergency involuntary medication decision demands—as the existence of a SOC Policy attests—meaningful administrative review of this deprivation of liberty, not merely the existence of collateral judicial mechanisms. Cf. *Ingraham* v. *Wright*, 430 U. S. 651 (1977).

[26] Lodging, Book 8, Oct. 27, 1982. Indeed, a "psychiatric security attendant," not a doctor, made the first recorded request for involuntary medication after Harper attempted to pull the guard's hand through a food slot. The guard filed a disciplinary "Infraction Report" which concluded: "Sug-

also indicated that Harper was prophylactically medicated absent symptoms that would qualify him for involuntary medication.[27]

The institutional bias that is inherent in the identity of the decisionmakers is unchecked by other aspects of Policy 600.30. The committee need not consider whether less intrusive procedures would be effective, or even if the prescribed medication would be beneficial to the prisoner, before approving involuntary medication. Findings regarding the severity or the probability of potential side effects of drugs and dosages are not required. And, although the Policy does not prescribe a standard of proof necessary for any factual determination upon which a medication decision rests, the Court gratuitously advises that the "clear, cogent, and convincing" standard adopted by the State Supreme Court would be unnecessary.[28]

---

gestion: This inmate is in need of involuntary medication. He is a threat to the safety + security of the institution." *Id.*, Book 1-2, Oct. 22, 1982. Five days later, Dr. Petrich, citing the incident, recommended involuntary medication. *Id.*, Book 8, Oct. 27, 1982.

[27] Harper was transferred on November 16, 1983, to Washington State Reformatory, where a psychiatrist on its Multidisciplinary Advisory Committee found:

"To this date, he has not exhibited behavior in the presence of any committee members or custody staff that would qualify him under involuntary medication policy. He does have a long history of recurrent difficulty and as best as we can tell SOC instituted the involuntary policy and *continued it on the basis of past bad faith;* however, we do not have any of that data available to us." *Id.*, Book 3, Nov. 30, 1983 (emphasis added).

See also *id.*, Book 8, May 1, 1985, Hearing ("[T]he inmate[']s behavior during the committee hearing did not meet the criteria for gravely disabled or self injurious behavior. Involuntary medication is continued on the basis of potential violent behavior towards others which has been well documented in the inmate's history").

[28] *Ante*, at 235. In *Addington* v. *Texas*, 441 U. S. 418 (1979), we held that the medical conditions for civil commitment must be proved by clear and convincing evidence. The purpose of this standard of proof, to reduce

Nor is the 600.30 hearing likely to raise these issues fairly and completely. An inmate recommended for involuntary medication is no more capable of "'speaking effectively for himself'" on these "issues which are 'complex or otherwise difficult to develop or present'" than an inmate recommended for transfer to a mental hospital. *Vitek*, 445 U. S., at 498 (Powell, J., concurring in part). Although single doses of some psychotropic drugs are designed to be effective for a full month, the inmate may not refuse the very medication he is contesting until 24 hours before his hearing.[29] Policy 600.30 also does not allow the inmate to be represented by counsel at hearings, but only to have present an adviser, who is appointed by the SOC. Lodging, Book 9, Policy 600.30, pp. 3–4. These advisers, of questionable loyalties and efficacy, cannot provide the "independent assistance" required for an inmate fairly to understand and participate in the hearing process. 445 U. S., at 498.[30] In addition, although the Policy gives the inmate a "limitable right to present testimony through his own witnesses and to confront and cross-examine witnesses," in the next paragraph it takes that right away for reasons that "include, but are not limited to such

---

the chances of inappropriate decisions, *id.*, at 427, is no less meaningful when the factfinders are professionals as when they are judges or jurors.

[29] Lodging, Book 9, Policy 600.30, p. 2. Prolixin decanoate, for example, is "a highly potent behavior modifier with a markedly extended duration of effect"; onset is between 24 to 72 hours after injection and effects can last 4–6 weeks. Physician's Desk Reference 1641–1642 (43d ed. 1989).

[30] The prisoner is introduced to, and may consult with, his appointed adviser at the commencement of the hearing. Harper's adviser on November 23, 1982, a nurse practitioner from Washington State Reformatory, asked Harper three questions in the hearing. Lodging, Book 8, Nov. 23, 1982, Hearing. The other five advisers appointed for Harper never spoke in the hearings. All five were apparently staff at the SOC: SOC Psychiatric Social Worker Hyden (who sat for the SOC Assistant Superintendent on the next 180-day committee that reapproved Harper's medication), a prison chaplain, two registered nurses, and a correctional officer. *Id.*, Book 8, Dec. 8, 1982, Dec. 30, 1983, Jan. 5, 1984, Oct. 31, 1984, and Nov. 7, 1984, Hearings.

things as irrelevance, lack of necessity, redundancy, possible reprisals, or other reasons relating to institutional interests of security, order, and rehabilitation." Lodging, Book 9, Policy 600.30, p. 3. Finally, because Policy 600.30 provides a hearing only for the 7-day committee, and just a paper record for the long-term committee, the inmate has no opportunity at all to present his objections to the more crucial decision to medicate him on a long-term basis.

In sum, it is difficult to imagine how a committee convened under Policy 660.30 could conceivably discover, much less be persuaded to overrule, an erroneous or arbitrary decision to medicate or to maintain a specific dosage or type of drug. See *Mathews* v. *Eldridge*, 424 U. S. 319, 335 (1976). Institutional control infects the decisionmakers and the entire procedure. The state courts that have reviewed comparable procedures have uniformly concluded that they do not adequately protect the significant liberty interest implicated by the forced administration of psychotropic drugs.[31] I agree with that conclusion. Although a review procedure administered by impartial, nonjudicial professionals might avoid the constitutional deficiencies in Policy 600.30, I would affirm the decision of the Washington Supreme Court requiring a judicial hearing, with its attendant procedural safeguards, as a remedy in this case.

---

[31] Many States require a judicial determination of incompetence, other findings, or a substituted judgment when a patient or inmate refuses psychotropic drugs. *E. g.*, *Riese* v. *St. Mary's Hospital and Medical Center*, 209 Cal. App. 3d 1303, 243 Cal. Rptr. 241 (1st Dist. 1988), review granted but dism'd, 774 P. 2d 698 (1989); *People* v. *Medina*, 705 P. 2d 961 (Colo. 1985) (en banc); *In re Boyd*, 403 A. 2d 744 (D. C. 1979); *In re Mental Commitment of M. P.*, 510 N. E. 2d 645 (Ind. 1987); *Rogers* v. *Commissioner of Dept. of Mental Health*, 390 Mass. 489, 458 N. E. 2d 308 (1983); *Jarvis* v. *Levine*, 418 N. W. 2d 139 (Minn. 1988); *Opinion of the Justices*, 123 N. H. 554, 465 A. 2d 484 (1983); *Rivers* v. *Katz*, 67 N. Y. 2d 485, 495 N. E. 2d 337 (1986); *In re Mental Health of K. K. B.*, 609 P. 2d 747 (Okla. 1980); *State ex rel. Jones* v. *Gerhardstein*, 141 Wis. 2d 710, 416 N. W. 2d 883 (1987).

I continue to believe that "even the inmate retains an unalienable interest in liberty—at the very minimum the right to be treated with dignity—which the Constitution may never ignore." *Meachum* v. *Fano*, 427 U. S. 215, 233 (1976) (dissenting opinion). A competent individual's right to refuse psychotropic medication is an aspect of liberty requiring the highest order of protection under the Fourteenth Amendment.[32] Accordingly, with the exception of Part II, I respectfully dissent from the Court's opinion and judgment.

[32] Only Harper's due process claim is before the Court. *Ante*, at 218, n. 5. His First Amendment, equal protection, state constitutional, and common-law tort claims have not yet been considered by the Washington state courts.

RIGGINS *v.* NEVADA

CERTIORARI TO THE SUPREME COURT OF NEVADA

No. 90–8466. Argued January 15, 1992—Decided May 18, 1992

When petitioner Riggins, while awaiting a Nevada trial on murder and robbery charges, complained of hearing voices and having sleep problems, a psychiatrist prescribed the antipsychotic drug Mellaril. After he was found competent to stand trial, Riggins made a motion to suspend the Mellaril's administration until after his trial, arguing that its use infringed upon his freedom, that its effect on his demeanor and mental state during trial would deny him due process, and that he had the right to show jurors his true mental state when he offered an insanity defense. After hearing the testimony of doctors who had examined Riggins, the trial court denied the motion with a one-page order giving no indication of its rationale. At Riggins' trial, he presented his insanity defense and testified, was convicted, and was sentenced to death. In affirming, the State Supreme Court held, *inter alia,* that expert testimony presented at trial was sufficient to inform the jury of the Mellaril's effect on Riggins' demeanor and testimony.

Held: The forced administration of antipsychotic medication during Riggins' trial violated rights guaranteed by the Sixth and Fourteenth Amendments. Pp. 133–138.

(a) The record narrowly defines the issues in this case. Administration of Mellaril was involuntary once Riggins' motion to terminate its use was denied, but its administration was medically appropriate. In addition, Riggins' Eighth Amendment argument that the drug's administration denied him the opportunity to show jurors his true mental condition at the sentencing hearing was not raised below or in the petition for certiorari and, thus, will not be considered by this Court. P. 133.

(b) A pretrial detainee has an interest in avoiding involuntary administration of antipsychotic drugs that is protected under the Due Process Clause. Cf. *Washington* v. *Harper,* 494 U. S. 210; *Bell* v. *Wolfish,* 441 U. S. 520, 545. Once Riggins moved to terminate his treatment, the State became obligated to establish both the need for Mellaril and its medical appropriateness. Cf. *Harper, supra,* at 227. Due process certainly would have been satisfied had the State shown that the treatment was medically appropriate and, considering less intrusive alternatives, essential for Riggins' own safety or the safety of others. The State also might have been able to justify the treatment, if medically appropriate, by showing that an adjudication of guilt or innocence could not be obtained by using less intrusive means. However, the trial court allowed the drug's administration to continue without making *any* determination of the need for this course or *any* findings about reasonable alternatives, and it failed to acknowledge Riggins' liberty interest in freedom from antipsychotic drugs. Pp. 133–137.

(c) There is a strong possibility that the trial court's error impaired Riggins' constitutionally protected trial rights. Efforts to prove or disprove actual prejudice from the record before this Court would be futile, and guesses as to the trial's outcome had Riggins' motion been granted would be speculative. While the precise consequences of forcing Mellaril upon him cannot be shown from a trial transcript, the testimony of doctors who examined Riggins establishes the strong possibility that his defense was impaired. Mellaril's side effects may have impacted not only his outward appearance, but also his testimony's content, his ability to follow the proceedings, or the substance of his communication with counsel. Thus, even if the expert testimony presented at trial allowed jurors to assess Riggins' demeanor fairly, an unacceptable risk remained that forced medication compromised his trial rights. Pp. 137–138.

(d) While trial prejudice can sometimes be justified by an essential state interest, the record here contains no finding to support a conclusion that administration of antipsychotic medication was necessary to accomplish an essential state policy. P. 138.

107 Nev. 178, 808 P. 2d 535, reversed and remanded.

O'CONNOR, J., delivered the opinion of the Court, in which REHNQUIST, C. J., and WHITE, BLACKMUN, STEVENS, and SOUTER, JJ., joined. KENNEDY, J., filed an opinion concurring in the judgment, *post*, p. 138. THOMAS, J., filed a dissenting opinion, in which SCALIA, J., joined except as to Part II–A, *post*, p. 146.

Mace J. Yampolsky argued the cause for petitioner. With him on the briefs were *Jay Topkis*, *Neal H. Klausner*, and *Steven C. Herzog*.

James Tufteland argued the cause for respondent. With him on the brief was *Rex Bell*.*

---

*Briefs of *amici curiae* urging reversal were filed for the Coalition for Fundamental Rights of Equality of Ex-patients by *Peter Margulies*, *Herbert Semmel*, and *Patrick Reilly*; for the National Association of Criminal

JUSTICE O'CONNOR delivered the opinion of the Court.

Petitioner David Riggins challenges his murder and robbery convictions on the ground that the State of Nevada unconstitutionally forced an antipsychotic drug upon him during trial. Because the Nevada courts failed to make findings sufficient to support forced administration of the drug, we reverse.

I

During the early hours of November 20, 1987, Paul Wade was found dead in his Las Vegas apartment. An autopsy revealed that Wade died from multiple stab wounds, including wounds to the head, chest, and back. David Riggins was arrested for the killing 45 hours later.

A few days after being taken into custody, Riggins told Dr. R. Edward Quass, a private psychiatrist who treated patients at the Clark County Jail, about hearing voices in his head and having trouble sleeping. Riggins informed Dr. Quass that he had been successfully treated with Mellaril in the past. Mellaril is the trade name for thioridazine, an antipsychotic drug. After this consultation, Dr. Quass prescribed Mellaril at a level of 100 milligrams per day. Because Riggins continued to complain of voices and sleep problems in the following months, Dr. Quass gradually increased the Mellaril prescription to 800 milligrams per day. Riggins also received a prescription for Dilantin, an antiepileptic drug.

In January 1988, Riggins successfully moved for a determination of his competence to stand trial. App. 6. Three

---

Defense Lawyers by *David M. Eldridge;* and for Nevada Attorneys for Criminal Justice by *Kevin M. Kelly.*

Briefs of *amici curiae* were filed for the State of Louisiana et al. by *William J. Guste, Jr.*, Attorney General of Louisiana, and *M. Patricia Jones* and *Kathleen E. Petersen*, Assistant Attorneys General, and by the Attorneys General for their respective States as follows: *Charles M. Oberly III* of Delaware and *Michael E. Carpenter* of Maine; and for the American Psychiatric Association by *Richard G. Taranto* and *Joel I. Klein.*

court-appointed psychiatrists performed examinations during February and March, while Riggins was taking 450 milligrams of Mellaril daily. Dr. William O'Gorman, a psychiatrist who had treated Riggins for anxiety in 1982, and Dr. Franklin Master concluded that Riggins was competent to stand trial. The third psychiatrist, Dr. Jack Jurasky, found that Riggins was incompetent. The Clark County District Court determined that Riggins was legally sane and competent to stand trial, *id.*, at 13, so preparations for trial went forward.

In early June, the defense moved the District Court for an order suspending administration of Mellaril and Dilantin until the end of Riggins' trial. *Id.*, at 20. Relying on both the Fourteenth Amendment and the Nevada Constitution, Riggins argued that continued administration of these drugs infringed upon his freedom and that the drugs' effect on his demeanor and mental state during trial would deny him due process. Riggins also asserted that, because he would offer an insanity defense at trial, he had a right to show jurors his "true mental state." *Id.*, at 22. In response, the State noted that Nevada law prohibits the trial of incompetent persons, see Nev. Rev. Stat. § 178.400 (1989), and argued that the court therefore had authority to compel Riggins to take medication necessary to ensure his competence. App. 31–32.

On July 14, 1988, the District Court held an evidentiary hearing on Riggins' motion. At the hearing, Dr. Master "guess[ed]" that taking Riggins off medication would not noticeably alter his behavior or render him incompetent to stand trial. Record 412. Dr. Quass testified that, in his opinion, Riggins would be competent to stand trial even without the administration of Mellaril, but that the effects of Mellaril would not be noticeable to jurors if medication continued. *Id.*, at 443–445. Finally, Dr. O'Gorman told the court that Mellaril made the defendant calmer and more relaxed but that an excessive dose would cause drowsiness. *Id.*, at 464–466. Dr. O'Gorman was unable to predict how Riggins might behave if taken off antipsychotic medication, yet he questioned the need to give Riggins the high dose he was receiving. *Id.*, at 474–476. The court also had before it a written report in which Dr. Jurasky held to his earlier view that Riggins was incompetent to stand trial and predicted that if taken off Mellaril the defendant "would most likely regress to a manifest psychosis and become extremely difficult to manage." App. 19.

The District Court denied Riggins' motion to terminate medication with a one-page order that gave no indication of the court's rationale. *Id.*, at 49. Riggins continued to receive 800 milligrams of Mellaril each day through the completion of his trial the following November.

At trial, Riggins presented an insanity defense and testified on his own behalf. He indicated that on the night of Wade's death he used cocaine before going to Wade's apartment. Riggins admitted fighting with Wade, but claimed that Wade was trying to kill him and that voices in his head said that killing Wade would be justifiable homicide. A jury found Riggins guilty of murder with use of a deadly weapon and robbery with use of a deadly weapon. After a penalty hearing, the same jury set the murder sentence at death.

Riggins presented several claims to the Nevada Supreme Court, among them that forced administration of Mellaril denied him the ability to assist in his own defense and prejudicially affected his attitude, appearance, and demeanor at trial. This prejudice was not justified, Riggins said in his opening brief, because the State neither demonstrated a need to administer Mellaril nor explored alternatives to giving him 800 milligrams of the drug each day. Record 1020. Riggins amplified this claim in his reply brief, objecting that the State intruded upon his constitutionally protected liberty interest in freedom from antipsychotic drugs without considering less intrusive options. Riggins argued:

> "In *United States v. Bryant*, 670 F. Supp. 840, 843 (Minn. 1987)[,] the court, in reference to medicating prisoners against their will, stated that 'courts have recognized a *protectable liberty interest* . . . in the freedom to avoid unwanted medication with such drugs.' The court in so stating cited *Bee v. Greaves*, 744 F. 2d 1387 (10th Cir. 1984)[,] which addressed the issue of medicating pre-trial detainees and stated that 'less restrictive alternatives, such as segregation or the use of less controversial drugs like tranquilizers or sedatives, should be ruled out before resorting to antipsychotic drugs.' In the case at bar, no less restrictive alternatives were utilized, considered or even proposed." Record 1070–1071 (emphasis in original).

The Nevada Supreme Court affirmed Riggins' convictions and death sentence. 107 Nev. 178, 808 P. 2d 535 (1991). With respect to administration of Mellaril, the court held that expert testimony presented at trial "was sufficient to inform the jury of the effect of the Mellaril on Riggins' demeanor and testimony." *Id.*, at 181, 808 P. 2d, at 538. Thus, although Riggins' demeanor was relevant to his insanity defense, the court held that denial of the defense's motion to terminate medication was neither an abuse of discretion nor a violation of Riggins' trial rights. In a concurring opinion, Justice Rose suggested that the District Court should have determined whether administration of Mellaril during trial was "absolutely necessary" by ordering a pretrial suspension of medication. *Id.*, at 185, 808 P. 2d, at 540 (concurring opinion). Justice Springer dissented, arguing that antipsychotic drugs may never be forced on a criminal defendant solely to allow prosecution. *Id.*, at 186, 808 P. 2d, at 541.

We granted certiorari, 502 U. S. 807 (1991), to decide whether forced administration of antipsychotic medication during trial violated rights guaranteed by the Sixth and Fourteenth Amendments.

II

The record in this case narrowly defines the issues before us. The parties have indicated that once the District Court denied Riggins' motion to terminate use of Mellaril, subsequent administration of the drug was involuntary. See, *e. g.*, Brief for Petitioner 6 (medication was "forced"); Brief for Respondent 14, 22, 28 (describing medication as "unwanted," "over objection," and "compelled"). This understanding accords with the determination of the Nevada Supreme Court. See 107 Nev., at 181; 808 P. 2d, at 537 (describing medication as "involuntary" and "forced"). Given the parties' positions on this point and the absence of any record evidence to the contrary, we adhere to the understanding of the State Supreme Court.

We also presume that administration of Mellaril was medically appropriate. Although defense counsel stressed that Riggins received a very high dose of the drug, at no point did he suggest to the Nevada courts that administration of Mellaril was medically improper treatment for his client.

Finally, the record is dispositive with respect to Riggins' Eighth Amendment claim that administration of Mellaril denied him an opportunity to show jurors his true mental condition at the sentencing hearing. Because this argument was presented neither to the Nevada Supreme Court nor in Riggins' petition for certiorari, we do not address it here.

With these considerations in mind, we turn to Riggins' core contention that involuntary administration of Mellaril denied him "a full and fair trial." Pet. for Cert. i. Our discussion in *Washington* v. *Harper*, 494 U. S. 210 (1990), provides useful background for evaluating this claim. In *Harper*, a prison inmate alleged that the State of Washington and various individuals violated his right to due process by giving him Mellaril and other antipsychotic drugs against his will. Although the inmate did not prevail, we agreed that his interest in avoiding involuntary administration of antipsychotic drugs was protected under the Fourteenth Amendment's Due Process Clause. "The forcible injection of medication into a nonconsenting person's body," we said, "represents a substantial interference with that person's liberty." *Id.*, at 229. In the case of antipsychotic drugs like Mellaril, that interference is particularly severe:

> "The purpose of the drugs is to alter the chemical balance in a patient's brain, leading to changes, intended to be beneficial, in his or her cognitive processes. While the therapeutic benefits of antipsychotic drugs are well documented, it is also true that the drugs can have serious, even fatal, side effects. One such side effect identified by the trial court is acute dystonia, a severe involuntary spasm of the upper body, tongue, throat, or eyes. The trial court found that it may be treated and reversed within a few minutes through use of the medication Cogentin. Other side effects include akathesia (motor restlessness, often characterized by an inability to sit still); neuroleptic malignant syndrome (a relatively rare condition which can lead to death from cardiac dysfunction); and tardive dyskinesia, perhaps the most discussed side effect of antipsychotic drugs. Tardive dyskinesia is a neurological disorder, irreversible in some cases, that is characterized by involuntary, uncontrollable movements of various muscles, especially around the face. . . . [T]he proportion of patients treated with antipsychotic drugs who exhibit the symptoms of tardive dyskinesia ranges from 10% to 25%. According to the American Psychiatric Association, studies of the condition indicate that 60% of tardive dyskinesia is mild or minimal in effect, and about 10% may be characterized as severe." *Id.*, at 229–230 (citations omitted).

Taking account of the unique circumstances of penal confinement, however, we determined that due process allows a mentally ill inmate to be treated involuntarily with antipsychotic drugs where there is a determination that "the inmate is dangerous to himself or others and the treatment is in the inmate's medical interest." *Id.*, at 227.

Under *Harper*, forcing antipsychotic drugs on a convicted prisoner is impermissible absent a finding of overriding justification and a determination of medical appropriateness. The Fourteenth Amendment affords at least as much protection to persons the State detains for trial. See *Bell* v. *Wolfish*, 441 U. S. 520, 545 (1979) ("[P]retrial detainees, who have not been convicted of any crimes, retain at least those constitutional rights that we have held are enjoyed by convicted prisoners"); *O'Lone* v. *Estate of Shabazz*, 482 U. S. 342, 349 (1987) ("[P]rison regulations . . . are judged under a 'reasonableness' test less restrictive than that ordinarily applied to alleged infringements of fundamental constitutional rights"). Thus, once Riggins moved to terminate administration of antipsychotic medication, the State became obligated to establish the need for Mellaril and the medical appropriateness of the drug.

Although we have not had occasion to develop substantive standards for judging forced administration of such drugs in the trial or pretrial settings, Nevada certainly would have satisfied due process if the prosecution had demonstrated, and the District Court had found, that treatment with antipsychotic medication was medically appropriate and, considering less intrusive alternatives, essential for the sake of Riggins' own safety or the safety of others. See *Harper*, *supra*, at 225–226; cf. *Addington* v. *Texas*, 441 U. S. 418 (1979) (Due Process Clause allows civil commitment of individuals shown by clear and convincing evidence to be mentally ill and dangerous). Similarly, the State might have been able to justify medically appropriate, involuntary treatment with the drug by establishing that it could not obtain an adjudication of Riggins' guilt or innocence by using less intrusive means. See *Illinois* v. *Allen*, 397 U. S. 337, 347

(1970) (Brennan, J., concurring) ("Constitutional power to bring an accused to trial is fundamental to a scheme of 'ordered liberty' and prerequisite to social justice and peace"). We note that during the July 14 hearing Riggins did not contend that he had the right to be tried without Mellaril if its discontinuation rendered him incompetent. See Record 424–425, 496, 500. The question whether a competent criminal defendant may refuse antipsychotic medication if cessation of medication would render him incompetent at trial is not before us.

Contrary to the dissent's understanding, we do not "adopt a standard of strict scrutiny." *Post*, at 156. We have no occasion to finally prescribe such substantive standards as mentioned above, since the District Court allowed administration of Mellaril to continue without making *any* determination of the need for this course or *any* findings about reasonable alternatives. The court's laconic order denying Riggins' motion did not adopt the State's view, which was that continued administration of Mellaril was required to ensure that the defendant could be tried; in fact, the hearing testimony casts considerable doubt on that argument. See *supra*, at 130–131. Nor did the order indicate a finding that safety considerations or other compelling concerns outweighed Riggins' interest in freedom from unwanted antipsychotic drugs.

Were we to divine the District Court's logic from the hearing transcript, we would have to conclude that the court simply weighed the risk that the defense would be prejudiced by changes in Riggins' outward appearance against the chance that Riggins would become incompetent if taken off Mellaril, and struck the balance in favor of involuntary medication. See Record 502 ("[T]hat he was nervous and so forth . . . can all be brought out [through expert testimony]. And when you start weighing the consequences of taking him off his medication and possibly have him revert into an incompetent situation, I don't think that that is a good experiment"). The court did not acknowledge the defendant's liberty interest in freedom from unwanted antipsychotic drugs.

This error may well have impaired the constitutionally protected trial rights Riggins invokes. At the hearing to consider terminating medication, Dr. O'Gorman suggested that the dosage administered to Riggins was within the toxic range, *id.*, at 483, and could make him "uptight," *id.*, at 484. Dr. Master testified that a patient taking 800 milligrams of Mellaril each day might suffer from drowsiness or confusion. *Id.*, at 416. Cf. Brief for American Psychiatric Association as *Amicus Curiae* 10–11 ("[I]n extreme cases, the sedation-like effect [of antipsychotic medication] may be severe enough (akinesia) to affect thought processes"). It is clearly possible that such side effects had an impact upon not just Riggins' outward appearance, but also the content of his testimony on direct or cross examination, his ability to follow the proceedings, or the substance of his communication with counsel.

Efforts to prove or disprove actual prejudice from the record before us would be futile, and guesses whether the outcome of the trial might have been different if Riggins' motion had been granted would be purely speculative. We accordingly reject the dissent's suggestion that Riggins should be required to demonstrate how the trial would have proceeded differently if he had not been given Mellaril. See *post*, at 149–150. Like the consequences of compelling a defendant to wear prison clothing, see *Estelle* v. *Williams*, 425 U. S. 501, 504–505 (1976), or of binding and gagging an accused during trial, see *Allen*, *supra*, at 344, the precise consequences of forcing antipsychotic medication upon Riggins cannot be shown from a trial transcript. What the testimony of doctors who examined Riggins establishes, and what we will not ignore, is a strong possibility that Riggins' defense was impaired due to the administration of Mellaril.

We also are persuaded that allowing Riggins to present expert testimony about the effect of Mellaril on his demeanor did nothing to cure the possibility that the substance of his own testimony, his interaction with counsel, or his comprehension at trial were compromised by forced administration of Mellaril. Even if (as the dissent argues, *post*, at 147–149) the Nevada Supreme Court was right that expert testimony allowed jurors to assess Riggins' demeanor fairly, an unacceptable risk of prejudice remained. See 107 Nev., at 181, 808 P. 2d, at 537–538.

To be sure, trial prejudice can sometimes be justified by an essential state interest. See *Holbrook* v. *Flynn*, 475 U. S. 560, 568–569 (1986); *Allen, supra*, at 344 (binding and gagging the accused permissible only in extreme situations where it is the "fairest and most reasonable way" to control a disruptive defendant); see also *Williams, supra*, at 505 (compelling defendants to wear prison clothing at trial furthers no essential state policy). Because the record contains no finding that might support a conclusion that administration of antipsychotic medication was necessary to accomplish an essential state policy, however, we have no basis for saying that the substantial probability of trial prejudice in this case was justified.

The judgment of the Nevada Supreme Court is reversed, and the case is remanded for further proceedings not inconsistent with this opinion.

It is so ordered.

JUSTICE KENNEDY, concurring in the judgment.

The medical and pharmacological data in the *amicus* briefs and other sources indicate that involuntary medication with antipsychotic drugs poses a serious threat to a defendant's right to a fair trial. In the case before us, there was no hearing or well-developed record on the point, and the whole subject of treating incompetence to stand trial by drug medication is somewhat new to the law, if not to medicine. On the sparse record before us, we cannot give full consideration to the issue. I file this separate opinion, however, to express my view that absent an extraordinary showing by the State, the Due Process Clause prohibits prosecuting officials from administering involuntary doses of antipsychotic medicines for purposes of rendering the accused competent for trial, and to express doubt that the showing can be made in most cases, given our present understanding of the properties of these drugs.

At the outset, I express full agreement with the Court's conclusion that one who was medicated against his will in order to stand trial may challenge his conviction. When the State commands medication during the pretrial and trial phases of the case for the avowed purpose of changing the defendant's behavior, the concerns are much the same as if it were alleged that the prosecution had manipulated material evidence. See *Brady* v. *Maryland,* 373 U. S. 83, 87 (1963) (suppression by the prosecution of material evidence favorable to the accused violates due process); *Arizona* v. *Youngblood,* 488 U. S. 51, 58 (1988) (bad-faith failure to preserve potentially useful evidence constitutes a due process violation). I cannot accept the premise of JUSTICE THOMAS' dissent that the involuntary medication order comprises some separate procedure, unrelated to the trial and foreclosed from inquiry or review in the criminal proceeding itself. To the contrary, the allegations pertain to the State's interference with the trial. Thus, review in the criminal proceeding is appropriate.

I also agree with the majority that the State has a legitimate interest in attempting to restore the competence of otherwise incompetent defendants. Its interest derives from the State's right to bring an accused to trial and from our holding in *Pate* v. *Robinson,* 383 U. S. 375, 378 (1966), that conviction of an incompetent defendant violates due process. Unless a defendant is competent, the State cannot put him on trial. Competence to stand trial is rudimentary, for upon it depends the main part of those rights deemed essential to a fair trial, including the right to effective assistance of counsel, the rights to summon, to confront, and to cross-examine witnesses, and the right to testify on one's own behalf or to remain silent without penalty for doing so. *Drope* v. *Missouri*, 420 U. S. 162, 171–172 (1975). Although the majority is correct that this case does not require us to address the question whether a defendant may waive his right to be tried while competent, in my view a general rule permitting waiver would not withstand scrutiny under the Due Process Clause, given our holdings in *Pate* and *Drope*. A defendant's waiver of the right to be tried while competent would cast doubt on his exercise or waiver of all subsequent rights and privileges through the whole course of the trial.

The question is whether the State's interest in conducting the trial allows it to ensure the defendant's competence by involuntary medication, assuming of course there is a sound medical basis for the treatment. The Court's opinion will require further proceedings on remand, but there seems to be little discussion about what is to be considered. The Court's failure to address these issues is understandable in some respects, for it was not the subject of briefing or argument; but to underscore my reservations about the propriety of involuntary medication for the purpose of rendering the defendant competent, and to explain what I think ought to be express qualifications of the Court's opinion, some discussion of the point is required.

This is not a case like *Washington* v. *Harper*, 494 U. S. 210 (1990), in which the purpose of the involuntary medication was to ensure that the incarcerated person ceased to be a physical danger to himself or others. The inquiry in that context is both objective and manageable. Here the purpose of the medication is not merely to treat a person with grave psychiatric disorders and enable that person to function and behave in a way not dangerous to himself or others, but rather to render the person competent to stand trial. It is the last part of the State's objective, medicating the person for the purpose of bringing him to trial, that causes most serious concern. If the only question were whether some bare level of functional competence can be induced, that would be a grave matter in itself, but here there are even more far reaching concerns. The avowed purpose of the medication is not functional competence, but competence to stand trial. In my view elementary protections against state intrusion require the State in every case to make a showing that there is no significant risk that the medication will impair or alter in any material way the defendant's capacity or willingness to react to the testimony at trial or to assist his counsel. Based on my understanding of the medical literature, I have substantial reservations that the State can make that showing. Indeed, the inquiry itself is elusive, for it assumes some baseline of normality that experts may have some difficulty in establishing for a particular defendant, if they can establish it at all. These uncertainties serve to underscore the difficult terrain the State must traverse when it enters this domain.

To make these concerns concrete, the effects of antipsychotic drugs must be addressed. First introduced in the 1950's, antipsychotic drugs such as Mellaril have wide acceptance in the psychiatric community as an effective treatment for psychotic thought disorders. See American Psychiatric Press Textbook of Psychiatry 770–774 (J. Talbott, R. Hales, & S. Yodofsky eds. 1988) (Textbook of Psychiatry); Brief for American Psychiatric Association as *Amicus Curiae* 6–7. The medications restore normal thought processes by clearing hallucinations and delusions. Textbook of Psychiatry 774. See also Brief for American Psychiatric Association as *Amicus Curiae* 9 ("The mental health produced by antipsychotic medication is no different from, no more inauthentic or alien to the patient than, the physical health produced by other medications, such as penicillin for pneumonia"). For many patients, no effective alternative exists for treatment of their illnesses. *Id.*, at 7, and n. 3.

Although these drugs have changed the lives of psychiatric patients, they can have unwanted side effects. We documented some of the more serious side effects in *Washington* v. *Harper*, *supra*, at 229–230, and they are mentioned again in the majority opinion. More relevant to this case are side effects that, it appears, can compromise the right of a medicated criminal defendant to receive a fair trial. The drugs can prejudice the accused in two principal ways: (1) by altering his demeanor in a manner that will prejudice his reactions and presentation in the courtroom, and (2) by rendering him unable or unwilling to assist counsel.

It is a fundamental assumption of the adversary system that the trier of fact observes the accused throughout the trial, while the accused is either on the stand or sitting at the defense table. This assumption derives from the right to be present at trial, which in turn derives from the right to testify and rights under the Confrontation Clause. *Taylor* v. *United States*, 414 U. S. 17, 19 (1973) *(per curiam)*. At all stages of the proceedings, the defendant's behavior, manner, facial expressions, and emotional responses, or their absence, combine to make an overall impression on the trier of fact, an impression that can have a powerful influence on the outcome of the trial. If the defendant takes the stand, as Riggins did, his demeanor can have a great bearing on his credibility and persuasiveness, and on the degree to which he evokes sympathy. The defendant's demeanor may also be relevant to his confrontation rights. See *Coy* v. *Iowa*, 487 U. S. 1012, 1016–1020 (1988) (emphasizing the importance of the face-to-face encounter between the accused and the accuser).

The side effects of antipsychotic drugs may alter demeanor in a way that will prejudice all facets of the defense. Serious due process concerns are implicated when the State manipulates the evidence in this way. The defendant may be restless and unable to sit still. Brief for American Psychiatric Association as *Amicus Curiae* 10. The drugs can induce a condition called parkinsonism, which, like Parkinson's disease, is characterized by tremor of the limbs, diminished range of facial expression, or slowed functions, such as speech. *Ibid.* Some of the side effects are more subtle. Antipsychotic drugs such as Mellaril can have a "sedation-like effect" that in severe cases may affect thought processes. *Ibid.* At trial, Dr. Jurasky testified that Mellaril has "a tranquilizer effect." Record 752. See also *ibid.* ("If you are dealing with someone very sick then you may prescribe up to 800 milligrams which is the dose he had been taking which is very, very high. I mean you can tranquilize an elephant with 800 milligrams"). Dr. Jurasky listed the following side effects of large doses of Mellaril: "Drowsiness, constipation, perhaps lack of alertness, changes in blood pressure. . . . Depression of the psychomotor functions. If you take a lot of it you become stoned for all practical purposes and can barely function." *Id.*, at 753.

These potential side effects would be disturbing for any patient; but when the patient is a criminal defendant who is going to stand trial, the documented probability of side effects seems to me to render involuntary administration of the drugs by prosecuting officials unacceptable absent a showing by the State that the side effects will not alter the defendant's reactions or diminish his capacity to assist counsel. As the American Psychiatric Association points out:

> "By administering medication, the State may be creating a prejudicial negative demeanor in the defendant—making him look nervous and restless, for example, or so calm or sedated as to appear bored, cold, unfeeling, and unresponsive. . . . That such effects may be subtle does not make them any less real or potentially influential." Brief for American Psychiatric Association as *Amicus Curiae* 13.

As any trial attorney will attest, serious prejudice could result if medication inhibits the defendant's capacity to react and respond to the proceedings and to demonstrate remorse or compassion. The prejudice can be acute during the sentencing phase of the proceedings, when the sentencer must attempt to know the heart and mind of the offender and judge his character, his contrition or its absence, and his future dangerousness. In a capital sentencing proceeding, assessments of character and remorse may carry great weight and, perhaps, be determinative of whether the offender lives or dies. See Geimer & Amsterdam, Why Jurors Vote Life or Death: Operative Factors in Ten Florida Death Penalty Cases, 15 Am. J. Crim. L. 1, 51–53 (1987–1988).

Concerns about medication extend also to the issue of cooperation with counsel. We have held that a defendant's right to the effective assistance of counsel is impaired when he cannot cooperate in an active manner with his lawyer. *Massiah* v. *United States*, 377 U. S. 201 (1964); *Geders* v. *United States*, 425 U. S. 80 (1976) (trial court order directing defendant not to consult with his lawyer during an overnight recess held to deprive him of the effective assistance of counsel). The defendant must be able to provide needed information to his lawyer and to participate in the making of decisions on his own behalf. The side effects of antipsychotic drugs can hamper the attorney-client relation, preventing effective communication and rendering the defendant less able or willing to take part in his defense. The State interferes with this relation when it administers a drug to dull cognition. See Brief for National Association of Criminal Defense Lawyers as *Amicus Curiae* 42 ("[T]he chemical flattening of a person's will can also lead to the defendant's loss of self-determination undermining the desire for self-preservation which is necessary to engage the defendant in his own defense in preparation for his trial").

It is well established that the defendant has the right to testify on his own behalf, a right we have found essential to our adversary system. *In re Oliver*, 333 U. S. 257, 273 (1948). We have found the right implicit as well in the Compulsory Process Clause of the Sixth Amendment. *Rock* v. *Arkansas*, 483 U. S. 44 (1987). In *Rock*, we held that a state rule excluding all testimony aided or refreshed by hypnosis violated the defendant's constitutional right to take the stand in her own defense. We observed that barring the testimony would contradict not only the right of the accused to conduct her own defense, but also her right to make this defense in person: "'It is the accused, not counsel, who must be "informed of the nature and cause of the accusation," who must be "confronted with the witnesses against him," and who must be accorded "compulsory process for obtaining witnesses in his favor."'" *Id.*, at 52, quoting *Faretta* v. *California*, 422 U. S. 806, 819 (1975). We gave further recognition to the right of the accused to testify in his or her own words, and noted that this in turn was related to the Fifth Amendment choice to speak "in the unfettered exercise of his own will." *Rock, supra*, at 53. In my view medication of the type here prescribed may be for the very purpose of imposing constraints on the defendant's own will, and for that reason its legitimacy is put in grave doubt.

If the State cannot render the defendant competent without involuntary medication, then it must resort to civil commitment, if appropriate, unless the defendant becomes competent through other means. If the defendant cannot be tried without his behavior and demeanor being affected in this substantial way by involuntary treatment, in my view the Constitution requires that society bear this cost in order to preserve the integrity of the trial process. The state of our knowledge of antipsychotic drugs and their side effects is evolving and may one day produce effective drugs that have only minimal side effects. Until that day comes, we can permit their use only when the State can show that involuntary treatment does not cause alterations raising the concerns enumerated in this separate opinion.

With these observations, I concur in the judgment reversing the conviction.

JUSTICE THOMAS, with whom JUSTICE SCALIA joins except as to Part II–A, dissenting.

Petitioner David Edward Riggins killed Paul William Wade by stabbing him 32 times with a knife. He then took cash, drugs, and other items from Wade's home. A Nevada jury convicted Riggins of first-degree murder and robbery with a deadly weapon and sentenced him to death. The Nevada Supreme Court affirmed. 107 Nev. 178, 808 P. 2d 535 (1991). This Court reverses the conviction, holding that Nevada unconstitutionally deprived Riggins of his liberty interest in avoiding unwanted medication by compelling him to take an antipsychotic drug. I respectfully dissent.

The Court's opinion, in my view, conflates two distinct questions: whether Riggins had a full and fair criminal trial and whether Nevada improperly forced Riggins to take medication. In this criminal case, Riggins is asking, and may ask, only for the reversal of his conviction and sentence. He is not seeking, and may not seek, an injunction to terminate his medical treatment or damages for an infringement of his personal rights. I agree with the positions of the majority and concurring opinions in the Nevada Supreme Court: Even if the State truly forced Riggins to take medication, and even if this medication deprived Riggins of a protected liberty interest in a manner actionable in a different legal proceeding, Riggins nonetheless had the fundamentally fair criminal trial required by the Constitution. I therefore would affirm his conviction.

I

Riggins contended in the Nevada Supreme Court that he did not have a " 'full and fair' trial" for two reasons, the first relating to exclusion of evidence of his mental condition and the second concerning his ability to assist in his defense. Record 1018. To the extent that Riggins' arguments below involved federal constitutional issues, I believe that the Nevada Supreme Court correctly rejected them.

A

Riggins first argued that the trial court improperly prevented him from presenting relevant evidence of his demeanor. As the Court notes, Riggins suffers from a mental illness and raised insanity as a defense at trial. When Riggins killed Wade, he was not using any antipsychotic medication. During his trial, however, Riggins was taking large doses of the antipsychotic drug Mellaril. Riggins believed that this drug would make his appearance at trial different from his appearance when he attacked Wade and that this difference might cause the jury to misjudge his sanity. To show his mental condition as it existed at the time of the crime, Riggins requested permission to appear before the jury in an unmedicated state. App. 20–24, 42–47. The trial court denied the request, and the Nevada Supreme Court affirmed.

This Court has no power to decide questions concerning the admissibility of evidence under Nevada law. *Estelle* v. *McGuire*, 502 U. S. 62, 67–68 (1991). We therefore may conduct only a limited review of a Nevada court's decision to exclude a particular form of demeanor evidence. Except in cases involving a violation of a specific constitutional provision such as the Confrontation Clause, see, *e. g., Ohio* v. *Roberts*, 448 U. S. 56 (1980), this Court may not reverse a state "trial judge's action in the admission of evidence" unless the evidentiary ruling "so infuse[s] the trial with unfairness as to deny due process of law." *Lisenba* v. *California*, 314 U. S. 219, 228 (1941). See also *Marshall* v. *Lonberger*, 459 U. S. 422, 438, n. 6 (1983); *Burgett* v. *Texas*, 389 U. S. 109, 113–114 (1967). In this case, I see no basis for concluding that Riggins had less than a full and fair trial.

The Court declines to decide whether Mellaril actually affected Riggins' appearance. On the basis of some pretrial psychiatric testimony it speculates only that Riggins might have looked less uptight, drowsy, or confused if he had not taken the drug. *Ante*, at 137. Other evidence casts doubt on this possibility. At least one psychiatrist believed that a jury would not "be able to notice whether or not [Riggins] was on Mellaril as compared to the period of the time when he was not medicated by that drug." Record 445. Yet, even if Mellaril noticeably affected Riggins' demeanor, the Court fails to explain why the medication's effects rendered Riggins' trial fundamentally unfair.

The trial court offered Riggins the opportunity to prove his mental condition as it existed at the time of the crime through testimony instead of his appearance in court in an unmedicated condition. Riggins took advantage of this offer by explaining to the jury the history of his mental health, his usage of Mellaril, and the possible effects of Mellaril on his demeanor. *Id.*, at 739–740. Riggins also called Dr. Jack A. Jurasky, a psychiatrist, who testified about Riggins' condition after his arrest and his likely mental state at the time of the crime. *Id.*, at 747–748. Dr. Jurasky also explained Riggins' use of Mellaril and how it might be affecting him. *Id.*, at 752–753, 760–761.

The Nevada Supreme Court concluded that this "testimony was sufficient to inform the jury of the effect of the Mellaril on Riggins' demeanor and testimony." 107 Nev., at 181, 808 P. 2d, at 538. Its analysis comports with that of other state courts that also have held that expert testimony may suffice to clarify the effects of an antipsychotic drug on a defendant's apparent demeanor. See *State* v. *Law*, 270 S. C. 664, 673, 244 S. E. 2d 302, 306 (1978); *State* v. *Jojola*, 89 N. M. 489, 493, 553 P. 2d 1296, 1300 (1976). Cf. *In re Pray*, 133 Vt. 253, 257–258, 336 A. 2d 174, 177 (1975) (reversing a conviction because no expert testimony explained how antipsychotic medicine affected the defendant's appearance). Having reviewed the record as a whole, I see no reason to disturb the conclusion of the Nevada Supreme Court. On the facts of this case, Riggins' inability to introduce evidence of his mental condition as he desired did not render his trial fundamentally unfair. See *Rock* v. *Arkansas*, 483

U. S. 44, 55, n. 11 (1987); *id.*, at 64–65 (REHNQUIST, C. J., dissenting).

B

Riggins also argued in the Nevada Supreme Court, although not in his briefs to this Court, that he did not have a "'full and fair' trial" because Mellaril had side effects that interfered with his ability to participate in his defense. Record 1018. He alleged, in particular, that the drug tended to limit his powers of perception. The Court accepts this contention, stating: "It is clearly *possible* that such side effects had an impact upon . . . the content of his testimony on direct or cross examination, his ability to follow the proceedings, or the substance of his communication with counsel." *Ante*, at 137 (emphasis added). I disagree. We cannot conclude that Riggins had less than a full and fair trial merely because of the possibility that Mellaril had side effects.

All criminal defendants have a right to a full and fair trial, and a violation of this right may occur if a State tries a defendant who lacks a certain ability to comprehend or participate in the proceedings. We have said that "the Due Process Clause guarantees the fundamental elements of fairness in a criminal trial," *Spencer* v. *Texas*, 385 U. S. 554, 563–564 (1967), and have made clear that "conviction of an accused person while he is legally incompetent violates due process," *Pate* v. *Robinson*, 383 U. S. 375, 378 (1966).

Riggins has no claim of legal incompetence in this case. The trial court specifically found him competent while he was taking Mellaril under a statute requiring him to have "sufficient mentality to be able to understand the nature of the criminal charges against him, and . . . to aid and assist his counsel in the defense interposed upon the trial." Nev. Rev. Stat. § 178.400(2) (1989). Riggins does not assert that due process imposes a higher standard.

The record does not reveal any other form of unfairness relating to the purported side effects of Mellaril. Riggins has failed to allege specific facts to support his claim that he could not participate effectively in his defense. He has not stated how he would have directed his counsel to examine or cross-examine witnesses differently. He has not identified any testimony or instructions that he did not understand. The record, moreover, does not even support his assertion that Mellaril made him worse off. As Justice Rose noted in his concurring opinion below: "Two psychiatrists who had prescribed Mellaril for Riggins, Dr. Quass and Dr. O'Gorman, testified that they believed it was helpful to him. Additional psychiatric testimony established that Mellaril may have increased Riggins' cognitive ability . . . ." 107 Nev., at 185, 808 P. 2d, at 540. See also *State* v. *Hayes*, 118 N. H. 458, 461, 389 A. 2d 1379, 1381 (1978) (holding a defendant's perception adequate because "[a]ll the expert evidence support[ed] the conclusion that the medication ha[d] a beneficial effect on the defendant's ability to function").[1] Riggins' competence, moreover, tends to confirm that he had a fair trial. See *State* v. *Jojola, supra,* at 492, 553 P. 2d, at 1299 (presuming, absent other evidence, that the side effects of an antipsychotic drug did not render a competent defendant unable to participate fully in his trial). I thus see no basis for reversing the Nevada Supreme Court.

II

Riggins also argues for reversal on the basis of our holding in *Washington* v. *Harper*, 494 U. S. 210, 221 (1990), that the Due Process Clause protects a substantive "liberty interest" in avoiding unwanted medication. Riggins asserts that Nevada unconstitutionally deprived him of this liberty interest by forcing him to take Mellaril. The Court agrees, ruling

[1] We previously have noted that "'[p]sychotropic medication is widely accepted within the psychiatric community as an extraordinarily effective treatment for both acute and chronic psychoses, particularly schizophrenia.'" *Washington* v. *Harper*, 494 U. S. 210, 226, n. 9 (1990) (quoting Brief for American Psychiatric Association et al. as *Amici Curiae*, O. T. 1989, No. 88-599, pp. 10-11).

that "the Nevada courts failed to make findings sufficient to support forced administration of the drug" in this case. *Ante*, at 129. I consider reversal on this basis improper.

A

Riggins may not complain about a deprivation of the liberty interest that we recognized in *Harper* because the record does not support his version of the facts. Shortly after his arrest, as the Court notes, Riggins told a psychiatrist at his jail that he was hearing voices and could not sleep. The psychiatrist prescribed Mellaril. When the prescription did not eliminate the problem, Riggins sought further treatment and the psychiatrist increased the dosage. Riggins thus began taking the drug voluntarily. *Ante*, at 129.

The Court concludes that the medication became involuntary when the trial court denied Riggins' motion for permission not to take the drug during the trial. *Ante*, at 133. I disagree. Although the court denied Riggins' motion, it did not order him to take any medication.[2] Moreover, even though Riggins *alleges* that the *state physicians* forced him to take the medication after the court's order, the record contains no finding of fact with respect to this allegation. The Court admits that it merely assumes that the physicians drugged him, and attempts to justify its assumption by observing that the Nevada Supreme Court also assumed that involuntary medication occurred. *Ibid.* The Nevada Supreme Court, however, may have made its assumption for the purpose of argument; the assumption, in its view, did

---

[2] Riggins' counsel confirmed this interpretation of the order at oral argument:

"QUESTION: . . . [D]id the court ever go further than saying I will not order the State to stop administering the medication? . . . It simply said . . . I won't intervene and enjoin the administration of this medication[.]

"MR. YAMPOLSKY: Yes . . . .

"QUESTION: So if [Riggins] had then said, well, I'm not going to take it, he wouldn't be in violation of the court order? . . .

"Mr. YAMPOLSKY: Apparently not." Tr. of Oral Arg. 10.

not change the result of the case. The Court cannot make the same assumption if it requires reversal of Riggins' conviction.

Riggins also cannot complain about a violation of *Harper* because he did not argue below for reversal of his conviction on the ground that Nevada had deprived him of a liberty interest. Riggins consistently maintained in the Nevada courts that he did not have a "full and fair trial" because the medication deprived him of the opportunity to present his demeanor to the jury and to participate in his defense. App. 20–24 (trial court motion); *id.*, at 42–47 (trial court reply); Record 1018–1021 (appellate brief); *id.*, at 1068–1071 (appellate reply brief). As counsel for Nevada put it at oral argument: "The way this issue was initially presented to the trial court was really a question of trial strategy. There was never an indication in this case that Mr. Riggins was a Harper-type defendant who did not want to be medicated." Tr. of Oral Arg. 23.[3]

Because the claims that Riggins raised below have no merit, Riggins has altered his theory of the case. The Court, therefore, should not condemn the Nevada courts because they "did not acknowledge the defendant's liberty interest in freedom from unwanted antipsychotic drugs." *Ante*, at 137. The Nevada courts had no reason to consider an argument that Riggins did not make. We have said quite recently that "[i]n reviewing the judgments of state courts under the jurisdictional grant of 28 U. S. C. § 1257, the Court has, with very rare exceptions, refused to consider petition-

[3] Riggins noted in his reply brief before the Nevada Supreme Court that the courts in *United States* v. *Bryant*, 670 F. Supp. 840, 843 (Minn. 1987), and *Bee* v. *Greaves*, 744 F. 2d 1387 (CA10 1984), had recognized a personal liberty interest in avoiding unwanted medication. Record 1070–1071. Yet, Riggins never asked for reversal because of a deprivation of this interest. He argued for reversal in that brief only on grounds that the medication "violated [his] right to a 'full and fair' trial because it denied him the ability to assist in his defense, and prejudiced his demeanor, attitude, and appearance to the jury." *Id.*, at 1068.

ers' claims that were not raised or addressed below." *Yee* v. *Escondido*, 503 U. S. 519, 533 (1992). Although "we have expressed inconsistent views as to whether this rule is jurisdictional or prudential in cases arising from state courts," *ibid.*, the Court does not attempt to justify its departure here.

Finally, we did not grant certiorari to determine whether the Nevada courts had made the findings required by *Harper* to support forced administration of a drug. We took this case to decide "[w]hether forced medication during trial violates a defendant's constitutional right to a full and fair trial." Pet. for Cert. The Court declines to answer this question one way or the other, stating only that a violation of *Harper* "may well have impaired the constitutionally protected trial rights Riggins invokes." *Ante*, at 137. As we have stated, "we ordinarily do not consider questions outside those presented in the petition for certiorari." *Yee* v. *Escondido*, *supra*, at 535. I believe that we should refuse to consider Riggins' *Harper* argument.

B

The *Harper* issue, in any event, does not warrant reversal of Riggins' conviction. The Court correctly states that Riggins, as a detainee awaiting trial, had at least the same liberty interest in avoiding unwanted medication that the inmate had in *Harper*. This case, however, differs from *Harper* in a very significant respect. When the inmate in *Harper* complained that physicians were drugging him against his will, he sought damages and an injunction against future medication in a civil action under 42 U. S. C. § 1983. See 494 U. S., at 217. Although Riggins also complains of forced medication, he is seeking a reversal of his criminal conviction. I would not expand *Harper* to include this remedy.

We have held that plaintiffs may receive civil remedies for all manner of constitutional violations under § 1983. See

Dennis v. *Higgins*, 498 U. S. 439, 443–451 (1991). This Court, however, has reversed criminal convictions only on the basis of two kinds of constitutional deprivations: those "which occu[r] during the presentation of the case" to the trier of fact, and those which cause a "structural defect affecting the framework" of the trial. *Arizona* v. *Fulminante*, 499 U. S. 279, 307, 310 (1991). The Court does not reveal why it considers a deprivation of a liberty interest in avoiding unwanted medication to fall into either category of reversible error. Even if Nevada failed to make the findings necessary to support forced administration of Mellaril, this failure, without more, would not constitute a trial error or a flaw in the trial mechanism. See 107 Nev., at 185, 808 P. 2d, at 540 (Rose, J., concurring). Although Riggins might be entitled to other remedies, he has no right to have his conviction reversed.[4]

---

[4] A State, however, might violate a defendant's due process right to a fundamentally fair trial if its administration of medication were to *diminish* substantially the defendant's mental faculties during the trial, even if he were not thereby rendered incompetent. See 3 E. Coke, Institutes *34 (1797) ("If felons come in judgement to answer, . . . they shall be out of irons, and all manner of bonds, so that their pain shall not take away any manner of reason, nor them constrain to answer, but at their free will"); Resolutions of the Judges upon the Case of the Regicides, Kelyng's Report of Divers Cases in Pleas of the Crown 10 (1708) (Old Bailey 1660) ("It was resolved that when Prisoners come to the Bar to be tryed, their Irons ought to be taken off, so that they be not in any Torture while they make their defense, be their Crime never so great"), reprinted in 5 How. St. Tr. 971, 979–980 (1816); *Trial of Christopher Layer*, 16 How. St. Tr. 94, 100 (1812) [K. B. 1722] ("[T]he authority is that [the defendant] is not to be 'in vinculis' during his trial, but should be so far free, that he should have the use of his reason, and all advantages to clear his innocence"); see also *State* v. *Williams*, 18 Wash. 47, 49–51, 50 P. 580, 581 (1897) ("'[T]he condition of the prisoner in shackles may, to some extent, deprive him of the free and calm use of all his faculties'") (quoting *State* v. *Kring*, 64 Mo. 591 (1877)). Riggins has not made (much less proved) any such allegation in this Court; indeed, the record indicates that Riggins' mental capacity was *enhanced* by his administration of Mellaril.

We applied a similar analysis in *Estelle* v. *Williams*, 425 U. S. 501 (1976). In that case, a prisoner challenged his conviction on grounds that the State had required him to wear prison garb before the jury. In reviewing the challenge, we did not ask whether the State had violated some personal right of the defendant to select his attire. Instead, we considered only whether the prison clothing had denied him a "fair trial" by making his appearance less favorable to the jury. *Id.*, at 503. Although we ultimately declined to reach the merits because the prisoner had waived the issue at trial, *id.*, at 512, we observed that lower courts had held that "a showing of actual prejudice must be made by a defendant seeking to have his conviction overturned on this ground," *id.*, at 504, n. 1. In my view, just as the validity of the conviction in *Estelle* v. *Williams* would depend on whether the prisoner had a fair trial, so does the validity of Riggins' conviction.

The need for requiring actual unfairness in this case (either in the form of a structural defect or an error in the presentation of evidence) becomes apparent when one considers how the Court might apply its decision to other cases. A State could violate *Harper* by forcibly administering *any* kind of medication to a criminal defendant. Yet, the Court surely would not reverse a criminal conviction for a *Harper* violation involving medications such as penicillin or aspirin. Perhaps Mellaril, in general, has a greater likelihood of affecting a person's appearance and powers of perceptions than these substances. As noted above, however, we have no indication in this case, considering the record as a whole, that Mellaril unfairly prejudiced Riggins.

I do not mean in any way to undervalue the importance of a person's liberty interest in avoiding forced medication or to suggest that States may drug detainees at their whim. Under *Harper*, detainees have an interest in avoiding unwanted medication that the States must respect. In appropriate instances, detainees may seek damages or injunctions against further medication in civil actions either under § 1983, as in *Harper*, or under state law. Yet, when this Court reviews a state-court criminal conviction of a defendant who has taken medication, it cannot undo any violation that already has occurred or punish those responsible. It may determine only whether the defendant received a proper trial, free of the kinds of reversible errors that we have recognized. Because Riggins had a full and fair trial in this case, I would affirm the Nevada Supreme Court.

C

For the foregoing reasons, I find it unnecessary to address the precise standards governing the forced administration of drugs to persons such as Riggins. Whether or not Nevada violated these standards, I would affirm Riggins' conviction. I note, however, that the Court's discussion of these standards poses troubling questions. Although the Court purports to rely on *Washington* v. *Harper*, the standards that it applies in this case differ in several respects.

The Court today, for instance, appears to adopt a standard of strict scrutiny. It specifically faults the trial court for failing to find either that the "continued administration of Mellaril was *required* to ensure that the defendant could be tried," *ante*, at 136 (emphasis added), or that "other *compelling* concerns outweighed Riggins' interest in freedom from unwanted antipsychotic drugs," *ibid.* (emphasis added). We specifically rejected this high standard of review in *Harper*. In that case, the Washington Supreme Court had held that state physicians could not administer medication to a prisoner without showing that it "was both necessary and effective for furthering a compelling state interest." 494 U. S., at 218. We reversed, holding that the state court "erred in refusing to apply the standard of reasonableness." *Id.*, at 223.

The Court today also departs from *Harper* when it says that the Nevada Supreme Court erred by not "considering less intrusive alternatives." *Ante*, at 135. The Court presumably believes that Nevada could have treated Riggins with smaller doses of Mellaril or with other kinds of therapies. In *Harper*, however, we imposed no such requirement. In fact, we specifically ruled that "[t]he alternative means proffered by [the prisoner] for accommodating his interest in rejecting the forced administration of antipsychotic drugs do not demonstrate the invalidity of the State's policy." 494 U. S., at 226.

This case differs from *Harper* because it involves a pretrial detainee and not a convicted prisoner. The standards for forcibly medicating inmates well may differ from those for persons awaiting trial. The Court, however, does not rely on this distinction in departing from *Harper;* instead, it purports to be applying *Harper* to detainees. *Ante*, at 135. Either the Court is seeking to change the *Harper* standards or it is adopting different standards for detainees without stating its reasons. I cannot accept either interpretation of the Court's opinion. For all of these reasons, I respectfully dissent.

STATE of Louisiana

v.

Michael Owen PERRY.

No. 91-KP-1324.

Supreme Court of Louisiana.

Oct. 19, 1992.

Dissenting Opinion by Justice Cole Nov. 9, 1992.

Rehearing Denied Nov. 25, 1992.

Defendant convicted of murder appealed imposition of death sentence. On remand, 498 U.S. 38, 111 S.Ct. 449, 112 L.Ed.2d 338, the Nineteenth Judicial District Court, East Baton Rouge Parish, reinstated order, and defendant applied for writ of certiorari. The Supreme Court, Dennis, J., held that state may not medicate incompetent death row prisoner against his will with antipsychotic drugs in order to carry out his death sentence while he is under influence of such drugs.

Affirmed in part and reversed in part.

Watson and Lemmon, JJ., concurred and filed opinions.

Hall, J., concurred in part and filed opinion.

Marcus, J., dissented and filed opinion and would grant rehearing.

Cole, J., dissented with reasons and would grant rehearing.

1. Constitutional Law ⚷46(1)

Court will not pass upon federal constitutional question, although properly presented by record, if there is also present some other ground upon which case may be disposed.

2. Constitutional Law ⚷18

So long as one party's state rights are expanded without infringement on another individual's federal right, State Constitution may be used to supplement or expand federally guaranteed constitutional rights.

3. Constitutional Law ⚷18

Where both state and federal constitutional issues are presented, state law should be applied first, especially in absence of readily applicable dispositive federal precepts.

4. Constitutional Law ⚷82(1)

Declaration of Rights of Louisiana Constitution provides more specific and broader protection of individual liberties than does Bill of Rights or other provisions of Federal Constitution. LSA-Const. Art. 1, § 1 et seq.; U.S.C.A. Const.Amends. 1-10.

5. Constitutional Law ⚷82(13)

Subject to legitimate requirements of prison discipline and security, prison inmates retain their fundamental constitutional rights and protections.

6. Constitutional Law ⚷82(7)

State constitutional right to privacy affords protection against government's unjustified physical invasion of person's body and brain or government's control by any means of person's mind and thoughts. LSA-Const. Art. 1, § 5.

7. Constitutional Law ⚷82(13)
Prisons ⚷17(2)

State may not medicate incompetent death row prisoner against his will with antipsychotic drugs in order to carry out his death sentence while he is under influence of such drugs; such forced medication would violate prisoner's bodily integrity, chemically alter his mind and will, and usurp his fundamental right to make decisions regarding his health and medical treatment, which, in absence of compelling state interest, would violate his constitutionally protected right to privacy. LSA-Const. Art. 1, § 5.

8. Criminal Law ⚷1213.10(3)
Prisons ⚷17(2)

State may not medicate incompetent death row prisoner against his will with antipsychotic drugs in order to carry out his death sentence while he is under influence of such drugs; such forced medication, which would impose significantly more indignity, pain and suffering than ordinarily was necessary for the extinguishment of life, constituted cruel and unusual punishment. LSA-Const. Art. 1, § 20.

9. **Constitutional Law ⟹18**
Criminal Law ⟹1213.1

Louisiana Constitution's prohibition against cruel and unusual punishment affords no less, and in some respects more, protection than that available to individuals under Eighth Amendment of Federal Constitution. U.S.C.A. Const.Amend. 8; LSA-Const. Art. 1, § 20.

10. **Criminal Law ⟹1213.8(1)**

In order to avoid violation of constitutional prohibition against cruel and unusual punishment, punishment must not be degrading to dignity of human beings, punishment must not be arbitrarily inflicted, punishment must not be excessive, and punishment must not be unacceptable to contemporary society. U.S.C.A. Const. Amend. 8; LSA-Const. Art. 1, § 20.

Keith B. Nordyke, June E. Denlinger, McGlinchey, Stafford, Cellini & Lang, Joseph I. Giarrusso, Jr., for applicant.

Richard Ieyoub, Atty. Gen., Douglas P. Moreau, Dist. Atty., Mary P. Jones, Kathleen E. Petersen, for respondent.

DENNIS, Justice.

The fundamental question raised by this case is whether the state can circumvent the centuries old prohibition against execution of the insane by medicating an incompetent death row prisoner against his will with antipsychotic drugs and carrying out his death sentence while he is under the influence of the drugs. After a hearing to determine whether the death row inmate was competent to be executed, the trial court, in effect, found that the inmate was insane but susceptible to being made able to understand the link between his crime and punishment by antipsychotic drugs. The trial court ordered the state to administer antipsychotic drugs to the prisoner for this purpose, without his consent if necessary. The prisoner did not consent to medication, but applied for review by this court, which denied writs, 543 So.2d 487 (La. 1989), and by the United States Supreme Court, which granted certiorari. *Perry v. Louisiana*, 494 U.S. 1015, 110 S.Ct. 1317, 108 L.Ed.2d 492 (1990). After entertaining briefs and oral argument, the Supreme Court vacated the trial court's order and remanded the case for further proceedings in light of *Washington v. Harper*, 494 U.S. 210, 110 S.Ct. 1028, 108 L.Ed.2d 178 (1990). *Perry v. Louisiana*, 498 U.S. 38, 111 S.Ct. 449, 112 L.Ed.2d 338 (1990). On remand, the trial court reinstated its order. We granted the prisoner's application for a writ of certiorari and stayed the trial court's forcible medication order. *State v. Perry*, 584 So.2d 1145 (La.1991).

We affirm in part and reverse in part. The trial court's determination that Perry is not competent for execution without the administration of antipsychotic drugs is affirmed. The court's order requiring the state to medicate Perry with antipsychotic drugs without his consent is reversed. The execution of the death sentence is stayed. The state may apply to this court for a modification of the stay of execution of the death sentence if Perry achieves or regains his sanity independently of and without the influence of antipsychotic drugs.

For centuries no jurisdiction has approved the execution of the insane. The state's attempt to circumvent this well-settled prohibition by forcibly medicating an insane prisoner with antipsychotic drugs violates his rights under our state constitution. La. Const.1974 Art. I, §§ 5, 20. First, it violates his right to privacy or personhood. Such involuntary medication requires the unjustified invasion of his brain and body with discomforting, potentially dangerous and painful drugs, the seizure of control of his mind and thoughts, and the usurpation of his right to make decisions regarding his health or medical treatment. Furthermore, implementation of the state's plan to medicate forcibly and execute the insane prisoner would constitute cruel, excessive and unusual punishment. This particular application of the death penalty fails to measurably contribute to the social goals of capital punishment. Carrying out this punitive scheme would add severity and indignity to the prisoner's punishment beyond that required for the mere extinguishment of life. This type of punitive treatment system is not accepted anywhere in contemporary society and is apt to be administered erroneously, arbitrarily or capriciously.

I. FACTS, PROCEDURAL HISTORY AND ISSUE

Michael Owen Perry was convicted and sentenced to death for murdering his mother, father, nephew and two cousins in a senseless criminal episode in 1983. Perry was 28 at the time of his offenses but had continued to live with his parents due to his long history of mental illness. At the age of 16, he was diagnosed as schizophrenic, and he was committed to mental institutions by his parents several times because of his psychotic symptoms. Although the record does not disclose any previous criminal conduct, he escaped from mental facilities twice and was made to sleep in a shed behind his parents' house due to his disruptive conduct.

Perry's mental illness raised legal issues throughout the criminal proceedings. Initially, two sanity commissions were convened to determine his competence to stand trial. *State v. Perry*, 502 So.2d 543, 547 (La.1986) cert. denied, 484 U.S. 872, 108 S.Ct. 205, 98 L.Ed.2d 156 (1987). Upon recommendation of the first commission, Perry was transferred to a state facility for treatment and psychiatric evaluation. Id. at 547–48. After being diagnosed as suffering from a long history of paranoid schizophrenia, Perry was placed on an antipsychotic drug treatment program, primarily consisting of doses of the drug Haldol. Eighteen months later, he was determined to be competent to stand trial, as recommended by the second sanity commission. Id. at 548. Following this, Perry was allowed by the court, contrary to advice of his counsel, to withdraw his insanity plea and proceed to trial on a simple plea of not guilty. Id. at 547, 550.

Perry was convicted of five counts of murder in 1985 and sentenced to death. On appeal this court affirmed his convictions and sentence, but stated that a determination of his competency to be executed "might be in order." *State v. Perry*, 502 So.2d 543, 564 (La.1987). Following the suggestion of this court, the trial court convened a sanity commission and conducted hearings. The medical experts reported that Perry suffers from an incurable schizoaffective disorder that causes his days to be a series of hallucinations, delusional and disordered thinking, incoherent speech, and manic behavior. These symptoms can be temporarily diminished with antipsychotic drugs, they testified, but his underlying insanity can never be permanently cured or quelled. After receiving this testimony, the court concluded that Perry was competent for execution only while he was being maintained by antipsychotic drugs in the form of Haldol. In effect, the trial court found that without the influence of antipsychotic drugs, Perry is insane and incompetent for execution. Accordingly, the court ordered the state to maintain Perry on this medication "as to be prescribed by the medical staff of said Department [of Corrections] and if necessary to administer said medication forcibly to defendant and over his objection."

After this court denied his writ and appeal, Perry sought and was granted a writ of certiorari by the United States Supreme Court. *Perry v. Louisiana*, 494 U.S. 1015, 110 S.Ct. 1317, 108 L.Ed.2d 492 (1990). After full briefing and oral argument, the high court vacated the trial court order and remanded the case to that court for reconsideration in light of *Washington v. Harper*, 494 U.S. 210, 110 S.Ct. 1028, 108 L.Ed.2d 178 (1990). *Perry v. Louisiana*, 498 U.S. 38, 111 S.Ct. 449, 112 L.Ed.2d 338 (1990). After considering the Supreme Court's remand, and without taking any additional evidence, the trial court reinstated its forcible medication order. Essentially, the trial court concluded that *Washington v. Harper* is inapplicable to a proceeding to determine competence for execution and does not require a different result from the trial court's original determination. This court granted a writ to review the trial court's action and issued a stay order to prevent the forcible medication of the prisoner. *State v. Perry*, 584 So.2d 1145 (La.1991).

This case hinges on whether the state constitutionally may forcibly medicate Perry and carry out his death sentence. There is no question but that Perry is incurably insane and incompetent for execution. Without the administration of antipsychotic drugs, Perry cannot pass any known test of competency. Nevertheless, when he is under the influence of antipsychotic drugs Perry sometimes is able to function at a minimum level of rationality. There is no contention by the state that Perry has consented to take the drugs. There is also no claim by Perry that the punishment would be unconstitutional if he were sane. The basic constitutional issue is, therefore, determinative and must be addressed.

The subsidiary issues raised are deferred because they will be rendered moot by our decision that the state's dual objective of forcible medication and execution is unconstitutional. The issues deferred include whether the trial court applied the appropriate standard for measuring competence for execution and whether the evidence in the present record is sufficient to support the trial court's finding that the inmate's mental competence can be maintained predictably and consistently with antipsychotic drugs. Moreover, our decision of these subsidiary issues in favor of Perry would not be dispositive of this case because the basic constitutional question would still control whether or not the state on remand would be permitted to medicate Perry and demonstrate while following correct legal precepts that he can be maintained forcibly with drugs at a consistent level of competence for execution.

II. PROHIBITION AGAINST EXECUTION OF THE INSANE

In *Ford v. Wainwright*, 477 U.S. 399, 106 S.Ct. 2595, 91 L.Ed.2d 335 (1986) the United States Supreme Court held that the Eighth and Fourteenth Amendments prohibit a state from inflicting the death penalty upon a prisoner who is insane. The court recognized that the common law's ancient prohibition of execution of the insane rested on multiple theories including moral, ethical and theological arguments together with the negligible deterrent and retributive value of executing the insane. Some authorities contended that the bar was justified as a way of preserving the defendant's ability to make arguments on his own behalf. See 1 M. Hale, Pleas of the Crown, 35 (1736) ("if after judgment he became of *non sane memory*, his execution shall be spared; for were he of sound memory he might allege somewhat in stay of judgement or execution"). Accord 4 W. Blackstone, Commentaries 388–89; 477 U.S. at 407–09, 106 S.Ct. at 2600–02. Other authorities agreed with Sir Edward Coke, who argued that because execution was intended to be an "example" to the living, the execution of "a mad man" was such a miserable spectacle ... of extreme inhumanity and cruelty" that it "can be no example to others". See 3 E. Coke, Institute 6 (1794).

Additional commentators postulated religious underpinnings: that it is uncharitable to dispatch an offender "into another world, when he is not of a capacity to fit himself for it," Hales, Remarks on the Trial of M. Charles Basement, 11 HOW.St.T. 474, 477 (1685). It is also said that execution serves no purpose in these cases because madness is its own punishment. Blackstone, supra, at 395. More recent authorities declare that the community's quest for "retribution"—the need to offset a criminal act by punishment of an equivalent "moral quality"—is not served by executing an insane person, which has a "lesser value" than that of the crime for which he is to be punished. See Hazard & Louisell, Death, the State and the Insane: Stay of Execution, 9 UCLA 381, 387 (1962). Faced with such a solid and widespread proscription, the Supreme Court concluded that, whether its aim is to protect the condemned from fear and pain without comfort of understanding, or to protect the dignity of society itself from the barbarity of exacting mindless vengeance, the prohibition against execution of the insane finds enforcement in the Eighth Amendment. 477 U.S. at 410, 106 S.Ct. at 2602.

Even before the Supreme Court constitutionalized the rule in Ford, no state in the union permitted the execution of the insane. At the time of its decision, 26 of the 41 death penalty jurisdictions had adopted statutes explicitly requiring the suspension of the execution of a prisoner who meets the legal test for incompetence. 477 U.S. at 408, n. 2, 106 S.Ct. at 2601 n. 2. Others had enacted more discretionary statutory procedures for suspension of sentence and transfer to mental facilities in such cases. Id. Still others, including Louisiana, had adopted the common law rule by judicial decision. Id.

For nearly a century it has been well-settled in Louisiana that one who has been convicted of a capital crime and sentenced to suffer the penalty of death, and who thereafter becomes insane, cannot be put to death while in that condition. *State v. Parker*, 80 So.2d 863 (La.1955); *State v. Allen*, 204 La. 513, 15 So.2d 870 (1943); *State v. Migues*, 194 La. 1081, 195 So. 545 (1940); *State v. Cannon*, 185 La. 395, 169 So. 446 (1936); *State v. Burnham*, 162 La. 737, 111 So. 79 (1926); *State v. Brodes*, 157 La. 162, 102 So. 190 (1924); *State ex rel. Paine v. Judge*, 49 La.Ann. 1500, 22 So. 738 (1897).

In Art. I, § 20 of the Louisiana Constitution of 1974, the people provided that "[n]o law shall subject any person to *euthanasia*, to *torture* or to cruel, *excessive*, or unusual punishment." (emphasis added.) The framers of our state constitution clearly intended for this guarantee to go beyond the scope of the Eighth Amendment in some respects and to provide at least the same level of protection as the Bill of Rights and the Fourteenth Amendment in all others. *State v. Sepulvado*, 367 So.2d 762 (La.1979); Hargrave, The Declaration of Rights of the Louisiana Constitution of 1974, 35 La.L.Rev. 1, 63 (1974). Consequently, the practice of executing the insane is thrice barred in our state, i.e., by the state and federal constitutions and by the decisions of this court.

III. DETERMINATION THAT STATE LAW IS APPLICABLE

The state's proposed medicate-to-execute scheme raises issues pertaining to fundamental guarantees under both the Louisiana and federal constitutions. Principles of jurisprudence, efficiency and federalism dictate that the appropriate procedure for deciding such a case is to analyze state law, including state constitutional provisions, before reaching a federal constitutional claim.

[1] Both the United States Supreme Court and this court adhere to the rule that the court will not pass upon a federal constitutional question, although properly presented by the record, if there is also present some other ground upon which the case may be disposed. See *Webster v. Reproductive Health Services*, 492 U.S. 490, 526, 109 S.Ct. 3040, 3060, 106 L.Ed.2d 410 (1989) (O'Connor, J., concurring), collecting authorities; *Ashwander v. TVA*, 297 U.S. 288, 346–347, 56 S.Ct. 466, 482–83, 80 L.Ed. 688 (1936) (Brandeis, J., concurring); *Benson & Gold Chevrolet Inc. v. La. Motor Veh. Com'n*, 403 So.2d 13 (La.1981) and authorities cited therein. Additionally, the Supreme Court has developed the Pullman doctrine, under which a federal court may decline to proceed though it has jurisdiction based on the federal constitution or statutes, in order to avoid decision of a federal constitutional question where the case may be disposed on questions of state law. *Texas v. Pullman, Co.*, 312 U.S. 496, 61 S.Ct. 643, 85 L.Ed. 971 (1941); See Wright, Law of Federal Courts, 302 et seq. (1983); see also *La. Power & Light Co. v. City of Thibodaux*, 360 U.S. 25, 79 S.Ct. 1070, 3 L.Ed.2d 1058 (1959); *Leiter Minerals, Inc. v. U.S.*, 352 U.S. 220, 77 S.Ct. 287, 1 L.Ed.2d 267 (1957). Therefore, an improper by-pass of a state constitutional or legal question by this court may result in an unnecessary federal constitutional decision, a remand of the case by the Supreme Court, or both.

[2] Greater judicial efficiency and coherence are promoted when we address state law issues first. See *Large v. Superior Court*, 148 Ariz. 229, 235, 714 P.2d 399, 405 (1986); *City of Portland v. Jacobsky*, 496 A.2d 646, 648 (Me.1985); *State v. Chaisson*, 125 N.H. 810, 486 A.2d 297, 301 (1984); *Sterling v. Cupp*, 290 Or. 611, 625

P.2d 123, 126 (1983); *State v. Coe*, 101 Wash.2d 364, 679 P.2d 353, 359 (1984); Developments in the Law: The Interpretation of State Constitutional Rights, 95 Harv. L.Rev. 1324, 1448 (1982). See also *Massachusetts v. Upton*, 466 U.S. 727, 736, 104 S.Ct. 2085, 2089, 80 L.Ed.2d 721 (1984) (Stevens, J., concurring). Because this court is the final arbiter of the meaning of the state constitution and laws, our disposition of a case on state grounds usually will terminate the litigation without the necessity of federal review. Furthermore, because our state Declaration of Rights incorporates or expands most of the federal Bill of Rights standards, a decision by this court upholding an individual's state constitutional right rarely will call for further review by the Supreme Court. Because of our oaths to support the constitution and laws of our state as faithfully and diligently as those of the federal government, La. Const. Art. X, § 30 (1974), we are obliged to independently interpret and apply our state constitution in each case. As long as one party's state rights are expanded without infringement on another individual's federal right, our state constitution may be used to supplement or expand federally guaranteed constitutional rights. See *Pruneyard Shopping Center v. Robins*, 447 U.S. 74, 100 S.Ct. 2035, 64 L.Ed.2d 741 (1980); Linde, E. Pluribus—Constitutional Theory and State Courts, 18 Ga.L.Rev. 165, 179 (1984); Developments in the Law: The Interpretation of State Constitutional Rights, 95 Harv. L.Rev. 1324, 1334 (1982).

[3] The very nature of our federal system and the vast differences between the federal and state constitutions and courts indicate that state law should be applied first. When the Founding Fathers assembled this nation, they recognized the primacy of the states in protecting individual rights. Mosk, State Constitutionalism: Both Liberal and Conservative, 63 Tex. L.Rev. 1081, 1083 (1985) citing The Federalist Nos. 14, 17, 32, 39, and 45. As Madison commented:

> The powers delegated by the proposed Constitution to the Federal Government, are few and defined. Those which are to remain in the State governments are numerous and indefinite. The former will be exercised principally on external objects, as war, peace, negotiation, and foreign commerce.... The powers reserved to the several States will extend to all the objects, which, in the ordinary course of affairs, concern the lives, liberties and properties of the people; and the internal order, improvement, and prosperity of the State.

The Federalist No. 45, at 313 (J. Madison) (J.E. Cooke ed. 1961).

Although not entirely proper, a state court's failure to apply state law first might be understandable when well-settled, clearly applicable federal precedent is available. However, the Supreme Court's remand of this case without decision evidences the unavailability of readily applicable dispositive federal precepts. Therefore, we set to one side, without deciding, the federal constitutional issues and proceed to resolve this case on state constitutional grounds.

IV. WASHINGTON v. HARPER DISTINGUISHED

Before applying the controlling state constitutional law, however, we consider the present case in light of Washington v. Harper, a case involving the forcible medical treatment of a mentally ill prisoner in his own best medical interest and for the safety of himself and others in the prison. We conclude that the present case is distinguishable for several reasons. First, forcing a prisoner to take antipsychotic drugs to facilitate his execution does not constitute medical treatment but is antithetical to the basic principles of the healing arts. Second, Harper held that due process requires the state to show that its prison regulation rationally seeks to further both the best medical interest of the prisoner and the state's own interest in prison safety before it may inject a prisoner with antipsychotic drugs against his will. The state in Perry's case has made neither showing but seeks forcible medication of a prisoner by court order as an instrument of his execution. Third, Harper not only fails to support the state's position; it strongly implies that forced administration of antipsychotic drugs may not be used by the state for the purpose of punishment.

A. Drugging For Execution: Punishment, Not Medical Treatment

> I swear by Apollo the physician, by Aesculapius, Hygeia, and Panacea, and I take to witness all the gods, all the goddesses, to keep according to my ability and my judgment the following Oath: ... I will prescribe regimen for the good of my patients according to my ability and my judgment and never do harm to anyone. To please no one will I prescribe a deadly drug, nor give advice which may cause his death ... I will preserve the purity of my life and my art ... In every house where I come I will enter only for the good of my patients, keeping myself far from all intentional ill-doing....

Hippocrates c. 460–400 B.C., Stedman's Medical Dictionary 647 (4th Unabridged Lawyer's Ed.1976).

Medical treatment does not consist merely of dispensing drugs; other ingredients are essential to the healing arts. The Hippocratic Oath, dating from the fifth century B.C., is the seminal source of the principles of medical ethics and the goals of medical treatment. Under the oath, the physician pledges to do no harm and to act only in the best medical interests of his patients. Consequently, medical treatment cannot occur when the state orders a physician to administer antipsychotic drugs to an insane prisoner in an attempt to render him competent for execution.

Because the physician is required by his oath both to alleviate suffering and to do no harm, the state's order forces him to act unethically and contrary to the goals of medical treatment. If any physician administers drugs forcibly and thereby enables the state to have the inmate declared competent for execution, the doctor knowingly handles the prisoner harmfully and contrary to his ultimate medical interest. The physician's abstention from dispensing the drugs, however, perpetuates suffering that ordinarily the physician is duty-bound to allay by treatment. If the drugs are forcibly administered by a person who is not a physician, what occurs is devoid of any pretense of medical treatment or compliance with the principles of medical ethics. Accord: Katz, Perry v. Louisiana: Medical Ethics on Death Row—Is Judicial Intervention Warranted?, 4 Geo.J.Leg.Ethics 707 (1991); Radelet & Barnard, Treating Those Found Incompetent for Execution: Ethical Chaos with Only One Solution, 16 Bull.Am.Acad.Psychiatry L. 297 (1988); Salguero, Medical Ethics and Competency to be Executed, 96 Yale L.J. 167 (1986); Evans, Perry v. Louisiana: Can a State Treat an Incompetent Prisoner to Ready Him for Execution?, 19 Bull.Am.Acad.Psychiatry L. 249 (1991); Ewing, Diagnosing and Treating Insanity on Death Row: Legal and Ethical Perspectives, 5 Behavioral Sciences and the Law 175 (1987). Therefore, the forcible medication of a prisoner merely to improve his mental comprehension as a means of rendering him competent for execution actually prevents the prisoner from receiving adequate medical treatment for his mental illness.

Several pernicious effects are caused by the forcible medicate-to-execute structure. First, the patient's autonomy rights are violated because he is not permitted to weigh the benefits and risks of a proposed course of treatment in consultation with his physician as is required in seeking the patient's best medical interest. See generally, E. Pellegrino & D. Thomasma, For the Patient's Good 37–50 (1988). Second, the forcible nature and lethal repercussions of the state's involuntary antipsychotic drug regimen preclude a trustful, communicative doctor-patient relationship that is essential to psychiatric therapy. Katz, supra, at 718. Third, since the physician cannot serve two masters, there is a substantial concern that the patient's well-being may be subordinated to the duty the doctor owes the state. Evans, supra, at 261; Salguero, supra, at 176. Fourth, for all of the foregoing reasons, and because of the incompatibility of the interests of the state and the prisoner, both of which the physician is required to further, the death penalty is apt to be implemented arbitrarily and capriciously. The aggregate of conditions surrounding the physician's determination of the prisoner's mental capacity at the time of execution does not yield room for well-informed and dispassionate medical judgment. Consequently, there is no genuine assurance that the "barbarity of exacting mindless vengeance" abhorred for centuries by all civilized societies will not occur under a modern scientific facade. Fifth, a psychiatrist's administration of involuntary medication may constitute being "a participant in a legally authorized execution" contrary to the ethical code of the American Medical Association, as adopted and interpreted by the American Psychiatric Association. APA, The Principles of Medical Ethics: With Annotations Especially Applicable to Psychiatry § 1, Annot. 4 (1989). Notably, the psychiatrist's involvement in the restoration of competence through forcible drug treatment raises further ethical concerns because it is more closely tied to the execution itself in comparison with other functions performed by psychiatrists in death penalty cases, e.g., determinations of competence for trial. By the same token, the physician's forcibly drugging an inmate for execution comes closer to being the cause of death in furthering the state's punishment goal than to the practice of medicine or treatment in the patient's best interest. See Katz, supra, at 715; Salguero, supra, at 176–77. Sixth, blurring the distinction between healing and punishing denigrates the "deep-seated social interest in preserving medical care, in actuality and in perception, as an unambiguously beneficent healing art." Katz, supra, at 724.

Accordingly, we conclude that a physician's prescription and administration of antipsychotic drugs to a prisoner against his will, pursuant to the order of a state court or other government official, for the purpose of carrying out the death penalty, does not constitute medical treatment but forms part of the capital punishment sought to be executed by the state. As Professor Opton succinctly put it:

> "[T]he difference between a violent punishment and a medical treatment lies not in the act itself, but in the intent of the actor. When a medical procedure is done at the request of the patient and for his benefit, it is a treatment. When the identical medical procedure is done against a person's interest or will, it is either a battery, if lacking legal sanction, or a punishment, if imposed by legal authority."

Opton, Psychiatric Violence Against Prisoners: When Therapy Is Punishment, 45 Miss.L.J. 605, 608 (1974).

B. Harper Does Not Authorize Medication For Punishment

In *Washington v. Harper*, the Supreme Court considered a state prisoner's substantive and procedural due process challenges to the State of Washington's prison regulation governing the forced medical treatment of inmates with antipsychotic drugs. Under the contested regulation, such medical treatment could be forced on a prisoner only when it was in his best medical interest and in the interest of his or others' safety in the prison. The regulation further provided that antipsychotic medication could be administered for no purpose other than medical treatment and then only under the direction of a licensed psychiatrist. *Washington v. Harper*, supra, 494 U.S. at 201 n. 8, 110 S.Ct. at 1024 n. 8.

The Supreme Court held that the forcible injection of medication into a nonconsenting person's body represents a substantial interference with that person's liberty, but that, taking into account the state's unique interest in prison safety and security, substantive due process allows a mentally ill inmate to be treated involuntarily with antipsychotic drugs where there is a determination that "the inmate is dangerous to himself or others and the treatment is in the inmate's medical interest." *Riggins v. Nevada*, —— U.S. ——, 112 S.Ct. 1810, 1815, 118 L.Ed.2d 479 (1992), quoting and interpreting *Washington v. Harper*, supra, 494 U.S. at 227, 110 S.Ct. at 1039. Therefore, under Harper, "forcing antipsychotic drugs on a convicted prisoner is impermissible absent a finding of overriding justification and a determination of medical appropriateness." Id.

The Supreme Court's holding in *Washington v. Harper* is inherently inapposite to the present case. The state's object here is to forcibly administer antipsychotic drugs to a prisoner in order to implement his execution. In contrast, the state's object in Harper was to require a prisoner to accept appropriate medical treatment that was in his own best medical interest. Therefore, in the present case, the state's involuntary use of drugs on Perry must be vindicated if at all as a procedure that legitimately forms part of his capital punishment. It cannot be justified under Harper because forcible administration of drugs to implement execution is not medically appropriate.

But even if we overlook the incongruity of applying a medical treatment precedent in a capital punishment context, Harper still cannot be applied to yield the result desired by the state. In Harper, the Supreme Court developed a substantive due process standard that requires the state to show that the prisoner is dangerous to himself or others and that the antipsychotic drug medical treatment is appropriate medically and in his best medical interest. The state's proof in the present case simply does not measure up to this due process standard. This, of course, is not surprising because the Harper standard has nothing to do with the issues with which the trial court and the parties dealt with below, viz., whether Perry was competent for execution and whether he could be consistently maintained with drugs at a level of competency and executed in that condition.

The present case, in which the state is represented by the prosecutorial arm of government, began as a proceeding to determine whether Perry was mentally competent to proceed with his execution and ended with a court determination that his competence could be maintained only by medication and an order authorizing and directing the state to forcibly medicate him for that purpose. In contrast, Harper was a proceeding initiated by medical doctors pursuant to a regulation carefully drawn by prison administrators governing forcible medical treatment of prisoners in the interest of their medical welfare and prison safety and security. The regulation forbade the use of antipsychotic drugs for any purpose other than by a psychiatrist for medical treatment. In the present case, the parties and the trial court directed the expert medical witnesses' attention and testimony to the subjects of whether Perry was sane without drugs and whether his ability to understand his punishment and its connection with his crimes could be maintained predictably and consistently with antipsychotic medicine. It is obvious that none of the participants considered that prison safety or the long term best medical interests of Perry were significant or determinative issues in the proceeding. Having conducted this proceeding with the single-minded purpose of forcibly medicating Perry in order to execute him, even in the United States Supreme Court, the state cannot now contend that it genuinely seeks to uphold the trial court's forced medication order merely to further Perry's best medical interest and the safety of Perry and others in the prison setting.

Furthermore, the majority opinion in Harper suggests that the substantive protections of the Due Process Clause prohibit the forced administration of antipsychotic drugs to any state prisoner whose best medical interest would not be advanced thereby. As Justice Stevens observed, the Court did not suggest that psychotropic drugs, any more than transfer for medical treatment, see *Vitek v. Jones,* 445 U.S. 480, 100 S.Ct. 1254, 63 L.Ed.2d 552 (1980), may be forced on prisoners as a necessary condition of their incarceration or as a disciplinary measure. *Washington v. Harper,* supra, 494 U.S. at 241–42, 110 S.Ct. at 1047–48 (Stevens, J., concurring and dissenting in part). The majority repeatedly noted and seemed to consider it crucial to its due process standard that the Washington prison policy required that the drugs "may be administered for no purpose other than treatment" and that "the treatment in question will be ordered only if it is in the prisoner's medical interests, given the legitimate needs of his institutional confinement." Id. at 227, 110 S.Ct. at 1039. From this Justice Stevens concluded that "[f]orced administration of antipsychotic medication may not be used as a form of punishment." Id. at 241, 110 S.Ct. at 1047. This inference seems to have been confirmed by the court's subsequent conclusion in *Riggins v. Nevada*, — U.S. ——, 112 S.Ct. 1810, 1815, 118 L.Ed.2d 479 (1992) that "[u]nder Harper, forcing antipsychotic drugs on a convicted prisoner is impermissible absent a finding of overriding justification and a determination of medical appropriateness."

Consequently, we conclude that *Washington v. Harper*, which is inherently inapposite and should not be applied to the present case, also sets forth a due process standard that the state has failed to meet, and strongly implies that antipsychotic drugs absolutely may not be used as a tool for punishment. For the reasons stated in the previous section of this opinion, however, we rest our decision not on inferences drawn from Harper, but on the state constitutional rights of privacy or personhood and humane treatment.

V. PRIVACY OR PERSONHOOD

The state's plan to force an insane prisoner to take antipsychotic drugs against his will as a necessary and integral antecedent to his execution infringes on several related interests protected by the right of privacy and personhood guaranteed by Art. I, § 5 of the 1974 Louisiana Constitution: the right to decide what is to be done medically with one's brain and body; the right to control one's own mind and thoughts; and the freedom from unwarranted physical interference with one's person. There is no compelling state interest that would be furthered measurably by the state's medicate-to-execute scheme. Therefore, the execution plan is unconstitutional and must be set aside.

[4] The decisions of this court indicate that the Declaration of Rights (Article I) of the 1974 Louisiana Constitution embody and often amplify the protection of certain individual rights afforded by the pre-existing United States Supreme Court interpretations of the Fourteenth Amendment and Bill of Rights. We have, for instance, held that the Louisiana Constitution provides greater protection of individual rights than does the federal constitution with respect to state rights phrased identically to federal counterparts, *State v. Church*, 538 So.2d 993 (La.1989); *State v. Hernandez*, 410 So.2d 1381 (La.1982), *State v. Breaux*, 329 So.2d 696 (La.1976); state rights phrased more specifically or broadly than the corresponding federal rights, e.g., *Sibley v. Board of Sup'rs of La. State Univ.*, 477 So.2d 1094 (La.1985), *State v. Sepulvado*, 367 So.2d 762 (La.1979); and state rights that have no explicit federal analog, e.g., *State v. Spooner*, 520 So.2d 336 (La.1988); *Title Research Corp. v. Rausch*, 450 So.2d 933 (La.1984). See Devlin, Privacy and Abortion Rights Under the Louisiana State Constitution: Could Roe v. Wade be Alive and Well in the Bayou State? 51 La.L.Rev. 685, 688–689 (1991); Comment, The Declaration of Rights of the Louisiana Constitution of 1974: The Louisiana Supreme Court and Civil Liberties, 51 La.L.Rev. 787 (1991) (authored by Richard Bullock). The consensus of the justices of this court has been that "our state constitution's declaration of individual rights ... represent[s] more specific ... [and] broader protection of the individual," *Guidry v. Roberts*, 335 So.2d 438, 448 (1976) (Tate, J.); and is "far broader and more definitely articulated than corresponding rights in the Federal Constitution." Id. 452, citing examples (Summers, J., dissenting). Moreover, there does not appear to have been a single instance in which this court has held that the Declaration of Rights affords less protection of individual liberties than did the Bill of Rights or other provisions of the federal constitution under the pre-existing Supreme Court interpretations.

A. Protected Privacy or Personhood Interests

Article I, § 5 of the 1974 Louisiana Constitution expressly guarantees that every individual shall be secure in his "person" against "unreasonable searches, seizures, or invasions of privacy." Since 1974, this court and our courts of appeal have interpreted the right to privacy declared in Article I, § 5 to incorporate protection for several different categories of privacy interests. In the area of invasion of privacy by unreasonable searches or seizures, this court has interpreted the right of privacy to afford even more stringent protection of individual liberty than the Fourth Amendment. *State v. Church*, 538 So.2d 993 (La. 1989); *State v. Hernandez*, 410 So.2d 1381 (La.1982); *State v. Kinnemann*, 337 So.2d 441 (La.1976). One Louisiana court of appeal has held that the "privacy" guarantee affords protection against the unreasonable compilation or disclosure of information about individuals. *Trahan v. Larivee*, 365 So.2d 294 (La.App. 3rd Cir.1978). See Devlin, supra, at 691–92; Hargrave, supra, at 21; Note, Toward a Right of Privacy as a Matter of State Constitutional Law, 5 Fla.St.U.L.Rev. 632 (1977).

In *Hondroulis v. Schuhmacher*, 553 So.2d 398, 410 (La.1989) this court held that Art. I, § 5 also establishes an affirmative right to privacy that impacts more than criminal search and seizure law, incorporates the principles of the United States Supreme Court privacy decisions in explicit statement, and includes the recognition of a patient's right to decide whether to obtain or reject medical treatment and what shall or shall not be done with his body. Relying principally on *Carey v. Population Services International*, 431 U.S. 678, 97 S.Ct. 2010, 52 L.Ed.2d 675 (1977) as containing a succinct statement of the privacy principles developed prior to the adoption of our state constitution we concluded: Although the federal constitution does not explicitly mention any right of privacy, the Supreme Court has recognized that one aspect of "liberty" protected by the Due Process Clause of the Fourteenth Amendment is a right of personal privacy or a guarantee of certain areas or zones of privacy. This right of personal privacy includes the interest in independence in making certain kinds of important decisions. While the outer limits of this aspect of privacy have not been marked by the Court, it is clear that among the decisions that an individual may make without unjustified government interference are personal decisions relating to marriage, procreation, contraception, family relationships, and child rearing and education. *Hondroulis v. Schuhmacher*, supra, at 414 (quoting and citing authorities).

In concluding that the decision to obtain or reject medical treatment should be recognized as falling within this cluster of constitutionally protected rights, this court noted that one federal court and numerous states had held that the right to privacy is broad enough to grant an individual the right to chart his or her own medical treatment plan. Id. citing *Rasmussen by Mitchell v. Fleming*, 154 Ariz. 207, 741 P.2d 674 (1987); *Bouvia v. Superior Court*, 179 Cal.App.3d 1127, 225 Cal.Rptr. 297 (1986); *Foody v. Manchester Memorial Hospital*, 40 Conn.Supp. 127, 482 A.2d 713 (1984); *Severns v. Wilmington Medical Center, Inc.*, 421 A.2d 1334 (Del.1980); *Satz v. Perlmutter*, 362 So.2d 160 (Fla. App. 4th Dist.1978); *Brophy v. New England Sinai Hospital, Inc.*, 398 Mass. 417, 497 N.E.2d 626 (1986); *Superintendent of Belchertown State School v. Saikewicz*, 373 Mass. 728, 370 N.E.2d 417 (1977); *In Matter of Farrell*, 212 N.J.Super. 294, 514 A.2d 1342 (1986); *Matter of Quinlan*, 70 N.J. 10, 355 A.2d 647 (1976), cert. denied sub nom. *Garger v. New Jersey*, 429 U.S. 922, 97 S.Ct. 319, 50 L.Ed.2d 289 (1976); *Leach v. Akron General Medical Center*, 68 Ohio Misc. 1, 426 N.E.2d 809 (1980); *Matter of Welfare of Colyer*, 99 Wash.2d 114, 660 P.2d 738 (1983); *Andrews v. Ballard*, 498 F.Supp. 1038 (S.D.Texas 1980). Cf. *In re P.V.W.*, 424 So.2d 1015 (La.1982).

Moreover, we concluded that the choice of whether to undergo surgery or other medical treatment is to an extraordinary degree an intrinsically personal decision. The patient alone must live with his disorder, encounter the risks of therapy, or reap the consequences of treatment. By the same token, the choice will profoundly affect his or her development or life. It may mean the difference between life and death, pain and pleasure, poverty and economic stability. 553 So.2d at 414–415, citing *Rasmussen by Mitchell v. Fleming*, supra; *Andrews v. Ballard,* supra. Accordingly, this court concluded that the Louisiana Constitution's right to privacy also provides for a right to decide whether to obtain or reject medical treatment. 553 So.2d at 415.

[5] We have no doubt that this and other interests that Perry has in avoiding the forcible administration of antipsychotic drugs are protected by Art. I, § 5 despite his status as a prisoner. It is generally accepted that conviction of a crime and incarceration, while limiting an inmate's right to freedom from confinement, do not extinguish his right to liberty altogether. *Vitek v. Jones,* 445 U.S. 480, 100 S.Ct. 1254, 63 L.Ed.2d 552 (1980); *Bell v. Wolfish,* 441 U.S. 520, 99 S.Ct. 1861, 60 L.Ed.2d 447 (1979). Subject to the legitimate requirements of prison discipline and security, prison inmates retain their fundamental constitutional rights and protections. *Hudson v. Palmer,* 468 U.S. 517, 104 S.Ct. 3194, 82 L.Ed.2d 393 (1984); *Brown v. State,* 117 Ariz. 476, 573 P.2d 876 (1978); *Moen v. Wilson,* 189 Colo. 85, 536 P.2d 1129 (1975); *Roque v. Warden,* 181 Conn. 85, 434 A.2d 348 (1980); *State v. Holmes,* 109 N.J.Super. 180, 262 A.2d 725 (1970); *Bush v. Canary,* 286 N.W.2d 536 (S.D. 1979); *Matter of Sinka,* 92 Wash.2d 555, 599 P.2d 1275 (1979).

In the evolution of the state constitution's Declaration of the Right of Due Process of Law, Art. I, § 2, the scope and nature of due process were understood not solely in terms of state jurisprudence under the prior due process clause, but also in light of the much broader contemporary federal due process developments. Also sought to be continued was the "fundamental fairness" analysis by which due process grows organically. Hargrave, supra, at 4. In view of this safeguard and the expanded protections of privacy and personhood afforded by Art. I, § 5, we conclude that the generally accepted principles regarding prisoners' retention of fundamental rights despite incarceration have been adopted by our state constitution.

Accordingly, because the involuntary medication was ordered as an integral and essential part of Perry's punishment and not because of any legitimate requirement of prison security or medical interest of Perry, we conclude that the medicate-to-execute scheme infringes on Perry's constitutionally protected interest in deciding whether to obtain or reject medical treatment and what shall be done medically with his mind and body.

[6] It is a matter of first impression whether Art. I, § 5 also affords protection against the government's unjustified physical invasion of a person's body and brain or the government's control by any means of a person's mind and thoughts. However, the United States Supreme Court recognized that these types of interests were protected under the Bill of Rights and the Fourteenth Amendment well before the adoption of our state constitution. See Henkin, Privacy and Autonomy, 47 Colum.L.Rev. 1410 (1974).

The concept of constitutional privacy as protecting an individual in the security of his or her body was first articulated long ago. In *U. Pacific R. Co. v. Botsford,* 141 U.S. 250, 11 S.Ct. 1000, 35 L.Ed. 734 (1891), the Court held that civil litigants could not be forced to submit to a surgical examination because "no right is held more sacred, or is more carefully guarded at common law, than the right of every individual to the possession and control of his own person ... 'to be let alone.'" Id. at 251, 11 S.Ct. at 1001. See also *Olmstead v. U.S.,* 277 U.S. 438, 478, 48 S.Ct. 564, 572, 72 L.Ed. 944 (1928) (Brandeis, J., dissenting). Governmental invasion of the body by stomach pumping "shocks the conscience" and was held to be a flagrant violation of substantive due process in *Rochin v. California,* 342 U.S. 165, 72 S.Ct. 205, 96 L.Ed. 183 (1952). Certain other governmental invasions have been treated as intrusions of a protected interest of privacy or personhood, although they eventually were upheld on a showing of clear necessity, procedural regularity, and lack of risk, trauma or pain to the individual. *Schmerber v. California,* 384 U.S. 757, 86 S.Ct. 1826, 16 L.Ed.2d 908 (1966) (blood tests); *Jacobson v. Massachusetts,* 197 U.S. 11, 25 S.Ct. 358, 49 L.Ed. 643 (1905) (compulsory vaccinations); see L. Tribe, American Constitutional Law, § 15–9, 1331–32 (2d ed. 1988). Indeed, "[c]ontrol over the body is the first form of autonomy and ... [a]ny plausible definition of privacy, then, whatever the sources of its normative commitments, must take the body as its first and most basic reference...." Gerety, Redefining Privacy, 12 Harv.Civ.Rts.—Civ.Lb.L.Rev. 233, 266 (1977).

An individual's constitutionally protected interest in his mind, thoughts and mental processes was also recognized by the Supreme Court prior to the adoption of our state constitution. The operations of the mind are absolutely beyond the power of government to control. See *Stanley v. Georgia,* 394 U.S. 557, 565–66, 89 S.Ct. 1243, 1248–49, 22 L.Ed.2d 542 (1969) (Government does not have "the power to control men's minds" or "the right to control the moral content of a person's thought." "[A]lso fundamental is the right to be free ... from unwarranted governmental intrusions into one's privacy."); *Paris Adult Theatre I v. Slaton,* 413 U.S. 49, 67, 93 S.Ct. 2628, 2640, 37 L.Ed.2d 446 (1973) ("The fantasies of a drug addict are his own and beyond the reach of government [unlike] regulation of drug sales...."); Tribe, supra, §§ 15–5 et seq. Although these cases involved governmental attempts to usurp mental control by nonphysical means, the decisions necessarily prohibit mind or thought control by physical or chemical means authorized or directed by the state.

[7] For all of these reasons, we conclude that the state's plan to medicate and execute Perry would violate his bodily integrity, chemically alter his mind and will, and usurp his fundamental right to make decisions regarding his health or medical treatment. Each of these interests is protected from unwarranted governmental intrusion by Art. I, § 5's right of privacy or personhood. Moreover, these invasions are particularly intrusive because the forcible administration of antipsychotic drugs creates a substantial risk of permanent injury and premature death.

B. Interference By Forcible Injection Of Antipsychotic Drugs

When antipsychotic drugs are forcibly administered to further the state's interest in carrying out capital punishment, and therefore *not* done in the prisoner's best medical interest, the intrusion represents an *extremely severe* interference with that person's liberty. The object of the intrusion is hostile in the utmost instead of beneficent, and the trustful, communicative doctor-patient relationship essential to the effective humane administration of antipsychotic drugs cannot exist. Under these circumstances, the nonconsenting recipient of antipsychotic drugs is much less likely to receive adequate protection from severely burdensome side effects.

As the Supreme Court has recognized, the forcible injection of antipsychotic drugs into a nonconsenting person's body, even when done in his medical interest with medical appropriateness, represents a particularly severe interference with that person's liberty. *Riggins,* supra, — U.S. at —, 112 S.Ct. at 1814; *Harper,* supra, 494 U.S. at 229, 110 S.Ct. at 1040. The Supreme Court summarized some of the potential effects of antipsychotic drugs as follows:

> The purpose of the drugs is to alter the chemical balance in a patient's brain, leading to changes, intended to be beneficial, in his or her cognitive processes. While the therapeutic benefits of antipsychotic drugs are well-documented, it is also true that the drugs can have serious, even fatal side effects. One such side effect identified by the trial court is acute dystonia, a severe involuntary spasm of the upper body, tongue, throat, or eyes. The trial court found that it may be treated and reversed within a few minutes through use of the medication Cogentin. Other side effects include akathesia (motor restlessness, often characterized by an inability to sit still); neuroleptic malignant syndrome (a relatively rare condition which can lead to death from cardiac dysfunction); and tardive dyskinesia, perhaps the most discussed side effect of antipsychotic drugs. Tardive dyskinesia is a neurological disorder, irreversible in some cases, that is

characterized by involuntary, uncontrollable movements of various muscles, especially around the face.... [T]he proportion of patients treated with antipsychotic drugs who exhibit the symptoms of tardive dyskinesia ranges from 10% to 25%. According to the American Psychiatric Association, studies of the condition indicate that 60% of tardive dyskinesia is mild or minimal in effect, and about 10% may be characterized as severe.

Riggins, supra, — U.S. at —, 112 S.Ct. at 1814 (quoting *Washington v. Harper*, supra, 494 U.S. at 229–30, 110 S.Ct. at 1040–41). Furthermore, even when antipsychotic drugs are administered purely as part of appropriate medical treatment, the drugs do not cure the mental disorder. Horton, Restoration of Competency For Execution: Furiosus Solo Furane Punitur, 44 Southwestern Law Journal 1191, 1204 (1990); Kenna, Current Status of Institutionalized Mental Health Patients' Right to Refuse Psychotropic Drugs, 6 J.Legal Med. 107, 110 (1985). They merely calm and mask the psychotic symptoms which usually return to debilitate the patient when medication is discontinued. Horton, Id.; Gutheil & Appelbaum, "Mind Control", "Synthetic Sanity", "Artificial Competence", and Genuine Confusion: Legally Relevant Effects of Antipsychotic Medication, 12 Hofstra L.Rev. 77, 99–101 (1983).

The interference by forcible injection of antipsychotic drugs is even more severe and dangerous when done for purposes of capital punishment. Therefore, further elaboration on the potential effects of the drugs is called for, including the description and detail of additional side effects not contained in the Supreme Court's summary.

Antipsychotic drugs regularly produce a variety of disorders in the control of posture, muscle tone and movement, presumably as a result of dysfunction of the extrapyramidal nervous system. R. Baldessarini, Chemotherapy in Psychiatry: Principles and Practice, 37 (1985). Accordingly, these side effects are often termed extrapyramidal syndrome or "EPS". The medical experts who examined Perry for the sanity hearing attested to these potential harms. The toxicity of antipsychotics on the central nervous system is manifested by several of these characteristic motor disorders. Another such disorder, akinesia, causes lethargy, drooling, rigidity of facial muscles, lessening of spontaneity, apathy, and a disinclination to initiate activity. Note, Antipsychotic Drugs and the Incompetent Defendant: A Perspective on the Treatment and Prosecution of Incompetent Defendants, 47 Wash. & Lee L.Rev. 1059, 1061 (1990). Other regularly occurring effects include feelings of heaviness, sluggishness, weakness, faintness, dry mouth, blurred vision, insomnia, anxiety, euphoria, agitation, drowsiness, depression, headache, confusion, vertigo, grand mal seizures, impaired liver function, hallucinations, jaundice, breast engorgement, impotence, constipation, diarrhea, nausea, vomiting, and anorexia. See, Physician's Desk Reference 1375 (42d ed. 1989) (hereinafter PDR); Baldessarini, supra, at 68–74.

Tardive Dyskinesia may develop even after relatively brief periods of treatment, even at low dosage levels. PDR at 1374. Tardive dyskinesia can in some cases seriously impair skills in self-care, feeding, and swallowing. There is no known treatment. The only way to effectively reduce the risk of tardive dyskinesia is to thoughtfully and conservatively use antipsychotic drugs and attempt to use alternative treatments. Baldessarini, supra, at 78. However, it is likely that such measures would be inconsistent with and impossible under a scheme of preparation for execution which considers only the remission of psychotic symptoms to a level at which the prisoner would be considered competent for execution. Also, recipients of antipsychotic medication run the danger of developing neuroleptic malignant syndrome, a potentially fatal condition manifested by hyperpyrexia, muscle rigidity, catatonia, and autonomic instability, including irregular pulse or blood pressure, tachycardia, and cardiac dysrhythmia. PDR at 1374.

Acute dystonia typically occurs early in treatment and usually with high-potency neuroleptics. Baldessarini, supra, at 69. This condition as a rule causes severe anxiety. Id. It is manifested by sustained uncontrollable excessive movement of the muscles of the neck, jaw, and tongue, as well as the eyes and trunk. Other symptoms may include trismus (lockjaw), opisthotonos (a condition of tetanic spasm of the muscles of the back, causing the head and lower limbs to bend backward and the trunk to arch forward), or tonic oculogyric movements or deviations of the eyes ("oculogyric crisis"). Facial grimacing, perioral spasms, protrusions or torsion of the tongue, sweating, fever and dysphagia are common. Laryngeal or pharyngeal spasm with dyspnea or life-threatening respiratory distress may develop, and a few fatalities have occurred. Id. These reactions are more likely to occur in young adult male patients.

Because of the many potentially harmful effects of antipsychotic drugs, the state's use of them to infringe upon a person's mind, body and medical autonomy as an instrument of capital punishment is far more invasive than other governmental interferences which have been held to be violative of the right of privacy or its forerunner, the right of substantive due process of law. In *Hondroulis v. Schuhmacher*, supra, the state statute at issue, as interpreted by the lower courts, impermissibly interfered with a person's right to decide what is to be done with his body by creating legal obstructions to his access to medical information from physicians. In *Griswold v. Connecticut*, supra, and the cases leading to *Griswold's* recognition of a separate, independent right to privacy implied by principles within the Bill of Rights, the state statutes at issue were held unconstitutional because they unduly interfered with an individual's right to make important decisions affecting himself, such as choices concerning contraception, procreation, marriage, family relationships, and child rearing and education. See authorities cited in *Hondroulis v. Schuhmacher*, supra, at 414. If the state is permitted to carry out its plan, Perry not only would be deprived of his right to make important medical choices affecting his mind, body and well-being, but he also would be forced to submit to the physical intrusion of powerful, dangerous and unpredictable drugs into his body and brain, and compelled to yield control of his thoughts and will to the state for the purpose of implementing his execution.

C. Application of the Compelling State Interest Test

Although the right to privacy or personhood is not absolute, we indicated in *Hondroulis v. Schuhmacher*, supra, that where a decision as fundamental as those included within the right of personal privacy is involved, state action imposing a burden on it may be justified only by a compelling state interest, and the state action must be narrowly confined so as to further only that compelling interest. Id. at 415. Only such strict judicial scrutiny is sufficiently protective of a person's right of privacy or personhood to avoid unwarranted governmental interference with his body, mind, and medical autonomy. Id.; accord: *Kramer v. Union Free School Dist.*, 395 U.S. 621, 89 S.Ct. 1886, 23 L.Ed.2d 583 (1969); *Shapiro v. Thompson*, 394 U.S. 618, 89 S.Ct. 1322, 22 L.Ed.2d 600 (1969); *Aptheker v. Secretary of State*, 378 U.S. 500, 84 S.Ct. 1659, 12 L.Ed.2d 992 (1964); *Cantwell v. Connecticut*, 310 U.S. 296, 60 S.Ct. 900, 84 L.Ed. 1213 (1940); *Sherbert v. Verner*, 374 U.S. 398, 83 S.Ct. 1790, 10 L.Ed.2d 965 (1963); *Griswold v. Connecticut*, 381 U.S. 479, 85 S.Ct. 1678, 14 L.Ed.2d 510 (1965); *People v. Medina*, 705 P.2d 961, 975 (Colo.1985); *Guardianship of Roe*, 383 Mass. 415, 421 N.E.2d 40 (1981).

We see no reason for the state's proposed action in the present case to be measured by a less rigorous standard or receive less than strict scrutiny simply because it is sought to be implemented by the state through a court order rather than by legislative enactment. We turn to question, therefore, whether the court order directing that the prisoner be forcibly medicated and maintained with antipsychotic drugs at a certain level of competency for purposes of execution, is necessary to promote a compelling state interest, and is narrowly drawn to further only that interest.

First, the state attempts to bring the involuntary drugging at issue in this case under the aegis of *Washington v. Harper*, supra, by arguing that although the forcible medication of Perry will further the state interests to be served by his execution, it will also advance Perry's medical interest and promote the state's interest in prison safety because his mental illness causes him to be a danger to himself and others. We believe these purposes were manufactured with the benefit of hindsight and did not in fact motivate the challenged court order. As we explained in distinguishing Harper above, the record reflects that the present proceeding was initiated by the trial court solely for the purpose of determining Perry's competence for execution, that the forcible medication was ordered solely to implement his execution and that forcible injection of antipsychotic drugs into his body to remove the obstacle to his execution is not in his ultimate medical interest.

Furthermore, even if prison safety and Perry's medical welfare were the state's true objectives, the trial court's order sweeps unnecessarily broadly and thereby invades the area of protected freedoms. See *Aptheker v. Secretary of State*, 378 U.S. at 508, 84 S.Ct. at 1664 and authorities cited therein. The state has within its power less drastic means of achieving the objectives of medically treating Perry for his own best interests and protecting others at the prison. La.R.S. 15:803.1 provides an example. Under this statute, a mentally ill prisoner may be medically treated involuntarily when "necessary to prevent harm or injury to the inmate or to others". Also he may be judicially committed to a treatment facility after a hearing at which the inmate is represented by counsel. Thus, the state action proposed in the present case is not narrowly confined to the interests of prison safety and the inmate's medical interest even if these were the state's objectives as asserted in argument.

Second, the state suggests alternatively that it has a compelling interest in medicating Perry in order to further the social goals to be advanced by the death penalty, i.e., the retribution and deterrence of capital crimes. For the reasons assigned in the next section of this opinion, however, we conclude that the execution of a forcibly medicated insane prisoner will not contribute to the goal of either retribution or deterrence of capital offenses. Consequently, the state has failed to demonstrate that its proposed infringement upon Perry's protected rights of privacy and personhood is outweighed by a compelling state interest that would be measurably advanced by carrying out the death sentence. The state's plan to use forcible medication as a means of effecting punishment is therefore unconstitutional and must be disallowed. However, because Perry's right of personhood and privacy is also protected under our state constitution's cruel, excessive and unusual punishment clause and cannot be adequately discussed without its consideration, we do not base our decision on Art. I, § 5 alone.

VI. HUMANE TREATMENT

[8] The specific issue we address here is whether death, combined with forcible administration of antipsychotic drugs, is punishment that subjects an insane capital offender to cruel, excessive or unusual punishment, that consequently, by virtue of Art. I, § 20 of the 1974 Louisiana Constitution, is beyond the power of the state to inflict. We conclude that the death penalty as applied to an insane offender under these circumstances is unconstitutional. The punishment is cruel because it imposes significantly more indignity, pain and suffering than ordinarily is necessary for the mere extinguishment of life, excessive because it imposes a severe penalty without furthering any of the valid social goals of punishment, and unusual because it subjects to the death penalty a class of offenders that has been exempt therefrom for centuries and adds novel burdens to the punishment of the insane which will not be suffered by sane capital offenders.

Article I, § 20 was derived from the Eighth Amendment and similar guarantees appearing in earlier state constitutions. La. Const.1921, Art. I, § 12; La. Const. 1913, Art. 12; La. Const.1898, Art. 12; La.

Const.1879, Art. 9; La. Const.1868, Art. 8; La. Const.1864, Arts. 94, 107. It adds, however, that no law shall subject any person to, "euthanasia", "torture", or "excessive punishment", broadening the prior prohibition against "excessive fines ... cruel and unusual punishment". La. Const.1921, Art. I, § 12; *State v. Sepulvado*, 367 So.2d 762 (La.1979). These additions expand in several instances the precepts that had evolved from the United States Supreme Court's interpretation of the Cruel and Unusual Punishments Clause of the Eighth Amendment. Hargrave, The Declaration of Rights of the Louisiana Constitution of 1974, 35 La.L.Rev. 1, 63 (1974); Jenkins, "The Declaration of Rights," 31 Loy.L.Rev. 9, 39–40 (1975).

The most significant example of expansion is the deliberate inclusion of a prohibition against "excessive" punishment, which has been interpreted to add a protection of individual liberty surpassing that provided by the Eighth Amendment. Because of this provision, a person is protected not only from punishment that is cruel, excessive or unusual per se or as applied to particular categories of crimes or classes of offenders, but also from any excessive feature of a particular sentence produced by an abuse of the sentencer's discretion, even though the sentence is otherwise within constitutional limits. *State v. Telsee*, 425 So.2d 1251 (La.1983); *State v. Sepulvado*, 367 So.2d 762 (La.1979).

[9] The enhancement of the safeguards in several particulars and the convention history in general indicate that Article I, § 20 affords no less, and in some respects more, protection than that available to individuals under the Cruel and Unusual Punishments Clause of the Eighth Amendment at the time of the adoption of our state constitution. Accordingly, this court has considered the United States Supreme Court opinions and other jurisprudence preexisting the adoption of the 1974 Louisiana Constitution as the threshold, but not the determinant, of the right to humane treatment declared by Art. I, § 20. See *State v. Sepulvado*, supra, at 746–66; see also Hargrave, supra, at 63.

In the leading case, *State v. Stetson*, 317 So.2d 172 (La.1975), this court was called upon to decide whether mandatory life imprisonment for the crime of distribution of heroin was cruel, excessive or unusual punishment. The court reviewed the concurring opinions of the Justices in *Furman v. Georgia*, 408 U.S. 238, 92 S.Ct. 2726, 33 L.Ed.2d 346 (1972) (Douglas, J., concurring); id. 408 U.S. at 257, 92 S.Ct. at 2735 (Brennan, J., concurring); id. at 306, 92 S.Ct. at 2760 (Stewart, J., concurring); id. at 310, 92 S.Ct. at 2762 (White, J., concurring); id. at 314, 92 S.Ct. at 2764 (Marshall, J., concurring) and other jurisprudence and derived four principles or generalized criteria for assessing the constitutional validity of punishments under Art. I, § 20: the punishment must not be (1) degrading to the dignity of human beings; (2) arbitrarily inflicted; (3) unacceptable to contemporary society; or (4) excessive, i.e., disproportionate to the crime or failing to serve a penal purpose more effectively than a less severe punishment. Id. at 177. Applying these principles, this court concluded that the penalty was constitutional. Id.

A. Background of the Principles of Humane Treatment

[10] The principles recognized by this court in the Stetson case as being appropriate for evaluating punishment under Art. I, § 20 were distilled by the Furman court's opinions from a rich background of jurisprudence. We refer to pertinent parts of that development for insight with which to apply the principles of humane treatment to the present case.

As this court stated in Stetson, the primary principle of the right to humane treatment is that a punishment must not be degrading to the dignity of human beings. This basic principle deals with society's obligation to itself and its members to treat each individual as a human being. The other three principles of humane treatment banning excessive, arbitrary and socially unacceptable punishment pertain to specific indicia of inhumane treatment and to the state's obligation to treat each individual or class of persons humanely in comparison with its treatment of others. We will describe each of these principles generally before applying them one by one to the circumstances of the present case.

The principal hallmark of any punishment that is degrading to the dignity of human beings is that it treats members of the human race as non-humans. This results when a person is treated as a thing or as a means to the state's ends, rather than as a fellow human, resulting in extremely degrading physical or mental suffering. *Trop v. Dulles*, 356 U.S. 86, 78 S.Ct. 590, 2 L.Ed.2d 630 (1958) (expatriation); *Weems v. U.S.*, 217 U.S. 349, 30 S.Ct. 544, 54 L.Ed. 793 (1910) (cadena temporal); *Wilkerson v. Utah*, 99 U.S. 130, 25 L.Ed. 345 (1878). The barbaric punishments condemned by history, "punishments which inflict torture, such as the rack, the thumbscrew, the iron boot, the stretching of limbs and the like," are, of course, "attended with acute pain and suffering." *O'Neil v. Vermont*, 144 U.S. 323, 339, 12 S.Ct. 693, 699, 36 L.Ed. 450 (1892) (Field, J., dissenting). The true significance of the unconstitutionality of these punishments, however, is their inconsistency with the fundamental premise of the Cruel and Unusual Punishments Clause that even the vilest criminal remains a human being both possessed and deserving of common human dignity. *Furman v. Georgia*, 408 U.S. 238, 273, 92 S.Ct. 2726–27, 33 L.Ed.2d 346 (1972) (Brennan, J., concurring). For example, in *Louisiana ex rel. Francis v. Resweber*, 329 U.S. 459, 464, 67 S.Ct. 374, 376, 91 L.Ed. 422 reh'g denied, 330 U.S. 853, 67 S.Ct. 673, 91 L.Ed. 1295 (1947), the Court concluded that it was not unconstitutional to force a prisoner to undergo a second effort to electrocute him after a mechanical malfunction thwarted the first attempt. The unsuccessful electrocution, although it caused mental anguish and physical pain, was the result of "an unforeseeable accident." Had the failure been intentional rather than a mishap, the punishment would have been, like torture, so degrading and indecent as to amount to a refusal to accord the offender human status. Id. 329 U.S. at 471–72, 67 S.Ct. at 380–81 (Frankfurter, J., concurring).

A state also may not constitutionally inflict punishment for the mere status one assumes in life, for to do so is to treat an individual as a thing rather than a fellow human being. Consequently, a state may not lawfully punish a person for being "mentally ill, or a leper, or ... afflicted with a venereal disease," or for being addicted to narcotics. *Robinson v. California*, 370 U.S. 660, 82 S.Ct. 1417, 8 L.Ed.2d 758 (1962). Furthermore, punishment may be degrading simply by reason of its enormity. A prime example is expatriation, a "punishment more primitive than torture," *Trop v. Dulles*, 356 U.S. at 101, 78 S.Ct. at 598; such punishment was held to be unconstitutional because it necessarily involves a denial by society of the individual's existence as a member of the human community. *Furman v. Georgia*, 408 U.S. at 273–74, 92 S.Ct. at 2743–44 (Brennan, J., concurring).

The remaining principles are complementary of the primary concept of human dignity. They prohibit the three archetypes of punishment that degrade the dignity of human beings i.e., excessive, arbitrary and socially unacceptable punishment. Frequently, they have been applied to prevent the state's application of a type of punishment to a particular class of offenders that would be inhumane in comparison with its treatment of others.

The second principle is that the state must not arbitrarily inflict a severe punishment. The very words "cruel and unusual punishment" imply condemnation of the arbitrary infliction of severe punishment. The state does not respect human dignity when it inflicts upon a person or a class of persons a severe punishment that it does not inflict on others for committing the same act or offense. *Furman v. Georgia*, supra 408 U.S. at 274, 92 S.Ct. at 2744 (Brennan, J., concurring).

While fear of torture was the central concern of the Framers of the Eighth Amendment, its English background indicates that the concern for regularity and generality in the imposition of severe punishment also underlies the Clause. A. Goldberg and A. Dershowitz, Declaring the

Death Penalty Unconstitutional, 83 Harv. L.Rev. 1773, 1789 (1970). The incident which prompted inclusion of the cruel and unusual punishment protection in the 1688 English Bill of Rights was the prosecution and punishment of Titus Oates, a minister of the Church of England, for two counts of perjury in 1685. Oates was convicted on both counts and sentenced to (1) pay a substantial fine, (2) life imprisonment, (3) whippings, (4) pilloring four times a year, and (5) to be defrocked. Id. Although none of these punishments was considered torture at that time, the English Parliament called for his release, calling the penalty "inhumane and unparalleled." Therefore, "cruel and unusual" seems to have originally meant a severe punishment unauthorized by statute and not within the jurisdiction of the court to impose. A. Grannuci, Nor Cruel and Unusual Punishments Inflicted: The Original Meaning, 57 Calif.L.Rev. 839, 859 (1969). See *Furman v. Georgia*, supra, 408 U.S. at 428, 92 S.Ct. at 2823 (Burger, C.J., dissenting).

By its attention to the use of a particular penalty outside of the jurisdiction involved, the United States Supreme Court implicitly affirmed the principle that for a punishment to withstand scrutiny under the Eighth Amendment, it must not be arbitrary. See *Wilkerson*, supra; *Weems*, supra; *Trop*, supra. Judicial scrutiny in this context reflects not only a measurement of evolving standards of decency but also a reference to the anomaly of the punishments in question. When an individual is singled out because of an accident of geography for unusually severe treatment, it seems particularly cruel. Moreover, as the Court observed in *Trop v. Dulles*, supra, 356 U.S. at 100–01 n. 32, 78 S.Ct. at 597–98 n. 32, "[i]f the word 'unusual' is to have any meaning apart from the word 'cruel' ... the meaning should be the ordinary one, signifying something different from that which is generally done." Goldberg & Dershowitz, supra 1789. Neither the cadena temporal in *Weems* nor the expatriation in *Trop* was authorized elsewhere. In *Wilkerson* the Court reviewed various treatises on military law in order to demonstrate that under "the custom of war," shooting was a common method of inflicting the punishment of death. 99 U.S. at 133–34.

The constitutional protection against arbitrary punishments was explicitly recognized in *Louisiana ex rel. Francis v. Resweber*, 329 U.S. 459, 67 S.Ct. 374, 91 L.Ed. 422 (1947). Focusing on the manner in which the first abortive attempt to electrocute Francis had been conducted, the Court spoke of the "[p]rohibition against wanton infliction of pain [that] has come into our law from the Bill of Rights of 1688." Id. 329 U.S. at 463, 67 S.Ct. at 376. In the Court's opinion, Francis had not been subject to the wanton or arbitrary infliction of pain; the extra pain he suffered was unavoidably accidental. See also Goldberg & Dershowitz, supra at 1791.

The third principle inherent in the guarantee of humane treatment is that a severe punishment must not be excessive. The inquiry into "excessiveness" has two aspects. First, the infliction of a severe punishment by the state cannot comport with human dignity when it is unnecessary and nothing more than the pointless infliction of suffering. A particular punishment, therefore, is unconstitutionally excessive if it does not make any measurable contribution to the goals that such punishment is intended to achieve. *Furman v. Georgia*, 408 U.S. 238, 279–80, 92 S.Ct. 2726, 2747, 33 L.Ed.2d 346 (1972) (Brennan, J., concurring); id. 408 U.S. at 311–12, 92 S.Ct. at 2763 (White, J., concurring); id. at 342–57, 92 S.Ct. at 2778–87 (Marshall, J., concurring); id. at 392–93, 92 S.Ct. at 2805–06 (Burger, C.J., dissenting); *Weems v. U.S.*, supra, 217 U.S. at 381, 30 S.Ct. at 554; *Wilkerson v. Utah*, 99 U.S. at 136. Second, the punishment must not be grossly out of proportion to the severity of the crime. *Trop v. Dulles*, supra, 356 U.S. at 100, 78 S.Ct. at 597 (plurality opinion); *Weems v. U.S.*, supra, 217 U.S. at 367, 30 S.Ct. at 549.

In *Gregg v. Georgia*, 428 U.S. 153, 96 S.Ct. 2909, 49 L.Ed.2d 859 (1976) the Supreme Court discussed the "excessiveness" inquiry with respect to the death penalty. Although *Gregg* was decided after the adoption of Art. I, § 20, the lead opinion relied primarily on decisions pre-existing our state constitution and therefore may be considered as an indication of the minimum level of protection afforded by the state constitutional right to humane treatment. The *Gregg* plurality stated that the death penalty is said to serve two principal social purposes: retribution and deterrence of capital crimes by prospective offenders. 428 U.S. at 183–84, 96 S.Ct. at 2929–30 (citing *Furman v. Georgia*, 408 U.S. at 394–95, 92 S.Ct. at 2806–07 (Burger, J., dissenting); id., at 452–54, 92 S.Ct. at 2835–36 (Powell, J., dissenting)); *Powell v. Texas*, 392 U.S. 514, 531, 88 S.Ct. 2145, 2153, 20 L.Ed.2d 1254 (1968). Therefore, when a particular application of the death penalty fails to measurably contribute to either of these goals it clearly is unnecessary and involves the wanton infliction of pain.

The final principle of humane treatment is that a severe punishment must not be unacceptable to contemporary society. As the Supreme Court has noted, the Cruel and Unusual Punishments Clause "must draw its meaning from the evolving standards of decency that mark the progress of a maturing society." *Trop v. Dulles*, supra, 356 U.S. at 101, 78 S.Ct. at 597. Rejection by society is a strong indication that a particular severe punishment does not comport with human dignity. In practice, most of the Supreme Court opinions prior to 1974 tended to rely upon objective indicia of attitudes actually prevailing among civilized people: historic usage of particular punishments, *Wilkerson v. Utah*, supra, (firing squad usage in Utah Territory and the Army); statutory authorization in other jurisdictions, *Weems v. U.S.*, supra (cadena temporal had no equivalent in the United States); *Trop v. Dulles*, supra, (expatriation unused by other civilized nations); general public opinion, *Louisiana ex rel. Francis v. Resweber*, 329 U.S. 459, 471, 67 S.Ct. 374, 380, 91 L.Ed. 422 (1947) (Frankfurter, J., concurring); and a combination of present acceptance with past usage, *Trop v. Dulles*, supra, 356 U.S. at 99, 78 S.Ct. at 597. See also *Robinson v. Calif.*, 370 U.S. 660, 82 S.Ct. 1417, 8 L.Ed.2d 758 (1962); *Weems v. U.S.*, 217 U.S. 349, 30 S.Ct. 544, 54 L.Ed. 793 (1910). Goldberg & Dershowitz, supra, at 1780–82.

Thus, whether there are objective factors from which a court can conclude that contemporary society considers a severe punishment unacceptable is the issue. Moreover, the acceptability of a severe punishment is measured by its actual use, not its availability, for it might become so offensive as never to be inflicted. *Furman v. Georgia*, 408 U.S. at 278–79, 92 S.Ct. at 2746–47 (Brennan, J., concurring). Objective evidence of contemporary notions of humanity and decency must be viewed, however, only as a threshold inquiry or the principle of humane treatment would merely legitimize advances already made and opinions already conventional. Goldberg & Dershowitz, supra, at 1782.

The four principles or generalized criteria provide the means by which a court can determine whether a challenged punishment is consistent with human dignity. They are, therefore, interrelated, and in most cases it will be their convergence that will justify the conclusion that a punishment is "cruel, excessive or unusual". The test, then, is a cumulative one: If a punishment is unusually degrading, if there is strong probability that it is inflicted arbitrarily, if it is substantially rejected by contemporary society, and if there is no reason to believe that it serves any valid goal of punishment more effectively than some less severe punishment, then the continued infliction of that punishment violates the command that the state may not inflict inhuman and uncivilized punishments upon those convicted of crimes. *Furman v. Georgia*, 408 U.S. at 282, 92 S.Ct. at 2748 (Brennan, J., concurring).

B. Application of Principles of Humane Treatment

The Stetson principles or generalized criteria of humane treatment, when applied to the punishment proposed by the state in the present case, converge to compel the conclusion that the forcible administration of antipsychotic drugs to induce competence for execution, compounded by execution itself, would be cruel, excessive, and unusual punishment. The state's medicate-for-execution scheme is thus unconstitutional.

The punishment intended for Perry is severely degrading to human dignity. It will involve far more than the mere extinguishment of human life. Unlike other death row prisoners, Perry will be forced to yield to the state the control of his mind, thoughts and bodily functions, ingest or absorb powerful toxic chemicals, and risk or suffer harmful, possibly fatal, drug side effects. He will not be afforded a humane exit but will suffer unique indignities and degradation. In fact, he will be forced to linger for a protracted period, stripped of the vestiges of humanity and dignity usually reserved to death row inmates, with the growing awareness that the state is converting his own mind and body into a vehicle for his execution. In short, Perry will be treated as a thing, rather than a human being, and deliberately subjected to "something inhuman, barbarous" and analogous to torture.

The punishment the state plans for Perry is arbitrary in its conception and is apt to be arbitrary in practice. The punishment is anomalous, irregular and without general application. No insane offender has been executed in the civilized world for centuries. There is no statute in this or any other jurisdiction authorizing the execution of an insane offender or the involuntary medication of a prisoner for this purpose. Moreover, the trial court by ordering the state to medicate Perry forcibly if necessary has created an opportunity for further arbitrariness in application. The trial court's order places any physician having a duty to treat Perry for his mental illness in a severe conflict of interest, as we have noted in distinguishing forcible medication for execution from forcible medical treatment for safety and health. In short, whether the doctor prescribes and administers antipsychotic drugs or refuses to do so, he must act contrary to his patient's best medical interests either by promoting the execution of his patient or by failing to alleviate suffering. In this ambiguous situation there is great risk that physicians who choose to forcibly administer drugs may pursue the clear goal of execution more vigorously than the vaguer duty of protecting the inmate from drug side effects; and there is danger that the involuntary dispensation may be removed effectively from physicians' hands altogether. Under these circumstances there will be increased danger of arbitrariness and capriciousness in both the forcible administration of drugs and the determination of competence for execution.

The punishment that the state seeks to carry out on Perry is excessive because it makes no measurable contribution to the acceptable goals of capital punishment and hence is nothing more than the purposeless and needless imposition of pain and suffering. Of the social goals of criminal punishment, the death penalty may be said to further only two, viz., retribution and deterrence of capital crimes. See *Gregg v. Georgia,* supra (restating principles advanced by members of the Court in *Furman v. Georgia,* supra, and prior decisions). Executing insane offenders after violating their rights of personhood by forcibly administering antipsychotic drugs to them against their wills, however, does not measurably further either the goal of deterrence or retribution.

The Supreme Court has noted that statistical attempts to evaluate the worth of the death penalty as a deterrent to crimes by potential offenders have been inconclusive. *Gregg v. Georgia,* supra, 428 U.S. at 184, 96 S.Ct. at 2930 (citations omitted). The Gregg plurality assumed that for some offenses and offenders the death penalty is a significant deterrent, viz., carefully contemplated murders, such as murder for hire, and murder by a life prisoner. Id. at 185–86, 96 S.Ct. at 2930–31. However, it is highly unlikely that the deterrent value of the death penalty will be increased measurably by including within the class of convicted offenders who may be executed a category that has been exempt from execution for centuries, viz., the insane. The likelihood is remote at best that a capital offender, capable of the kind of cost-benefit analysis that would make him susceptible to being deterred by the possibility of execution, would attach crucial weight to the fact that he cannot be executed should he become insane after being apprehended, convicted and sentenced to death. Cf. *Thompson v. Oklahoma*, 487 U.S. 815, 108 S.Ct. 2687, 101 L.Ed.2d 702 (1988); *Penry v. Lynaugh*, 492 U.S. 302, 109 S.Ct. 2934, 106 L.Ed.2d 256 (1989) (Brennan, J., dissenting); *Enmund v. Florida*, 458 U.S. 782, 102 S.Ct. 3368, 73 L.Ed.2d 1140 (1982). Under these circumstances, the threat of execution is too attenuated to be of substantial service to criminal justice. See *Furman v. Georgia*, supra, 408 U.S. at 391, 92 S.Ct. at 2804 (White, J., concurring).

Furthermore, the state's execution of insane prisoners by means of forcible medication does not measurably contribute to the social goal of retribution. The pursuit of retribution, like that of any single social aim, has its restrictive qualifiers. H.L.A. Hart, Responsibility and Punishment, 10 (1968). The principles limiting the unqualified pursuit of retribution include respect for human dignity and equivalence between crime and punishment. Because the punishment planned by the state in the present case would violate these restrictive principles we conclude that the state cannot legitimately further the goal of retribution by this means. See J.G. Murphy, Retribution, Justice, and Therapy 227 (1979) (citing I. Kant, The Philosophy of Law (W. Hastie trans. 1887)); H.L.A. Hart, Punishment and Responsibility: Essays in the Philosophy of Law 231 (1968).

The retributory theory of punishment presupposes that each human being possesses autonomy, a kind of rational freedom which entitles him or her to dignity and respect as a person which is morally sacred and inviolate, but that an original social contract was entered by which the people constituted themselves a state. Murphy, supra at 68, 65; Murphy, Kant: The Philosophy of Right, Ch. 4 (1970); Kant, The Philosophy of Law (1887). Accordingly, in order to enjoy the benefits that a legal system makes possible, each person must make the sacrifice of obeying the law even when it is personally undesirable. If the system is to remain just, therefore, it must be guaranteed that those who disobey will not gain unfair advantage over those who abide by the law. Criminal punishment is used to maintain the proper balance by insuring that the law breaker derives no profit from wrongdoing. The criminal who chooses not to sacrifice by exercising self-restraint and obedience elects, in effect, to sacrifice in another way—namely, by paying the prescribed penalty. Murphy, supra at 83, citing Kant, Metaphysische Anfangsgrunde der Rechtslehre, 331, 332, 335 (1797).

In strictest or most severe form the theory of retribution asserts, among other things, that a person's punishment must in some way match, or be the equivalent of, the wickedness of his offense. H.L.A., Punishment and Responsibility, 231 (1968). To many this is the most perplexing feature of the strict model of retributory theory. The simple equivalencies of an eye for an eye or a death for a death seem either repugnant or inapplicable to most offenses. Therefore, instead of equivalence between particular punishments and particular crimes, modern retributive theory is concerned with proportionality. Id. 233–34.

Because retribution is a theory which respects human dignity, regards human beings as responsible agents and not merely as things or resources to be manipulated for the social good, however, even strict retributivists agree that there are some things which should not be done to a criminal even if he has done them to others. Murphy, supra, 85, 90, citing Rechtslehre at 363. Immanuel Kant, the leading defender of the severe form of retribution, argued that the state should never do anything to a criminal that humiliates and degrades his dignity as a human being. Id.

Speaking of the death penalty, in a passage having great significance to the present case, Kant argued that, while a murderer must forfeit his life as a match or equivalent to his crime, the state cannot inflict suffering more than necessary to take his life: "[w]hoever has committed murder must die.... His death, however, must be kept free from all maltreatment that would make the humanity suffering in his person loathsome or abominable." Kant, The Philosophy of Law, supra, at

198. Consequently, we conclude that even the strictest retributivist would disapprove of the forcible administration of antipsychotic drugs to implement prisoners' executions because this would violate the cardinal principle of retribution that the state cannot degrade human dignity or maltreat any criminal.

As members of the Supreme Court have noted, "retribution is not inconsistent with our respect for human dignity." *Furman v. Georgia*, 408 U.S. at 394–395, 92 S.Ct. at 2806–07 (Burger, C.J., dissenting); id., at 452–454, 92 S.Ct. at 2835–36 (Powell, J. dissenting); *Powell v. Texas*, 392 U.S. 514, 531, 535–536, 88 S.Ct. 2145, 2153, 2155–56, 20 L.Ed.2d 1254 (1968) (plurality opinion). Indeed, the opinions of the Court have, in effect, adhered strongly to the concept that to exact significantly more punishment than death simpliciter from a capital offender would be maltreatment or torture demeaning his dignity and not a proportionate or even an equivalent punishment. See *Louisiana ex rel. Francis v. Resweber*, supra; *Wilkerson v. Utah*, supra; *In re Kemmler*, 136 U.S. 436, 10 S.Ct. 930, 34 L.Ed. 519 (1890). Moreover, if retribution could serve as justification for heaping an extra amount of indignity and suffering on a murderer because his crime was particularly vile, the "cruel, excessive and unusual" language would be read out of the Constitution; torture and atrocities would be permissible despite their being historically the clearest cases of forbidden inhumane punishment. *Furman v. Georgia*, supra, 408 U.S. at 408–10, 92 S.Ct. at 2813–14 (Marshall, J., concurring).

In light of these principles, we are convinced that the regime of punishment proposed by the trial court's order does not measurably contribute to the goal of retribution. Rather than calling upon Perry to suffer only the extinguishment of his life in a humane manner, the state would have him undergo a course of maltreatment that is inherently loathsome and degrading to his dignity as a human being. Unlike sane death row prisoners who retain dignity until the end, Perry would be forced to endure the usurpation of control of his body and mind by the state and the deprivation of medical treatment in his best interests before he is dispatched by the lethal injection. He must experience an indefinite period of indignity, anxiety and fear, assimilating unwanted antipsychotic drugs into his brain and body against his will at the risk of harmful and fatal side effects. He will go through this painful test involving his intimate mental and bodily processes without the aid of a trusted physician acting in his welfare and in whom he can confide. There is in this process of executing the death sentence no match, equivalence or proportionality. These circumstances amount to more than the mere extinguishment of life; they degrade human dignity and reach a sum in which there is something inhuman, barbarous, and analogous to torture.

Finally, we conclude that the compound of forcible medication and death that the state seeks to impose on Perry is a severe punishment unacceptable to contemporary society. After taking into account objective evidence of contemporary values, it is evident that the punishment would offend civilized standards of decency.

The prohibition against executing a prisoner who has lost his sanity has impressive historical and contemporary credentials. After being observed in the common law for centuries, it took root in America where it is followed unanimously today. Of the 36 death penalty jurisdictions, more than 20 have enacted statutory provisions prohibiting the execution of insane capital offenders. See Ala.Code § 15–16–23 (1982); Ariz. Rev.Stat.Ann. § 13–402 (1982); Ark.Code Ann. § 16–90–506 (1987); Cal.Penal Code §§ 3700–3704 (West 1982); Colo.Rev.Stat. § 16–8–110 (1986); Conn.Gen.Stat. § 54–101 (1985); Fla.Stat.Ann. § 922.07 (West 1985); Ga.Code Ann. § 17–10–61 to –63 (Harrison 1990); Ill.Rev.Stat. ch. 38, ¶ 1005–2–3 (1982); Kan.Stat.Ann. § 22–4006 (1988); Ky.Rev.Stat. § 431.240 (1985); Md.Code Ann. art. 27, § 75A(a)(2)(ii) (1990); Mass.Gen.Laws Ann. ch. 279, § 62 (West Supp.1992); Miss.Code Ann. § 99–19–57 (Supp.1985); Mo.Ann.Stat. § 552.060 (Vernon 1989); Mont.Code Ann. §§ 46–19–201 to –202 (1985); Neb.Rev.Stat. § 29–2537 to -2538 (1978); Nev.Rev.Stat. §§ 176.415 to 455 (1986); N.M.Stat.Ann. § 31-14-4 to 31-14-7 (1984); N.Y.Correct.Law §§ 655-57 (McKinney 1987); Ohio Rev.Code Ann. § 2949.28-30 (Baldwin 1992); Okla. Stat.Ann. tit. 22 §§ 1005-1008 (1986); Utah Code Ann. § 77-15-3 to -5 and § 77-19-8 to -13 (1990); Wyo.Stat. §§ 7-13-901 to -903 (1987). Other states provide for the transfer of all mentally incompetent prisoners to the state hospital. See Del.Code Ann. tit. 11, § 406 (1987); Ind.Code Ann. § 11-10-4-1 to 11-10-4-5 (Burns 1988); N.C.Gen.Stat. § 15A-1001 to 1002 (1988); S.C.Code Ann. § 44-23-210 (Law.Co-op. 1985); Va.Code § 19.2-177.1 (1990). Four states have adopted, by case law, the common law rule prohibiting the execution of the insane. *State v. Allen*, 204 La. 513, 15 So.2d 870 (1943); *Commonwealth v. Moon*, 383 Pa. 18, 117 A.2d 96 (1955); *Jordan v. State*, 124 Tenn. 81, 135 S.W. 327 (1911); *State v. Davis*, 6 Wash.2d 696, 108 P.2d 641 (1940) (dictum). Idaho has a statute that provides for the adoption of the common law absent an explicit statutory provision. Idaho Code § 73-116 (1989). In sum, the overwhelming weight of objective evidence of contemporary values in state statutes and common law indicates that society will not tolerate any exception to the widely and deeply held prohibition against executing the insane.

The ethical standards of the medical profession reinforce this view and constitute further objective evidence of this standard of decency. Both the American Medical Association and the American Psychiatric Association have strongly urged physicians not to participate in legalized state executions. See Ewing, Diagnosing and Treating "Insanity" on Death Row: Legal and Ethical Perspectives, 5 Behav.Sci. & L. 175, 176 (1987). Like the use of lethal injections, forcible medication in an attempt to restore competency constitutes a part of capital punishment that inherently conflicts with medical ethics. Horton, 44 S.W.L.J. at 1213; Sargent, Treating the Condemned to Death, Hastings Center Report at 6 (Dec. 1986); Salguero, Medical Ethics and Competency to be Executed, 96 Yale L.J. 167 at 178, n. 64.

Furthermore, the state cannot avoid contending with the force of this objective evidence by invoking the deferential judicial review standards adopted by the United States Supreme Court in assessing the constitutionality of a state's particular statutory punishment under the Eighth Amendment. In such cases, the Supreme Court has said that it will presume the validity of the statute and that a heavy burden rests on those who challenge the statute. *Gregg v. Georgia*, 428 U.S. 153, 96 S.Ct. 2909, 49 L.Ed.2d 859 (1976). The reasons cited for these rules were the deference the court owes to state legislatures under our federal system, its reluctance to become the arbiter of the standards of criminal responsibility throughout the country, and the difficulty of changing the high court's interpretations through constitutional amendment. Id.

The present case is clearly distinguishable from those in which the United States Supreme Court announced its Eighth Amendment review standards. *Perry* does not attack a death penalty statute in this case on the grounds of newly evolved standards of decency. Instead, *Perry* seeks to uphold the prohibition against executing the insane that was jurisprudentially adopted by this court and has been part of our law for nearly a century. Because the prohibition has not been expressly modified by the legislature, it must be presumed to have been tacitly approved by the lawmakers. Therefore, the state's role in the present case is not that of a defender of a statute but a proponent of a novel interpretation of this court's jurisprudential rule. Furthermore, we do not consider *Perry's* Eighth Amendment attack in this opinion but resolve this case on state grounds alone. Accordingly, this case does not bring into play the deference that the United States Supreme Court owes to the state legislatures under the principles of federalism.

Considering that it is the state, and not the prisoner, that seeks a change in the status quo, in the form of a novel interpretation of the law and the recognition of a new exception to a well-established norm, we conclude that the burden of justifying the proposed new legal precept must be allocated to the state, as its proponent and potential beneficiary. Accordingly, the state has the duty to present objective, persuasive evidence that it would not offend civilized standards of decency for a jurisdiction to medicate an insane prisoner against his will with antipsychotic drugs and use his involuntarily controlled mental condition as the means of his execution.

The state does not present any unequivocal objective evidence to show that the execution of the insane via forcible medication is acceptable to society. The state mainly begs the question by basing its conclusion that forcible medication renders the execution acceptable upon its own unproven assumption that only the insane prisoner's lack of comprehension stands in the way of an execution comporting with standards of decency. However, the state's invasion of the inmate's body, mind and autonomy in order to chemically alter his mental condition for execution is in itself inhumane treatment violating his right of personhood and privacy and has not been proven to be acceptable to society. Moreover, the insane prisoner's lack of understanding of his punishment is only one of the civilized qualms about executing the insane. The prohibition stems as well from other concerns, such as religious atonement, lack of deterrence and retribution, the insane person's inability to report exculpatory or mitigating evidence or to assist counsel, madness viewed as its own punishment, and the dignity of society itself. In the absence of objective proof to the contrary, we cannot say that these concerns are no longer important to society or that they can be dispelled by the forcible administration of antipsychotic drugs.

The evidence adduced by the state is equivocal and fails to prove that contemporary values have changed so as to require us to create an exception to the solid ban against executing the insane. The state first argues that the laws of other states permit the forcible administration of drugs to insane prisoners as a means of implementing executions. Specifically, the state relies on the provisions of some state statutes that reinstate the execution of the death penalty when an incompetent prisoner regains his sanity. We disagree with the state's interpretation of those statutes. The clear legislative intent of such laws is simply to adopt the common law rule under which an incompetent inmate may be executed if he should ever regain *genuine* sanity. The statutes do not authorize forcible drugging or the execution of an inmate during a temporary abatement of his psychotic symptoms by chemical means. The common law rule and many of its statutory adoptions antedate the use of antipsychotic drugs for the medical treatment of the mentally ill in this country. Therefore, the lawmakers could not have contemplated that the statutes would be used for such purpose. No state court has ever approved such a statutory interpretation or usage. In our opinion, these statutes do not constitute objective evidence of society's acceptance of forcible administration of antipsychotic drugs as a tool of capital punishment.

Secondly, the state relies on a Maryland statute which provides that "[a]n inmate is not incompetent merely because his or her competence is dependent upon continuing treatment, including the use of medication" but also states that "[i]f the court finds the inmate to be incompetent it shall revoke the warrant to execute the death sentence and remand the case to the court in which the sentence of death was imposed, which shall strike the sentence of death and enter in its place a sentence of life imprisonment without the possibility of parole." Md. Code Ann. art. 27, 75(1)(a)(2)(ii) (1990). Reading the Maryland statute as outsiders without special competence in Maryland law, we have little confidence in our interpretation and application of that law in particular situations. However, under the statute, it is clear that once an inmate is found to be incompetent his death sentence must be converted to a sentence of life imprisonment and that his sentence cannot be changed again to capital punishment. It is also clear that the statute does not expressly authorize the state to medicate an inmate *forcibly* in an attempt to make an insane prisoner competent for execution. In the absence of an explicit authorization we have grave doubts that a court could or should read such a meaning into the statute. Therefore, the Maryland law can hardly be considered objective evidence that the people of that state approve of the practice of forcible administration of antipsychotic drugs to prisoners as a means of implementing their executions. Furthermore, there is no indication that Maryland has ever attempted to use the statute to medicate an inmate forcibly for execution purposes. The acceptability of a severe punishment is measured by its use, not by its availability, for it might be so offensive to society as never to be inflicted. *Furman v. Georgia,* 408 U.S. at 279, 92 S.Ct. at 2746 (Brennan, J., concurring). Finally, no matter how the single Maryland statute is interpreted, the current judgment with respect to execution of the forcibly medicated insane would still weigh overwhelmingly on the side of rejecting the death penalty under such circumstances as being inhumane punishment. Cf. *Penry v. Lynaugh,* 492 U.S. 302, 109 S.Ct. 2934, 106 L.Ed.2d 256 (1989); *Enmund v. Florida,* 458 U.S. 782, 102 S.Ct. 3368, 73 L.Ed.2d 1140 (1982).

The execution of the insane, merged with the invasions of personhood inherent in the forcible administration of antipsychotic drugs for this purpose, therefore, is inconsistent with all four principles of humane treatment under our state constitution. Death under these circumstances is an unusually degrading and severe punishment. There is a strong probability that it will be inflicted arbitrarily. Its rejection by contemporary society is total. Such punishment is excessive because it does not serve either retribution or deterrence of potential capital offenses, the only recognized goals of capital punishment.

When this nation began death was not a unique punishment but was imposed as the penalty for numerous crimes. Execution of the insane, however, had been considered inhumane for centuries and was forbidden. Since that time, successive restrictions on the death penalty, imposed against the background of a continuing moral controversy, have drastically curtailed the use of capital punishment. For a state at this stage of the history of the usage of the death penalty to subject insane prisoners to execution under the pretense that they can be made "sane" by forcibly invading their minds, bodies and personhood with antipsychotic drugs, clearly would constitute cruel, excessive and unusual punishment.

VII. CONCLUSION

The trial court's determination and order are affirmed in part and reversed in part. The trial court's effective determination that Perry is insane and incompetent for execution is affirmed. The trial court's order authorizing and requiring the state to administer antipsychotic drugs to Perry against his will for purposes of execution is reversed. The execution of the death sentence upon Perry is stayed. In order to modify this stay order the state must demonstrate to this court that Perry has achieved or regained his sanity and competence for execution independently of the effects or influence of antipsychotic drugs.

IT IS SO ORDERED.

WATSON, J., joins the opinion and adds brief additional reasons.

LEMMON, J., concurs and assigns reasons.

HALL, J., concurs to note that he joins in the opinion but does not fully subscribe to all that is said in Section V of the opinion.

MARCUS, J., dissents and assigns reasons.

COLE, J., dissents for reasons to be assigned.

WATSON, Justice, concurring.

I join the opinion and concur to note that the basic question—whether civilized society can medicate an insane person to make him temporarily sane in order to kill him—almost answers itself. There is no overwhelming need to execute this crazy man. Such barbarous action requires strong penological interest, not present here.

LEMMON, Justice, concurring.

I join in Section VI of the majority opinion holding that the trial court's order authorizing and requiring the state to administer antipsychotic drugs to defendant against his will for the sole purpose of execution constitutes cruel, excessive and unusual punishment in violation of La. Const. art. I, § 20.

Capital punishment, while constitutionally permissible for a sane person guilty of first degree murder, is an inappropriate punishment for a person who cannot understand the nature of the penalty or the reason for his being subjected to that penalty unless he is forcibly medicated for the sole purpose of being made competent to undergo execution. The state can achieve its legitimate penological interest in enforcing its criminal laws (which prescribe *either* death *or* imprisonment for life without benefit of parole as the penalties for first degree murder), and societal order can be preserved, without the necessity of executing a person who is spending the remainder of his life in prison and who is insane except for forcibly administered medication.

MARCUS, Justice (dissenting).

In 1985, Michael Owen Perry was convicted of five counts of first degree murder of five family members.[1] The jury subsequently recommended that Perry be sentenced to death on all five counts. On appeal, this court affirmed his convictions and sentences.[2] The court noted that under *State v. Allen,* 204 La. 513, 15 So.2d 870 (1943) and *Ford v. Wainwright,* 477 U.S. 399, 106 S.Ct. 2595, 91 L.Ed.2d 335 (1986), the state is prohibited from executing one who has become insane subsequent to his conviction of a capital crime; therefore, counsel for defendant may apply to the trial court for appointment of a sanity commission to determine whether Perry has become insane subsequent to his convictions and lacks the capacity to understand the death penalty.

On January 21, 1988, the trial court appointed a sanity commission to determine Perry's present sanity. Based upon recommendations from the state and defense, the trial court appointed Drs. Glen Estes, Aris Cox, Theresita Jimenez, and Curtis Vincent, a clinical psychologist. Following the appointment of the sanity commission, the trial court granted defense counsel's *ex parte* motion authorizing him to represent Perry in these proceedings and to make decisions on Perry's behalf as deemed necessary and in his best interest. On March 14, 1988, Perry's counsel instructed the state prison authorities to remove Perry from all psychotropic medication.[3]

The trial court held its first sanity hearing on April 20, 1988, after Perry was fully evaluated by the sanity commission. The commission unanimously agreed that Perry suffered from schizo-affective disorder. The commission also expressed the opinion that psychotropic medication relieved the symptoms of that disorder; however, the commission was somewhat divided on the issue of competence to undergo execution with the majority expressing an opinion that Perry was competent to undergo execution. Dr. Jimenez, a psychiatrist who had examined Perry in the past, testified that Perry "does understand that he is convicted of the death of his family and he does understand that the penalty is death." Dr. Cox, also a psychiatrist who had examined Perry in the past and was Perry's treating physician at Angola, testified that Perry was "aware that he could be killed by the electrocution, and he was aware of why he was there." He also testified that

1. Prior to trial, the trial court appointed a sanity commission to determine Perry's capacity to proceed. The commission diagnosed Perry as having a long history of paranoid schizophrenia; therefore, the trial court ordered that Perry be sent to the Feliciana Forensic Facility for evaluation and treatment. Subsequently, upon motion by the state, a second sanity commission was appointed to evaluate Perry. At the second sanity hearing, all three physicians unanimously agreed that Perry was mentally competent and could assist counsel in his defense. The trial court agreed and ruled accordingly.

2. *State v. Perry,* 502 So.2d 543 (La.1986).

3. Specifically, Perry was given Haldol to control the symptoms of his schizo-affective disorder.

when he examined Perry, Perry was on psychotropic medication and "functioning about as well" as he had ever seen him function. Dr. Vincent, a clinical psychologist who had also examined Perry in the past, testified that Perry "has the understanding that if an individual murders somebody and they can be found guilty and then could be executed legally." Dr. Estes, a psychiatrist who had met with Perry only once for about an hour, testified that he "did not conclude that he [Perry] understood his sentence, his punishment for what he did wrong."

The trial court took the matter under advisement. Shortly after the hearing (April 29, 1988), Perry's counsel authorized the state prison authorities to resume Perry's treatment with psychotropic medication. The trial court later requested the prison authorities to provide the court with periodic updated reports regarding Perry's mental status. Soon thereafter, Perry filed an objection to the introduction of his updated mental health reports into evidence. Additionally, as a result of the trial court's request for those reports, Perry's counsel requested the prison authorities to discontinue Perry's treatment with psychotropic medication.

A few months later, the trial court overruled Perry's objection to the introduction of the status reports into evidence. The court also vacated its prior order authorizing Perry's counsel to make decisions on his behalf. Based on the newly-introduced status reports prepared by the prison authorities, the trial court concluded that there was a change in circumstances in Perry's mental health warranting a new evaluation. Therefore, a second sanity hearing was scheduled for September 30, 1988. The court requested two of the four physicians on the original sanity commission (Drs. Cox and Jimenez) to re-evaluate Perry. The trial court also ordered that Perry be forcibly maintained on psychotropic medication pending the second sanity hearing; however, upon Perry's application, this court stayed the order authorizing forcible medication.

At the second sanity hearing (October 21, 1988), the physicians again testified that Perry suffered from schizo-affective disorder; however, they again found that administration of psychotropic medicine would render Perry competent for execution. After the hearing, the trial court rendered the following judgment:

> It is ordered that the defendant, Michael Owen Perry, is competent for purposes of execution in that he is aware of the punishment he is about to suffer and he is aware of the reason that he is to suffer said punishment.
>
> It is further ordered that defendant's competency is achieved through the use of antitropic or antipsychotic drugs including Haldol and the Louisiana Department of Public Safety and Corrections is further ordered to maintain defendant on the above medication as to be prescribed by the medical staff of said Department and if necessary to administer said medication forcibly to defendant and over his objection.

Perry filed an application for supervisory writs to this court which was denied.[4] Perry then filed a petition for a writ of certiorari to the United States Supreme Court which was granted.[5] After briefing and argument, the Court vacated the judgment and remanded the case to the trial court "for further consideration in light of *Washington v. Harper*, 494 U.S. 210, 110 S.Ct. 1028, 108 L.Ed.2d 178 (1990)."[6] On remand, the trial court reaffirmed and reinstated its original judgment, distinguishing Perry's case from *Harper*. The court noted that *Harper* involved prison regulations governing the forced medication of inmates in the interest of prison safety and security; whereas Perry's case involves forced medication of a death row inmate to render him competent for execution. The court held that the state's interest in obtaining

4. *State v. Perry*, 543 So.2d 487, *reh'g denied*, 545 So.2d 1049 (La.1989).

5. 494 U.S. 1015, 110 S.Ct. 1317, 108 L.Ed.2d 492 (1990).

6. *Perry v. Louisiana*, 498 U.S. 38, 111 S.Ct. 449, 112 L.Ed.2d 338 (1990) (per curiam), *reh'g denied*, — U.S. ——, 111 S.Ct. 804, 112 L.Ed.2d 865 (1991).

and satisfying the jury verdict (the death penalty) in this case outweighs Perry's right to refuse medication. In addition, the court found (for purposes of argument) that Perry was a danger to others and that the medication was in his best medical interest. Upon *Perry's* application, we granted certiorari to review the correctness of that decision.[7]

As I see it, the issues presented are 1) what level or standard of competency is necessary to undergo execution; 2) whether Perry can be forcefully medicated against his will so that he might achieve a level of competency sufficient to undergo execution; and 3) what procedural due process requirements are necessary before a death row inmate can be forcefully medicated for execution.

I. Mental Standard Required to Undergo Execution

It is well settled in this state that if a person convicted of a capital crime and sentenced to death later becomes insane, then that person cannot be executed. *State v. Perry,* 502 So.2d 543 (La.1986); *State v. Allen,* 204 La. 513, 15 So.2d 870 (1943). In *Perry,* this court stated that the state will not impose the death penalty on a person who becomes insane subsequent to his conviction for first degree murder if he "lacks the capacity to understand the death penalty." The United States Supreme Court addressed the issue in *Ford v. Wainwright,* 477 U.S. 399, 106 S.Ct. 2595, 91 L.Ed.2d 335 (1986). The majority held that execution of the mentally insane constituted cruel and unusual punishment under the Eighth Amendment to the United States Constitution; however, the majority did not address the level or standard of competency necessary to undergo execution. Noting the majority's failure to explain that standard, Justice Powell confronted the issue in a concurring opinion. He found that the minimum level of competency necessary under the Eighth Amendment to execute those under a sentence of death is an awareness of the punishment and why they are to suffer that punishment.

Perry argues that a capacity to understand the proceedings against him and an ability to assist counsel as interpreted in *State v. Bennett,* 345 So.2d 1129 (La.1977), are implicit in the mental standard to undergo execution. In *Ford,* 477 U.S. 399, 106 S.Ct. 2595, Justice Powell, in addressing a similar argument, *i.e.*, the lack of an ability to make arguments on one's own behalf, found "slight merit" to that argument in a post-conviction setting. He noted that "modern practice provides for more extensive review of sentences and convictions than did the common law" and with that review it would be "unlikely indeed that a defendant could go to his death with knowledge of undiscovered trial error that might set him free." *Ford,* 477 U.S. at 420, 106 S.Ct. at 2607. Under the Louisiana Code of Criminal Procedure, the very nature of post-conviction proceedings precludes the necessity of an awareness of the proceedings and an ability to assist counsel.[8] I consider the minimum standard of competency necessary to undergo execution set forth in *Ford* to be a proper standard. I would therefore adopt the *Ford* standard, *i.e.*, the ability of one to understand the death penalty and the reason one is to suffer that penalty, as the standard to undergo execution in this state.[9]

7. 584 So.2d 1145 (La.1991).

8. La.Code Cr.Pro. art. 930.3 provides:
If the petitioner is in custody after sentence for conviction for an offense, relief shall be granted only on the following grounds:
(1) The conviction was obtained in violation of the constitution of the United States or the state of Louisiana;
(2) The court exceeded its jurisdiction;
(3) The conviction or sentence subjected him to double jeopardy;
(4) The limitations on the institution of prosecution has expired;
(5) The statute creating the offense for which he was convicted and sentenced is unconstitutional; or
(6) The conviction or sentence constitute the ex post facto application of law in violation of the constitution of the United States or the state of Louisiana.

9. The trial court, noting that there were no express statutory rules of procedure to determine competency for execution, used the procedure outlined in La.Code Crim.P. art. 641 *et seq.* We note that this procedure satisfies the procedural due process requirements outlined in *Ford*

A trial judge's determination of mental capacity is entitled to great weight, especially where the evaluation of credibility or the resolution of conflicting well-founded medical testimony is concerned. *State v. Flores*, 315 So.2d 772 (La.1975). Based on the testimony of the sanity commission, I would find that the trial judge did not abuse his discretion in holding Perry competent to be executed.

II. Can a Death Row Inmate Be Forcibly Medicated For Purposes of Execution

In its order, the U.S. Supreme Court directed the trial court to review its decision in light of *Washington v. Harper*, 494 U.S. 210, 110 S.Ct. 1028, 108 L.Ed.2d 178 (1990). In *Harper*, the issue before the Court was "what factual circumstances must exist before the state may administer antipsychotic drugs to the prisoner against his will." *Harper*, 494 U.S. at 220, 110 S.Ct. at 1036. Specifically, the Special Offender Center of the state of Washington promulgated Policy 600.30 which provides for the involuntary administration of psychotropic medication to an inmate in the event a special committee of psychiatrists finds that the inmate suffers from a mental disorder and is gravely disabled or dangerous. The defendant, who was forcefully medicated under this policy, challenged the constitutionality of Policy 600.30, claiming his constitutional rights were violated as he had a protected liberty interest in refusing medication.

The Court recognized the defendant's liberty interest in refusing medication. According to the Court, that liberty interest was created by the justifiable expectation that Policy 600.30 prohibited the arbitrary administration of antipsychotic medication. Additionally, the Court found defendant possessed a significant liberty interest created by the Due Process Clause of the Fourteenth Amendment in refusing the unwanted medication. The Court explained, however, that "the extent of a prisoner's right under the Clause to avoid the unwanted administration of antipsychotic drugs must be defined in the context of the inmate's confinement." *Harper*, 494 U.S. at 222, 110 S.Ct. at 1037. The Court noted that it had previously held in *Turner v. Safley*, 482 U.S. 78, 107 S.Ct. 2254, 96 L.Ed.2d 64 (1987), and *O'Lone v. Estate of Shabazz*, 482 U.S. 342, 107 S.Ct. 2400, 96 L.Ed.2d 282 (1987), that "the proper standard for determining the validity of a prison regulation claimed to infringe on an inmate's constitutional rights is to ask whether the regulation is reasonably related to legitimate penological interests." *Harper*, 494 U.S. at 222, 110 S.Ct. at 1037. In other words, when a prison regulation impinges on an inmate's constitutional rights, the regulation is valid if it is reasonably related to legitimate penological interests. Finding that Policy 600.30 was a rational means of furthering the state's legitimate objectives, *i.e.*, prison safety and security, the Court held that the Due Process Clause permitted the state to treat a prison inmate who has a serious mental illness with antipsychotic drugs against his will if the inmate is dangerous to himself or others and the treatment is in the inmate's medical interest.

Under the guidance of *Harper*, I believe we must determine whether the instant case presents sufficient factual circumstances to warrant the administration of unwanted psychotropic medication to Perry. I have no doubt that under the Due Process Clauses of both the federal and state constitutions, Perry possesses a significant liberty interest to be free from unwanted medication. However, the Court in *Harper* noted that the liberty interest must be defined in the context of the inmate's confinement.

Finding that Perry possesses a liberty interest in refusing medication, I would

v. Wainwright, 477 U.S. 399, 106 S.Ct. 2595, 91 L.Ed.2d 335 (1986), namely:

1) Inclusion of the defendant in the truth seeking process;
2) The opportunity to cross examine in an adversarial setting; and
3) Inclusion of the judiciary in the decision making process (either in an active capacity or a reviewing capacity).

A specific statutory rule of procedure to determine competency for execution addresses itself to the legislature.

examine the state's interest in forcibly medicating Perry and decide whether his forced medication is reasonably related to that interest. Clearly, the state possesses a significant interest in the enforcement of its criminal laws. "One of the primary functions of government is the preservation of societal order through enforcement of criminal law...." *Procunier v. Martinez*, 416 U.S. 396, 412, 94 S.Ct. 1800, 1811, 40 L.Ed.2d 224 (1974). Except as constitutionally limited, a state may choose means to protect itself and its people against criminal violation of its laws. *Commonwealth ex rel. Sullivan v. Ashe*, 302 U.S. 51, 55, 58 S.Ct. 59, 60, 82 L.Ed. 43 (1937). In *Gregg v. Georgia*, 428 U.S. 153, 96 S.Ct. 2909, 49 L.Ed.2d 859 (1976), the Court explained:

> The death penalty is said to serve two principal social purposes: retribution and deterrence of capital crimes by prospective offenders.
>
> In part, capital punishment is an expression of society's moral outrage at particularly offensive conduct. This function may be unappealing to many, but it is essential in an ordered society that asks its citizens to rely on legal processes rather than self-help to vindicate their wrongs.

Having found a legitimate penological interest in the enforcement of its criminal laws, the final analysis mandated by *Harper* requires a determination of whether Perry's forced medication is reasonably related to this state interest. Apparently, the only way Perry can achieve a level of competence sufficient to undergo execution is through the administration of psychotropic medication. There does not seem to be any alternative method of treating Perry for his illness. Under *Ford*, a death row inmate must understand the nature of the death penalty and the reason he is to suffer that penalty. The administration of medication produces the required level of competence for Perry to undergo execution and is therefore consistent with his sentence. Since the forcible medication of Perry renders him competent for execution, society's objective in the enforcement of its criminal penalties is accomplished. I would conclude that under the rational relation test espoused in *Harper*, the forcible medication of Perry is reasonably related to a legitimate penological interest. Therefore, I would find Perry may be forcefully medicated to render him competent for execution.

Perry argues that under *Harper* and La. R.S. 15:830.1, an inmate can be forcibly medicated only after a finding that the inmate is a threat to himself or others and the administration of unwanted medication is in his best medical interest.[10] However, *Harper* and La.R.S. 15:830.1 contemplate the forced administration of antipsychotic medication in the context of the penological interest of prison safety and security. Neither *Harper* nor La.R.S. 15:830.1 addresses or precludes forced medication for execution, which is the penological interest involved in this case. While dangerousness and best medical interest are proper considerations in terms of forced medication to insure prison safety and security, they are not pertinent inquiries in the context of forced medication for execution. The state's objective in administering unwanted medication for execution is to render the inmate competent to undergo execution; whereas the state's objective under La.R.S. 15:830.1 and *Harper* is to insure prison safety and security. Therefore, Perry's argument is without merit.[11] In any event,

10. In *Harper*, the Court held that under the Due Process Clause, the state could "treat a prison inmate who has a serious mental illness with antipsychotic drugs against his will, *if the inmate is dangerous to himself or others and the treatment is in the inmate's medical interest.*" (Emphasis added). Similarly, La.R.S. 15:830.1 provides: "Whenever a mentally ill or mentally retarded inmate refuses treatment and any staff physician, staff psychiatrist, or consulting psychiatrist of the institution certifies that the treatment is necessary *to prevent harm or injury to the inmate or others*, such treatment will be permitted...." (Emphasis added).

11. Perry also asserts that he is afforded a constitutionally protected right to refuse medication by a consent decree adopted by the United States District Court for the Middle District of Louisiana in *Head v. King*, No. 84-209-B (M.D.La. Mar. 5, 1991). First, given the evidence in the record, the scope and effect of the consent decree is unknown. Second, the pro-

the trial court found Perry to be a danger to others, and the sanity commission was of the opinion that psychotropic medication relieved the symptoms of Perry's disorder with minimal side effects and was in his best medical interest.[12]

III. Procedural Due Process Necessary to Forcefully Medicate Perry

In *Harper*, the Court was also confronted with the issue of whether the procedure outlined in Policy 600.30 provided the defendant with procedural due process protections before he could be forcefully medicated. Under the Policy, a psychiatrist decided whether an inmate suffered from a mental disorder and was gravely disabled or posed a threat of harm to himself or others. If the inmate refused medication, he was entitled to a hearing before a special committee consisting of a psychiatrist, psychologist, and the Associate Superintendent of the Special Offender Center (none of whom were involved in the treatment of the inmate). The inmate would be given 24 hours notice of the hearing. He would also be given the right to attend the hearing, to present evidence, to cross-examine the witnesses, and the right to the assistance of a lay advisor who understood the psychiatric issues involved. If a majority of the committee found that the inmate suffered a mental disorder and was either gravely disabled or posed a threat of harm to himself or others, then the inmate could be medicated against his will. The inmate would be given the right to appeal to the Superintendent of the Center and the right to seek judicial review of the Center's decision by means of a personal restraint petition or extraordinary writ. The Court held that these procedures satisfied the defendant's right to procedural due process.

In the instant case, upon the recommendations of state and defense, the trial court appointed a sanity commission consisting of three psychiatrists and one psychologist to determine Perry's present sanity. The trial court held a contradictory sanity hearing after Perry was fully evaluated by the sanity commission. The trial court required the prison authorities to provide the court with periodic updated reports regarding Perry's mental health status. Finding a change in Perry's mental health, the trial court requested two of the four physicians on the original sanity commission to reevaluate Perry. Subsequently, a second contradictory sanity hearing was held. Perry was represented by two attorneys throughout the proceedings. Finally, the trial court's decision was subject to review by this court. Clearly, the procedures adopted by the trial court satisfied Perry's right to procedural due process.[13]

CONCLUSION

In conclusion, I would adopt the *Ford* standard, *i.e.*, the ability of one to understand the death penalty and the reason one is to suffer that penalty, as the required level of competency to undergo execution in this state. In addition, I would find that the trial judge did not abuse his discretion in finding that Perry was competent to be executed while maintained on psychotropic medication. Furthermore, I would hold that under the rational relation test es-

posed plan detailing the use of psychotropic medication on an involuntary basis merely follows the procedure provided in La.R.S. 15:830.1. The proposed plan does not address medication for execution and is therefore inapplicable to this case.

12. Additionally, Perry argues that by forcibly medicating him solely for the purpose of carrying out execution makes that medication a part of his punishment not authorized by the legislature. The commission recommended that Perry be treated with psychotropic medication to control his mental disorder. He was voluntarily administered the medication prior to his sanity hearings. Additionally, his attorney authorized the state prison authorities to resume treatment of Perry with psychotropic medication after the sanity hearing of April 20, 1988. Since the medication actually benefits Perry, it cannot be viewed as a form of punishment.

13. The trial court, noting there was no express statutory procedure to determine whether one should be forcefully medicated for purposes of execution, adopted the procedure outlined in La.Code Crim.P. art. 641 *et seq.* (as it did for the competency determination. *See supra* note 10). A specific statutory rule of procedure to permit forced medication for execution addresses itself to the legislature.

poused in *Harper*, the forcible medication of Perry is reasonably related to the legitimate penological interest in enforcing the death penalty. Finally, the procedures adopted by the trial court in determining whether Perry could be medicated for execution satisfied his right to procedural due process.

For these reasons, I respectfully dissent and would affirm the judgment of the district court.

COLE, Justice, dissenting.

Our constitution is not intended to embody a particular sociological theory. Rather, "[i]t is made for people of fundamentally differing views, and the accident of our finding certain opinions natural and familiar or novel and even shocking ought not to conclude our judgment upon the question whether [the state's position] embodying them conflict[s] with the [c]onstitution...." *Lochner v. New York*, 198 U.S. 45, 76, 25 S.Ct. 539, 547, 49 L.Ed. 937 (1905) (Holmes, J., dissenting).

Because I view the majority's fundamental premises as unsound, and because the result reached is one compelled neither by the language of the constitution nor the intent of its drafters, I respectfully dissent and briefly outline the areas of my disagreement.

I.

First, I disagree that providing one with medication to reduce or alleviate his distress is in some way not in his "best medical interest" merely because at some point thereafter a lawfully imposed death sentence may be carried out. The majority contends that because a physician is bound by oath both to alleviate suffering and to do no harm, he is not permitted to administer antipsychotic drugs "forcibly" since by doing so he knowingly handles the patient "harmfully and contrary to his ultimate medical interest." Administering the medication to one who thereafter is rendered competent for execution is claimed to prevent the prisoner from receiving adequate medical treatment for his mental illness. Even the majority acknowledges, however, that "[t]he physician's abstention from dispensing the drugs ... perpetuates suffering that ordinarily the physician is duty-bound to allay...." *Supra* at 752. This statement, to me, is indicative of the majority's quest to halt the execution of Perry because it offends the sensibilities of the majority. If, in fact, a physician is sworn to do no harm and to act only in the best medical interests of his patients, I fail to see how administering an antipsychotic drug manufactured to *alleviate suffering* in those for whom it is indicated, i.e., those manifesting overt psychotic symptoms, can reasonably be construed as doing harm or acting against the patient's best medical interests. The fact that subsequent to the treatment the patient recovers sufficiently to be subjected to the lawfully imposed death sentence does not somehow retroactively render the treatment medically contraindicated. To the contrary, it would seem the majority's consigning Perry to a life term not only in the state penitentiary but to a life term as the prisoner of his own delusions is far more pernicious than any of the effects brought about by the so-called medicate-to-execute structure. Prescribing and administering appropriate medication can scarcely be deemed punishment, at least not by any generally accepted definition of the term.

II.

The majority errs also in concluding that administering medically indicated antipsychotic drugs violates Perry's asserted rights under LA.CONST. art. I, § 5 [1] to decide what is to be done medically with one's mind and body; to control one's own mind and thoughts; and to be free from unwarranted physical interference with one's brain and body.

Here, the majority seeks to have it both ways. On the one hand, the majority con-

1. It is interesting to note the majority's effort to ensure this case is decided solely on state law grounds, thus barring further, perhaps unfavorable, review by the Supreme Court of the United States.

tends Perry is so incompetent as to be unable to appreciate his surroundings, circumstances, or the nature of and reasons for the lawful sentence. Accordingly, the sentence cannot lawfully be imposed while he remains in his separate reality. On the other hand, the majority ascribes to the same individual the capacity to chart his own medical treatment plan, the ability to decide rationally what is to be done medically and what limits he wishes to impose, and, most curiously, the ability to control his own mind and thoughts.

The majority concludes that administering the drug to Perry and perhaps subsequently executing him would "usurp his fundamental right to make decisions regarding his health or medical treatment." *Supra* at 758. It is difficult to conceive of the state usurping a right to make decisions when the person whose right to make the decision is unable to make any rational decision or to appreciate the world around him.

The majority also catalogues in great detail the possible adverse effects of the medication sought to be imposed. The Physician's Desk Reference ("PDR"), quoted in the opinion, typically lists *all* reported side effects, no matter how infrequent the occurrence. One could, with little difficulty, peruse the PDR in search of a similar parade of horribles and find virtually all prescription medications may produce adverse, unintended consequences. That is precisely why they are sold only by prescription of a physician. That does not, however, render them instruments of torture any more than the occasional adverse consequences make Haldol monstrous, notwithstanding the majority's implication to the contrary. When it comes to a decision to treat psychosis with an available, proven treatment, or to allow the psychotic to remain in his disconnected state, it cannot be deemed unconstitutionally violative of some amorphous right of the psychotic to choose neglect over treatment.

III.

The majority has determined that executing a previously insane criminal, after administering to the criminal, purportedly against his "will," antipsychotic drugs, is unconstitutional because it subjects the individual to cruel, excessive, or unusual punishment, in violation of LA.CONST. art. I, § 20. To reach its conclusion, the majority employs the criteria set forth in *State v. Stetson*, 317 So.2d 172 (La.1975), namely, that the punishment must not be: degrading to the dignity of human beings; arbitrarily inflicted; unacceptable to contemporary society; or excessive, i.e., disproportionate to the crime or failing to serve a penal purpose more effectively than a less severe punishment. I disagree with both the premises and the conclusions of the majority as to each consideration.

A.

First, because I do not believe appropriate medical treatment can be deemed "punishment," I disagree with the majority that administering antipsychotic drugs to Perry while he remains in a psychotic state forms any part of the punishment to be meted out by the state. The fact that at some point thereafter, when Perry regains his competence, the state may carry out the lawfully imposed death sentence is of no moment. The death penalty has not been found to be degrading to human dignity. In fact, some have thought capital punishment indispensable to redeem, or restore, the dignity of the person executed. *See, e.g.*, G. HEGEL, PHILOSOPHY OF RIGHT (T.M. Knox trans., 1962); I. KANT, THE PHILOSOPHY OF LAW: METAPHYSICAL PRINCIPLES OF THE SCIENCE OF RIGHT, pt. II 194–205 (W. Hastie, B.D. trans., 1887). The death penalty has been upheld by both state and federal courts as a legitimate means of expressing society's outrage at people who commit crimes such as the ones Perry committed.

The punishment intended for Perry, being executed by means of a lethal injection is most assuredly less severe than being electrocuted. As electrocution has been determined not to be unreasonably severe, a lethal injection administered while the prisoner is lying on a hospital gurney is certainly not.

B.

The punishment intended for Perry is not being arbitrarily applied. Perry was accorded every due process right to which he is entitled, before, during, and after his trial. A jury convicted him of five counts of first degree murder and recommended the death penalty on all counts. This Court affirmed all convictions and sentences. *State v. Perry,* 502 So.2d 543 (La.1986). There is nothing arbitrary about seeking to carry out a lawfully imposed sentence.

What seems arbitrary to me is the fact that the survivors of the victims of Perry's crimes, as well as society at large, should be deprived of a just resolution of the matter through the fortuity of Perry's having become insane after conviction and sentence but before the sentence could be carried out. He was, after all, found sane at the time he committed the crimes, sane at trial (and thus able to assist in his defense), and sane at the time of conviction and sentence (so that he understood the nature of the punishment and the reason for its imposition). It seems to me arbitrary in the extreme that he should escape sentence for such heinous crimes while others who have not managed to become insane, and who perhaps truly repent, do not. One thing that will *not* be arbitrary but will be fairly predictable, however, is the number of present and future death row inmates who become "insane" upon reading the majority's opinion.

C.

The death penalty is, by virtue of its widespread support [2] and statutory enactment, not unacceptable to contemporary society. The fact that one has been previously adjudged insane, has been treated by legitimate medical procedures, and has, as a result, regained sanity sufficient to be exposed to the death penalty,[3] does not render the sentence unacceptable to contemporary society. Rather, I believe the converse to be true. American citizens grow increasingly appalled by, and alienated from, a legal system that affords criminals greater rights than law-abiding taxpayers. Contemporary society is awash with callous, cold-blooded killers who themselves are provided room, board, clothing, and medical care at taxpayers' expense for an average of 8–15 years from the time of the crime to the time (if ever) of execution. Restoring a convicted murderer to sanity and subsequently carrying out the sentence is in no way unacceptable to contemporary society.

D.

The majority asserts the punishment the state "seeks to carry out on Perry is excessive because it makes no measurable contribution to the acceptable goals of capital punishment and hence is nothing more than the purposeless and needless imposition of pain and suffering." *Supra* at 766. Nothing could be further from the truth.

As previously noted, the survivors of Perry's victims, as well as society at large, are entitled to retribution for the heinous acts Perry committed. The fact that he fortuitously, perhaps conveniently, became insane prior to his execution does not detract from the legitimacy of his sentence. Likewise, the fact that he may be chemically restored to sanity, and then executed, does not denigrate the verdict, the sentence, or the process. Society is entitled to express its legitimate outrage at those who have served notice on it that they are unwilling to abide by its most basic principles. Retribution, indeed, "is a legitimate dimension of the punishment of crimes." *Furman v. Georgia,* 408 U.S. 238, 394, 92 S.Ct. 2726, 2806, 33 L.Ed.2d 346 (1972) (Burger, C.J., dissenting).

2. "According to polls more than eighty percent of Americans favor the death penalty." Ernest van den Haag, *Why Capital Punishment?,* 54 Albany L.Rev. 501, 501 (1990).

3. The majority opinion asserts that there is *no question* that Perry is incurably insane and incompetent for execution but also concedes that, while medicated, Perry *is able* to function at a minimum level of rationality. At such a level of rationality, Perry can understand the nature of the punishment to be imposed and the reasons for its imposition. That is sufficient to pass constitutional muster.

The majority cites Immanuel Kant, noting his belief that the state's punishment must respect human dignity by making the punishment equivalent to the crime and that the execution must be kept free from all maltreatment which would make the "humanity suffering in his person loathsome or abominable." *Supra* at 767 (emphasis omitted). In this case, the punishment, execution by lethal injection, is indeed disproportionate to the crime. It is disproportionately low.

Having written the opinion of the Court affirming the convictions and sentences on direct appeal, I cannot help but be reminded of the gruesome, hideous crime scenes resulting from Perry's handiwork. Blasting five human beings, including a child, to death with handguns and a shotgun is not an offense that should be minimized by the subsequent onset of Perry's present psychiatric difficulties. In an exercise of gross understatement, the majority deems this rampage a "senseless criminal episode." *Supra* at 748. I deem this "episode" loathsome and abominable, far more so than a simple administration of Haldol. The retributive value of Perry's execution would not be diminished by the fact that his competence had been previously chemically restored. "Punishment is to vindicate the law and the social order undermined by the crime." Ernest van den Haag, *The Ultimate Punishment: A Defense*, 99 Harvard L.Rev. 1662, 1667 (1986).

The equally laudable goal of deterring crime by potential criminals is served in this case as well. Society has the right to protect itself from those who would commit murder and seek to avoid their legitimate punishment by a subsequently contracted, or feigned, insanity. Medical restoration of sanity, where possible, is a humane goal. Executing murderers who have been restored to sanity sends a message to a potential murderer that his act will not go unpunished. Contrived or sought after mental illness will not be factored into the balance for would-be killers, and the marginal effect, even if minuscule, is a positive factor weighing against the sentence in this case being deemed excessive.

IV.

Notwithstanding my disagreement with the majority's conclusion that administration of antipsychotic drugs would violate Perry's rights under La. Const. art. I, §§ 5 and 20, I feel compelled to point out the limitations of the majority's holding.

The majority's finding of constitutional infirmities under La.Const. art. I, § 5 (the Right to Privacy) is expressly premised on the lack of any legitimate state interest in administering the antipsychotic drugs to Perry. ("Because the involuntary medication was ordered as an integral and essential part of Perry's punishment *and not because of any legitimate requirement of prison security or medical interest of Perry*, we conclude that the medicate-to-execute scheme infringes on Perry's constitutionally protected interests...." *Supra* at 757 (emphasis added). Presumably a different result would obtain if the drugs were being administered under different circumstances, such as pursuant to a finding that Perry was a danger to himself or others (satisfying La.R.S. 15:830.1(A)), and that administration of the drugs was appropriate medically and in Perry's best interest (meeting the *Washington v. Harper* standards for administration of antipsychotic drugs).

Similarly, the majority's finding that administration of antipsychotic drugs to Perry would violate his Art. I, Section 20 rights against cruel, unusual, or excessive punishment is premised on its conclusion that administration of the drugs *for the purpose of preparing him for execution*, would, itself, be part of the punishment. ("Accordingly, we conclude that ... administration of antipsychotic drugs to a prisoner against his will, pursuant to the order of a state court or other official, *for the purpose of carrying out the death penalty, ... forms part of the capital punishment* sought to be executed by the state." *Supra* at 753 (emphasis added). Again, if the sanity-inducing medication were administered for other than punitive purposes (e.g., to protect Perry or others around him), the constitutional infirmities which the majority finds under LA. CONST. art. I, Section 20 would not be present.

The majority's opinion makes clear its belief that the "medicate-to-execute" scheme violates several of this state's constitutional protections. This holding is legally buttressed against the majority's findings of constitutional infirmities in a scheme wherein a defendant is medicated *so that* he may be rendered sane for execution (i.e., the finding of constitutional infirmities is based on the "purpose" which administration of the drugs is sought to achieve). Were Perry administered the drugs for constitutionally permissible purposes, his resulting sanity would merely be a "by-product" of this treatment. That being so, I do not view the majority's opinion as prohibiting the state from seeking to carry out Perry's lawfully imposed sentence should that situation arise.

I reach this conclusion notwithstanding the majority's overbroad statement "[i]n order to modify this stay order the state must demonstrate to this court that Perry has achieved or regained his sanity and competence for execution *independently of the effects or influence of antipsychotic drugs.*" *Supra* at 771 (emphasis added). This statement follows the majority's lengthy, in-depth constitutional analysis of the "medicate-to-execute" scheme, yet the majority's opinion provides no support for the stated proposition beyond that scheme. Indeed, the majority's opinion lacks any discussion whatsoever of the constitutionality of carrying out Perry's sentence if he is rendered competent through the use of antipsychotic drugs for purposes unrelated to the execution of his sentence. For these reasons, I conclude this statement simply did not contemplate the situation discussed above, *viz.*, Perry being administered antipsychotic drugs in a constitutionally permissible manner. Accordingly, I do not believe the majority's opinion would bar execution of Perry's sentence in that situation.

V.

Finally, it is appropriate to require that if Perry has a constitutional right to refuse the drugs, and thereby presumably avoid the death sentence, he should not thereafter be permitted to take the drugs at any time. If he prefers to remain in a self-induced psychotic state, and the majority endorses that choice, he should be allowed to do so, but he should simply not be allowed to have it both ways. I find nothing in the majority opinion addressing the predictable probability that Perry will now voluntarily take the drugs and continue to do so until the state again seeks to carry out the lawfully imposed sentence. With or without the advice of counsel, Perry should not be permitted to alternatively choose sanity and insanity. This tactic places Perry above and beyond the reach of the law and is the bottom line of the majority opinion.

VI.

For these reasons and for the additional reasons assigned by Justice MARCUS in dissent, I would affirm the order of the district court in its entirety.

Syllabus

GODINEZ, WARDEN *v.* MORAN

CERTIORARI TO THE UNITED STATES COURT OF APPEALS FOR THE NINTH CIRCUIT

No. 92-725. Argued April 21, 1993—Decided June 24, 1993

After respondent Moran pleaded not guilty to three counts of first-degree murder and two psychiatrists concluded that he was competent to stand trial, he informed the Nevada trial court that he wished to discharge his attorneys and change his pleas to guilty. The court found that Moran understood "the nature of the criminal charges against him" and was "able to assist in his defense"; that he was "knowingly and intelligently" waiving his right to the assistance of counsel; and that his guilty pleas were "freely and voluntarily" given. He was ultimately sentenced to death. When Moran subsequently sought state postconviction relief, the trial court held an evidentiary hearing before rejecting his claim that he was mentally incompetent to represent himself, and the State Supreme Court dismissed his appeal. A Federal District Court denied his petition for a writ of habeas corpus, but the Court of Appeals reversed. It concluded that due process required the trial court to hold a hearing to evaluate and determine Moran's competency before it accepted his decisions to waive counsel and plead guilty. It also found that the postconviction hearing did not cure the error, holding that the trial court's ruling was premised on the wrong legal standard because competency to waive constitutional rights requires a higher level of mental functioning than that required to stand trial. The court reasoned that, while a defendant is competent to stand trial if he has a rational and factual understanding of the proceedings and is capable of assisting his counsel, he is competent to waive counsel or plead guilty only if he has the capacity for reasoned choice among the available alternatives.

Held: The competency standard for pleading guilty or waiving the right to counsel is the same as the competency standard for standing trial: whether the defendant has "sufficient present ability to consult with his lawyer with a reasonable degree of rational understanding" and a "rational as well as factual understanding of the proceedings against him," *Dusky* v. *United States*, 362 U. S. 402 *(per curiam)*. There is no reason for the competency standard for either of those decisions to be higher than that for standing trial. The decision to plead guilty, though profound, is no more complicated than the sum total of decisions that a defendant may have to make during the course of a trial, such as whether to testify, whether to waive a jury trial, and whether to cross-examine witnesses for the prosecution. Nor does the decision to waive counsel require an appreciably higher level of mental functioning than the decision to waive other constitutional rights. A higher standard is not necessary in order to ensure that a defendant is competent to represent himself, because the ability to do so has no bearing upon his competence to *choose* self-representation, *Faretta* v. *California*, 422 U. S. 806, 836. When, in *Westbrook* v. *Arizona*, 384 U. S. 150 *(per curiam)*, this Court vacated a lower court ruling because there had been no "hearing or inquiry into the issue of [the petitioner's] competence to waive his constitutional right to the assistance of counsel," it did not mean to suggest that the *Dusky* formulation is not a high enough standard in cases in which the defendant seeks to waive counsel. Rather, the "competence to waive" language was simply a shorthand for the "intelligent and competent waiver" requirement of *Johnson* v. *Zerbst*, 304 U. S. 458, 468. Thus, *Westbrook* stands only for the unremarkable proposition that when a defendant seeks to waive his right to counsel, a determination that he is competent to stand trial is not enough; the waiver must also be intelligent and voluntary before it can be accepted. While States are free to adopt competency standards that are more elaborate than the *Dusky* formulation, the Due Process Clause does not impose them. Pp. 396–402.

972 F. 2d 263, reversed and remanded.

THOMAS, J., delivered the opinion of the Court, in which REHNQUIST, C. J., and WHITE, O'CONNOR, and SOUTER, JJ., joined, and in Parts I, II–B, and III of which SCALIA and KENNEDY, JJ., joined. KENNEDY, J., filed an opinion concurring in part and concurring in the judgment, in which SCALIA, J., joined, *post*, p. 402. BLACKMUN, J., filed a dissenting opinion, in which STEVENS, J., joined, *post*, p. 409.

David F. Sarnowski, Chief Deputy Attorney General of Nevada, argued the cause for petitioner. With him on the brief were *Frankie Sue Del Papa*, Attorney General, and *Brooke A. Nielsen*, Assistant Attorney General.

Amy L. Wax argued the cause for the United States as *amicus curiae* urging reversal. With her on the brief were *Acting Solicitor General Bryson, Acting Assistant Attorney General Keeney*, and *Joel M. Gershowitz.*

Cal J. Potter III, by appointment of the Court, 506 U. S. 1046, argued the cause for respondent. With him on the brief was *Edward M. Chikofsky*.*

JUSTICE THOMAS delivered the opinion of the Court.

This case presents the question whether the competency standard for pleading guilty or waiving the right to counsel is higher than the competency standard for standing trial. We hold that it is not.

I

On August 2, 1984, in the early hours of the morning, respondent entered the Red Pearl Saloon in Las Vegas, Nevada, and shot the bartender and a patron four times each with an automatic pistol. He then walked behind the bar and removed the cash register. Nine days later, respondent arrived at the apartment of his former wife and opened fire on her; five of his seven shots hit their target. Respondent then shot himself in the abdomen and attempted, without success, to slit his wrists. Of the four victims of respondent's gunshots, only respondent himself survived. On August 13, respondent summoned police to his hospital bed and confessed to the killings.

After respondent pleaded not guilty to three counts of first-degree murder, the trial court ordered that he be examined by a pair of psychiatrists, both of whom concluded that he was competent to stand trial.[1] The State thereafter an-

---

**Kent S. Scheidegger* and *Charles L. Hobson* filed a brief for the Criminal Justice Legal Foundation as *amicus curiae* urging reversal.

Briefs of *amici curiae* urging affirmance were filed for the American Civil Liberties Union et al. by *Steven R. Shapiro, Diann Y. Rust-Tierney, John A. Powell*, and *Bruce J. Winick;* for the American Psychiatric Association et al. by *James W. Ellis* and *Barbara E. Bergman;* and for the National Association of Criminal Defense Lawyers by *Jon May*.

[1] One of the psychiatrists stated that there was "not the slightest doubt" that respondent was "in full control of his faculties" insofar as he had the "ability to aid counsel, assist in his own defense, recall evidence and . . .

nounced its intention to seek the death penalty. On November 28, 1984, 2½ months after the psychiatric evaluations, respondent again appeared before the trial court. At this time respondent informed the court that he wished to discharge his attorneys and change his pleas to guilty. The reason for the request, according to respondent, was to prevent the presentation of mitigating evidence at his sentencing.

On the basis of the psychiatric reports, the trial court found that respondent

> "is competent in that he knew the nature and quality of his acts, had the capacity to determine right from wrong; that he understands the nature of the criminal charges against him and is able to assist in his defense of such charges, or against the pronouncement of the judgment thereafter; that he knows the consequences of entering a plea of guilty to the charges; and that he can intelligently and knowingly waive his constitutional right to assistance of an attorney." App. 21.

The court advised respondent that he had a right both to the assistance of counsel and to self-representation, warned him of the "dangers and disadvantages" of self-representation, *id.*, at 22, inquired into his understanding of the proceedings and his awareness of his rights, and asked why he had chosen to represent himself. It then accepted respondent's waiver of counsel. The court also accepted respondent's guilty pleas, but not before it had determined that respondent was not pleading guilty in response to threats or promises, that he understood the nature of the charges against him and the consequences of pleading guilty, that he was aware of the

---

give testimony if called upon to do so." App. 8. The other psychiatrist believed that respondent was "knowledgeable of the charges being made against him"; that he had the ability to "assist his attorney, in his own defense, if he so desire[d]"; and that he was "fully cognizant of the penalties if convicted." *Id.*, at 17.

rights he was giving up, and that there was a factual basis for the pleas. The trial court explicitly found that respondent was "knowingly and intelligently" waiving his right to the assistance of counsel, *ibid.*, and that his guilty pleas were "freely and voluntarily" given, *id.*, at 64.[2]

On January 21, 1985, a three-judge court sentenced respondent to death for each of the murders. The Supreme Court of Nevada affirmed respondent's sentences for the Red Pearl Saloon murders, but reversed his sentence for the murder of his ex-wife and remanded for imposition of a life sentence without the possibility of parole. *Moran* v. *State*, 103 Nev. 138, 734 P. 2d 712 (1987).

On July 30, 1987, respondent filed a petition for postconviction relief in state court. Following an evidentiary hearing, the trial court rejected respondent's claim that he was "mentally incompetent to represent himself," concluding that "the record clearly shows that he was examined by two psychiatrists both of whom declared [him] competent." App. to Pet. for Cert. D–8. The Supreme Court of Nevada dismissed respondent's appeal, *Moran* v. *Warden*, 105 Nev. 1041, 810 P. 2d 335, and we denied certiorari, 493 U. S. 874 (1989).

Respondent then filed a habeas petition in the United States District Court for the District of Nevada. The District Court denied the petition, but the Ninth Circuit reversed. 972 F. 2d 263 (1992). The Court of Appeals concluded that the "record in this case" should have led the trial court to "entertai[n] a good faith doubt about [respondent's] competency to make a voluntary, knowing, and intelligent

[2] During the course of this lengthy exchange, the trial court asked respondent whether he was under the influence of drugs or alcohol, and respondent answered as follows: "Just what they give me in, you know, medications." *Id.*, at 33. The court made no further inquiry. The "medications" to which respondent referred had been prescribed to control his seizures, which were a byproduct of his cocaine use. See App. to Pet. for Cert. D–4.

waiver of constitutional rights," *id.*, at 265,[3] and that the Due Process Clause therefore "required the court to hold a hearing to evaluate and determine [respondent's] competency . . . before it accepted his decision to discharge counsel and change his pleas," *ibid.* Rejecting petitioner's argument that the trial court's error was "cured by the postconviction hearing," *ibid.*, and that the competency determination that followed the hearing was entitled to deference under 28 U. S. C. § 2254(d), the Court of Appeals held that "the state court's postconviction ruling was premised on the wrong legal standard of competency," 972 F. 2d, at 266. "Competency to waive constitutional rights," according to the Court of Appeals, "requires a higher level of mental functioning than that required to stand trial"; while a defendant is competent to stand trial if he has "a rational and factual understanding of the proceedings and is capable of assisting his counsel," a defendant is competent to waive counsel or plead guilty only if he has "the capacity for 'reasoned choice' among the alternatives available to him." *Ibid.* The Court of Appeals determined that the trial court had "erroneously applied the standard for evaluating competency to stand trial, instead of the correct 'reasoned choice' standard," *id.*, at 266–267, and further concluded that when examined "in light of the correct legal standard," the record did not support a finding that respondent was "mentally capable of the reasoned choice required for a valid waiver of constitutional rights," *id.*, at 267.[4] The Court of Appeals accordingly in-

[3] The specific features of the record upon which the Court of Appeals relied were respondent's suicide attempt; his desire to discharge his attorneys so as to prevent the presentation of mitigating evidence at sentencing; his "monosyllabic" responses to the trial court's questions; and the fact that he was on medication at the time he sought to waive his right to counsel and plead guilty. 972 F. 2d, at 265.

[4] In holding that respondent was not competent to waive his constitutional rights, the court placed heavy emphasis on the fact that respondent was on medication at the time he sought to discharge his attorneys and plead guilty. See *id.*, at 268.

structed the District Court to issue the writ of habeas corpus within 60 days, "unless the state court allows [respondent] to withdraw his guilty pleas, enter new pleas, and proceed to trial with the assistance of counsel." *Id.*, at 268.

Whether the competency standard for pleading guilty or waiving the right to counsel is higher than the competency standard for standing trial is a question that has divided the Federal Courts of Appeals[6] and state courts of last re-

[6] While the Ninth Circuit and the District of Columbia Circuit, see *United States* v. *Masthers*, 176 U. S. App. D. C. 242, 247, 539 F. 2d 721, 726 (1976), have employed the "reasoned choice" standard for guilty pleas, every other Circuit that has considered the issue has determined that the competency standard for pleading guilty is identical to the competency standard for standing trial. See *Allard* v. *Helgemoe*, 572 F. 2d 1, 3–6 (CA1), cert. denied, 439 U. S. 858 (1978); *United States* v. *Valentino*, 283 F. 2d 634, 635 (CA2 1960) *(per curiam)*; *United States ex rel. McGough* v. *Hewitt*, 528 F. 2d 339, 342, n. 2 (CA3 1975); *Shaw* v. *Martin*, 733 F. 2d 304, 314 (CA4), cert. denied, 469 U. S. 873 (1984); *Malinauskas* v. *United States*, 505 F. 2d 649, 654 (CA5 1974); *United States* v. *Harlan*, 480 F. 2d 515, 517 (CA6), cert. denied, 414 U. S. 1006 (1973); *United States ex rel. Heral* v. *Franzen*, 667 F. 2d 633, 638 (CA7 1981); *White Hawk* v. *Solem*, 693 F. 2d 825, 829–830, n. 7 (CA8 1982), cert. denied, 460 U. S. 1054 (1983); *Wolf* v. *United States*, 430 F. 2d 443, 444 (CA10 1970); *United States* v. *Simmons*, 961 F. 2d 183, 187 (CA11 1992), cert. denied, 507 U. S. 989 (1993). Three of those same Circuits, however, have indicated that the competency standard for waiving the right to counsel is "vaguely higher" than the competency standard for standing trial, see *United States ex rel. Konigsberg* v. *Vincent*, 526 F. 2d 131, 133 (CA2 1975), cert. denied, 426 U. S. 937 (1976); *United States* v. *McDowell*, 814 F. 2d 245, 250 (CA6), cert. denied, 484 U. S. 980 (1987); *Blackmon* v. *Armontrout*, 875 F. 2d 164, 166 (CA8), cert. denied, 493 U. S. 939 (1989), and one of them has stated that the two standards "may not always be coterminous," *United States* v. *Campbell*, 874 F. 2d 838, 846 (CA1 1989). Only the Ninth Circuit applies the "reasoned choice" standard to waivers of counsel, and only the Seventh Circuit, see *United States* v. *Clark*, 943 F. 2d 775, 782 (1991), cert. pending, No. 92–6439, has held that the competency standard for waiving counsel is identical to the competency standard for standing trial. The Fourth Circuit has expressed the view that the two standards are "closely linked." *United States* v. *McGinnis*, 384 F. 2d 875, 877 (1967) *(per curiam)*, cert. denied, 390 U. S. 990 (1968).

sort.[6] We granted certiorari to resolve the conflict. 506 U. S. 1033 (1992).

II

A criminal defendant may not be tried unless he is competent, *Pate* v. *Robinson*, 383 U. S. 375, 378 (1966), and he may not waive his right to counsel or plead guilty unless he does so "competently and intelligently," *Johnson* v. *Zerbst*, 304 U. S. 458, 468 (1938); accord, *Brady* v. *United States*, 397 U. S. 742, 758 (1970). In *Dusky* v. *United States*, 362 U. S. 402 (1960) *(per curiam)*, we held that the standard for competence to stand trial is whether the defendant has "sufficient present ability to consult with his lawyer with a reasonable degree of rational understanding" and has "a rational as well as factual understanding of the proceedings against him." *Ibid.* (internal quotation marks omitted). Accord, *Drope* v. *Missouri*, 420 U. S. 162, 171 (1975) ("[A] person whose mental condition is such that he lacks the capacity to understand the nature and object of the proceedings against him, to consult with counsel, and to assist in preparing his defense may not be subjected to a trial"). While we have described the standard for competence to stand trial, however, we have never expressly articulated a standard for competence to plead guilty or to waive the right to the assistance of counsel.

Relying in large part upon our decision in *Westbrook* v. *Arizona*, 384 U. S. 150 (1966) *(per curiam)*, the Ninth Circuit adheres to the view that the competency standard for pleading guilty or waiving the right to counsel is higher than the competency standard for standing trial. See *Sieling* v. *Eyman*, 478 F. 2d 211, 214–215 (1973) (first Ninth Circuit

[6] Compare, *e. g.*, *State* v. *Sims*, 118 Ariz. 210, 215, 575 P. 2d 1236, 1241 (1978) (heightened standard for guilty plea); and *Pickens* v. *State*, 96 Wis. 2d 549, 567–568, 292 N. W. 2d 601, 610–611 (1980) (heightened standard for waiver of counsel), with *People* v. *Heral*, 62 Ill. 2d 329, 334, 342 N. E. 2d 34, 37 (1976) (identical standard for pleading guilty and standing trial); and *People* v. *Reason*, 37 N. Y. 2d 351, 353–354, 334 N. E. 2d 572, 574 (1975) (identical standard for waiving counsel and standing trial).

decision applying heightened standard). In *Westbrook*, a two-paragraph *per curiam* opinion, we vacated the lower court's judgment affirming the petitioner's conviction, because there had been "a hearing on the issue of [the petitioner's] competence to stand trial," but "no hearing or inquiry into the issue of his competence to waive his constitutional right to the assistance of counsel." 384 U. S., at 150. The Ninth Circuit has reasoned that the "clear implication" of *Westbrook* is that the *Dusky* formulation is not "a high enough standard" for determining whether a defendant is competent to waive a constitutional right. *Sieling, supra*, at 214.[7] We think the Ninth Circuit has read too much into *Westbrook*, and we think it errs in applying two different competency standards.[8]

A

The standard adopted by the Ninth Circuit is whether a defendant who seeks to plead guilty or waive counsel has the capacity for "reasoned choice" among the alternatives available to him. How this standard is different from (much less higher than) the *Dusky* standard—whether the defendant has a "rational understanding" of the proceedings—is not readily apparent to us. In fact, respondent himself opposed certiorari on the ground that the difference between the two standards is merely one of "terminology," Brief in Opposition 4, and he devotes little space in his brief on the merits to a defense of the Ninth Circuit's standard, see, *e. g.*, Brief for

[7] A criminal defendant waives three constitutional rights when he pleads guilty: the privilege against self-incrimination, the right to a jury trial, and the right to confront one's accusers. *Boykin* v. *Alabama*, 395 U. S. 238, 243 (1969).

[8] Although this case comes to us by way of federal habeas corpus, we do not dispose of it on the ground that the heightened competency standard is a "new rule" for purposes of *Teague* v. *Lane*, 489 U. S. 288 (1989), because petitioner did not raise a *Teague* defense in the lower courts or in his petition for certiorari. See *Parke* v. *Raley*, 506 U. S. 20, 26 (1992); *Collins* v. *Youngblood*, 497 U. S. 37, 41 (1990).

Respondent 17–18, 27, 32; see also Tr. of Oral Arg. 33 ("Due process does not require [a] higher standard, [it] requires a separate inquiry").[9] But even assuming that there is some meaningful distinction between the capacity for "reasoned choice" and a "rational understanding" of the proceedings, we reject the notion that competence to plead guilty or to waive the right to counsel must be measured by a standard that is higher than (or even different from) the *Dusky* standard.

We begin with the guilty plea. A defendant who stands trial is likely to be presented with choices that entail relinquishment of the same rights that are relinquished by a defendant who pleads guilty: He will ordinarily have to decide whether to waive his "privilege against compulsory self-incrimination," *Boykin* v. *Alabama*, 395 U. S. 238, 243 (1969), by taking the witness stand; if the option is available, he may have to decide whether to waive his "right to trial by jury," *ibid.;* and, in consultation with counsel, he may have to decide whether to waive his "right to confront [his] accusers," *ibid.*, by declining to cross-examine witnesses for the prosecution. A defendant who pleads not guilty, moreover, faces still other strategic choices: In consultation with his attorney, he may be called upon to decide, among other things, whether (and how) to put on a defense and whether to raise one or more affirmative defenses. In sum, *all* criminal defendants—not merely those who plead guilty—may be required to make important decisions once criminal proceedings have been initiated. And while the decision to plead guilty is undeniably a profound one, it is no more complicated than the sum total of decisions that a defendant may be called upon to make during the course of a trial. (The decision to plead guilty is also made over a shorter period of

[9] We have used the phrase "rational choice" in describing the competence necessary to withdraw a certiorari petition, *Rees* v. *Peyton*, 384 U. S. 312, 314 (1966) *(per curiam)*, but there is no indication in that opinion that the phrase means something different from "rational understanding."

time, without the distraction and burden of a trial.) This being so, we can conceive of no basis for demanding a higher level of competence for those defendants who choose to plead guilty. If the *Dusky* standard is adequate for defendants who plead not guilty, it is necessarily adequate for those who plead guilty.

Nor do we think that a defendant who waives his right to the assistance of counsel must be more competent than a defendant who does not, since there is no reason to believe that the decision to waive counsel requires an appreciably higher level of mental functioning than the decision to waive other constitutional rights. Respondent suggests that a higher competency standard is necessary because a defendant who represents himself "'must have greater powers of comprehension, judgment, and reason than would be necessary to stand trial with the aid of an attorney.'" Brief for Respondent 26 (quoting Silten & Tullis, Mental Competency in Criminal Proceedings, 28 Hastings L. J. 1053, 1068 (1977)). Accord, Brief for National Association of Criminal Defense Lawyers as *Amicus Curiae* 10–12. But this argument has a flawed premise; the competence that is required of a defendant seeking to waive his right to counsel is the competence to *waive the right*, not the competence to represent himself.[10] In *Faretta* v. *California*, 422 U. S. 806 (1975), we

[10] It is for this reason that the dissent's reliance on *Massey* v. *Moore*, 348 U. S. 105 (1954), is misplaced. When we said in *Massey* that "[o]ne might not be insane in the sense of being incapable of standing trial and yet lack the capacity to stand trial without benefit of counsel," *id.*, at 108, we were answering a question that is quite different from the question presented in this case. Prior to our decision in *Gideon* v. *Wainwright*, 372 U. S. 335 (1963), the appointment of counsel was required only in those state prosecutions in which "special circumstances" were present, see *id.*, at 350–351 (Harlan, J., concurring), and the question in *Massey* was whether a finding that a defendant is competent to stand trial compels a conclusion that there are no "special circumstances" justifying the appointment of counsel. The question here is not whether a defendant who is competent to stand trial has no right to have counsel appointed; it is

held that a defendant choosing self-representation must do so "competently and intelligently," *id.*, at 835, but we made it clear that the defendant's "technical legal knowledge" is "not relevant" to the determination whether he is competent to waive his right to counsel, *id.*, at 836, and we emphasized that although the defendant "may conduct his own defense ultimately to his own detriment, his choice must be honored," *id.*, at 834. Thus, while "[i]t is undeniable that in most criminal prosecutions defendants could better defend with counsel's guidance than by their own unskilled efforts," *ibid.*, a criminal defendant's ability to represent himself has no bearing upon his competence to *choose* self-representation.[11]

B

A finding that a defendant is competent to stand trial, however, is not all that is necessary before he may be permitted to plead guilty or waive his right to counsel. In addition to determining that a defendant who seeks to plead guilty or waive counsel is competent, a trial court must satisfy itself that the waiver of his constitutional rights is knowing and voluntary. *Parke* v. *Raley*, 506 U. S. 20, 28–29 (1992) (guilty plea); *Faretta*, *supra*, at 835 (waiver of counsel). In this

---

whether such a defendant is competent to waive the right to counsel that (after *Gideon*) he under all circumstances has.

[11] We note also that the prohibition against the trial of incompetent defendants dates back at least to the time of Blackstone, see *Medina* v. *California*, 505 U. S. 437, 446 (1992); *Drope* v. *Missouri*, 420 U. S. 162, 171–172 (1975); *Youtsey* v. *United States*, 97 F. 937, 940 (CA6 1899) (collecting "common law authorities"), and that "[b]y the common law of that time, it was not representation by counsel but self-representation that was the practice in prosecutions for serious crime," *Faretta* v. *California*, 422 U. S., at 823; accord, *id.*, at 850 (BLACKMUN, J., dissenting) ("self-representation was common, if not required, in 18th century English and American prosecutions"). It would therefore be "difficult to say that a standard which was designed to determine whether a defendant was capable of defending himself" is "inadequate when he chooses to conduct his own defense." *People* v. *Reason*, 37 N. Y. 2d, at 354, 334 N. E. 2d, at 574.

sense there *is* a "heightened" standard for pleading guilty and for waiving the right to counsel, but it is not a heightened standard of *competence.*[12]

This two-part inquiry[13] is what we had in mind in *Westbrook.* When we distinguished between "competence to stand trial" and "competence to waive [the] constitutional right to the assistance of counsel," 384 U. S., at 150, we were using "competence to waive" as a shorthand for the "intelligent and competent waiver" requirement of *Johnson* v. *Zerbst.* This much is clear from the fact that we quoted that very language from *Zerbst* immediately after noting that the trial court had not determined whether the petitioner was competent to waive his right to counsel. See 384 U. S., at 150 ("'This protecting duty imposes the serious and weighty responsibility upon the trial judge of determining whether there is an intelligent and competent waiver by the accused'") (quoting *Johnson* v. *Zerbst,* 304 U. S., at 465). Thus, *Westbrook* stands only for the unremarkable proposi-

---

[12] The focus of a competency inquiry is the defendant's mental capacity; the question is whether he has the *ability* to understand the proceedings. See *Drope* v. *Missouri, supra,* at 171 (defendant is incompetent if he "lacks the *capacity* to understand the nature and object of the proceedings against him") (emphasis added). The purpose of the "knowing and voluntary" inquiry, by contrast, is to determine whether the defendant actually *does* understand the significance and consequences of a particular decision and whether the decision is uncoerced. See *Faretta* v. *California, supra,* at 835 (defendant waiving counsel must be "made aware of the dangers and disadvantages of self-representation, so that the record will establish that 'he knows what he is doing and his choice is made with eyes open'") (quoting *Adams* v. *United States ex rel. McCann,* 317 U. S. 269, 279 (1942)); *Boykin* v. *Alabama,* 395 U. S., at 244 (defendant pleading guilty must have "a full understanding of what the plea connotes and of its consequence").

[13] We do not mean to suggest, of course, that a court is required to make a competency determination in every case in which a defendant seeks to plead guilty or to waive his right to counsel. As in any criminal case, a competency determination is necessary only when a court has reason to doubt the defendant's competence. See *Drope* v. *Missouri, supra,* at 180–181; *Pate* v. *Robinson,* 383 U. S. 375, 385 (1966).

tion that when a defendant seeks to waive his right to counsel, a determination that he is competent to stand trial is not enough; the waiver must also be intelligent and voluntary before it can be accepted.[14]

III

Requiring that a criminal defendant be competent has a modest aim: It seeks to ensure that he has the capacity to understand the proceedings and to assist counsel. While psychiatrists and scholars may find it useful to classify the various kinds and degrees of competence, and while States are free to adopt competency standards that are more elaborate than the *Dusky* formulation, the Due Process Clause does not impose these additional requirements. Cf. *Medina* v. *California*, 505 U. S. 437, 446–453 (1992). The judgment of the Court of Appeals is reversed, and the case is remanded for further proceedings consistent with this opinion.

So ordered.

JUSTICE KENNEDY, with whom JUSTICE SCALIA joins, concurring in part and concurring in the judgment.

I am in full agreement with the Court's decision that the competency standard for pleading guilty and waiving the right to counsel is the same as the test of competency to stand trial. As I have some reservations about one part of the Court's opinion and take a somewhat different path to reach my conclusion, it is appropriate to make some further observations.

The Court compares the types of decisions made by one who goes to trial with the decisions required to plead guilty and waive the right to counsel. This comparison seems to suggest that there may have been a heightened standard of

[14] In this case the trial court explicitly found both that respondent was competent and that his waivers were knowing and voluntary. See *supra*, at 392–393.

competency required by the Due Process Clause if the decisions were not equivalent. I have serious doubts about that proposition. In discussing the standard for a criminal defendant's competency to make decisions affecting his case, we should not confuse the content of the standard with the occasions for its application.

We must leave aside in this case any question whether a defendant is absolved of criminal responsibility due to his mental state at the time he committed criminal acts and any later question about whether the defendant has the minimum competence necessary to undergo his sentence. What is at issue here is whether the defendant has sufficient competence to take part in a criminal proceeding and to make the decisions throughout its course. This is not to imply that mental competence is the only aspect of a defendant's state of mind that is relevant during criminal proceedings. Whether the defendant has made a knowing, intelligent, and voluntary decision to make certain fundamental choices during the course of criminal proceedings is another subject of judicial inquiry. That both questions might be implicated at any given point, however, does not mean that the inquiries cease to be discrete. And as it comes to us, this case involves only the standard for determining competency.

This Court set forth the standard for competency to stand trial in *Dusky* v. *United States*, 362 U. S. 402 (1960) *(per curiam):* "[T]he 'test must be whether [the defendant] has sufficient present ability to consult with his lawyer with a reasonable degree of rational understanding—and whether he has a rational as well as factual understanding of the proceedings against him.'" *Ibid.* In my view, both the Court of Appeals and respondent read "competency to stand trial" in too narrow a fashion. We have not suggested that the *Dusky* competency standard applies during the course of, but not before, trial. Instead, that standard is applicable from the time of arraignment through the return of a verdict. Although the *Dusky* standard refers to "ability to consult with [a] lawyer," the crucial component of the inquiry is the defendant's possession of "a reasonable degree of rational understanding." In other words, the focus of the *Dusky* formulation is on a particular level of mental functioning, which the ability to consult counsel helps identify. The possibility that consultation will occur is not required for the standard to serve its purpose. If a defendant elects to stand trial and to take the foolish course of acting as his own counsel, the law does not for that reason require any added degree of competence. See *ante*, at 399–400, n. 10.

The Due Process Clause does not mandate different standards of competency at various stages of or for different decisions made during the criminal proceedings. That was never the rule at common law, and it would take some extraordinary showing of the inadequacy of a single standard of competency for us to require States to employ heightened standards. See *Medina* v. *California*, 505 U. S. 437, 446–447 (1992). Indeed, we should only overturn Nevada's use of a single standard if it "'offends some principle of justice so rooted in the traditions and conscience of our people as to be ranked as fundamental.'" *Ibid.* (quoting *Patterson* v. *New York*, 432 U. S. 197, 202 (1977)).

The historical treatment of competency that supports Nevada's single standard has its roots in English common law. Writing in the 18th century, Blackstone described the effect of a defendant's incompetence on criminal proceedings:

> "[I]f a man in his sound memory commits a capital offence, and before arraignment for it, he becomes mad, he ought not to be arraigned for it; because he is not able to plead to it with that advice and caution that he ought. And if, after he has pleaded, the prisoner becomes mad, he shall not be tried; for how can he make his defence?" 4 W. Blackstone, Commentaries *24.

Accord, 1 M. Hale, Pleas of the Crown *34–*35.

Blackstone drew no distinction between madness for purposes of pleading and madness for purposes of going to trial. An English case arising in the Crown Court in 1865 indicates that a single standard was applied to assess competency at the time of arraignment, the time of pleading, and throughout the course of trial. See *Regina* v. *Southey*, 4 Fos. & Fin. 864, 872, n. a, 176 Eng. Rep. 825, 828, n. a (N. P. 1865) ("Assuming the prisoner to be insane at the time of arraignment, he cannot be tried *at all*, with or without counsel, for, even assuming that he has appointed counsel at a time when he was sane, it is not fit that he should be tried, as he cannot understand the evidence, nor the proceedings, and so is unable to instruct counsel, or to withdraw his authority if he acts improperly, as a prisoner may always do"); *id.*, at 877, n. a, 176 Eng. Rep., at 831, n. a ("[I]f [the defendant] be so insane as not to understand the nature of the proceedings, he cannot plead").

A number of 19th-century American cases also referred to insanity in a manner that suggested there was a single standard by which competency was to be assessed throughout legal proceedings. See, *e. g.*, *Underwood* v. *People*, 32 Mich. 1, 3 (1875) ("[I]nsanity, when discovered, was held at common law to bar any further steps against a prisoner, at whatever stage of the proceedings"); *Crocker* v. *State*, 60 Wis. 553, 556, 19 N. W. 435, 436 (1884) ("At common law, if a person, after committing a crime, became insane, he was not arraigned during his insanity, but was remitted to prison until such incapacity was removed. The same was true where he became insane after his plea of not guilty and before trial"); *State* v. *Reed*, 41 La. Ann. 581, 582, 7 So. 132 (1889) ("It is elementary that a man cannot plead, or be tried, or convicted, or sentenced, while in a state of insanity"). See also 2 J. Bishop, Commentaries on Law of Criminal Procedure §§664, 667 (2d ed. 1872) ("[A] prisoner cannot be tried, sentenced, or punished" unless he is "mentally competent to make a rational defense").

Other American cases describe the standard by which competency is to be measured in a way that supports the idea that a single standard, parallel to that articulated in *Dusky*, is applied no matter at what point during legal proceedings a competency question should arise. For example, in *Freeman* v. *People*, 4 Denio 2 (N. Y. 1847), it was held: "If . . . a person arraigned for a crime, is capable of understanding the nature and object of the proceedings going on against him; if he rightly comprehends his own condition in reference to such proceedings, and can conduct his defence in a rational manner, he is, for the purpose of being tried, to be deemed sane." *Id.*, at 24–25. Because the competency question was posed in *Freeman* at the time the defendant was to be arraigned, *id.*, at 19, the *Freeman* court's conception of competency to stand trial was that of a single standard to be applied throughout.

An even more explicit recitation of this common-law principle is found in *Hunt* v. *State*, 27 So. 2d 186 (Ala. 1946). In the course of the opinion in that case, there was a discussion of the common-law rule regarding a defendant's competency to take part in legal proceedings:

> "The rule at common law . . . is that if at any time while criminal proceedings are pending against a person accused of a crime, the trial court either from observation or upon suggestion of counsel has facts brought to his attention which raise a doubt of the sanity of defendant, the question should be settled before further steps are taken. . . . The broad question to be determined then is whether the defendant is capable of understanding the proceedings and of making his defense, and whether he may have a full, fair and impartial trial." *Id.*, at 191 (citation omitted).

At common law, therefore, no attempt was made to apply different competency standards to different stages of criminal proceedings or to the variety of decisions that a defendant must make during the course of those proceedings. See *Commonwealth* v. *Woelfel*, 88 S. W. 1061, 1062 (Ky. 1905); *Jordan* v. *State*, 135 S. W. 327, 328–329 (Tenn. 1911); *State* v. *Seminary*, 115 So. 370, 371–372 (La. 1927); *State ex rel. Townsend* v. *Bushong*, 146 Ohio St. 271, 272, 65 N. E. 2d 407, 408 (1946) *(per curiam)*; *Moss* v. *Hunter*, 167 F. 2d 683, 684–685 (CA10 1948). Commentators have agreed that the common-law standard of competency to stand trial, which parallels the *Dusky* standard, has been applied throughout criminal proceedings, not just to the formal trial. See H. Weihofen, Mental Disorder as a Criminal Defense 428–429, 431 (1954) ("It has long been the rule of the common law that a person cannot be required to plead to an indictment or be tried for a crime while he is so mentally disordered as to be incapable of making a rational defense"); S. Brakel, J. Parry, and A. Weiner, The Mentally Disabled and the Law 695–696 (3d ed. 1985) ("It has traditionally been presumed that competency to stand trial means competency to participate in all phases of the trial process, including such pretrial activities as deciding how to plead, participating in plea bargaining, and deciding whether to assert or waive the right to counsel").

That the common law did not adopt heightened competency standards is readily understood when one considers the difficulties that would be associated with more than one standard. The standard applicable at a given point in a trial could be difficult to ascertain. For instance, if a defendant decides to change his plea to guilty after a trial has commenced, one court might apply the competency standard for undergoing trial while another court might use the standard for pleading guilty. In addition, the subtle nuances among different standards are likely to be difficult to differentiate, as evidenced by the lack of any clear distinction between a "rational understanding" and a "reasoned choice" in this case. See *ante*, at 398.

It is true, of course, that if a defendant stands trial instead of pleading guilty, there will be more occasions for the trial court to observe the condition of the defendant to determine his mental competence. Trial courts have the obligation of conducting a hearing whenever there is sufficient doubt concerning a defendant's competence. See *Drope* v. *Missouri*, 420 U. S. 162, 180–181 (1975). The standard by which competency is assessed, however, does not change. Respondent's counsel conceded as much during oral argument, making no attempt to defend the contrary position of the Court of Appeals. See, *e. g.*, Tr. of Oral Arg. 22 ("This is not a case of heightened standards"); *id.*, at 31 ("We didn't argue a heightened standard. We did not argue a heightened standard to the Ninth Circuit, nor did we necessarily argue a heightened standard at any juncture in this case"); *id.*, at 33 ("Due process does not require this higher standard, but requires a separate inquiry").

A single standard of competency to be applied throughout criminal proceedings does not offend any " 'principle of justice so rooted in the traditions and conscience of our people as to be ranked as fundamental.' " *Medina*, 505 U. S., at 446. Nothing in our case law compels a contrary conclusion, and adoption of a rule setting out varying competency standards for each decision and stage of a criminal proceeding would disrupt the orderly course of trial and, from the standpoint of all parties, prove unworkable both at trial and on appellate review.

I would avoid the difficult comparisons engaged in by the Court. In my view, due process does not preclude Nevada's use of a single competency standard for all aspects of the criminal proceeding. Respondent's decision to plead guilty and his decision to waive counsel were grave choices for him to make, but as the Court demonstrates in Part II–B, there is a heightened standard, albeit not one concerned with competence, that must be met before a defendant is allowed to make those decisions.

With these observations, I concur in the judgment and in Parts I, II–B, and III of the Court's opinion.

JUSTICE BLACKMUN, with whom JUSTICE STEVENS joins, dissenting.

Today, the majority holds that a standard of competence designed to measure a defendant's ability to consult with counsel and to assist in preparing his defense is constitutionally adequate to assess a defendant's competence to waive the right to counsel and represent himself. In so doing, the majority upholds the death sentence for a person whose decision to discharge counsel, plead guilty, and present no defense well may have been the product of medication or mental illness. I believe the majority's analysis is contrary to both common sense and longstanding case law. Therefore, I dissent.

I

As a preliminary matter, the circumstances under which respondent Richard Allan Moran waived his right to an attorney and pleaded guilty to capital murder bear elaboration. For, although the majority's exposition of the events is accurate, the most significant facts are omitted or relegated to footnotes.

In August 1984, after killing three people and wounding himself in an attempt to commit suicide, Moran was charged in a Nevada state court with three counts of capital murder. He pleaded not guilty to all charges, and the trial court ordered a psychiatric evaluation. At this stage, Moran's competence to represent himself was not at issue.

The two psychiatrists who examined him therefore focused solely upon his capacity to stand trial with the assistance of counsel. Dr. Jack A. Jurasky found Moran to be "in full control of his faculties insofar as his ability to aid counsel, assist in his own defense, recall evidence and to give testimony if called upon to do so." App. 8. Dr. Jurasky, however, did express some reservations, observing: "Psychologically, and perhaps legally speaking, this man, because he is expressing and feeling considerable remorse and guilt, may be inclined to exert less effort towards his own defense." *Ibid.* Nevertheless, under the circumstances, Dr. Jurasky felt that Moran's depressed state of mind was not "necessarily a major consideration." *Ibid.* Dr. William D. O'Gorman also characterized Moran as "very depressed," remarking that he "showed much tearing in talking about the episodes that led up to his present incarceration, particularly in talking about his ex-wife." *Id.*, at 15–16. But Dr. O'Gorman ultimately concluded that Moran "is knowledgeable of the charges being made against him" and "can assist his attorney, in his own defense, if he so desires." *Id.*, at 17.

In November 1984, just three months after his suicide attempt, Moran appeared in court seeking to discharge his public defender, waive his right to counsel, and plead guilty to all three charges of capital murder. When asked to explain the dramatic change in his chosen course of action, Moran responded that he wished to represent himself because he opposed all efforts to mount a defense. His purpose, specifically, was to prevent the presentation of any mitigating evidence on his behalf at the sentencing phase of the proceeding. The trial judge inquired whether Moran was "presently under the influence of any drug or alcohol," and Moran replied: "Just what they give me in, you know, medications." *Id.*, at 33. Despite Moran's affirmative answer, the trial judge failed to question him further regarding the type, dosage, or effect of the "medications" to which he referred. Had the trial judge done so, he would have discovered that Moran was being administered simultaneously four different prescription drugs—phenobarbital, dilantin, inderal, and vistaril. Moran later testified to the numbing effect of these drugs, stating: "I guess I really didn't care about anything . . . . I wasn't very concerned about anything that was going on . . . as far as the proceedings and everything were going." *Id.*, at 92.[1]

Disregarding the mounting evidence of Moran's disturbed mental state, the trial judge accepted Moran's waiver of counsel and guilty pleas after posing a series of routine questions regarding his understanding of his legal rights and the offenses, to which Moran gave largely monosyllabic answers. In a string of affirmative responses, Moran purported to acknowledge that he knew the import of waiving his constitutional rights, that he understood the charges against him, and that he was, in fact, guilty of those charges. One part of this exchange, however, highlights the mechanical character of Moran's answers to the questions. When the trial judge asked him whether he killed his ex-wife "deliberately, with premeditation and malice aforethought," Moran unexpectedly responded: "No. I didn't do it—I mean, I wasn't looking to kill her, but she ended up dead." *Id.*, at 58. Instead of probing further, the trial judge simply repeated the question, inquiring again whether Moran had acted deliberately. Once again, Moran replied: "I don't know. I mean, I don't know what you mean by deliberately. I mean, I pulled the trigger on purpose, but I didn't plan on doing it; you know what I mean?" *Id.*, at 59. Ignoring the ambiguity of Moran's responses, the trial judge reframed the question to elicit an affirmative answer, stating: "Well, I've previously explained to you what is meant by deliberation and premeditation. Deliberate means that you arrived at or determined as a result of careful thought and weighing the consideration

[1] Moran's medical records, read in conjunction with the Physician's Desk Reference (46 ed. 1992), corroborate his testimony concerning the medications he received and their impact upon him. The records show that Moran was administered dilantin, an antiepileptic medication that may cause confusion; inderal, a beta-blocker antiarrhythmic that may cause light-headedness, mental depression, hallucinations, disorientation, and short-term memory loss; and vistaril, a depressant that may cause drowsiness, tremors, and convulsions. App. 97–98.

for and against the proposed action. Did you do that?" This time, Moran responded: "Yes." *Ibid.*

It was only after prodding Moran through the plea colloquy in this manner that the trial judge concluded that he was competent to stand trial and that he voluntarily and intelligently had waived his right to counsel. Accordingly, Moran was allowed to plead guilty and appear without counsel at his sentencing hearing. Moran presented no defense, called no witness, and offered no mitigating evidence on his own behalf. Not surprisingly, he was sentenced to death.

II

It is axiomatic by now that criminal prosecution of an incompetent defendant offends the Due Process Clause of the Fourteenth Amendment. See *Medina* v. *California*, 505 U. S. 437 (1992); *Riggins* v. *Nevada*, 504 U. S. 127, 138 (1992) (KENNEDY, J., concurring); *Drope* v. *Missouri*, 420 U. S. 162, 171 (1975); *Pate* v. *Robinson*, 383 U. S. 375, 378 (1966). The majority does not deny this principle, nor does it dispute the standard that has been set for competence to stand trial with the assistance of counsel: whether the accused possesses "the capacity to understand the nature and object of the proceedings against him, to consult with counsel, and to assist in preparing his defense." *Drope*, 420 U. S., at 171. Accord, *Dusky* v. *United States*, 362 U. S. 402 (1960). My disagreement with the majority turns, then, upon another standard—the one for assessing a defendant's competence to waive counsel and represent himself.

The majority "reject[s] the notion that competence to plead guilty or to waive the right to counsel must be measured by a standard that is higher than (or even different from)" the standard for competence to stand trial articulated in *Dusky* and *Drope*. *Ante*, at 398. But the standard for competence to stand trial is specifically designed to measure a defendant's ability to "consult with counsel" and to "assist in preparing his defense." A finding that a defendant is competent to stand trial establishes only that he is capable of aiding his attorney in making the critical decisions required at trial or in plea negotiations. The reliability or even relevance of such a finding vanishes when its basic premise—that counsel will be present—ceases to exist. The question is no longer whether the defendant can proceed with an attorney, but whether he can proceed alone and uncounseled. I do not believe we place an excessive burden upon a trial court by requiring it to conduct a specific inquiry into that question at the juncture when a defendant whose competency already has been questioned seeks to waive counsel and represent himself.

The majority concludes that there is no need for such a hearing because a defendant who is found competent to stand trial with the assistance of counsel is, *ipso facto,* competent to discharge counsel and represent himself. But the majority cannot isolate the term "competent" and apply it in a vacuum, divorced from its specific context. A person who is "competent" to play basketball is not thereby "competent" to play the violin. The majority's monolithic approach to competency is true to neither life nor the law. Competency for one purpose does not necessarily translate to competency for another purpose. See Bonnie, The Competence of Criminal Defendants: A Theoretical Reformulation, 10 Behav. Sci. & L. 291, 299 (1992); R. Roesch & S. Golding, Competency to Stand Trial 10–13 (1980). Consistent with this commonsense notion, our cases always have recognized that "a defendant's mental condition may be relevant to more than one legal issue, each governed by distinct rules reflecting quite different policies." *Drope,* 420 U. S., at 176. See *Jackson* v. *Indiana,* 406 U. S. 715, 739 (1972). To this end, this Court has required competency evaluations to be specifically tailored to the context and purpose of a proceeding. See *Rees* v. *Peyton,* 384 U. S. 312, 314 (1966) (directing court "to determine [petitioner's] mental competence in the present posture of things").

In *Massey* v. *Moore*, 348 U. S. 105, 108 (1954), for example, the Court ruled that a defendant who had been found competent to stand trial with the assistance of counsel should have been given a hearing as to his competency to represent himself because "[o]ne might not be insane in the sense of being incapable of standing trial and yet lack the capacity to stand trial without benefit of counsel."[2] And in *Westbrook* v. *Arizona*, 384 U. S. 150 (1966), the Court reiterated the requirement that the determination of a defendant's competency be tailored to the particular capacity in question, observing: "Although petitioner received a hearing on the issue of his competence to stand trial, there appears to have been no hearing or inquiry into the issue of his competence to waive his constitutional right to the assistance of counsel and proceed, as he did, to conduct his own defense." See also *Medina*, 505 U. S., at 446–448 (distinguishing between a claim of incompetence and a plea of not guilty by reason of insanity); *Riggins*, 504 U. S., at 140–144 (KENNEDY, J., concurring) (distinguishing between functional competence and competence to stand trial).

Although the Court never has articulated explicitly the standard for determining competency to represent oneself, it has hinted at its contours. In *Rees* v. *Peyton*, *supra*, it required an evaluation of competence that was designed to measure the abilities necessary for a defendant to make a decision under analogous circumstances. In that case, a capital defendant who had filed a petition for certiorari ordered his attorney to withdraw the petition and forgo further legal proceedings. The petitioner's counsel advised the Court that he could not conscientiously do so without a psychiatric examination of his client because there was some doubt as to

[2] The majority's attempt to distinguish *Massey* as a pre-*Gideon* v. *Wainwright*, 372 U. S. 335 (1963), case, *ante*, at 399–400, n. 10, is simply irrelevant. For, as the majority itself concedes, *Massey* stands only for the proposition that the two inquiries are different—competency to stand trial with the assistance of counsel is not equivalent to competency to proceed alone.

his client's mental competency. Under those circumstances, this Court directed the lower court to conduct an inquiry as to whether the defendant possessed the "capacity to appreciate his position and make a *rational choice* with respect to continuing or abandoning further litigation or on the other hand whether he is suffering from a mental disease, disorder, or defect which may substantially affect his capacity in the premises." 384 U. S., at 314 (emphasis added). Certainly the competency required for a capital defendant to proceed *without the advice of counsel* at trial or in plea negotiations should be no less than the competency required for a capital defendant to proceed *against the advice of counsel* to withdraw a petition for certiorari. The standard applied by the Ninth Circuit in this case—the "reasoned choice" standard—closely approximates the "rational choice" standard set forth in *Rees.*[3]

Disregarding the plain language of *Westbrook* and *Massey*, the majority in effect overrules those cases *sub silentio.*[4] From the constitutional right of self-representation established in *Faretta* v. *California*, 422 U. S. 806 (1975), the majority extrapolates that "a criminal defendant's ability to represent himself has no bearing upon his competence to *choose*

[3] According to the majority, "there is no indication . . . that the phrase ['rational choice'] means something different from 'rational understanding.'" *Ante*, at 398, n. 9. What the majority fails to recognize is that, in the distinction between a defendant who possesses a "rational understanding" of the proceedings and one who is able to make a "rational choice," lies the difference between the capacity for passive and active involvement in the proceedings.

[4] According to the majority, "*Westbrook* stands only for the unremarkable proposition" that a determination of competence to stand trial is not sufficient to waive the right to counsel; "the waiver must also be intelligent and voluntary before it can be accepted." *Ante*, at 401–402. But the majority's attempt to transform a case about the competency to waive counsel into a case about the voluntariness of a waiver needlessly complicates this area of the law. Perhaps competence to waive rights is incorporated into a voluntariness inquiry, but there is no necessary link between the two concepts.

self-representation." *Ante,* at 400. But *Faretta* does not confer upon an *incompetent* defendant a constitutional right to conduct his own defense. Indeed, Faretta himself was "literate, competent, and understanding," and the record showed that "he was voluntarily exercising his informed free will." 422 U. S., at 835. "Although a defendant need not himself have the skill and experience of a lawyer," *Faretta's* right of self-representation is confined to those who are able to choose it "competently and intelligently." *Ibid.* The *Faretta* Court was careful to emphasize that the record must establish that the defendant "'knows what he is doing and his choice is made with eyes open.'" *Ibid.,* quoting *Adams* v. *United States ex rel. McCann,* 317 U. S. 269, 279 (1942).

The majority asserts that "the competence that is required of a defendant seeking to waive his right to counsel is the competence to *waive the right,* not the competence to represent himself." *Ante,* at 399. But this assertion is simply incorrect. The majority's attempt to extricate the competence to waive the right to counsel from the competence to represent oneself is unavailing, because the former decision necessarily entails the latter. It is obvious that a defendant who waives counsel must represent himself. Even Moran, who pleaded guilty, was required to defend himself during the penalty phase of the proceedings. And a defendant who is utterly incapable of conducting his own defense cannot be considered "competent" to make such a decision, any more than a person who chooses to leap out of a window in the belief that he can fly can be considered "competent" to make such a choice.

The record in this case gives rise to grave doubts regarding respondent Moran's ability to discharge counsel and represent himself. Just a few months after he attempted to commit suicide, Moran essentially volunteered himself for execution: He sought to waive the right to counsel, to plead guilty to capital murder, and to prevent the presentation of any mitigating evidence on his behalf. The psychiatrists' reports supplied one explanation for Moran's self-destructive behavior: his deep depression. And Moran's own testimony suggested another: the fact that he was being administered simultaneously four different prescription medications. It has been recognized that such drugs often possess side effects that may "compromise the right of a medicated criminal defendant to receive a fair trial . . . by rendering him unable or unwilling to assist counsel." *Riggins*, 504 U. S., at 142 (KENNEDY, J., concurring). Moran's plea colloquy only augments the manifold causes for concern by suggesting that his waivers and his assent to the charges against him were not rendered in a truly voluntary and intelligent fashion. Upon this evidence, there can be no doubt that the trial judge should have conducted another competency evaluation to determine Moran's capacity to waive the right to counsel and represent himself, instead of relying upon the psychiatrists' reports that he was able to stand trial with the assistance of counsel.[6]

To try, convict, and punish one so helpless to defend himself contravenes fundamental principles of fairness and impugns the integrity of our criminal justice system. I cannot condone the decision to accept, without further inquiry, the self-destructive "choice" of a person who was so deeply medicated and who might well have been severely mentally ill. I dissent.

---

[6] Whether this same evidence implies that Moran's waiver of counsel and guilty pleas were also involuntary remains to be seen. Cf. *Miller* v. *Fenton*, 474 U. S. 104 (1985) (voluntariness is a mixed question of law and fact entitled to independent federal review).

COOPER *v.* OKLAHOMA

CERTIORARI TO THE COURT OF CRIMINAL APPEALS OF OKLAHOMA

No. 95–5207. Argued January 17, 1996—Decided April 16, 1996

Oklahoma law presumes that a criminal defendant is competent to stand trial unless he proves his incompetence by clear and convincing evidence. Applying that standard, a judge found petitioner Cooper competent on separate occasions before and during his trial for first-degree murder, despite his bizarre behavior and conflicting expert testimony on the issue. In affirming his conviction and death sentence, the Court of Criminal Appeals rejected his argument that the State's presumption of competence, combined with its clear and convincing evidence standard, placed such an onerous burden on him as to violate due process.

Held: Because Oklahoma's procedural rule allows the State to try a defendant who is more likely than not incompetent, it violates due process. Pp. 354–369.

(a) It is well settled that the criminal trial of an incompetent defendant violates due process. *Medina* v. *California,* 505 U. S. 437, 449, establishes that a State may presume that the defendant is competent and require him to prove incompetence by a preponderance of the evidence. Such a presumption does not offend a "'principle of justice so rooted in the traditions and conscience of our people as to be ranked as fundamental,'" *id.,* at 445, for it affects the outcome "only in a narrow class of cases . . . where the evidence that a defendant is competent is just as strong as the evidence that he is incompetent," *id.,* at 449. This case, however, presents the quite different question whether a State may proceed with a criminal trial after a defendant has shown that he is more likely than not incompetent. Pp. 354–356.

(b) Oklahoma's rule has no roots in historical practice. Both early English and American cases suggest that the common-law standard of proof was preponderance of the evidence. That this same standard is currently used by 46 States and the federal courts indicates that the vast majority of jurisdictions remain persuaded that Oklahoma's heightened standard is not necessary to vindicate the State's interest in prompt and orderly disposition of criminal cases. The near-uniform application of a standard that is more protective of the defendant's rights than Oklahoma's rule supports the conclusion that the heightened standard offends a deeply rooted principle of justice. Pp. 356–362.

(c) Oklahoma's rule does not exhibit "fundamental fairness" in operation. An erroneous determination of competence has dire consequences for a defendant who has already demonstrated that he is more likely than not incompetent, threatening the basic fairness of the trial itself. A defendant's inability to communicate effectively with counsel may leave him unable to exercise other rights deemed essential to a fair trial—*e. g.*, choosing to plead guilty, waiving his privilege against compulsory self-incrimination by taking the witness stand, or waiving his rights to a jury trial or to cross-examine witnesses—and to make a myriad of smaller decisions concerning the course of his defense. These risks outweigh the State's interest in the efficient operation of its criminal justice system. Difficulty in ascertaining whether a defendant is incompetent or malingering may make it appropriate to place the burden of proof on him, but it does not justify the additional onus of an especially high standard of proof. Pp. 362–367.

(d) Although it is normally within a State's power to establish the procedures through which its laws are given effect, the power to regulate procedural burdens is subject to proscription under the Due Process Clause when, as here, the procedures do not sufficiently protect a fundamental constitutional right. *Patterson* v. *New York*, 432 U. S. 197, distinguished. The decision herein is in complete accord with the ruling in *Addington* v. *Texas*, 441 U. S. 418, that due process requires a clear and convincing evidence standard of proof in involuntary civil commitment proceedings. That ruling protects an individual's fundamental liberty interest, while the ruling in this case safeguards the fundamental right not to stand trial while incompetent. Pp. 367–369.

889 P. 2d 293, reversed and remanded.

STEVENS, J., delivered the opinion for a unanimous Court.

Robert A. Ravitz argued the cause and filed briefs for petitioner.

W. A. Drew Edmondson, Attorney General of Oklahoma, argued the cause for respondent. With him on the brief was *Sandra D. Howard*, Assistant Attorney General.*

---

*Briefs of *amici curiae* urging reversal were filed for the American Association on Mental Retardation et al. by *James W. Ellis* and *Barbara E. Bergman;* and for the National Association of Criminal Defense Lawyers by *Charles D. Weisselberg, Dennis E. Curtis, Denise Meyer*, and *Larry J. Fleming.*

A brief of *amicus curiae* urging affirmance was filed for the State of Utah et al. by *Jan Graham*, Attorney General of Utah, *J. Kevin Murphy,*

JUSTICE STEVENS delivered the opinion of the Court.

In Oklahoma the defendant in a criminal prosecution is presumed to be competent to stand trial unless he proves his incompetence by clear and convincing evidence. Okla. Stat., Tit. 22, § 1175.4(B) (1991). Under that standard a defendant may be put to trial even though it is more likely than not that he is incompetent. The question we address in this case is whether the application of that standard to petitioner violated his right to due process under the Fourteenth Amendment.

I

In 1989 petitioner was charged with the brutal killing of an 86-year-old man in the course of a burglary. After an Oklahoma jury found him guilty of first-degree murder and recommended punishment by death, the trial court imposed the death penalty. The Oklahoma Court of Criminal Appeals affirmed the conviction and sentence.

Petitioner's competence was the focus of significant attention both before and during his trial. On five separate occasions a judge considered whether petitioner had the ability to understand the charges against him and to assist defense counsel. On the first occasion, a pretrial judge relied on the opinion of a clinical psychologist employed by the State to find petitioner incompetent. Based on that determination, he committed petitioner to a state mental health facility for treatment.

Assistant Attorney General, and *Carol Clawson*, Solicitor General, *John M. Bailey*, Chief State's Attorney of Connecticut, and by the Attorneys General for their respective States as follows: *Gale A. Norton* of Colorado, *M. Jane Brady* of Delaware, *Margery S. Bronster* of Hawaii, *Alan G. Lance* of Idaho, *Carla J. Stovall* of Kansas, *Michael C. Moore* of Mississippi, *Don Stenberg* of Nebraska, *Frankie Sue Del Papa* of Nevada, *Tom Udall* of New Mexico, *Betty D. Montgomery* of Ohio, *Thomas W. Corbett, Jr.*, of Pennsylvania, *Jeffrey B. Pine* of Rhode Island, and *James S. Gilmore III* of Virginia.

Upon petitioner's release from the hospital some three months later, the trial judge heard testimony concerning petitioner's competence from two state-employed psychologists. These experts expressed conflicting opinions regarding petitioner's ability to participate in his defense. The judge resolved the dispute against petitioner, ordering him to proceed to trial.

At the close of a pretrial hearing held one week before the trial was scheduled to begin, the lead defense attorney raised the issue of petitioner's competence for a third time. Counsel advised the court that petitioner was behaving oddly and refusing to communicate with him. Defense counsel opined that it would be a serious matter "if he's not faking." App. 6. After listening to counsel's concerns, however, the judge declined to revisit his earlier determination that petitioner was competent to stand trial.

Petitioner's competence was addressed a fourth time on the first day of trial, when petitioner's bizarre behavior prompted the court to conduct a further competency hearing at which the judge observed petitioner and heard testimony from several lay witnesses, a third psychologist, and petitioner himself.[1] The expert concluded that petitioner was

---

[1] During the hearing petitioner, who had refused to change out of prison overalls for the trial because the proffered clothes were "burning" him, Tr. of Pretrial Motions and Competency Hearings 3–4 (May 4–5, 1992), talked to himself and to an imaginary "spirit" who petitioner claimed gave him counsel. On the witness stand petitioner expressed fear that the lead defense attorney wanted to kill him.

In his argument at the close of the proceeding, defense counsel reminded the court of an incident that occurred during petitioner's testimony:

"Every time I would get close to his space where he is seated in this little witness enclave . . . he would stand up and he would get away from me as far as he could and so I would back off and I'd give him a little space. . . . So, I've approached him from every side. . . . except I haven't approached him from the front. So yesterday, I approach him from the front. And that's the last thing I did. I regret doing that.

"He stood up and he got as far back against the rail behind the witness chair as he could get. I edged closer. He got as far back and he got up

presently incompetent and unable to communicate effectively with counsel, but that he could probably achieve competence within six weeks if treated aggressively. While stating that he did not dispute the psychologist's diagnosis, the trial judge ruled against petitioner. In so holding, however, the court voiced uncertainty:

> "Well, I think I've used the expression . . . in the past that normal is like us. Anybody that's not like us is not normal, so I don't think normal is a proper definition that we are to use with incompetence. My shirtsleeve opinion of Mr. Cooper is that he's not normal. Now, to say he's not competent is something else.
>
> . . . . .
>
> "But you know, all things considered, I suppose it's possible for a client to be in such a predicament that he can't help his defense and still not be incompetent. I suppose that's a possibility, too.
>
> "I think it's going to take smarter people than me to make a decision here. I'm going to say that I don't believe he has carried the burden by clear and convincing evidence of his incompetency and I'm going to say we're going to go to trial." *Id.*, at 42–43.

---

on that rail. So I've got him up on the rail and I'm thinking, hey, what can I lose? Let me just see what he does now because he can go no further back, but as the Court knows, there's a space of about two-and-a-half feet behind this rail and a marble wall.

"Without looking for his safety at all and looking what's behind him, when I moved the least bit and I didn't move very far towards him, he fell to get away from me. He fell. He hit his head. The thud on that marble when he jackknifed backward off of that railing into that marble could be heard at the back of that courtroom. . . .

"We got him back up here in the witness enclave, he's just busted his head, tears are streaming down his eyes and he does not respond in any normal fashion." App. 37–38.

Incidents that occurred during the trial,[2] as well as the sordid history of petitioner's childhood that was recounted during the sentencing phase of the proceeding, were consistent with the conclusions expressed by the expert. In a final effort to protect his client's interests, defense counsel moved for a mistrial or a renewed investigation into petitioner's competence. After the court summarily denied these motions, petitioner was convicted and sentenced to death.

In the Court of Criminal Appeals, petitioner contended that Oklahoma's presumption of competence, combined with its statutory requirement that a criminal defendant establish incompetence by clear and convincing evidence, Okla. Stat., Tit. 22, § 1175.4(B) (1991),[3] placed such an onerous burden on him as to violate his right to due process of law. The appellate court rejected this argument. After noting that it can be difficult to determine whether a defendant is malingering, given "the inexactness and uncertainty attached to [competency] proceedings," the court held that the standard was justified because the "State has great interest in assuring its citizens a thorough and speedy judicial process," and because a "truly incompetent criminal defendant, through his attorneys and experts, can prove incompetency with relative ease." 889 P. 2d 293, 303 (1995). We granted certiorari to review the Court of Criminal Appeals' conclusion that appli-

[2] Petitioner did not communicate with or sit near defense counsel during the trial. Through much of the proceedings he remained in prison overalls, crouching in the fetal position and talking to himself.

[3] Section 1175.4(B) provides, in relevant part: "The court, at the hearing on the application [for determination of competency], shall determine, by clear and convincing evidence, if the person is incompetent. The person shall be presumed to be competent for the purposes of the allocation of the burden of proof and burden of going forward with the evidence."

Section 1175.4 was amended in 1991, during the pretrial period of petitioner's prosecution. The amendment did not alter the text of subsection B.

cation of the clear and convincing evidence standard does not violate due process. 516 U. S. 910 (1995).

II

No one questions the existence of the fundamental right that petitioner invokes. We have repeatedly and consistently recognized that "the criminal trial of an incompetent defendant violates due process." *Medina* v. *California*, 505 U. S. 437, 453 (1992); *Drope* v. *Missouri*, 420 U. S. 162, 171–172 (1975); *Pate* v. *Robinson*, 383 U. S. 375, 378 (1966). Nor is the significance of this right open to dispute. As JUSTICE KENNEDY recently emphasized:

> "Competence to stand trial is rudimentary, for upon it depends the main part of those rights deemed essential to a fair trial, including the right to effective assistance of counsel, the rights to summon, to confront, and to cross-examine witnesses, and the right to testify on one's own behalf or to remain silent without penalty for doing so. *Drope* v. *Missouri*, 420 U. S. 162, 171–172 (1975)." *Riggins* v. *Nevada*, 504 U. S. 127, 139–140 (1992) (opinion concurring in judgment).[4]

The test for incompetence is also well settled. A defendant may not be put to trial unless he "'has sufficient present ability to consult with his lawyer with a reasonable degree of rational understanding . . . [and] a rational as well as factual understanding of the proceedings against him.'" *Dusky* v. *United States*, 362 U. S. 402, 402 (1960) *(per curiam)*.[5]

---

[4] Indeed, the right not to stand trial while incompetent is sufficiently important to merit protection even if the defendant has failed to make a timely request for a competency determination. See *Pate* v. *Robinson*, 383 U. S. 375, 384 (1966).

[5] The Oklahoma statute defines competence as "the present ability of a person arrested for or charged with a crime to understand the nature of the charges and proceedings brought against him and to effectively and

Our recent decision in *Medina* v. *California*, 505 U. S. 437 (1992), establishes that a State may presume that the defendant is competent and require him to shoulder the burden of proving his incompetence by a preponderance of the evidence. *Id.*, at 449. In reaching that conclusion we held that the relevant inquiry was whether the presumption "'offends some principle of justice so rooted in the traditions and conscience of our people as to be ranked as fundamental.'" *Id.*, at 445 (quoting *Patterson* v. *New York*, 432 U. S. 197, 202 (1977)). We contrasted the "deep roots in our common-law heritage" underlying the prohibition against trying the incompetent with the absence of any settled tradition concerning the allocation of the burden of proof in a competency proceeding. 505 U. S., at 446. Our conclusion that the presumption of competence offends no recognized principle of "fundamental fairness" rested in part on the fact that the procedural rule affects the outcome "only in a narrow class of cases where the evidence is in equipoise; that is, where the evidence that a defendant is competent is just as strong as the evidence that he is incompetent." *Id.*, at 449.[6]

The question we address today is quite different from the question posed in *Medina*. Petitioner's claim requires us to consider whether a State may proceed with a criminal trial after the defendant has demonstrated that he is more likely than not incompetent. Oklahoma does not contend that it may require the defendant to prove incompetence beyond a reasonable doubt.[7] The State maintains, however, that the clear and convincing standard provides a reasonable accom-

---

rationally assist in his defense." Okla. Stat., Tit. 22, § 1175.1(1) (Supp. 1996).

[6] In her concurring opinion, JUSTICE O'CONNOR expressed the view that placing the burden on the defendant in this limited group of cases was permissible because it provided the defendant with an incentive to cooperate with the information-gathering process necessary to a reliable competency determination. *Medina*, 505 U. S., at 455.

[7] Tr. of Oral Arg. 46–48.

modation of the opposing interests of the State and the defendant. We are persuaded, by both traditional and modern practice and the importance of the constitutional interest at stake, that the State's argument must be rejected.

III

"Historical practice is probative of whether a procedural rule can be characterized as fundamental," *Medina*, 505 U. S., at 446. In this case, unlike in *Medina*, there is no indication that the rule Oklahoma seeks to defend has any roots in prior practice. Indeed, it appears that a rule significantly more favorable to the defendant has had a long and consistent application.

We turn first to an examination of the relevant common-law traditions of England and this country. The prohibition against trying the incompetent defendant was well established by the time Hale and Blackstone wrote their famous commentaries. 4 W. Blackstone, Commentaries *24 ("[I]f a man in his sound memory commits a capital offence . . . [a]nd if, after he has pleaded, the prisoner becomes mad, he shall not be tried: for how can he make his defence?"); 1 M. Hale, Pleas of the Crown *34–*35 (same). The English cases which predate our Constitution provide no guidance, however, concerning the applicable standard of proof in competency determinations. See *Trial of Charles Bateman* (1685), reported in 11 How. St. Tr. 464, 467 (1816), and Hawles, *Remarks on the Trial of Mr. Charles Bateman*, 11 How. St. Tr. 474, 476 (1816) (noting that the court in the 1685 trial incurred "censure" for proceeding to trial with a doubt as to the defendant's competence); *Kinloch's Case* (1746), 18 How. St. Tr. 395, 411 (1813); *King* v. *Steel*, 1 Leach 452, 168 Eng. Rep. 328 (1787).

Beginning in the late 18th century, cases appear which provide an inkling of the proper standard. In *King* v. *Frith*, 22 How. St. Tr. 307 (1790), for example, the court instructed the jury to "diligently inquire . . . whether John Frith, the now prisoner at the bar . . . be of sound mind and understanding or not . . . ." *Id.*, at 311. Some 50 years later the jurors received a nearly identical admonition in *Queen* v. *Goode*, 7 Ad. & E. 536, 112 Eng. Rep. 572 (K. B. 1837): "'You shall diligently inquire, and true presentment make . . . whether John Goode . . . be insane or not . . . .'" *Id.*, at 536, n. *(a)*, 112 Eng. Rep., at 572–573, n. *(a)*2.[8] Similarly, in *King* v. *Pritchard*, 7 Car. & P. 303, 173 Eng. Rep. 135 (1836), the court empaneled a jury to consider "whether the prisoner is mute of malice or not; secondly, whether he can plead to the indictment or not; thirdly, whether he is of sufficient intellect to comprehend the course of proceedings on the trial . . . ." *Ibid.* See also *King* v. *Dyson*, 73 Car. & P. 305, n. *(a)*, 173 Eng. Rep. 135–136, n. *(a)* (1831); *Queen* v. *Southey*, 4 F. & F. 864, 895, 176 Eng. Rep. 825, 838 (1865); *Queen* v. *Berry*, 1 Q. B. Rep. 447, 449 (1876). *Ibid.*[9]

These authorities, while still speaking less clearly than we might wish, are instructive. By phrasing the inquiry in a simple disjunctive, *Frith*, *Goode*, and *Pritchard* suggest that traditional practice required the jury to determine whether the defendant was "more likely than not" incompetent. Nothing in the jury instructions of these cases will bear the interpretation of a clear and convincing standard. What is more, the cases contain no indication that the use of a pre-

[8] Courts often referred to the prisoner's insanity (or present insanity) rather than incompetence, even when the proceeding concerned the defendant's competence to stand trial. Beginning with the earliest cases, the issue at a sanity or competency hearing has been "whether the prisoner has sufficient understanding to comprehend the nature of this trial, so as to make a proper defence to the charge." *King* v. *Pritchard*, 7 Car. & P. 303, 304, 173 Eng. Rep. 135 (1836).

[9] In 1800 England codified the common-law rule that a court could empanel a jury to determine whether a defendant charged with treason, murder, or a felony offense was competent to stand trial. Criminal Lunatics Act, 1800, 39 & 40, Geo. 3, ch. 94, § 2.

ponderance standard represented a departure from earlier (pre-Constitution) practice.[10]

Modern English authority confirms our interpretation of these early cases as applying a preponderance standard. Relying on "principles . . . laid down in a number of cases," including *Pritchard* and *King* v. *Dyson*, 7 Car. & P. 305, n. *(a)*, 173 Eng. Rep. 135, n. *(a)* (1831), the court in *Queen* v. *Podola*, 43 Crim. App. 220, 3 All E. R. 418 (1959), ruled:

> "If the contention that the accused is insane is put forward by the defence and contested by the prosecution, there is, in our judgment, a burden upon the defence of satisfying the jury of the accused's insanity. In such a case, as in other criminal cases in which the onus of proof rests upon the defence, the onus is discharged if the jury are satisfied on the balance of probabilities that the accused's insanity has been made out." *Id.*, at 235, 3 All E. R., at 429.[11]

---

[10] Indeed, although in *Medina* we concluded that it is permissible for a State to require the defendant to shoulder the burden of demonstrating his incompetence, we noted that some 19th-century English authorities placed the burden on the prosecutor once competence was put in issue. *Medina* v. *California*, 505 U. S., at 447. See *Queen* v. *Davies*, 3 Car. & K. 328, 329, 175 Eng. Rep. 575, 575 (1853) (judge ruled that "[the prosecutor] should begin, and call his witnesses, to show that the prisoner is sane, and capable of pleading"); *Ley's Case*, 1 Lewin 239, 240, 168 Eng. Rep. 1026 (1828) ("'If there be a doubt as to the prisoner's sanity . . . you cannot say that he is in a fit state to be put upon his trial'"). See also Halsbury, 10 Laws of England 403 (3d ed. 1955) ("Where a jury is so empanelled [to determine competency], the onus is on the prosecution to prove the sanity of the defendant"). But see *Queen* v. *Podola*, 43 Crim. App. 220, 236, 3 All E. R. 418, 430 (1959) (explicitly rejecting the suggestion that the prosecutor must prove the defendant's competence to stand trial). Given the disagreement among English courts concerning which party bore the burden of proof, it is unlikely that in cases in which the burden was placed on the defendant that burden was as weighty as clear and convincing evidence.

[11] The *Podola* court opined that the tests laid down in *Pritchard* "have been followed so often that they may be said to be firmly embodied in our law." 43 Crim. App., at 238, 3 All E. R., at 431.

Likewise, we are aware of no decisional law from this country suggesting that any State employed Oklahoma's heightened standard until quite recently. Rather, the earliest available sources typically refer to English authorities, see, *e. g., Freeman* v. *People*, 47 Am. Dec. 216, 223–225 (N. Y. 1847), *State* v. *Harris*, 78 Am. Dec. 272, 272–275 (N. C. 1860) (adopting procedures outlined in *King* v. *Dyson*, 7 Car. & P. 305, n. *(a)*, 173 Eng. Rep. 135, n. *(a)* (1831), and *King* v. *Pritchard*, 7 Car. & P. 303, 173 Eng. Rep. 135 (1836)), and employ the disjunctive language used by the English courts, see, *e. g., Commonwealth* v. *Hathaway*, 13 Mass. 299 (1816); *People* v. *Kleim*, 1 N. Y. 13, 15 (1845); *Harris*, 78 Am. Dec., at 275; *United States* v. *Chisolm*, 149 F. 284, 290 (SD Ala. 1906).[12] By the turn of the 20th century, however, American courts were explicitly applying a preponderance standard. In 1896, Ohio juries were instructed that "[t]he burden is upon the prisoner to show by a preponderance of the proof that he is insane." *State* v. *O'Grady*, 5 Ohio Dec. 654, 655 (1896).[13] Some 15 years later, the Tennessee Supreme Court described the competency determination as

[12] In *Commonwealth* v. *Braley*, 1 Mass. 102, 103 (1804), a case decided shortly after the Constitution was ratified, the court instructed the jury to consider "whether [the accused] neglected or refused to plead to the indictment against him for murder, of his free will and malice, or whether he did so neglect by the act of God." This instruction may be a precursor to the "sane or insane" disjunctive.

[13] See also *State* v. *Tyler*, 7 Ohio N. P. 443, 444 (1898) ("What I mean by the preponderance of the evidence is that the accused must show that he is now at the time of this trial probably not sane"). Cf. *People* v. *Ah Ying*, 42 Cal. 18, 20 (1872) (jury should find defendant presently insane if "satisfied" by the evidence supporting that conclusion).

Both *Tyler* and *State* v. *O'Grady* are instructive concerning the proper interpretation of the authorities which articulate no standard of proof but phrase the inquiry in the disjunctive. In each case the jury was told that its task was to determine whether the accused "is or is not sane," *Tyler*, 7 Ohio N. P., at 443, see also *O'Grady*, 5 Ohio Dec., at 654, and then explicitly instructed that the defendant bore the burden of proof by a preponderance of the evidence. *Tyler*, 7 Ohio N. P., at 443; *O'Grady*, 5 Ohio Dec., at 655.

"controlled by the preponderance of the proof," *Jordan* v. *State*, 124 Tenn. 81, 89, 135 S. W. 327, 329 (1911), and the highest court of Pennsylvania held that competence is "decided by a preponderance of the evidence," *Commonwealth* v. *Simanowicz*, 242 Pa. 402, 405, 89 A. 562, 563 (1913).[14] These early authorities are bereft of language susceptible of supporting a clear and convincing evidence standard.[15]

Contemporary practice demonstrates that the vast majority of jurisdictions remain persuaded that the heightened standard of proof imposed on the accused in Oklahoma is not necessary to vindicate the State's interest in prompt and orderly disposition of criminal cases. Only 4 of the 50 States presently require the criminal defendant to prove his incompetence by clear and convincing evidence.[16] None of the re-

---

[14] See also *State* v. *Arnold*, 12 Iowa 479, 484 (1861) ("A doubt must be raised whether at the time there is such mental impairment . . . as to render it probable that the prisoner can not, as far as may devolve upon him, have a full, fair and impartial trial"); *People* v. *McElvaine*, 125 N. Y. 596, 608, 26 N. E. 929, 933 (1891) (the court "was familiar with the appearance and conduct of the prisoner during the period of that trial, and had sufficient grounds before it to judge as to the probability of his present sanity"). See also *Crocker* v. *State*, 19 N. W. 435, 436 (Wis. 1884); *United States* v. *Chisolm*, 149 F. 284, 290 (SD Ala. 1906).

Several of the early cases explicitly mention the common-law roots of the State's statutory procedure for determining competency. See *People* v. *McElvaine*, 125 N. Y., at 608, 26 N. E., at 932 ("We do not think the Code of Criminal Procedure has made any radical change in the mode of procedure or the character of the [competency] proceedings"); *French* v. *State*, 67 N. W. 706, 710 (Wis. 1896) ("The statute . . . providing for an inquisition, where there is a probability that the accused is, at the time of his trial, insane, and thereby incapacitated to act for himself, to determine whether he is so insane, is substantially a provision in affirmance of a power the court had at common law in such cases, as abundantly appears from the authorities").

[15] Oklahoma all but concedes that early common law and statutory decisions employed a standard of proof lower than clear and convincing. See Brief for Respondent 21–23.

[16] Conn. Gen. Stat. § 54–56d(b) (1995); Okla. Stat., Tit. 22, § 1175.4 (1991); 50 Pa. Cons. Stat. § 7403(a) (Supp. 1995); and R. I. Gen. Laws § 40.1–5.3–3 (Supp. 1995). The adoption of the clear and convincing evidence standard

maining 46 jurisdictions imposes such a heavy burden on the defendant.[17] Indeed, a number of States place no burden on the defendant at all, but rather require the prosecutor to

---

by Oklahoma and Connecticut may have been a response to this Court's decision in *Addington* v. *Texas*, 441 U. S. 418 (1979). We discuss *Addington infra*, at 368–369.

[17] See *Lackey* v. *State*, 615 So. 2d 145, 151–152 (Ala. Crim. App. 1992); *McCarlo* v. *State*, 677 P. 2d 1268, 1272 (Alaska App. 1984); Cal. Penal Code Ann. § 1369(f) (West 1982); Colo. Rev. Stat. § 16–8–111(2) (1986); *Diaz* v. *State*, 508 A. 2d 861, 863 (Del. 1986); *Flowers* v. *State*, 353 So. 2d 1259, 1270 (Fla. App. 1978); *Johnson* v. *State*, 209 Ga. App. 514, 516, 433 S. E. 2d 717, 719 (1993); Haw. Rev. Stat. §§ 704–404 and 704–411 (1993); Ill. Comp. Stat., ch. 725, § 5/104–11(c) (1992); *Montano* v. *State*, 649 N. E. 2d 1053, 1057–1058 (Ind. App. 1995); *State* v. *Rhode*, 503 N. W. 2d 27, 35 (Iowa App. 1993); *State* v. *Seminary*, 165 La. 67, 72, 115 So. 370, 372 (1927); *Jolley* v. *State*, 282 Md. 353, 365, 384 A. 2d 91, 98 (1978); *Commonwealth* v. *Prater*, 420 Mass. 569, 573–574, 651 N. E. 2d 833, 837 (1995); Minn. Rule Crim. Proc. 20.01 (1995); *Griffin* v. *State*, 504 So. 2d 186, 191 (Miss. 1987); *State* v. *Zorzy*, 136 N. H. 710, 714–715, 622 A. 2d 1217, 1219 (1993); *State* v. *Lambert*, 275 N. J. Super. 125, 129, 645 A. 2d 1189, 1191 (1994); *State* v. *Chapman*, 104 N. M. 324, 327, 721 P. 2d 392, 395 (1986); *People* v. *Santos*, 43 App. Div. 2d 73, 75, 349 N. Y. S. 2d 439, 442 (1973); *State* v. *Heger*, 326 N. W. 2d 855, 858 (N. D. 1982); Ohio Rev. Code Ann. § 2945.37 (1993); *State* v. *Nance*, 466 S. E. 2d 349, 351 (S. C. 1996); S. D. Codified Laws § 23A–10A–6.1 (1988); *Jordan* v. *State*, 124 Tenn. 81, 89, 135 S. W. 327, 329 (1911); *Blacklock* v. *State*, 820 S. W. 2d 882, 886 (Tex. App. 1991); Utah Code Ann. § 77–15–5(10) (1995); Va. Code Ann. § 19.2–169.1(E) (1995); Wash. Rev. Code § 10.77.090 (1994); W. Va. Code § 27–6A–2(b) (1992); Wis. Stat. § 971.14(4)(b) (1985 and Supp. 1995); *Loomer* v. *State*, 768 P. 2d 1042, 1045 (Wyo. 1989).

The burden imposed in the remaining States is unclear. Nothing in the competency statutes or case law of these States suggests, however, that the defendant bears the burden of proving incompetence by clear and convincing evidence. See Ariz. Rule Crim. Proc. 11.5 (1987 and Supp. 1995); *Mitchell* v. *State*, 323 Ark. 116, 120, 913 S. W. 2d 264, 266 (1996); Idaho Code § 18–212 (1987); Kan. Stat. Ann. § 22–3302 (1995); Ky. Rev. Stat. Ann. § 504.100 (Michie 1990); Me. Rev. Stat. Ann., Tit. 15, § 101–B (Supp. 1995); Mich. Comp. Laws § 330.2020 (1992); *State* v. *Clark*, 546 S. W. 2d 455, 468 (Mo. App. 1976); Mont. Code Ann. § 46–14–221 (1992 and Supp. 1995); Neb. Rev. Stat. § 29–1823 (1989); Nev. Rev. Stat. § 178.415 (1992); N. C. Gen. Stat. § 15A–1002 (1988); Ore. Rev. Stat. §§ 161.360–161.370 (Supp. 1994); and Vt. Stat. Ann., Tit. 13, § 4817 (1974).

prove the defendant's competence to stand trial once a question about competency has been credibly raised.[18] The situation is no different in federal court. Congress has directed that the accused in a federal prosecution must prove incompetence by a preponderance of the evidence. 18 U. S. C. § 4241.

The near-uniform application of a standard that is more protective of the defendant's rights than Oklahoma's clear and convincing evidence rule supports our conclusion that the heightened standard offends a principle of justice that is deeply "rooted in the traditions and conscience of our people." *Medina* v. *California*, 505 U. S., at 445 (internal quotation marks omitted). We turn next to a consideration of whether the rule exhibits "'fundamental fairness' in operation." *Id.*, at 448 (quoting *Dowling* v. *United States*, 493 U. S. 342, 352 (1990)).

IV

Contemporary and historical procedures are fully consistent with our evaluation of the risks inherent in Oklahoma's practice of requiring the defendant to prove incompetence by clear and convincing evidence. In *Addington* v. *Texas*, 441 U. S. 418, 423 (1979), we explained that:

> "The function of a standard of proof, as that concept is embodied in the Due Process Clause and in the realm of factfinding, is to 'instruct the factfinder concerning the degree of confidence our society thinks he should have in the correctness of factual conclusions for a particular type of adjudication.' *In re Winship*, 397 U. S. 358, 370 (1970) (Harlan, J., concurring)."

The "more stringent the burden of proof a party must bear, the more that party bears the risk of an erroneous decision."

---

[18] See, *e. g.*, Haw. Rev. Stat. §§ 704–404 and 704–411 (1993); Ill. Comp. Stat., ch. 725, § 5/104–11(c) (1992); S. D. Codified Laws § 23A–10A–6.1 (1988); Wis. Stat. § 971.14(4)(b) (Supp. 1994 and Supp. II 1995).

Cruzan v. *Director, Mo. Dept. of Health,* 497 U. S. 261, 283 (1990). For that reason, we have held that due process places a heightened burden of proof on the State in civil proceedings in which the "individual interests at stake . . . are both 'particularly important' and 'more substantial than mere loss of money.'" *Santosky* v. *Kramer,* 455 U. S. 745, 756 (1982) (termination of parental rights) (quoting *Addington,* 441 U. S., at 424).[19]

Far from "jealously guard[ing]," *Jacob* v. *New York City,* 315 U. S. 752, 752–753 (1942), an incompetent criminal defendant's fundamental right not to stand trial, Oklahoma's practice of requiring the defendant to prove incompetence by clear and convincing evidence imposes a significant risk of an erroneous determination that the defendant is competent. In *Medina* we found no comparable risk because the presumption would affect only the narrow class of cases in which the evidence on either side was equally balanced.

[19] See also *Addington* v. *Texas* (involuntary civil commitment); *Woodby* v. *INS,* 385 U. S. 276, 285–286 (1966) (deportation); *Chaunt* v. *United States,* 364 U. S. 350, 353 (1960) (denaturalization); *Schneiderman* v. *United States,* 320 U. S. 118, 125 (1943) (denaturalization).

Our opinions in *Cruzan* v. *Director, Mo. Dept. of Health,* 497 U. S. 261 (1990), and *Ohio* v. *Akron Center for Reproductive Health,* 497 U. S. 502 (1990), are not to the contrary. In *Cruzan* we held that the Due Process Clause does not prohibit Missouri from requiring a third party who seeks to terminate life-sustaining treatment to demonstrate by clear and convincing evidence that the incompetent person receiving such treatment would wish that step to be taken. 497 U. S., at 280. We reasoned that the heightened standard of proof was permissible because the decisionmaker was a surrogate for the incompetent individual, *id.,* at 280–281, and because the consequences of an erroneous decision were irreversible, *id.,* at 283. In *Akron Center for Reproductive Health* we upheld an Ohio statute that required an unmarried, unemancipated minor woman who sought to obtain an abortion without notifying a parent to prove by clear and convincing evidence that judicial bypass of the notification requirement was appropriate in her case. We approved the heightened standard of proof in that case largely because the proceeding at issue was *ex parte.* 497 U. S., at 515–516.

"Once a State provides a defendant access to procedures for making a competency evaluation," we stated, there is "no basis for holding that due process further requires the State to assume the burden of vindicating the defendant's constitutional right by persuading the trier of fact that the defendant is competent to stand trial." 505 U. S., at 449. Unlike the presumption at issue in *Medina*, however, Oklahoma's clear and convincing evidence standard affects a class of cases in which the defendant has already demonstrated that he is more likely than not incompetent.

For the defendant, the consequences of an erroneous determination of competence are dire. Because he lacks the ability to communicate effectively with counsel, he may be unable to exercise other "rights deemed essential to a fair trial." *Riggins* v. *Nevada*, 504 U. S., at 139 (KENNEDY, J., concurring in judgment). After making the "profound" choice whether to plead guilty, *Godinez* v. *Moran*, 509 U. S. 389, 398 (1993), the defendant who proceeds to trial

> "will ordinarily have to decide whether to waive his 'privilege against compulsory self-incrimination,' *Boykin* v. *Alabama*, 395 U. S. 238, 243 (1969), by taking the witness stand; if the option is available, he may have to decide whether to waive his 'right to trial by jury,' *ibid.*; and, in consultation with counsel, he may have to decide whether to waive his 'right to confront [his] accusers,' *ibid.*, by declining to cross-examine witnesses for the prosecution." *Ibid.*

With the assistance of counsel, the defendant also is called upon to make myriad smaller decisions concerning the course of his defense. The importance of these rights and decisions demonstrates that an erroneous determination of competence threatens a "fundamental component of our criminal justice system"[20]—the basic fairness of the trial itself.

[20] *United States* v. *Cronic*, 466 U. S. 648, 653 (1984).

By comparison to the defendant's interest, the injury to the State of the opposite error—a conclusion that the defendant is incompetent when he is in fact malingering—is modest. To be sure, such an error imposes an expense on the state treasury and frustrates the State's interest in the prompt disposition of criminal charges. But the error is subject to correction in a subsequent proceeding and the State may detain the incompetent defendant for "the reasonable period of time necessary to determine whether there is a substantial probability that he will attain [competence] in the foreseeable future." *Jackson* v. *Indiana*, 406 U. S. 715, 738 (1972).[21]

The Oklahoma Court of Criminal Appeals correctly observed that the "inexactness and uncertainty" that characterize competency proceedings may make it difficult to determine whether a defendant is incompetent or malingering. 889 P. 2d, at 303. We presume, however, that it is unusual for even the most artful malingerer to feign incompetence successfully for a period of time while under professional care.[22] In this regard it is worth reiterating that only four jurisdictions currently consider it necessary to impose on the criminal defendant the burden of proving incompetence by clear and convincing evidence. Moreover, there is no reason to believe that the art of dissimilation is new. Eighteenth and nineteenth century courts, for example, warned jurors charged with making competency determinations that "'there may be great fraud in this matter,'" *King* v. *Dyson*, 7 Car. & P. 305, n. *(a)*, 173 Eng. Rep., at 136, n. *(a)* (quoting

[21] Under *Jackson*, if the defendant regains competence or is found to be malingering, the State may proceed to trial.

[22] Sir John Hawles, Solicitor General to King William III (who reigned from 1689–1702), noted that "there is a great difference between pretences and realities, and *sana* and *non sana memoria* hath been often tryed in capital matters, and the prisoners have reaped so little benefit by their pretences, it being always discovered, that we rarely hear of it." Hawles, *Remarks on the Trial of Mr. Charles Bateman* (1685), 11 How. St. Tr. 474, 478 (1816).

1 Hale, Pleas of the Crown, at *35), and that "[i]t would be a reproach to justice if a guilty man . . . postponed his trial upon a feigned condition of mind, as to his inability to aid in his defense," *United States* v. *Chisolm*, 149 F., at 288.[23] Although they recognized this risk, the early authorities did not resort to a heightened burden of proof in competency proceedings. See Part III, *supra*.

More fundamentally, while the difficulty of ascertaining where the truth lies may make it appropriate to place the burden of proof on the proponent of an issue, it does not justify the additional onus of an especially high standard of proof. As the *Chisolm* Court continued,

> "[I]t would be likewise a reproach to justice and our institutions, if a human being . . . were compelled to go to trial at a time when he is not sufficiently in possession of his mental faculties to enable him to make a rational and proper defense. The latter would be a more grievous error than the former; since in the one case an individual would go unwhipped of justice, while in the other the great safeguards which the law adopts in the punishment of crime and the upholding of justice would be rudely invaded by the tribunal whose sacred duty it is to uphold the law in all its integrity." 149 F., at 288.

A heightened standard does not decrease the risk of error, but simply reallocates that risk between the parties. See *Cruzan* v. *Director, Mo. Dept. of Health*, 497 U. S., at 283. In cases in which competence is at issue, we perceive no sound basis for allocating to the criminal defendant the large share of the risk which accompanies a clear and convincing evidence standard. We assume that questions of competence will arise in a range of cases including not only those in which one side will prevail with relative ease, but also those in which it is more likely than not that the defendant

[23] See also *People* v. *Lake*, 2 N. Y. 215, 220, 222 (1855); *State* v. *Harris*, 78 Am. Dec. 272, 274 (N. C. 1860); *State* v. *Tyler*, 7 Ohio N. P., at 444.

is incompetent but the evidence is insufficiently strong to satisfy a clear and convincing standard. While important state interests are unquestionably at stake, in these latter cases the defendant's fundamental right to be tried only while competent outweighs the State's interest in the efficient operation of its criminal justice system.

V

Oklahoma makes two additional arguments in support of its procedural rule that warrant discussion. First, Oklahoma correctly reminds us that it is normally within the power of the State to establish the procedures through which its laws are given effect, including those related to the burden of producing evidence and the burden of persuasion. See *Patterson* v. *New York*, 432 U. S., at 201–202. In *Patterson* we upheld New York's requirement that in a prosecution for second-degree murder the defendant must bear the burden of proving the affirmative defense of extreme emotional disturbance in order to reduce the crime to manslaughter. *Id.*, at 207–208. After observing that the rule was consistent with common-law practice, *id.*, at 202, we held that "[t]he Due Process Clause . . . does not put New York to the choice of abandoning [statutory] defenses or undertaking to disprove their existence in order to convict of a crime which otherwise is within its constitutional powers to sanction by substantial punishment," *id.*, at 207–208.

Although we found no violation in *Patterson*, we noted that the State's power to regulate procedural burdens was subject to proscription under the Due Process Clause if it "offends some principle of justice so rooted in the traditions and conscience of our people as to be ranked as fundamental," *id.*, at 201–202 (internal quotation marks omitted). This case involves such a rule. Unlike *Patterson*, which concerned procedures for proving a statutory defense, we consider here whether a State's procedures for guaranteeing a fundamental constitutional right are sufficiently protective of that right. The deep roots and fundamental character of the defendant's right not to stand trial when it is more likely than not that he lacks the capacity to understand the nature of the proceedings against him or to communicate effectively with counsel mandate constitutional protection.

Finally, Oklahoma suggests that our decision in *Addington* v. *Texas*, 441 U. S. 418 (1979), in which we held that due process requires a clear and convincing standard of proof in an involuntary civil commitment proceeding, supports imposition of such a rule in competency proceedings. The argument is unpersuasive because commitment and competency proceedings address entirely different substantive issues. Although we have not had the opportunity to consider the outer limits of a State's authority to civilly commit an unwilling individual, *O'Connor* v. *Donaldson*, 422 U. S. 563, 573–574 (1975), our decision in *Donaldson* makes clear that due process requires at a minimum a showing that the person is mentally ill and either poses a danger to himself or others or is incapable of "surviving safely in freedom," *id.*, at 573–576. The test for competence to stand trial, by contrast, is whether the defendant has the present ability to understand the charges against him and communicate effectively with defense counsel. *Dusky* v. *United States*, 362 U. S., at 402. Even if we were to uphold Oklahoma's imposition of the clear and convincing evidence rule in competency proceedings, the comparable standards in the two proceedings would not guarantee parallel results.[24]

More importantly, our decision today is in complete accord with the basis for our ruling in *Addington*. Both cases concern the proper protection of fundamental rights in circumstances in which the State proposes to take drastic action against an individual. The requirement that the grounds for civil commitment be shown by clear and convincing evidence

[24] For example, a mentally retarded defendant accused of a nonviolent crime may be found incompetent to stand trial but not necessarily be subject to involuntary civil commitment.

protects the individual's fundamental interest in liberty. The *prohibition* against requiring the criminal defendant to demonstrate incompetence by clear and convincing evidence safeguards the fundamental right not to stand trial while incompetent. Because Oklahoma's procedural rule allows the State to put to trial a defendant who is more likely than not incompetent, the rule is incompatible with the dictates of due process.[25]

VI

For the foregoing reasons, the judgment is reversed, and the case is remanded to the Oklahoma Court of Criminal Appeals for further proceedings not inconsistent with this opinion.

It is so ordered.

---

[25] We note that *Addington* did not purport to resolve any question concerning the rights of the defendant in a criminal proceeding. To the contrary, in his opinion for the Court, Chief Justice Burger contrasted the appropriate standard in civil commitment proceedings with the rules applicable in criminal cases in which "the interests of the defendant are of such magnitude that historically and without any explicit constitutional requirement they have been protected by standards of proof designed to exclude as nearly as possible the likelihood of an erroneous judgment." 441 U. S., at 423.

FEATURE

THERAPEUTIC JURISPRUDENCE AND CRIMINAL JUSTICE MENTAL HEALTH ISSUES

*by David B. Wexler and Bruce J. Winick**

I. Introduction

Mental health law, which originated only about 20 years ago,[1] has reached a turning point. Born in the aftermath of the civil rights movement, and seizing the momentum of the revolution in criminal procedure and prisoners' rights, the field was built on a constitutional foundation that grew out of concern for protecting the rights of patients. But that constitutional foundation is now crumbling, and as a result, mental health law seems to have lost its driving force and much of its lustre.

Bruce Ennis, appropriately described as the founder of the mental health bar,[2] set the stage for advocacy and scholarship in a 1971 article which argued that "if persons are involuntarily to be confined because of mental illness, the standards and procedures for confinement should guarantee no fewer rights than those afforded criminal defendants."[3] While early case law seemed to embrace this premise, the attraction soon wore off. Indeed, even in the heyday of mental health law, the courts rarely accorded mental patients the full-blown rights accorded to criminal defendants. In any event, the criminal procedure revolution surely has been quelled, leading to a concomitant calm in the evolution of mental health law. A new perspective is needed to rejuvenate the field and to infuse it with academic appeal. The time has come to conceptualize new approaches and research directions.

Our research interests have increasingly focused on what we have come to call "therapeutic jurisprudence" – the extent to which substantive rules, legal procedures, and the roles of lawyers and judges produce therapeutic or antitherapeutic consequences.[4] The purpose of this essay is to describe what we mean by therapeutic jurisprudence, and to explain how the therapeutic jurisprudence perspective can be applied to illustrative criminal justice/mental health issues.

**David B. Wexler is the John D. Lyons Professor of Law and Professor of Psychology at the University of Arizona; Bruce J. Winick is a Professor of Law at the University of Miami. Portions of this essay are drawn from their book* Essays In Therapeutic Jurisprudence *(1991).*

II. The Approach of Therapeutic Jurisprudence

Therapeutic jurisprudence is interdisciplinary, empirical, and international in its orientation. It seeks to sensitize legal policy makers to a frequently ignored aspect of mental health law policy analysis – the therapeutic impact of legal rules and procedures – and to serve as a tool to frame a new and useful research agenda. Ironically, mental health law – potentially one of the most interdisciplinary of legal fields – has fallen considerably short of accomplishing its interdisciplinary potential. Not only has far too little empirical work been done in the field, but much of what has been done focused on questions that are not especially significant to legal decisionmakers. As a result, the impact of such research too often has been minimal.

One empirical question rarely asked concerns the therapeutic implications of various legal rules and practices. Is a particular legal rule, either presently in effect or proposed, therapeutic or antitherapeutic to patients (and perhaps to society as a whole)? Legal decisionmaking should consider not only economic factors, public safety, and the protection of patients' rights, but should also take into account the therapeutic implications of a rule and its alternatives. For example, the decision whether to abolish the legal insanity defense should turn, at least in part, on the therapeutic implications that abolition would have on patients and on society as a whole. In addition, governmental policies in a variety of areas not as closely related to mental health law per se, should take into account the therapeutic impact in any rational decisionmaking process that assesses the effects of alternative legal approaches.

Let us emphasize, at the outset, that therapeutic jurisprudence does not embrace a vision of law, or even mental health law, as serving exclusively or primarily therapeutic ends. We do not call for a return to the "therapeutic state" or extol what Wexler once called "therapeutic justice."[5] The law serves many ends, and our suggestion that the impact of legal rules and practices on therapeutic values should be analyzed does not mean that therapeutic values should predominate over others. Nor do we suggest that the law should assume a deferential posture toward clinical expertise. Many of the issues at the heart of mental health law are legal, not clinical, in nature. Legal issues should not be permitted to masquerade as clinical ones; indeed, rather than deference, the law should adopt a healthy skepticism toward claims of clinical expertise.

Legal judgments are often based on factual predicates that remain unexamined empirically and that might prove false. Some legal judgments disregard the potential impact they may have on therapeutic values. Our aim is to suggest that legal decisionmakers take this impact into account explicitly, that they become more sophisticated about and make better use of the insights and methods of the behavioral sciences, and that behavioral scientists audit the law's success or failure in this regard.

We are sensitive to the potential criticism of therapeutic jurisprudence that has often been made of law and economics scholarship. By suggesting the need to identify the therapeutic and antitherapeutic consequences of legal rules and practices, we do not necessarily suggest that such rules and practices be recast to accomplish therapeutic ends or to avoid antitherapeutic results. Whether they should is, of course, a normative question that calls for a weighing of other potentially relevant normative values as well, such as patient autonomy, constitutional rights, and community safety.

Therapeutic jurisprudence simply seeks to focus attention on an often neglected ingredient in the calculus necessary for performing a sensible policy analysis of mental health law and practice – the therapeutic dimension – and to call for its systematic empirical examination. To identify this as a significant consideration is not intended to suggest that it trumps other considerations.

We assume there is general agreement that, other things being equal, mental health law should be restructured to better accomplish therapeutic values. But whether other things are equal in a given context is often a matter of dispute. Although therapeutic jurisprudence seeks to illuminate the therapeutic implications of legal practices, it does not resolve this dispute, which requires analysis of the impact of alternative practices on other relevant values.

III. Therapeutic Jurisprudence Applied to Criminal Justice Mental Health Issues

In our recent book *Essays in Therapeutic Jurisprudence* (Carolina Academic Press 1991), we provide a more complete explanation of therapeutic jurisprudence and illustrate its application and potential as a tool of policy analysis in a number of contexts. This essay looks at criminal justice mental health issues through the lens of therapeutic jurisprudence. Our hope is to bring a new perspective to an area that has not received much attention since the American Bar Association's *Criminal Justice Mental Health Standards* were adopted in 1984. We will examine three topics to demonstrate the approach of therapeutic jurisprudence: (1) whether incompetent death row inmates have a right to refuse treatment; (2) the provision of treatment to defendants found incompetent to stand trial; and (3) the effects on sex offenders of existing plea bargaining practices.

A. Treatment for Incompetent Death Row Inmates

In *Ford v. Wainwright*, the Supreme Court decided that the cruel and unusual punishment clause of the eighth amendment prohibits a state from executing a defendant whose mental health has so deteriorated while on death row that he has become incompetent to be executed.[6] Virtually all states had previously recognized, either by statute or case law, that a death row inmate who had become incompetent should not be executed during the period of incompetency, and that execution could occur only following mental health treatment which succeeds in restoring the defendant's ability to understand and appreciate the reason for the execution. Although the Supreme Court's opinion in *Ford* constitutionalized this practice and imposed procedural due process requirements for determining the incompetency-to-be-executed issue, the Court's decision did not address whether the state could coercively treat the incompetent death row inmate in order to restore him to competency so that the death penalty could be administered.

In 1990, however, in *Perry v. Louisiana*,[7] the Supreme Court granted *certiorari* to consider this previously unresolved question: Do such death row inmates possess a right to refuse treatment that is designed to restore them to competency? *Perry* presents the right to refuse treatment question in a difficult ethical context for clinicians. The American Medical Association and the American Psychiatric Association submitted a joint *amicus curiae* brief arguing that such coercive treatment placed clinicians in an untenable ethical role.[8] Aside from this submission, *Perry* was briefed and argued along conventional constitutional lines, with the right to refuse treatment contending against the state's interest in administering capital punishment. The Supreme Court decided to remand the case to the state court for reconsideration in light of its intervening decision in *Washington v. Harper*,[9] which had rejected the claim of a constitutional right to refuse antipsychotic medication by a dangerous prison inmate.[10] The constitutional issue framed by *Perry* thus remains unresolved.

Therapeutic jurisprudence suggests an important dimension that should be considered in resolving the *Perry* issue: What are the therapeutic implications of permitting the state to coercively treat a defendant found incompetent to be executed? First, the consequences to the healing professions, the psychiatrists and psychologists asked to provide such treatment, should be considered. Does the use of therapists in this way undermine their primary role as healers? Does it corrode their sense of themselves as members of a healing profession? Does it raise ethical and emotional conflicts that would deter many good clinicians from working in the correctional context? Does it decrease the standing of these subgroups with their peers? Does it breed distrust among patients generally? If the answer to at least some of these questions is yes, then the practice of coercive treatment of incompetent death row inmates could seriously diminish the quality of treatment that prisoners (and perhaps other institutionalized populations) receive, and drive many ethical and sensitive practitioners from the criminal field or deter them from entering it.

Second, is such "therapy" efficacious? Death row inmates facing execution upon successful treatment would inevitably be motivated to attempt to resist and, indeed, to frustrate such treatment. Even organic treatment like psychotropic drugs may require a degree of patient compliance to succeed. Moreover, expectancy theory and other strands of cognitive psychology would suggest that psychological mechanisms which play an essential role in treatment success might also be important ingredients in the success of organic treatment techniques.[11] Therefore, it could be predicted that patients are likely to exhibit a behavioral response to such treatment that sets up failure or, at a minimum, makes success difficult. This is not to say that patients cannot be restored to competency by involuntary treatment, but only that it probably will be difficult, frustrating, and ultimately dehumanizing for both clinician and patient.

Although members of this class of patients are incompetent for some purposes, such as execution, their incompetency will not necessarily prevent them from responding behaviorally to what they undoubtedly will understand to be the consequence of successful treatment, i.e., their execution.[12] This is a salient example of what in therapeutic jurisprudence terminology is known as "law-related psychological dysfunction" or "juridical psychopathology,"[13] in which the therapeutic enterprise is undermined by the consequences of the legal rule or practice.

Permitting involuntary treatment of death row inmates found incompetent to be executed predictably will have a number of strongly negative implications for therapeutic values for both professionals and patients. The existence and extent of these negative therapeutic implications are empirical questions deserving careful research as a predicate to the sensible resolution of the issue left open in *Perry*. If shown to exist, these negative implications should be factored into the inevitable balancing that the courts will need to perform in analyzing the constitutionality of involuntary treatment in this context. Furthermore, they should be considered by legislators seeking to fashion legislative responses to the problem, and by courts seeking to adopt rules of procedure to deal with it.

A countervailing therapeutic implication can be invoked, however. If death row inmates found incompetent to be executed are not subject to involuntary treatment, they presumably would remain in a permanent incompetent state. This too could be seen as a law-produced dysfunctional effect, one that would have to be counted as a negative therapeutic implication. What should we do with such defendants? In their joint *amicus* brief in *Perry*, the American Medical Association and American Psychiatric Association suggest that we automatically commute their sentences to life imprisonment, and this seems a sensible and humane proposal.[14] Defendants then could be offered voluntary treatment, which presumably would be accepted free of the disincentives that would produce the strongly negative motivation for treatment that execution would obviously provide. Such treatment probably would be effective in restoring such patients to a greater degree of mental health. This result would have only positive therapeutic implications. It also would avoid the presumably negative impact that coerced treatment has on professionals.

Unfortunately, the automatic commutation of sentences would make the status of being found incompetent to be executed more desirable, and probably would produce a predictable behavioral response on the part of death row inmates. But this identical behavioral response already is encouraged by the Supreme Court's constitutional holding in *Ford v. Wainwright*.[15] Because *Ford* requires that death row inmates found incompetent to be executed have their executions suspended, they already will be provided with an incentive to become incompetent or to pretend to be so.[16]

Conducting a therapeutic jurisprudence assessment of compulsory treatment of death row inmates who are incompetent to be executed involves difficult and unexamined empirical questions. Therapeutic jurisprudence identifies these questions as critical ones that need to be probed as part of the difficult balancing required to resolve the question of coercive treatment for incompetent death row inmates. It thus suggests a research agenda for social scientists, and the Supreme Court's remand in *Perry*, by leaving the constitutional question open, at least for now, paves the way for comparative research in states that take differing approaches to the issue.

B. Treatment for Defendants Found Incompetent to Stand Trial

Although much work has been done on the assessment of competency to stand trial, little empirical research has examined the treatment process for criminal defendants found incompetent to stand trial. As a result, almost nothing is known about the treatment provided to defendants placed in this status. Because of the confusion documented in the literature by clinical evaluators who frequently equate the incompetency-to-stand-trial standard with the existence of mental illness,[17] it is likely that most defendants found incompetent are treated like civil patients presenting the same psychiatric diagnosis. Treatment probably is rarely tailored to the specific abilities needed to be competent to stand trial. Treatment probably focuses on the patient's psychopathology, rather than the short-term goal of restoration to trial competence, or more appropriately, to competency to perform the specific trial-related task the defendant has been found incapable of performing adequately.

Based upon the literature on the psychology of choice,[18] it can be hypothesized that the potential for successful treatment of defendants who are incompetent to stand trial increases when the defendant accepts treatment voluntarily, rather than as a result of court coercion, typically involving an incompetency commitment to a forensic facility. Thus, Winick has suggested that a system of trial continuances replace the formal competency process now existing for defendants asserting their incompetency as a bar to trial.[19] A continuance of reasonable duration would be granted to the defendant based on a certificate of counsel that the defendant is, in counsel's opinion, incompetent. The continuance would be conditioned on the defendant's acceptance of the treatment of his choice, and its extension would be conditioned on progress toward restoration of competency. Accordingly, Winick's proposal can be viewed as an application of therapeutic jurisprudence.

Whether Winick's proposal for restructuring the incompetency-to-stand-trial process would bring about more effective treatment for incompetent defendants is an empirical question that deserves examination. A jurisdiction wishing to experiment with the continuance alternative to the traditional formal competency evaluation process can be matched with one that does not, to see whether defendants permitted to choose treatment for their incompetency will do better than those compelled to accept such treatment.

Winick's proposal for voluntary treatment as a condition for the granting of a trial continuance could be joined with his "wagering" proposal,[20] to suggest a new approach to treatment for trial incompetency under which the defendant and the court would enter into a contingency contract. Under the contract, the defendant would receive the requested trial continuance in exchange for his agreement to participate in an appropriate treatment program and for making periodic progress toward the goal of restoration to trial competency. This contingency contract or "wager" with the court may well enhance the efficacy of a treatment program for trial incompetency, and the validity of this hypothesis could be tested empirically.

One problem with a wagering model in this context is that for many defendants, the goal of seeking incompetency-to-stand-trial status is to avoid trial indefinitely or even permanently. As a result, such defendants may have a disincentive to show progress toward the goal of restoration to competency. An additional reinforcer is thus needed to offset this disincentive.

In many jurisdictions, the defendant does not automatically receive credit against his ultimate sentence for time spent in incompetency commitment.[21] Other jurisdictions, however, mandate such sentence credit. The American Bar Association's *Criminal Justice Mental Health Standards* recommend that such sentencing credit be given,[22] but this proposal may be criticized from a therapeutic jurisprudence standpoint. Predictably, providing sentencing credit will strengthen the disincentive for incompetent defendants to be restored to competency quickly. This would further illustrate law-produced psychological dysfunction.

Psychological theory suggests that we should reward competency, not incompetency. In jurisdictions that do not mandate sentence credit, such credit could be provided contingent upon demonstrated progress towards restoration to trial competency, thereby functioning as a reinforcer in the proposed contingency contract. Specific credit against any ultimate sentence can be given for meeting intermediate treatment goals on schedule, and eventually for reaching the goal of restoration to trial competency. To prevent shamming near the point of restoration, the court may take away or reduce sentence credit already earned for meeting intermediate treatment goals if the defendant, following a hearing, is found to be malingering.

Restructuring the incompetency-to-stand-trial process so that it substitutes the use of trial continuances for the formal competency evaluation process and permits the contingency contracting described, should expedite efficacious treatment and successful restoration to competency. Of course, the success of such a proposal depends upon the availability to incompetent defendants of a range of effective treatment methods and programs tailored to their needs. Recent literature has proposed a number of innovative treatment programs for defendants found incompetent to stand trial, including a structured cognitive problem-solving group therapy approach focusing on incompetency-to-stand-trial issues, and a psychoeducational intervention using videotape, a model of a courtroom, and discussions with defendant-patients concerning the trial process.[23] Such innovative treatment programs designed specifically for incompetent defendants present a fruitful area for research.

Whether hospitals or other treatment facilities use innovative treatment programs or conventional approaches, research would be desirable concerning the suggested applications of therapeutic jurisprudence in the competency-to-stand-trial context. This research, if conducted with the court's permission, would not seem to violate legal requirements. There seems to be no constitutional impediment to replacing much of the existing competency evaluation process with a system of trial continuances. Moreover, to the extent that a statutory right to formal competency evaluation exists, the granting of a continuance requested by the defendant and his counsel (although not necessarily its denial) could simply be conditioned upon the waiver of that right. With judicial approval, researchers could conduct a study of the proposed trial continuances model.

Would it work? Would attorneys seek to manipulate it for delay? Can judges exercise sufficient controls to minimize abuse? Would it save money? Would it provide incentives for more expeditious competency restoration? These are several questions that could be examined. Researchers could select jurisdictions for study that deny automatic sentence credit for time spent undergoing treatment so that sentence credit could be used as a reinforcer in the contingency contract. This discussion illustrates how therapeutic jurisprudence can be used to frame new proposals for changes in the law, and to identify new areas of empirical research that can be extremely useful in guiding law reform.

C. Sex Offenders and the Plea Process

One of the most striking features of sex offenders – and in particular of child molesters – is their heavy "denial and minimization"[24] of their behavior. These "cognitive distortions"[25] have been studied and classified by clinicians (e.g., "nothing happened," or "something happened but it wasn't my idea," or "something happened and it was my idea but it wasn't sexual," etc.).[26] Moreover, mental health professionals believe that "the key issues . . . of offender denial, motivation to change and cooperation in the process of treatment . . . are all aspects of the offender's functioning which are just as amenable to analysis and modification as the sex offending behavior itself."[27] In fact, there are treatment manuals for child molesters that cover such matters as "cognitive restructuring."[28] One approach to cognitive restructuring uses the technique of role-reversal: "the therapist role-plays being a child molester who uses the various . . . cognitive distortions," and "the patients are asked to take the role of a probation officer, a policeman, a family member, or anyone who might interact with a chid molester, and attempt to confront the beliefs role-played by the therapist."[29] The role-reversal process is used to lead the offenders to "rethink their own cognitions."[30]

A therapeutic jurisprudence approach to the sex offender problem might ask whether the law (rules, procedures, or roles of lawyers and judges) in the context of sex offenders operates therapeutically or anti-therapeutically. For example, does the law in this area promote cognitive restructuring? Or does it instead promote cognitive distortion (and thus perhaps contribute to psychological dysfunction and criminality)? It may well be, as one British psychologist has observed, that "many aspects of the justice system are inadvertently geared towards fostering offender denial."[31] In that connection, the therapeutic jurisprudence approach applied to the sex offender context produces the following suggestions.

Because sex offenders are usually extremely unwilling to admit guilt, even when the state's evidence is impressive, they often seek to plead "no contest" (*nolo contendere*),[32] a plea that, without trial, permits them to accept the consequences of a conviction without admitting their guilt. Indeed, some will seek to enter so-called *Alford* pleas – whereby a defendant is permitted to plead guilty while at the same time *protesting his innocence*.[33]

Courts may and often do accept such pleas, although they generally[34] are under no obligation to do so.[35] Note, however, that the acceptance of *nolo* and *Alford* pleas from sex offenders may reinforce cognitive distortions and denial. This may lead the offenders to reject offers of treatment directed at decreasing their deviant sexual arousal, increasing their nondeviant sexual arousal, and increasing their social/sexual skills.[36] In the alternative, it may undermine the potential that such treatment will be successful even if the offender is persuaded or required to participate in it.

Moreover, judicial willingness to accept *nolo* and *Alford* pleas may make it easy (perhaps too easy) for defense attorneys to arrange plea bargains acceptable to their clients. If judges refused to accept pleas in sex offender cases unaccompanied by an admission of guilt, defense lawyers would need to more actively coax those clients who lack plausible defenses to admit guilt and accept the bargain.

> It may often be a lawyer's duty to emphasize in harsh terms the force of the prosecution's evidence: "What about this fact? Is it going to go away? How the hell would you vote if you were a juror in your case?" It may sometimes be a lawyer's duty to say bluntly, "I cannot possibly beat this case. You are going to spend a long time in jail, and the only question is how long."[37]

Thus, if jurisdictions refused to recognize *nolo* and *Alford pleas* – or if judges refused or were less willing to accept them in sex offender cases – in essence, the law would induce defense lawyers to engage their clients in an exercise of "cognitive restructuring," role-reversal and all ("How the hell would you vote if you were a juror in your case?") The result would be a revised legal arrangement that would restructure the role of the defense lawyer in a way that would promote therapeutic values.

The therapeutic potential of the role of the judge could also be enhanced. Judges could help break through offender denial, not only by rejecting *nolo* and *Alford* pleas in sex offender cases, but by engaging in detailed[38] questioning of the defendant about the factual basis of the plea.[39] In fact, the judge might specifically address on the record some of the matters typically subject to cognitive distortion by sex offenders. In his classic study of guilty pleas, Donald Newman describes a post-plea-of-guilty hearing where, "after receiving . . . a guilty plea from a defendant . . . the court requires the defendant to take the stand, under oath, and state that he did commit the crime and exactly how he committed it."[40] Pleas with full admissions of guilt might be further buttressed by a judicial sentencing policy particularly unsympathetic to sex offenders who stand trial and offer a defense rejected by the jury and considered perjurious by the judge.[41]

A plea procedure that encourages a sex offender to make a detailed admission of guilt[42] should, therefore, work against denial and cognitive distortion and toward cognitive restructuring. Moreover, should the offender oscillate and deny his guilt when in a correctional institution or community treatment program, an "adequate record with which to confront the person"[43] may induce him again to accept responsibility, and perhaps "to participate in institutional therapy programs"[44] or to participate more meaningfully in such programs.

A final factor perhaps relevant to "cognitive restructuring through law" relates to the type of plea bargain offered a sex offender. An offender might be charged with the actual crime the state believes he committed, and might receive a sentence concession for an "on-the-nose" plea to that charge.[45] Alternatively, he may be charged with the actual crime, but allowed to plead to a reduced charge.[46] "Charge" bargaining, rather than "sentence" bargaining, is particularly prevalent in jurisdictions where mandatory sentencing has shifted discretion from the courts (in sentencing) to the prosecution (in charging).[47] An interesting and generally unasked question regarding the wisdom of alternative sentencing and bargaining schemes is whether "charge" bargaining feeds into cognitive distortion more so than does "sentence" bargaining.

A therapeutic jurisprudence perspective on sex offenders and the plea process would thus suggest a revision of existing practices which, together with the consequent reshaping of the role of judges and defense lawyers, could uproot the law's current reinforcement of denial and cognitive distortion by sex offenders and promote their rehabilitation through cognitive restructuring. Note that this type of therapeutic jurisprudence exploration, although substantively distinct from what is traditionally viewed as "mental health law," is surely "law and mental health." Traditional mental health law would include the two incompetency topics discussed earlier, but it would not include topics such as plea bargaining and *nolo contendere* and *Alford* pleas. Thus, besides revisiting traditional mental health law issues, therapeutic jurisprudence will take us to many law/mental health intersection points, both civil and criminal, that fall outside the substantive core of mental health law.

IV. Conclusion

The law and mental health field needs new directions. We have suggested one reflecting the assumption that law should serve rather than disserve the mental health of those it affects. Substantive rules, and the practices and procedures that implement them, should be analyzed to determine their impact on therapeutic values. This frequently ignored dimension should be systematically examined with the tools of the behavioral sciences, and the results should factor into the policy analysis that must precede sensible law reform efforts. In this essay we have applied therapeutic jurisprudence to three illustrative criminal justice mental health topics and shown how this approach can be used to identify, for empirical testing, critical policy questions that might otherwise be ignored.

The law has much to contribute to improving the condition and well-being of patients. To reach its full potential, it must become more empirical and truly interdisciplinary. We propose an approach in which behavioral scientists and legal analysts join together to forge a new generation of exciting and pertinent scholarship and law reform.

Endnotes

1. *See* B. Ennis, *Prisoners of Psychiatry* (1972); *see also* Brooks & Winick, "Foreword: Mental Disability Law Comes of Age," 39 *Rutgers L. Rev.* 235, 235 (1987).

2. R. Isaac & V. Armat, *Madness In the Streets: How Psychiatry and the Law Abandoned the Mentally Ill* 109 (1990).

3. Ennis, "Civil Liberties and Mental Illness," 7 *Crim. L. Bull.* 101, 108 (1971).

4. D. Wexler & B. Winick, *Essays in Therapeutic Jurisprudence* (1991); *see* D. Wexler, *Therapeutic Jurisprudence: The Law as a Therapeutic Agent* (1990).

5. Wexler, "Therapeutic Justice," 57 *Minn. L. Rev.* 289, 291 (1972).

6. 477 U.S. 399, 410 (1986), 10 MPDLR 278.

7. 110 S. Ct. 1317 (1990), 14 MPDLR 115.

8. Brief for the American Psychiatric Association and the American Medical Association as *Amici Curiae* at 16, *Perry v. Louisiana*, 111 S. Ct. 449 (1990) (No. 89-5120) [hereinafter *Amici* Brief].

9. 110 S. Ct. 1028 (1990), 14 MPDLR 124.

10. *Id.* at 1039-40.

11. *See, e.g., Harper*, 110 S. Ct. at 1050 n.15 (Stevens, J., dissenting); *Rennie v. Klein*, 462 F. Supp. 1131, 1144 (D.N.J. 1978), 3 MDLR 95, *aff'd in part, modified in part, and remanded*, 653 F.2d 836 (3d Cir. 1981), 5 MDLR 322, *vacated and remanded*, 458 U.S. 1119 (1982); Durham & LaFond, "A Search for the Missing Premise of Involuntary Therapeutic Commitment: Effective Treatment of the Mentally Ill," 40 *Rutgers L. Rev.* 303, 367-68 (1988); Winick, "Competency to Consent to Treatment: The Distinction Between Consent and Objection," 28 *Hous. L. Rev.* 15, 50 & n. 118 (1991).

12. *See* B. Braginsky, D. Braginsky, & K. Ring, *Methods of Madness: The Mental Hospital as a Last Resort* 49-52 (1969); Wexler, "Token and Taboo: Behavior Modification, Token Economies, and the Law," 61 *Calif. L. Rev.* 81, 84-87 (1973) (describing examples of rational, self-regarding behavior of mental patients).

13. D. Wexler, *supra* note 4, at 5.

14. *See Amici* Brief, *supra* note 8, at 25.

15. 477 U.S. 399 (1986), 10 MPDLR 278.

16. In this respect, *Ford* exemplifies "law-related psychological dysfunction." *See* D. Wexler, *supra* note 4, at 5. Although perhaps dysfunctional, the *Ford* decision is justifiable based on considerations other than those relating to therapeutic values – the notion that it does not comport with human dignity to execute a defendant who is so mentally ill that he is unable to understand and appreciate why he is being put to death. This analysis illustrates that therapeutic values, although relevant to a great many legal decisions, may not be dispositive of the legal issue.

17. *See, e.g.*, R. Roesch & S. Golding, *Competency to Stand Trial* 83-91 (1980); Winick, "Restructuring Competency to Stand Trial," 32 *UCLA L. Rev.* 921, 982 (1985).

18. *See* Winick, *supra* note 11, at 46-53.

19. *See* Winick, "Incompetency to Stand Trial: An Assessment of Costs and Benefits, and a Proposal for Reform," 39 *Rutgers L. Rev.* 243, 281-84 (1987) [hereinafter Winick, Incompetency to Stand Trial]; Winick, *supra* note 17, at 979-83.

20. *See* Winick, "Harnessing the Power of the Bet: Wagering with the Government as a Mechanism for Social and Individual Change," 45 *U. Miami L. Rev.* 737 (1991).

21. *See* Winick, *supra* note 17, at 947.

22. *See ABA Criminal Justice Mental Health Standards* §7-4.15 (1989).

23. *See* Siegel & Elwork, "Treating Incompetence to Stand Trial," 14 *Law & Hum. Behav.* 57 (1990).

24. Perkins, "Clinical Work With Sex Offenders in Secure Settings," in *Clinical Approaches to Sex Offenders and Their Victims* 151, 168 (C. Hollin & K. Howells eds. 1991).

25. Pollock & Hashmall, "The Excuses of Child Molesters," 9 *Behav. Sci. & L.* 53, 54 (1991). *See also* Abel, Becker & Cunningham-Rathner, "Complications, Consent, and Cognitions in Sex Between Children and Adults," 7 *Int'l J. L. & Psychiatry* 89 (1984).

26. Pollock & Hashmall, *supra* note 25, at 57.

27. Perkins, *supra* note 24, at 152.

28. G. Abel, J. Becker, J. Cunningham-Rathner, M. Kaplan, & J. Rouleau, "Treatment Manual for Child Molesters" (unpublished, undated).

29. *Id.* at 39.

30. *Id.*

31. Perkins, *supra* note 24, at 152.

32. *In re Guilty Plea Cases*, 235 N.W. 2d 132, 147 (Mich. Sup. Ct. 1975) (court accepting *nolo* plea must give justifying reasons, and reluctance to admit a sordid crime, such as sexual assault on a child, appears to be such a reason).

33. *North Carolina v. Alford*, 400 U.S. 25 (1970); Note, "The *Alford* Plea: A Necessary but Unpredictable Tool for the Criminal Defendant," 72 *Iowa L. Rev.* 1063 (1987). *See* Alschuler, "The Defense Attorney's Role in Plea Bargaining," 84 *Yale L. J.* 1179, 1280, 1286 n. 290 (1975) (discussing pleas in sex cases).

34. An occasional case suggests that trial courts ordinarily must accept such pleas. *E.g.*, *United States v. Gaskins*, 485 F.2d 1046 (D.C. Cir. 1973).

35. *North Carolina v. Alford*, 400 U.S. at 38 n. 11.

36. Perkins, *supra* note 24, at 161-67 (discussing treatment techniques).

37. *Cf.* Alschuler, *supra* note 33, at 1309 (discussing lawyer's role in helping client understand the often harsh reality of the strength of the prosecution's case).

38. Uviller, "Pleading Guilty: A Critique of Four Models," 41 *Law & Contemp. Probs.* 102, 121 (1977) (judicial discretion re form and quantity of inquiry).

39. Judges already have an obligation to probe the factual basis of the plea. *See, e.g.*, Fed. R. Crim. P. 11. *But see Arizona v. Brooks*, 586 P.2d 1270 (Ariz. Sup. Ct. 1978) (upholding guilty plea in child molestation case despite absence of explicit statement by defendant that acts were motivated by abnormal sexual interest in children).

40. *See* D. Newman, *Conviction: The Determination of Guilt or Innocence Without Trial* 19-20 (1966).

41. *See United States v. Grayson*, 438 U.S. 41 (1978) (proper for court in imposing sentence to consider perjury committed during defense of criminal case). *Compare United States v. Dunnigan*, 49 Crim. L. Rep. 1505 (4th Cir. Aug. 30, 1991) (discussing "obstruction of justice" section of U.S. Sentencing Guidelines).

42. *But see United States v. Miller*, 910 F.2d 1321 (6th Cir. 1990) (discouraging full acceptance of responsibility by increasing sentence under U.S. Sentencing Guidelines for admitting other relevant conduct in interview with probation officer). *Compare United States v. Faulkner*, 934 F.2d 190 (9th Cir. 1991) (court cannot increase sentence by taking into account matters dismissed or uncharged pursuant to plea agreement).

43. D. Newman, *supra* note 40, at 222.

44. *Id.*

45. Uviller, *supra* note 38, at 109.

46. *Id.* at 108. *See* D. Newman, *supra* note 40, 105-08, 119 (lesser pleas in sex cases).

47. Alschuler, "Sentencing Reform and Prosecutorial Power: A Critique of Recent Proposals for 'Fixed' and 'Presumptive' Sentencing," 126 *U. Pa. L. Rev.* 550 (1978).

Law, Ideology, and Critical Inquiry: the Case of Treatment Refusal for Incompetent Prisoners Awaiting Execution

Bruce A. Arrigo, Ph.D.*
Christopher R. Williams**

I. INTRODUCTION

The behavioral and social sciences have recently re-examined decisions regarding prisoner's competency to be executed, especially in the context of their implications for mental health law and policy in general[1] and mentally disordered death-row prisoners in particular.[2] The essential debate focuses upon those conditions wherein the state may, without abridging an inmate's constitutionally protected liberty interests, terminate the life of a citizen awaiting execution.[3] This is an extremely contentious

---

* Professor of Criminology and Forensic Psychology, and Director of the Institute of Psychology, Law, and Public Policy at the California School of Professional Psychology-Fresno; Ph.D. Administration of Justice, The Pennsylvania State University, 1993; M.A. in Sociology, Duquesne University, 1987; M.A. in Psychology, Duquesne University, 1985; B.A. Politics, Saint Joseph's University, 1982. The authors gratefully acknowledge the support and consultation of Dr. Beth Arrigo who provided considerable assistance in the preparation of an earlier draft of this manuscript.

** Ph.D. candidate in Forensic Psychology at the California School of Professional Psychology; B.A. Psychology, Wright State University, 1995.

1. BRUCE J. WINICK, THE RIGHT TO REFUSE MENTAL HEALTH TREATMENT (1997).

2. *See, e.g.*, Bruce Arrigo & Jeffrey Tasca, *Right to Refuse Treatment, Competency to be Executed, and Therapeutic Jurisprudence: Toward A Systematic Analysis*, 24 L. & PSYCHOL. REV. 1, 1-47 (1999). *See also* Bruce Winick, *Competency to be Executed: A Therapeutic Jurisprudence Perspective*, 10 BEHAV. SCI. & L. 317, 317-37 (1992) [hereinafter *Competency to be Executed*].

3. The legal history of this debate can be traced to the matter of *Nobles v. Georgia*, 168 U.S. 399 (1897). Interestingly, the Court concluded that no competency for execution hearing was constitutionally required when the death row prisoner was mentally incompetent. In the wake of *Nobles*, courts and legislatures

matter and, as a result, the debate remains mostly unresolved by the Court. For example, questions persist as to whether the execution of a convicted mentally ill offender is, under particular circumstances, in the best interest of the state and, thus, society,[4] or whether it is the quintessential expression of judicially sponsored inhumanity.[5]

Although doctrinal legal analyses and classical legal reasoning are useful approaches by which to assess this question, other more non-traditional methods of legal inquiry can provide compelling insight into the implicit social forces that influence the courts and legislatures,[6] as well as the unconscious clinicolegal processes that underscore psychiatric justice.[7] Discourse analysis is one way to investigate whether the execution of mentally disordered offenders serves the interests of society or advances legal harm. The pivotal feature of discourse analysis is that all language is method,[8] and that hidden assumptions and implicit values within a text

---

routinely found that there was no legal basis to execute an incompetent death row prisoner. *See Competency to be Executed*, *supra* note 2, at 319. As we will demonstrate, however, this standard was substantially amended by the United States Supreme Court. *See infra* note 4 and accompanying text.

4. The three most compelling cases exploring the legal boundaries of this issue include: *Ford v. Wainwright*, 477 U.S. 399 (1986); *Washington v. Harper*, 494 U.S. 210 (1990); and *Perry v. Louisiana*, 494 U.S. 1015 (1990). The related case of *Riggins v. Nevada*, 504 U.S. 127 (1992), while worth noting, is not specifically germane to our investigation. *Riggins* involved medication refusal during the pretrial and trial stage and *not* while the individual was incarcerated. Indeed, the expressed purpose of *Riggins* was to explore the conditions under which a mentally ill person resisting anti-psychotic medication could be rendered "competent to stand trial." *Riggins*, 504 U.S. at 140 (Kennedy, J., dissenting). Clearly, then, *Riggins* was not a death row inmate case or one addressing the rights of incompetent prisoners. *See* Arrigo & Tasca, *supra* note 2, at 2.

5. *See generally* ROBERT JOHNSON, DEATH WORK: A STUDY OF THE MODERN EXECUTION PROCESS (1998); ABU-JAMAL, LIVE FROM DEATH ROW (1995); SAMUEL DICKS, DEATH ROW: INTERVIEWS WITH INMATES, THEIR FAMILIES, AND OPPONENTS OF CAPITAL PUNISHMENT (1990); HUGO BEDAU, DEATH IS DIFFERENT: STUDIES IN MORALITY, LAW, AND POLITICS OF CAPITAL PUNISHMENT (1987); HUGO BEDAU, THE CASE AGAINST THE DEATH PENALTY (1987).

6. For the systematic application of a postmodern semiotic method applied to the laws of civil commitment, *see* BRUCE ARRIGO, MADNESS, LANGUAGE, AND THE LAW 59-105 (1994).

7. *See* BRUCE A. ARRIGO, THE CONTOURS OF PSYCHIATRIC JUSTICE: A POSTMODERN CRITIQUE OF MENTAL ILLNESS, CRIMINAL INSANITY, AND THE LAW (1996) [hereinafter CONTOURS].

8. The notion that all language is a method represents an important theme contained in the structural and post-structural sociology of knowledge process. The structural approach (here aligned with our structural legal semiotic analysis) focuses on the "underlying rules which organize phenomena into a social system . . ." STEVEN BEST & DOUGLAS KELLNER, POSTMODERN THEORY: CRITICAL

(e.g., a state statute, an appellate transcript, a legal brief) can be deciphered, much like a coded message, through a careful assessment of the words and/or phrases in use.[9] Thus, it is through this discursive method of critical inquiry that the ideology embedded in the law, often concealed through and masked by a myriad of holdings, *stare decisis*, dicta, and the like, becomes increasingly transparent.[10] For purposes of our investiga-

---

INTERROGATIONS 18 (1991). The post-structural approach (here aligned with our legal deconstruction investigation) claims that root assumptions, foundational truths, linear cause-effect relations, and the neutrality of the scientific method are not ascertainable because language structures are thought in ways which are never neutral. *See generally* DIANE MACDONELL, THEORIES OF DISCOURSE (1986); RICHARD RORTY, PHILOSOPHY IN THE MIRROR OF NATURE (1979). Deconstructionism points to the "hierarchy of values which attempt not only to guarantee truth [falsely], but also serve to exclude and devalue allegedly inferior terms or position[s] [values]." BEST & KELLNER, *supra* note 8, at 21. For a practical assessment of deconstructionism with relevant sociolegal implications, *see* Stephan Fuchs & Steven Ward, *What is Deconstruction, and Where and When Does it Take Place: Making Facts in Science, Building Cases in Law*, 59 AM. SOC. R. 481, 481-500. For more direct applications to the sociology of law, *see* DRAGAN MILOVANOVIC, A PRIMER IN THE SOCIOLOGY OF LAW 155-56 (1994); and for a general overview of structural and post-structural thought in law and justice studies, *see* Bruce Arrigo, *The Peripheral Core of Law and Criminology: On Postmodern Social Theory and Conceptual Integration*, 12 JUST. Q. 447, 447-72 (1995) [hereinafter *Peripheral Core*]. For more on the development of what discourse analysis is and how it furthers critical inquiry into the nature of social phenomena, *see, e.g.*, MICHEL FOUCAULT, THE ARCHEOLOGY OF KNOWLEDGE AND THE DISCOURSE ON LANGUAGE 21-71 (A.M. Sheridan Smith trans. 1972); MICHEL FOUCAULT, THE ORDER OF THINGS 157-62 (R.D. Laing ed. 1973); JULIA KRISTEVA, DESIRE IN LANGUAGE: A SEMIOTIC APPROACH TO LITERATURE AND ART 23-35 (Leon S. Roudiez ed., Thomas Gora et al. trans. 1980); JULIA KRISTEVA, REVOLUTION IN POETIC LANGUAGE 13-17 (1986); JACQUES LACAN, *ECRITS: A SELECTION* 30-113 (Alan Sheridan trans. 1977); ROLAND BARTHES, THE SEMIOTIC CHALLENGE 217-93 (Richard Howard trans. 1988); JACQUES DERRIDA, OF GRAMMATOLOGY 165-268 (Gayatri Chakravorty Spivak trans. 1976); JACQUES DERRIDA, WRITING AND DIFFERENCE 278-93 (Alan Bass trans. 1976) [hereinafter WRITING]; ALGIRDAS GREIMAS, THE SOCIAL SCIENCES: A SEMIOTIC VIEW 9-184 (Paolo Fabbri & Frank A. Collins trans. 1990).

9. Unpacking the concealed assumptions and covert values embedded in a text through various discourse analysis methodologies reveals something more or something other about the unconscious intent of the text and/or its author. This additive feature is not detectable through standard legal analysis. *See* ARRIGO, *supra* note 6, at 128-40.

10. This logic was originally developed by the Critical Legal Studies (CLS) Movement. *See generally* THE POLITICS OF LAW: A PROGRESSIVE CRITIQue (David Kairys ed. 1982); Mark Tushnet, *Critical Legal Studies: An Introduction to Its Origins and Underpinnings*, 36 J. LEGAL EDUC. 505, 505-17 (1986); Mark Tushnet, *Critical Legal Studies: A Political History*, 100 YALE L. J. 1515, 1515-44 (1991) [hereinafter *Political History*]; ROBERTO MANGABEIRA UNGER, THE

tion, then, discourse analysis is helpful in that the language of confinement law is placed "under the microscope." The central issue we consider is as follows: what does the United States Supreme Court "really" intend when, in certain instances, it endorses the execution of incompetent mentally ill prisoners on death row who invoke a right to refuse treatment? Put another way, what values, assumptions, and/or meanings are privileged through the legally sanctioned act of capital punishment for psychiatrically disordered offenders?

To focus the investigation, we begin with a standard, though brief, assessment of the precedent-setting mental health case law on the execution of mentally disordered inmates.[11] This assessment considers the evolution of related issues such as the mentally ill prisoner's right to refuse drug treatment and the conditions under which a finding of incompetency does or does not mitigate capital punishment. We then provide a detailed overview of two methods for engaging in discourse analysis: structural semiotics[12] and deconstructionism.[13] These are not the only two approaches representing discourse analysis but, as we contend, each provides unique insight into the unconscious intent of the Court. The overview lays the necessary theoretical foundation for the application that follows it. Next, we consider how discourse analysis, based on principles found in structural legal semiotics and legal deconstructionism, furthers our understanding of the United States Supreme Court's more covert meaning when sustaining capital punishment for incompetent mentally ill offenders on death row. In this context, we specifically consider the words "incompetency" and " treatment" as linguistic artifacts (i.e., coded messages) that signify implicit values and hidden assumptions for the Court regarding the mentally ill and disordered death row inmates. We conclude by speculating on the implications of our analysis for the future of mental health confinement law and policy and for the execution of psychiatrically disordered offenders.

CRITICAL LEGAL STUDIES MOVEMENT (1986); Alan Hunt, *The Theory of Critical Legal Studies*, 6 OXFORD J. LEGAL STUD. 1, 1-45 (1986); ANDREW ALTMAN, CRITICAL LEGAL STUDIES: A LIBERAL CRITIQUE (1990). We note, however, that the CLS Movement is still developing and searching for a unified theory. *See* MILOVANOVIC, *supra* note 8, at 95. Further, we submit that the CLS agenda has yet to fully and systematically incorporate discourse analysis principles, as we describe them, into a unified theory of legal thought and action. *But see* J.M. Balkin, *Deconstructive Practice and Legal Theory*, 96 YALE L.J. 743, 743-86 (1987).

11. *See supra* note 4 and accompanying text.

12. *See infra* notes 49-72 and accompanying text.

13. *See infra* notes 73-97 and accompanying text.

II. EXECUTING THE MENTALLY ILL: LEGAL ANALYSIS

A. Mental Illness and Capital Offenders

A substantial number of incarcerated individuals suffer from mental illness in one form or another.[14] Thus, it is not surprising that mental illness is a significant factor affecting the legal system's response to serious crimes where punishment can and does amount to a death sentence.[15] In this section we are interested, in terms of law, in whether an individual's mental illness affects his or her future as a death row prisoner. This concern draws specific attention to the matter of one's psychological competency and legal right to refuse treatment.[16] Indeed, outside of competency to be executed determinations, death row prisoners have little opportunity of forestalling the inevitable execution that awaits them.[17] Thus, the

---

14. *See, e.g.*, HENRY STEADMAN ET AL., THE MENTALLY ILL IN JAIL: PLANNING FOR ESSENTIAL SERVICES 3-87 (John Monahan et al. eds. 1989); Rudolph Alexander, *Determining Appropriate Criteria in the Evaluation of Correctional Mental Health Treatment for Inmates*, 18 J. OFFENDER REHABILITATION 119, 122 (1992); H. Richard Lamb & Linda E. Weinberger, *Persons With Severe Mental Illness in Jails and Prisons: A Review*, 49 PSYCHIATRIC SERVICES 483, 483-92 (1998); TREATMENT OF OFFENDERS WITH MENTAL DISORDERS (Robert W. Wettstein ed. 1998); James Ogloff et al., *Mental Health Services in Jails and Prisons: Legal, Clinical, and Policy Issues*, 18 L. & PSYCHOL. REV. 109, 109 (1994). Jeffrey Metzner, *An Introduction to Correctional Psychiatry: Part III*, 26 J. AM. ACAD. PSYCHIATRY & L. 107, 107-15 (1998).

15. *See Competency to be Executed*, *supra* note 2, at 317; *see also* R. Andrew Shultz-Ross, *Theoretical Difficulties in the Treatment of Mentally Ill Prisoners*, 38 J. FORENSIC SCI. 426, 428 (1993); Fred Cohen, *Inmates with Mental Disorders: A Guide to Law and Practice*, 16 MENTAL & PHYSICAL DISABILITY L. REP. 339, 339-46 (1992); Faith Liebman & Neil Leibman, *Developing Trends in Prisoners' Rights to Mental Health Treatment*, 9 AM. J. PSYCHIATRY 19, 19-20 (1991).

16. *See, e.g.*, Arrigo & Tasca, *supra* note 2.

17. We recognize that the appellate process can question on Constitutional grounds related matters such as whether a trial was fair and whether a lawyer's representation was adequate. The former is secured under the Due Process Clause of the Fifth and Fourteenth Amendments of the U.S. Constitution. *See, e.g.*, Nebraska Press Association v. Stuart, 427 U.S. 539 (1976); Gannett Co. v. De Pasquale, 443 U.S. 368 (1979); Press-Enterprise Co v. Superior Court, 478 U.S. 1 (1986). The latter is guaranteed under the Sixth Amendment of the United States Constitution. *See, e.g.*, Powell v. Alabama, 287 U.S. 45 (1932); Gideon v. Wainwright, 392 U.S. 1 (1963); Argersinger v. Hamlin, 407 U.S. 25 (1972). What we allude to, however, is the fate of mentally disordered inmates and their capacity to exercise their treatment rights while on death row in order not to be restored to competency for the sole purpose of execution. *See* WINICK, *supra* note 1, at 299-300. *See, e.g.*, State v. Perry, 610 So.2d 746 (La. 1992), in which the Court concluded that "forcing a prisoner to take anti-psychotic drugs [to restore competency

situation for the mentally disordered offender on death row is quite profound. The prevalence of psychiatric illness that predated sentencing and imprisonment, the exacerbating conditions of incarceration and pending execution, and the legal assertion of incompetency to be executed as a "last chance" for circumventing capital punishment, represents a complex clustering of variables significantly impacting the life or death of criminally confined individuals.[18]

B. The Case of Ford v. Wainwright[19]

The 1986 case of *Ford v. Wainwright* addressed whether the Federal Constitution's prohibition on "cruel and unusual punishment"[20] applied to the involuntary administration of mental health treatment for patients and offenders.[21] The critical question examined in the *Ford* case was "whether

---

and] to facilitate his execution does not constitute treatment." *Id.* at 751. Such a determination amounts to "medical punishment." *Id. See also Competency to be Executed, supra* note 2, at 328-32.

18. As Johnson describes it:

> 'Death row is the most total of institutions, the penitentiary most demanding of penitence, the prison most debilitating and disabling in its confinement. On death row the allegorical pound of flesh is just the beginning. Here the whole person is consumed. The spirit is captured and gradually worn down, then the body is disposed of . . . .'

See JOHNSON *supra* note 5, at 70-71. This troubling reality is intensified when the medicolegal tension of drug treatment or its refusal is considered for incompetent prisoners awaiting execution. *See* Kirk Heilbrun et al., *The Debate on Treating Individuals Incompetent for Execution*, 149 AM. J. PSYCHIATRY 596, 596-97 (1992).

19. 477 U.S. 399 (1986).

20. U.S. CONST. amend. VIII.

21. *See* WINICK, *supra* note 1, at 223. For the development of this right under the Federal Constitution, *see* Estelle v. Gamble, 429 U.S. 97 (1976); Robinson v. California, 370 U.S. 660 (1962). Alvin Ford was convicted of murder in the state of Florida in 1974 and subsequently received a sentence of death. *See id.* at 401. There was no indication that he was incompetent at the time of the offense, during the trial, or at the sentencing phase of the case. *See id.* at 401-02. Ford, however, exhibited considerable behavioral changes sometime after he received his sentence. For example, he believed he was part of a complex Ku Klux Klan conspiracy, inducing obsessive suicidal thoughts, that his female relatives were being sexually abused in the prison, and that his family members and friends were held hostage. After fourteen months of psychiatric evaluation, Ford was diagnosed as a paranoid schizophrenic with suicidal potential. Ford's counsel argued that this major mental disorder impaired his ability to assist in the defense of his life, violating the competency to be executed statute under Florida law. Subsequent psychiatric evaluation was sought by the Governor's office. Ford's condition deteriorated. His thought and speech became incomprehensible. In 1986, the case was argued before the United States Supreme Court. Justice Marshall, in delivering the opinion of the Court, drew attention to the Eighth Amendment's prohibition of a

intrusive treatment administered essentially for reasons of punishment (to enable the state to carry out the death penalty) would offend contemporary standards of decency and therefore constitute cruel and unusual punishment in violation of the Eight[h] Amendment."[22] In the *Ford* case, the administration of medical treatment (drug therapy) gave rise to his competency to be executed. Thus, the Court considered whether said treatment amounted to "medical punishment."[23]

In response to this matter, the Court recognized the "ancestral legacy" of prohibiting the execution of the mentally ill, noting its historical regard as "savage and inhuman."[24] To support this contention, the Court cited Blackstone, and the English common law roots of stay of execution for the insane:

> 'Idiots and lunatics are not chargeable for their own acts, if committed when under these incapacities .... Also, if a man in his sound memory commits a capital offence, and before arraignment for it, he becomes mad, he ought not be arraigned for it: because he is not able to plead to it with that advice and caution that he ought. And if, after he has pleaded, the prisoner becomes mad, he shall not be tried: for how can he make his defence? If, after he be tried and found guilty, he loses his senses before judgement, judgement shall not be pronounced; *and if, after judgement, he becomes of nonsane memory, execution shall be stayed: for peradventure, says the humanity of the English law, had the prisoner been of sound memory, he might have alleged some-*

State's execution of an "insane" prisoner. Thus, as Justice Marshall opined, "Florida's statutory procedures for determining a condemned prisoner's sanity provide inadequate assurance of accuracy . . . and . . . having been denied a fact finding procedure adequate to afford a full and fair hearing, . . . petitioner is entitled to a *de novo* evidentiary hearing in the District Court on the question of his competency to be executed." Ford v. Wainwright, 477 U.S. 399, 400 (1986). The United States Court of Appeals heard oral arguments on these matters in September 1990. This notwithstanding, the Eleventh Circuit never ruled on Ford's appeal. He died before such an evidentiary trial could conclude in February of 1991.

22. Ford v. Wainwright, 477 U.S. at 408; WINICK, *supra* note 1, at 299.

23. In related matters, the U.S. Supreme Court had previously and summarily found unconstitutional interventions amounting to medical punishment. *See, e.g.*, Bee v. Greaves 744 F.2d 1387 (1984) (addressing the administration of psychotropic medication, absent an emergency, for institutional control or discipline of an adult patient); *see also* Nelson v. Heyne, 491 F.2d 352 (7th Cir. 1974), *cert. denied*, 417 U.S. 976 (1976) (for a similar finding within a juvenile correctional context); Mackey v. Procunier, 477 F.2d 877 (9th Cir. 1973) (discussing the use of the paralyzing "fright drug" succinylcholine in a prison aversive conditioning program). We note, however, that in the *Ford* decision the Court did *not* address the related matter of whether a state could *coercively treat* (and thus restore to competency) a mentally disordered prisoner awaiting execution for purposes of capital punishment. *See* WINICK, *supra* note 1, at 299-300.

24. *Ford*, 477 U.S. at 406.

> *thing in stay of judgement or execution.'*[25]

While stay of execution for the incompetent death row prisoner had been generally practiced as common law prior to the *Ford* decision, the Court reaffirmed this notion in regard to medical treatment of a prisoner awaiting execution. As the Court explained:

> the various reasons put forth in support of the common-law restriction have no less logical, moral, and practical force than they did when first voiced. For today, no less than before, we may seriously question the retributive value of executing a person who has no comprehension of why he has been singled out and stripped of his fundamental right to life.[26]

Thus, *Ford* was the first case in which the United States Supreme Court held that a prisoner had constitutional safeguards prohibiting execution while the person remained incompetent.[27] Indeed, the Court concluded that the Eighth Amendment prohibits a State from carrying out a sentence of death upon a prisoner who is insane.[28] This prohibition against executing an incompetent prisoner has since been adopted by the majority of states.[29]

While *Ford* addressed the larger issue of protecting the Eighth Amendment rights of an incompetent death row prisoner who refused medical intervention, it fell short of offering viable standards for determining

25. *Id.* at 406-07 (quoting 4 W. BLACKSTONE, COMMENTARIES 24-25) (emphasis added).

26. *Id.* at 405.

27. *See* Arrigo & Tasca, *supra* note 2, at 18-23; *see also Competency to be Executed, supra* note 2, at 319-21.

28. *See Competency to be Executed, supra* note 2, at 319-21. For relevant literature on behavior, social science, and the law exploring the contours of this determination, *see generally* Paul Appelbaum, *Competency to be Executed: Another Conundrum for Mental Health Professionals*, 37 HOSP. & COMMUNITY PSYCHIATRY 682, 682-84 (1986); Robert D. Miller, *Evaluation of and Treatment to Competency to be Executed: A National Survey and Analysis*, 16 J. PSYCHIATRY & L. 67, 67-90 (1988); Donald H. Wallace, *Incompetency for Execution: The Supreme Court Challenges the Ethical Standards of the Mental Health Professions*, 8 J. LEGAL MED. 265, 265-81 (1987); Charles Patrick Ewing, *Diagnosing and Treating "Insanity" on Death Row: Legal and Ethical Perspectives*, 5 BEHAV. SCI. & L. 175, 175-85 (1987).

29. *See* WINICK, *supra* note 1, at 299-300. The U.S. Supreme Court has previously held that the state does possess a legitimate penal interest in capital punishment sufficient to withstand Eighth Amendment scrutiny. *See, e.g.*, Gregg v. Georgia, 428 U.S. 153 (1976); Proffit v. Florida, 428 U.S. 242 (1976). The Court, however, in *Ford* found that the administration of medical treatment, within a correctional context for an incompetent death row inmate, was an intrusive intervention that could not overcome the Eighth Amendment challenge. *See* Ford v. Wainwright, 477 U.S. 399, 416-17 (1986).

competency.[30] Moreover, the U.S. Supreme Court in *Ford* did not consider the more complex question of whether a state could *coercively* treat a mentally disordered death row inmate for purposes of restoring his competency and eventual execution. In addition, it did not determine whether medical intervention and anti-psychotic drug therapy were necessary in those cases where an incompetent prisoner, who refused treatment, was found to be dangerous to other inmates and correctional staff. This latter issue was squarely addressed in the case of *Washington v. Harper*.[31]

C. The Case of Washington v. Harper

Harper is the seminal decision on the matter of treatment refusal for incompetent prisoners suffering from mental illness.[32] The primary issue before the United States Supreme Court was whether the involuntary administration of medical treatment for an incompetent, though dangerous,

---

30. We note that the presence of mental illness alone does not equate with incompetency. However, the standards used to define incompetency and their operation in particular cases vary considerably. *See* WINICK, *supra* note 1, at 349. For a general assessment of how the legal question of competency is often a confusing matter for clinicians in their assessments impacting the accuracy of their determinations and patient and prisoner outcomes, *see, e.g.*, Bruce Winick, *The Side Effects of Incompetency Labeling and the Implication for Mental Health Law*, 1 PSYCHOL. PUB. POL'Y & L. 6, 30-33 (1995) [hereinafter *Side Effects*]; Paul J. Appelbaum & Thomas Grisso, *The MacArthur Treatment Competence Study, I: Mental Illness and Competence to Consent to Treatment*, 19 L. & HUM. BEHAV. 105, 111-18 (1995).

31. 494 U.S. 210 (1989). We recognize that the U.S. Supreme Court originally granted certiorari in *Perry v. Louisiana*, 498 U.S. 38 (1990), to assess the "treatment to execute" matter prior to its determination in *Harper*. The Court, however, chose to remand *Perry* to the State Supreme Court of Louisiana for further consideration, which temporarily left unresolved the matter presented to it in *Perry*. By presenting legal background on *Harper* before an analysis of *Perry*, we draw attention to the progression of constitutional and legal thought in the area of treatment-refusal rights for prisoners, competency determinations, and death row executions. In addition, we demonstrate the apparent legal uncertainty inherent in the Court's assessment of these weighty issues.

32. *See* WINICK, *supra* note 1, at 3. We note further, however, that the Court's decision to address this substantive issue did not occur in a vacuum. *See, e.g.*, Mills v. Rogers 457 U.S. 291, where the Court initially sidestepped the issue in a case involving the right of hospital patients to refuse anti-psychotic drugs. *See also In re Guardianship of Roe*, 421 N.E.2d 40 (1981), in which the Court recognized the right to treatment refusal at the state level; Rogers v. Commissioner, 458 N.E.2d 308 (Mass. 1983), where the Supreme Judicial Court of Massachusetts further endorsed this state right; Rogers v. Okin, 738 F.2d 1 (1st Cir. 1984), where the Court of Appeals opined that the Massachusetts state guidelines wherein treatment refusal could be invoked were "equal [to] or [in excess of] the rights provided in the federal Constitution." *Id.* at 9.

prisoner violated the prohibition on cruel and unusual punishment guaranteed under the Eighth Amendment.[33] Further, the Court considered whether respondent *Harper* possessed a "significant liberty interest" in "resisting such unwanted treatment."[34] The Court found that the police powers of the state to forcibly medicate outweighed the prisoner's constitutionally protected liberty interest from such intrusiveness, provided the administered treatment was necessary to "maintain . . . the security of the prison,"[35] and was in the inmate's medical interest.[36] This concern for institutional security extended to the safety of correctional personnel, as well as other prisoners.[37]

The significance of the *Harper* decision cannot be under estimated. For the first time, the United States Supreme Court made expressly clear that the state has a compelling and superseding interest in controlling and treating incompetent inmates who resisted drug therapy. The decision in *Harper* is consistent with prior and related rulings in which the Supreme Court demonstrated a preference for institutional policy, extending considerable deference to such facilities as legitimate agents of the state.[38]

---

33. Walter Harper had been imprisoned in the state of Washington following a 1976 conviction for robbery. He received psychiatric treatment for six years, including the involuntary consumption of psychotropic medication. In 1982, while incarcerated, Harper refused to take the anti-psychotic drugs prescribed to him and, consequently, his condition deteriorated to the degree that he engaged in violent conduct. Under Washington's Department of Corrections and the Special Offender Center (SOC), it was determined that Harper suffered from a mental disorder, was gravely disabled, and posed a likelihood of serious harm to himself and others in the prison. Given these findings, Harper was forced to consume anti-psychotic medication. He filed a suit alleging that the SOC failed to provide him with a judicial hearing before involuntarily medicating him in violation of his Fourteenth Amendment Due Process protections and his Eighth Amendment rights against cruel and unusual punishment.

34. Washington v. Harper, 494 U.S. 210, 229 (1990). This issue was of considerable consequence for Harper's Due Process Rights. As the Court indicated, "[w]e have no doubt that . . . respondent possesses a significant liberty interest in avoiding the unwanted administration of anti-psychotic drugs under the Due Process Clause of the Fourteenth Amendment." *Id.*

35. WINICK, *supra* note 1, at 3; *see also Washington*, 494 U.S. at 227; Arrigo & Tasca, *supra* note 2, at 27.

36. As the Court indicated, "[t]he drugs may be administered for no purpose other than treatment, and only under the direction of a licensed psychiatrist." *Washington*, 494 U.S. at 226.

37. *See id.* at 227. During an administrative hearing and within the time frame that Harper had ceased taking his medications, he responded violently toward correctional staff member. *See id.* at 248 n. 18. This further solidified the Court's concern for Harper posing some demonstrable danger when refusing treatment.

38. For other cases reflecting this non-intrusive posture, *see, e.g.*, Youngberg v. Romeo, 457 U.S. 307 (1982) (on the rights of the mentally retarded); Thornburgh

Further, we note that *Harper* endeavored to balance treatment needs with liberty demands within a prison context, suggesting that the incompetency of the inmate expressed through an implied or actual risk of danger was the most dispositive on the issue of forced medication.

Consistent with the holding in *Ford*, *Harper* examined what was in the best interest of the prisoner in relation to the state (i.e., the correctional facility, its constituency groups, and society in general). Where the *Ford* case found unconstitutional the execution of an incompetent death row inmate without further, though unspecified, justification, *Harper* determined that unwanted medical intervention for mentally disordered offenders was similarly unconstitutional, *unless* compelling state interests could be articulated. The Court concluded in *Harper* that when a prisoner poses a dangerous threat to others in the correctional facility and when the inmate's treatment is in his or her best medical interest, then coercive intervention is constitutionally permissible. Left unresolved, however, was whether the logic of *Ford* and *Harper* applied equally to incompetent death row inmates who invoked their right to refuse treatment. This matter was addressed in *Perry v. Louisiana*.[39]

D. Perry v. Louisiana

The case of *Perry v. Louisiana* is significant for purposes of scrutinizing and ascertaining the government's interests in requiring that the psychiatric intervention forcibly administered to incompetent prisoners be medically appropriate.[40] In other words, the *Harper* decision did not address the full context in which a right to refuse drug therapy could be successfully asserted within the correctional milieu, although it seemed to imply it. In *Perry*, the particular correctional context was death row. At issue was whether an incompetent mentally ill offender enjoyed the right to refuse drug treatment, as secured under the Eighth and Fourteenth Amendments, when said treatment was administered for purposes of competency restoration and execution.[41]

---

v. Abbot, 409 U.S. 401 (1989) (for related prison rights); and Parham v. J.R., 442 U.S. 584 (1979) (for the rights of mentally ill juveniles). For a theoretical and legal analysis of the Court's deference in these matters, *see* Bruce Arrigo, *The Logic of Identity and the Politics of Justice: Establishing a Right to Community-Based Treatment for the Institutionalized Mentally Disabled*, 18 NEW ENG. J. CRIM. & CIV. CONFINEMENT 1, 23-29 (1992) [hereinafter *Logic*].

39. Perry v. Louisiana, 498 U.S. 38 (1990).

40. As Winick posits, "[w]as the requirement that medication be medically indicated an element of the Court's constitutional standard, or merely a factor contained in the record that allowed the majority to feel more comfortable about its decision?" WINICK, *supra* note 1, at 272-73.

41. *See* WINICK, *supra* note 1, at 273. At the trial stage, the court argued that

Although the Court granted *certiorari* to hear the constitutional question raised by *Perry*, resolution of the matter was avoided following oral arguments, given the intervening decision in *Washington v. Harper*.[42] Thus, the case was remanded to the Louisiana State Supreme Court. Relying on the *Harper* ruling, the Louisiana Supreme Court found that an incompetent death row prisoner could not be forcibly medicated for the primary purpose of restoring competency for execution.[43] Indeed, the Court distinguished *Perry* from *Harper* by stating that coercive medication of the inmate awaiting execution neither improved prison safety and staff welfare nor served the best medical interest of the psychiatrically disordered offender.[44] Thus, while *Harper* acknowledged coercive treatment for incompetent prisoners under constitutionally legitimate and clearly specified conditions, *Perry* essentially limited such intrusiveness.[45]

We note, however, that the *Harper-Perry* distinction does not reflect a substantial difference in approach to treatment, competency, and execution issues regarding the mentally ill as originally developed in *Ford*. Instead, there is a more consistent line of legal thought at work with these three cases. Indeed, the holding in *Perry* merely *limits* the scope of execution for incompetent death row offenders who invoke their treatment refusal rights. In other words, the applicability of *Perry* only extends to those cases in which the state admits its purpose: medicate to execute. Under these conditions, treatment administered for the sole purpose of

---

forcible medication was necessary and reasonable because the state interest in carrying out the verdict imposed by the jury overrode any interest that Mr. Perry had in avoiding unwanted medication. Perry appealed, arguing that he had a right to refuse treatment in the form of anti-psychotic medication. The U.S. Supreme Court remanded the case to the state for reconsideration, given the intervening matter of *Washington v. Harper*, 494 U.S. 210 (1990). The Supreme Court of Louisiana addressed the concern posed in *Perry* in *State v. Perry*, 610 So.2d 746 (La. 1992).

42. 494 U.S. 210 (1990). *See also* WINICK, *supra* note 1, at 299.

43. *See* Arrigo & Tasca, *supra* note 2, at 23-26; *see also Competency to be Executed*, *supra* note 2, at 328-32.

44. In particular, the court concluded that the administration of forced medical treatment to facilitate execution did not "further the best medical interest of the prisoner and the state's own interest in prison safety . . . [nor could] forced administration of anti-psychotic drugs . . . be used by the state for the purpose of punishment." State v. Perry, 610 So.2d at 751-752.

45. As Justice Dennis stated, commenting on the contrasting nature of the two cases, "the program of forcible medication at issue in the *Perry* case was initiated by the prosecutorial arm of the state and . . . would ultimately result in the patient's execution, not his best interests, medical or otherwise." State v. Perry, 610 So.2d at 747. Unlike *Harper*, the regimen of drug treatment in *Perry* was not essential for medical treatment; rather, it was an integral part of the execution process. *See* Arrigo & Tasca, *supra* note 2.

competency restoration and execution is medical punishment, ostensibly prohibited under the Federal Constitution.[46] Forcibly injecting dangerous mind altering drugs into a prisoner, in order to make a death row inmate competent circumvents the holding in *Ford*. Interestingly this does not guarantee that mentally ill prisoners awaiting execution and asserting a right to refuse treatment would, in all instances, be protected from capital punishment, despite Eighth and Fourteenth Amendment safeguards. Indeed, consistent with the holding in *Harper*, to the extent that an inmate presented a dangerous risk to other prisoners, to correctional staff, and to himself, forced drug therapy could be constitutionally ordered. This result could follow, notwithstanding an inmate's liberty interest in refusing involuntary psychiatric treatment and in avoiding medical punishment. This weighty matter has yet to be addressed by the U.S. Supreme Court.

While the decisions in *Ford*, *Harper*, and *Perry* collectively represent the state of the restrictions imposed by constitutional law on treatment refusal for incompetent inmates, they provide a somewhat uncertain legal standard regarding the execution of mentally ill offenders. This uncertainty is directly linked not only to whether the U.S. Supreme Court would concur with Louisiana's decision in *Perry*, but whether it would, consistent with *Harper*, forcibly treat violent and aggressive death row prisoners suffering from a mental disorder. In the latter instance, while the inmate would no longer pose a risk of danger to self or others, his or her renewed competency would give rise to execution in contravention of the prisoner's right to refuse unwanted medication.[47] We contend that answering these matters is, in part, related to how the Court understands the meaning of competency and treatment in relation to the mentally ill offender and the death row prisoner. In order to assist the Court in evaluating its implicit assumptions and hidden values on these important issues, we rely on several insights contained in critical legal theory and discourse analysis.

---

46. *See Competency to be Executed*, *supra* note 2, at 330; *see also supra* note 44 and accompanying text. As Winick observes, "'[m]edical punishment' is a concept alien to American constitutional tradition and does not comport with human dignity. Therefore, it would arguably constitute cruel and unusual punishment." WINICK, *supra* note 1, at 300.

47. It is also worth noting that there are several clinical and ethical implications involved in restoring to competency a prisoner on death row, even when, ostensibly, it is in the offender's best medical interest. The effect is that while the individual would be restored and made psychologically "well," he or she would then be executed following the administered psychiatric treatment. *See supra* note 28 and accompanying text.

III. THEORETICAL DEVELOPMENTS: ON STRUCTURAL LEGAL SEMIOTICS AND LEGAL DECONSTRUCTIONISM

A. Semiotics, Structuralism, and Structural Legal Semiotics

Critical theory building in law has developed considerably during the past two decades, and its growth has been particularly appreciable in the area of discourse analysis.[48] One expression of discourse analysis is semiotics.[49] Semiotics contains a variety of forms as developed and applied in the legal sphere.[50] The particular brand of legal semiotics we draw atten-

48. For a lucid account of the various critical approaches in the sociology of law developed over the last two decades including postmodern feminist jurisprudence, constitutive theory and law, critical race theory, legal deconstructionism, and legal semiotics *see* MILOVANOVIC, *supra* note 8, at 141-84.

49. Semiotics is the study of "signs" and "sign systems." A sign is any written or verbal expression. It can be a word, phrase, gesture, extra-verbal cue, silence, noise, etc., provided it conveys some meaning beyond what is written, spoken, or observed. Thus, a sign signifies something beyond itself; that is, beyond what is written, spoken, or observed. When signs are clustered together within a particular domain of inquiry (e.g., sports, war, computer science), we may speak of a system of signs or a sign language system. *See* THOMAS SEBEOK, ENCYCLOPEDIC DICTIONARY OF SEMIOTICS (1986). Law, and more particularly, law and psychiatry, function as a sign system because medicolegal discourse utilizes specialized expressions, words, or phrases that convey unique meaning within its own system of communication. *See* ARRIGO, *supra* note 6, at 135-40; *see also* CONTOURS, *supra* note 7, at 151-74, 203-04. For more on the general development of semiotics, *see generally* FERDINAND DE SAUSSURE, COURSE IN GENERAL LINGUISTICS (Charles Bally & Sechaye eds., Wade Baskin trans. 1966); BENJAMIN WHORF, LANGUAGE, THOUGHT, AND REALITY (Wohn B. Carroll ed. 1966); FERRUCCIO ROSSI-LANDI, LINGUISTICS AND ECONOMICS (1977); CHARLES PEIRCE, THE PHILOSOPHY OF PEIRCE: SELECTED WRITINGS (Justus Bulcher ed. 1956); CHARLES PEIRCE, COLLECTED PAPERS OF CHARLES SANDERS PEIRCE (Charles Hartshorne & Paul Weiss, eds. 1965); UMBERTO ECO, A THEORY OF SEMIOTICS (1979).

50. For a comprehensive overview of the vagaries of legal semiotics, *see generally* Susan W. Tiefenbrun, *Legal Semiotics*, 5 CARDOZO ARTS & ENT. L. J. 89, 89-156 (1986). For a more practical and philosophical analysis of legal semiotics, *see* ARRIGO, *supra* note 6, at 27-58. For a much more detailed assessment featuring *the Peircean model, see, e.g.*, ROBERTA KEVELSON, THE LAW AS A SYSTEM OF SIGNS (1988); ROBERTA KEVELSON, CHARLES S. PEIRCE'S METHOD OF METHODS (1987); ROBERTA KEVELSON, PEIRCE, PARADOX, PRAXIS: THE IMAGE, THE CONFLICT, AND THE LAW (Thomas Sebock et al., eds. 1990); for *the Greimasian model see generally* BERNARD JACKSON, SEMIOTICS AND LEGAL THEORY (1985); and for *the Lacanian model, see generally* CONTOURS, *supra* note 7, at 175-201; DRAGAN MILOVANOVIC, POSTMODERN LAW AND DISORDER: PSYCHOANALYTIC SEMIOTICS, CHAOS AND JURIDIC EXEGESES (1992) [hereinafter DISORDER]; DRAGAN MILOVANOVIC, POSTMODERN CRIMINOLOGY (1997) [hereinafter CRIMINOLOGY]; DAVID S. CAUDILL, LACAN AND THE SUBJECT OF LAW: TOWARD A

tion to is structural[51] legal semiotics. The term "structure" derives from the Latin *struere* which means "to build" or "to contrive." Structuralism, then, denotes the act or process of building, and structural semiotics refers to the search for identifiable *foundations* embedded in all language systems.[52] Structuralism is based, in part, on the linguistic work of Ferdinand de Saussure.[53] It also draws from Russian formalism and literary criticism inspired by Roman Jakobson, the anthropology of Claude Levi-Strauss, and the narrative analyses of Roland Barthes and Algirdas Greimas.[54]

The search for essential stabilities, underlying truths, and fundamental "laws" of human existence are found, for example, in the 19th and 20th century structuralist accounts of the mind,[55] culture,[56] and society.[57] According to the structuralist tradition, every object of inquiry must necessarily be conceived as a structure or as a whole.[58] This sense of complete-

---

PSYCHOANALYTICAL CRITICAL LEGAL THEORY (1997).

51. For more extensive descriptions of structuralism and the structuralist project, *see generally* THE STRUCTURALISTS FROM MARX TO LEVI-STRAUSS (Richard DeGeorge and Fernande DeGeorge eds. 1972); TERENCE HAWKES, STRUCTURALISM AND SEMIOTICS (1977); STRUCTURALISM AND SINCE: FROM LEVI-STRAUSS TO DERRIDA (John Sturrock ed. 1979); ART BERMAN, FROM THE NEW CRITICISM TO DECONSTRUCTIONISM: THE RECEPTION OF STRUCTURALISM AND POST-STRUCTURALISM (1988).

52. Here we refer to the deep structures of meaning (e.g., cultural, biological, physical, psychological) that account for all social phenomena and human social interaction, conveyed through the activity of speech or writing. *See* GREIMAS, *supra* note 8, at 3-10.

53. *See generally* SAUSSURE, *supra* note 49.

54. *See* BERMAN, *supra* note 51, at 114-222; *see also* Tiefenbrun, *supra* note 49, at 113-47. We note that many other linguistic, literary criticism, and anthropological contributions on the nature of structuralism can be traced to the work of additional commentators. In linguistics, *see generally* C.K. OGDEN & I.A. RICHARDS, THE MEANING OF MEANING: A STUDY OF THE INFLUENCE OF LANGUAGE UPON THOUGHT AND OF THE SCIENCE OF SYMBOLISM (1926); in literary criticism, *see, e.g.*, JONATHAN CULLER, THE PURSUIT OF SIGNS: SEMIOTICS, LITERATURE, DECONSTRUCTION (1981); in anthropology, *see generally* A.J. ARNAUD, ESSAI D'ANALYSE STRUCTURALE DU CODE CIVIL FRANCAIS (1973).

55. *See, e.g.*, SIGMUND FREUD, THE EGO AND THE ID (Joan Riviere trans. 1927) (discussing the id, ego, and superego structures of the mind).

56. *See generally* CLAUDE LEVI-STRAUSS, THE SAVAGE MIND (1962) (discussing the anthropological studies on the similarity between "primitive" and "cultured" thinking which, Levi-Strauss believed, revealed a general, universal structure of human culture).

57. *See generally* KARL MARX, CAPITAL (1967) (addressing the formulation of society as composed of a super*structure* and infra*structure* or base). According to Marx, we can locate an overall structure and several substructures within each of them.

58. This emphasis on wholeness is in opposition to the atomistic view of the world in which things exist only in relation to other things, and these relationships

ness gives order to an otherwise fragmented and uncertain future.[59] The subject, and all of our unsubstantiated claims to autonomy, efficacy, causality, are supplanted by scientific rigor, totalizing truths, and objectivist knowledge.[60]

As previously noted, structuralism extensively employs Saussure's linguistic model. Thus, language is an essential determinant of structure. Structuralists maintain that language shapes the world, and the world, in turn, is known and determined by the non-referential language system in use:[61] it is a closed system of communication. Language, understood semiotically, then, implies that it is possible to uncover the structural meanings (hidden values or implicit assumptions) conveyed in a system of communication. Law is one example of such a linguistic coordinate system,[62] and the intersection of law and psychiatry (i.e., medicolegal discourse) is a more specialized variation of it.[63] Given our appreciation for semiotics and structuralism, we understand, therefore, that structural legal

---

exist only as part of a whole. Philosophically, then, structuralism is the very antithesis of the existentialist-humanist notion of a world in which each subject or individual is understood as an individual rather than merely a part of the whole. *See generally* JEAN PAUL SARTRE, BEING AND NOTHINGNESS (Hazel E. Barnes trans. 1956); EXISTENTIALISM FROM DOSTOEVSKY TO SARTRE (William Kaufmann ed. 1956); MARTIN HEIDEGGER, THE QUESTION OF BEING (William Kluback & Jean T. Wilde trans. 1958); GABRIEL MARCEL, THE MYSTERY OF BEING (1950-51).

59. This wholeness was a search for order within the cosmos. As Barthes explains, "[t]he aim of all structuralist activity, in the fields of both thought and poetry, is to reconstitute an object, and, by this process, to make known the rules of functioning, or "functions," of this object. Th[is] structure . . . brings out something that remained invisible, or, if you like, unintelligible in the natural object." ROLAND BARTHES, ESSAIS CRITIQUES 213 (1964).

60. As a result, structuralists celebrated the disappearance of the subject. "The subject was dismissed, or radically decentered, as merely an effect of language, culture, or the unconscious, and denied casual or creative efficacy." BEST & KELLNER, *supra* note 8, at 19.

61. For example, Levi-Strauss appropriated his anthropologically-inspired linguistic model to a structural investigation of kinship systems, mythology, and rituals. *See generally* CLAUDE LEVI- STRAUSS, STRUCTURAL ANTHROPOLOGY (1963). The early Lacan developed his psychoanalytically-informed semiotics to a structural and mathematical account of desire (*De sir*). *See generally* LACAN, *supra* note 8. Althusser applied his modernist political economy rationale to a structural rendition of Marxism. *See generally* LOUIS ALTHUSSER, LENIN AND PHILOSOPHY AND OTHER ESSAYS (Ben Brewster trans. 1971).

62. *See, e.g.*, Dragan Milovanovic, *Juridico-Linguistic Communicative Markets: Towards a Semiotic Analysis*, 10 CONTEMP. CRISES 281, 285-96 (1986) [hereinafter *Juridico-Linguistic*]; Dragan Milovanovic, *Jailhouse Lawyers and Jailhouse Lawyering*, 16 INT'L J. SOC. L. 455, 455-75 (1988) [hereinafter *Jailhouse*].

63. *See* ARRIGO, *supra* note 6, at 135-40; *see also* CONTOURS, *supra* note 7, at 47-93.

semiotics is the study of legal language, understood to be a collection of "signs."[64] The two particular medicolegal signs we investigate is this Article include "treatment" and "competency."

The model of structural legal semiotics we appropriate is borrowed from Bernard Jackson.[65] His model utilizes the "semiotic square"[66] or semiotic grid, which is designed to tell us more about the process of meaning creation and the various interpretations that attach to the grouping of words and/or phrases specifically selected to convey our thoughts.[67] As applied to law, his schema is referred to as the narrative coherence model.[68] Methodologically, the semiotic square is helpful to legal inquiry in that it allows one to chart and lay out some of the discernible, though concealed, meanings lodged in the more formalistic language of law.[69]

---

64. *See supra* note 58 and accompanying text. There are differing perspectives on the meaning of signs. *See* Bruce Arrigo, *Insanity Defense Reform and the Sign of Abolition: Re-visiting Montana's Experience*, 10 INT'L J. SEMIOTICS L. 191, 195-210 (1997) [hereinafter *Reform*] (for useful descriptions of three semiotic sign models with a targeted law-psychology example). For purposes of this Article, given our more structural orientation, we rely on the *Greimasian* approach (through the linguistics of Saussure) as appropriated by Bernard Jackson. *See* JACKSON, *supra* note 50 and accompanying text. Accordingly, a sign is constituted by a "signifier" and a "signified." The signifier is the acoustic-visual image (i.e., the naming of a thought). The signified is the content we assign, through spoken or written language, to the signifier. For example, words or phrases such as "diminished capacity," "informed consent," "execution," "right to refuse treatment," "mental illness," "guilty but mentally ill," "dangerous," "reasonableness," and the like are signifiers. We fill in their meaning, give them value, through other words or phrases that express these ideas. "Language is a 'system of signs that expresses ideas, or signifieds, through differing signifiers that produce meaning." BEST & KELLNER, *supra* note 8, at 19; *see also* SAUSSURE, *supra* note 49, at 120-22.

65. *See generally* BERNARD JACKSON, MAKING SENSE IN LAW (1995) [hereinafter LAW]; *see also* JACKSON, *supra* note 50 and accompanying text.

66. The semiotic square was originally developed by Greimas and it represents the most rudimentary element of Greimasian structural semiotics. *See, e.g.*, ALGIRDAS GREIMAS, ON MEANING: SELECTED WRITINGS (Paul J. Perron and Frank H. Collins trans. 1987). For application to law, *see* GREIMAS, *supra* note 8, at 108-114 (1990).

67. *See* LAW, *supra* note 65, at 140-63; *see also* JACKSON, *supra* note 50, at 74-110, 117; MILOVANOVIC, *supra* note 8, at 114-18.

68. Jackson is interested in uncovering the "underlying non-verbalized narrative (deep) structure" cloaked by the superficial structure of legal discourse and decision making. MILOVANOVIC, *supra* note 8, at 117-18. This deeper level of signification reveals an "unconscious rationality which transmits cultural values and which is expressed in cultural products [e.g., U.S. Supreme Court rulings], albeit it in an often transformed manner." LAW, *supra* note 65, at 93.

69. As a pedagogical tool, the semiotic square "allow[s] the investigator to discover how otherwise concealed meaning is generated from and embedded within deeply hidden language structures, thereby producing coherent narrative construc-

Thus, as a research tool, the grid permits one, in a novel and creative way, to discover something more about the unconscious intent behind what jurists say and what they mean.[70]

DIAGRAM 1: SEMIOTIC SQUARE

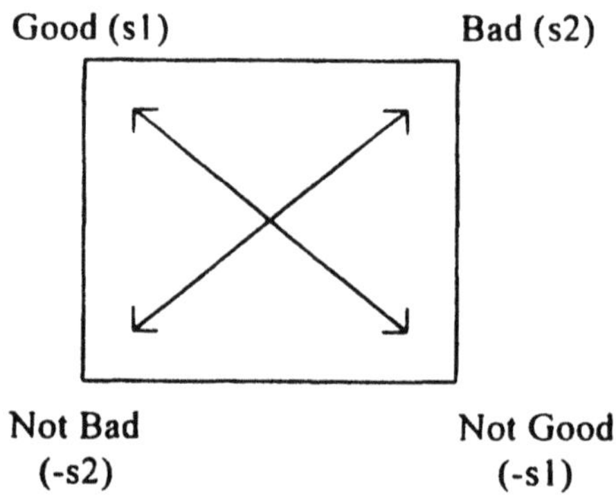

As Diagram 1 indicates, the semiotic square is fashioned around binary oppositions and the interplay of meaning at work in these relationships. These include contraries (strong oppositions) and contradictions (clear negations). Examples of binary oppositions that are contraries include "day versus night," "right versus wrong," "healthy versus ill," "good versus bad." Examples of binary opposition that are contradictions include "not day versus not night," "not right versus not wrong," "not healthy versus not ill," "not good versus not bad." By indicating the dominant term in the binary opposition (e.g., "day," "right," "healthy," and "good"), the negations are immediately implied ("not day," "not right," "not healthy," and "not good").

There is a built-in logic to this structural model of legal analysis demonstrating the subtlety of language and producing coherence in thought where semantic differences are examined closely for what they communicate.[71] To illustrate, the term "not good" includes something other than bad (e.g., problematic, difficult, troubling), and the term "not bad" includes something other than good (e.g., marginally acceptable, satisfactory, okay). Operationally, the semiotic square is designed in such a way

---

tions." *Reform*, *supra* note 64, at 197-98.

70. As Balkin accurately points out in his presentation of Derridean legal deconstructionism, "(as everyone thinks) we mean more than we say, we also say more than we mean. Our words seem to perform tricks that we had not intended, establish connections that we had not considered, lead to conclusions that were not present in our minds when we spoke or wrote." Balkin, *supra* note 10, at 778.

71. *See Reform*, *supra* note 64, at 198.

that the identification of one term in the grid makes possible the discovery of the other three terms, given the function of contraries and contradictions.[72]

In this Article's following section, we rely on the logic of the semiotic square, as our method for conducting structural legal semiotic analysis, to discover the deeper, unconscious meanings, for the signs "treatment" and "competency." We contend that this particular form of legal inquiry tells us more about the U.S. Supreme Court's understanding of mentally disordered prisoners and their death row executions. Before we engage in this process, however, we consider how the theory of legal deconstructionism will also assist in our overall evaluative task.

B. Post-Structuralism, Deconstruction, and Legal Deconstructionism

Post-structuralism emerged as a critical rebuttal of the structuralist assumptions regarding mind, culture, and society.[73] Where the aims of structuralism included a search for foundational truths, absolute certainty, objectivist knowledge, and systemic wholeness,[74] post-structuralism waged "war" on all totalizing forms of reason, logic, and rationality.[75] Post-structuralists alleged that such structures were illusions of science and contrivances of politics because of the intervening variable of language. Unlike the structuralists who advocated the importance of discourse within narrowly confined parameters of meaning (i.e., the code of speech in use as non-referential), post-structuralists celebrated the essential undecidability of meaning inherent in what we say or in what we write.[76]

One explanation for the convictions of post-structuralist thought is contained in the deconstructionist work of Jacques Derrida.[77] Derrida

---

72. *See* JACKSON, *supra* note 50, at 77.

73. *See* BEST & KELLNER, *supra* note 8, at 20; BERMAN, *supra* note 51, at 199-200.

74. *See supra* note, 51-52 and accompanying text.

75. *See Peripheral Core*, *supra* note 8, at 450. The post-structuralist movement embraced incompleteness, fragmentation, uncertainty, different forms of consciousness, multiplicities of identities, and the instability of meaning. *See* BEST & KELLNER, *supra* note 8, at 20-21.

76. As Derrida explains, "the meaning of meaning is [of] infinite implication. [There is an] indefinite referral of signifier to signified . . . . Its force is a certain pure and infinite equivocality which gives signified meaning no respite, no rest . . . it always signifies again and differs." JACQUES DERRIDA, SPEECH AND PHENOMENA AND OTHER ESSAYS ON HUSSERL'S THEORY OF SIGNS 43 (1973) [hereinafter SPEECH].

77. *See generally* JACQUES DERRIDA, POSITIONS (1981) [hereinafter POSITIONS]; JACQUES DERRIDA, MARGINS OF PHILOSOPHY (1981) [hereinafter PHILOSOPHY]; DERRIDA, *supra* note 8; SPEECH, *supra* note 76. For an accessible and general

offers a substantial critique of Western philosophy and thought he terms the "metaphysics of presence."[78] The metaphysics of presence is an effort to expose hierarchical oppositions implied or embedded in words or phrases used to convey meaning.[79] Examples of hierarchical oppositions include "objective/subjective," "real/appearance," "straight/gay," "positive/negative," "normal/abnormal." In each instance, the former term is valued and privileged as presence, while the corresponding latter term is devalued and relegated as absence.[80] These value positions are troubling because they connote certain shared and unstated beliefs in the primacy of the first term *over and against* the second one.[81] Potentially, this is extremely problematic, particularly in relation to what are defined as acceptable forms of human social interaction, appropriate modes of sense making, and customary ways of being. Ultimately, this can lead to the privileging of certain ideas over others.[82]

Deconstruction,[83] then, can expose the biases or preferences contained within the simplest of notions (i.e., hierarchical oppositions).[84] This is not

overview of Derrida's thought highlighting his distinction between speaking and writing, *see* Iddo Landau, *Early and Later Deconstruction in the Writings of Jacques Derrida*, 14 CARDOZO L. REV. 1895, 1895-1909 (1993).

78. *See* Balkin, *supra* note 10, at 746-51. Elaborating upon this Derridean notion, Culler contends that "philosophy has been a 'metaphysics of presence,' the only metaphysics we know." JOHNATHAN CULLER, ON DECONSTRUCTION: THEORY AND CRITICISM AFTER STRUCTURALISM 92 (1982).

79. *See* Balkin, *supra* note 10, at 746-51.

80. *See* MILOVANOVIC, *supra* note 8, at 101.

81. This notion of "privileging" the first term in binary oppositions is termed "logocentricism" by Derrida. *See* DERRIDA, *supra* note 8, at 3. The implied centrality of the dominant position's logic represented by the first value position masks the interdependence of the two terms. In Western thought, there is a "hidden premise that what is most apparent to our consciousness—what is most simple, basic, or immediate—is most real, true, foundational, or important." Balkin, *supra* note 10, at 747-48.

82. Balkin, *supra* note 10, at 746-51. For applications to medical justice and the hierarchical oppositions it employs, *see* Bruce Arrigo, *Martial Metaphors and Medical Justice: Implications for Law, Crime, and Deviance*, 24 J. POL. MIL. SOC. (forthcoming Fall 1999) [hereinafter *Martial Metaphors*].

83. Clearly, the radicality of deconstruction we propose is not a complete destabilization of meaning *ad infinitum*. More specifically, we are not rejecting the modernist notions of progress, emancipation, reason, and the subject in a wholesale fashion. *See* Fuchs & Ward, *supra* note 8, at 483. This would be a revolutionary project in law and, more particularly, medicolegal discourse beyond the scope of the present Article. What we are contesting, however, is the legitimacy and institutional authority that follows from ossified meaning, privileged as the *dominant* interpretation rendering alternatives readings and, consequently, different expressions in law and legal thought non-justiciable. *See id.* at 486-88.

84. *See* BEST & KELLNER, *supra* note 8, at 229; *see also* BERMAN, *supra* note 51,

to imply that deconstructionism functions as a totalizing proscription for social change. It merely reveals and de-centers, although incompletely and temporarily, how legal arguments often disguise ideological positions.[85] Derrida's insights are important to our project because several of his major philosophical tenets direct our attention to the unconscious intent of the U.S. Supreme Court on matters of refusing treatment for incompetent mentally ill prisoners awaiting execution. In order to demonstrate where and how legal deconstructionism is useful in this regard, we briefly review three Derridean concepts. These three concepts include: (1) the reversal of hierarchies; (2) differance and trace; and (3) arguments that undo themselves.[86]

1. Reversal of Hierarchies

By inverting privileged value positions, Derrida does not intend that one create new and permanent power relations. The logic of reversal is simply to ascertain what additional insights might be contained in the value positions and their newly articulated or scripted arrangement once having switched them.[87] In addition, however, this deconstructive activity is quite revealing because it shows the mutual interdependence of the two value positions. Consider, for example, the term "sanity" as used in the mental health criminal and civil law context.[88] Deconstructionists argue that, in the first instance, insanity is a derivative concept based on the other value or term. Thus, we have a binary opposition. On closer inspection, however, we note that the sanity of person "A" depends on the insanity of person "B" and vice versa. The meanings we assign to one are dependent

---

at 204-08.

85. As Balkin concludes:

> [d]econstruction by its very nature is an analytic tool and not a synthetic one. It can displace a hierarchy momentarily, it can shed light on otherwise hidden dependencies of concepts, but it cannot propose new hierarchies of thought or substitute new foundations. These are by definition logocentric projects, which deconstruction defines itself against.

Balkin, *supra* note 10, at 786.

86. A fourth concept worth mentioning is the logic of the supplement. *See* Derrida, *supra* note 8, at 141-64. This notion is developed more systematically in relation to Derrida's position on arguments that unground themselves. *See infra* note 96 and accompanying text. Although we identify the supplement as an important component to deconstructionism, its utility is marginal for purposes of our legal deconstruction of the U.S. Supreme Court's view of competency and treatment issues related to mentally disordered prisoners on death row. For more on the application of the supplement in the legal sphere, *see* Balkin, *supra* note 10, at 758-61.

87. *See id.* at 746-51.

88. *See, e.g.*, RALPH REISNER & CHRISTOPHER SLOBOGIN, LAW AND THE MENTAL HEALTH SYSTEM: CRIMINAL AND CIVIL ASPECTS (1997).

upon the meanings we assign to the other. What we thought was the privileged value (i.e., sanity) is itself dependent upon the concept it was privileged over (i.e., insanity). Thus, not only is neither term foundational, but both mutually rely upon each other to express thought and action. This leads us to ponder what replacement forms of logic would be presented if the hierarchical arrangement was indeed reversed.

2. Differance and the Trace

The concept of mutual interdependence given the two terms in a binary opposition is important to Derrida's notion of "differance" (with an "a"). The use of the word "differance" intends always and already three separate but related meanings.[89] As Balkin describes it:

> *Differance* simultaneously indicates that (1) the terms of an oppositional hierarchy are differentiated from each other (which is what determines them); (2) each term in the hierarchy defers the other (in the sense of making the other term wait for the first term); and (3) each term in the hierarchy defers *to* the other (in the sense of being fundamentally dependent upon the other).[90]

Let us return to our example of "sanity versus insanity" for further explication. "Differance" signals how the two value positions are different; how, given the metaphysics of presence and absence, the spoken or written term postpones, suspends, or represses the other, and how both values are mutually interdependent on one another for their identities.[91] Again, the play of differences and dependencies described here operate simultaneously.

"Differance," however, is significant to the deconstructionist agenda for a related reason. Derrida's idea of trace implies that the two values in the binary opposition rely for their clarity and cohesion on the differentiation between them.[92] In other words, each term (i.e., "sanity" and "insanity") contains the vestige of the other within it, and it is this lingering trace which anchors "differance" making the deconstruction of hierarchical oppositions possible.[93] The task of a legal deconstructionist analysis, then, is

89. *See* PHILOSOPHY, *supra* note 77, at 3; *see also* POSITIONS, *supra* note 77, at 39-40; Balkin, *supra* note 10, at 752.

90. Balkin, *supra* note 10, at 752.

91. *See* MILOVANOVIC, *supra* note 8, at 101; *see also Martial Metaphors*, *supra* note 82.

92. *See* Balkin, *supra* note 10, at 752; *see also* DERRIDA, *supra* note 8, at 46-47.

93. *See* DERRIDA, *supra* note 8, at 46-47. Milovanovic described the Derridean notion of trace in relation to legal deconstruction as follows:

> in deconstructive strategies, one must start with the idea that any term (presence) always implies a hidden one (absence); both are essential to any meaning of each. The *trace* is that part that exists in each and maintains the relation. In many ways, it is the "glue." For those prac-

to identify the play of differances and the mutual interdependencies between terms in a hierarchical opposition, as a way of demonstrating the positional, relational and provisional nature of all phenomena.[94]

3. Arguments That Undo Themselves

Inverting hierarchies in binary oppositions can be quite illuminating. One of the things this activity can point to is that the arguments supporting the privileging of the dominant term may be the reasons for endorsing the other value. There is a logic of justification that is undone or ungrounded through this deconstructive agenda.[95]

Consider, for example, the values assigned to being mentally healthy versus being mentally ill.[96] The logic of psychological health implies that one behaves appropriately, thinks rationally, speaks coherently, feels naturally, lives ordinarily, and simply *is* normal. There is a certain predictabil-

---

> ticing deconstruction, the challenge is to identify the absent term which maintains the term that is felt as present.

MILOVANOVIC, *supra* note 8, at 101-02.

94. We note, too, that the concepts of "differance" and trace are not *essentialist* terms in Derrida's epistemology. This thinking is antithetical to the deconstructionist project. Indeed, as Rorty contends, such notions cannot be "divinized." *See* Richard Rorty, *Philosophy as a Kind of Writing: An Essay on Derrida*, 10 NEW LITERARY HIST. 141, 153 (1978). "Differance" and trace fleetingly capture the "foundationless, provisional . . . , or reversibl(e)" nature of meaning in human affairs. Balkin, *supra* note 10, at 752 n. 26.

95. Perhaps the most widely discussed and debated example of "ungrounding" comes from Derrida's investigation of speech and writing. *See* DERRIDA, *supra* note 8, at 30-44, 166-67. Drawing attention to the work of Rousseau, Levi-Strauss, and Saussure, Derrida notes that there is a non-accidental preference for speech over writing in their respective philosophies. *See id.* at 29-44 (discussing Saussure); *see id.* at 101-268 (discussing Levi- Strauss and Rousseau). The former term is privileged as presence, while the corresponding latter term is delegitimized as absence. Derrida demonstrates that, notwithstanding all the limitations of writing, "speech is a kind of 'writing' that suffers from the same inadequacies attributed to writing." Balkin, *supra* note 10, at 757. Thus, the logocentricism of speech is undone by deconstructing the terms in the binary opposition.

96. For a sociological analysis, *see generally* THOMAS SCHEFF, BEING MENTALLY ILL (1984). For a sociolegal analysis, *see generally* CAROL A.B. WARREN, THE COURT OF LAST RESORT: MENTAL ILLNESS AND THE LAW (1982). For an historical and philosophical review, *see generally* MICHEL FOUCAULT, MADNESS AND CIVILIZATION: A HISTORY OF INSANITY IN THE AGE OF REASON (Richard Howard trans. 1965); MICHEL FOUCAULT, MENTAL ILLNESS AND PSYCHOLOGY (1976). For a medicolegal assessment, *see generally* THOMAS SZASZ, LAW, LIBERTY, AND PSYCHIATRY: AN INQUIRY INTO THE SOCIAL USES OF MENTAL HEALTH PRACTICES (1963); THOMAS SZASZ, INSANITY: THE IDEA AND ITS CONSEQUENCES (1987) [hereinafter INSANITY]. For a postmodern psycholegal analysis, *see generally supra* notes 6-7 and accompanying text.

ity, routinization, control, homogeneity, and order implied in this model; however, some degree of deviation is availed to all individuals. Interestingly, we endorse appreciable departures from psychological health, even some forms of extreme dysfunction, provided the pathology produces meaningful results. The elite athlete who engages in intense physical training in order to play better, run faster, and jump higher, is not diagnosed with an obsessive-compulsive disorder. The actor or model who carefully monitors all caloric intake in order to maintain the fashionable waif image portrayed on film or in print is not diagnosed with acute anorexia nervosa. The artist who paints hauntingly surreal images in order to convey the shocking and astonishing conditions of our times is not diagnosed with paranoid schizophrenia. The musician who suffers through atypical sleeping patterns in order to craft beautiful and deeply personal love ballets is not diagnosed with depression.

Each of these examples is an argument that undoes the dominant value position of being mental healthy. In addition, each illustration demonstrates how psychological wellness (i.e., optimal success at sports, entertainment, art, and music) is really a kind of mental illness. Finally, each instance shows how the limitations of psychological illness also represent the inadequacies of emotional wellness.[97]

---

97. The most glaring of limitations is that, just as we cannot say with absolute certainty what mental illness really is, we cannot say with absolute certainty what good mental health is either. Indeed, as the examples suggest, on some occasions it is even better to be more "crazy" than not. This notion of how arguments undo themselves gives rise to Derrida's logic of the supplement. *See* DERRIDA, *supra* note 8, at 144; *see also* Balkin, *supra* note 10, at 758-59. There are two meanings for the term "supplement." The first of these refers to adding something to an already sufficient thing. For example, a professor gives a complete lecture to a class but places on reserve in the university's library the previously prepared notes for the lecture. The notes represent the lecture. The second meaning of the term "supplement" is to fill something in with what it lacks in order to make it self-sufficient. The lecture needs the notes in order to be complete for the students. The logic of the supplement demonstrates how the second term in a hierarchical position (e.g., being mentally ill or insane) can only supplement the first term (e.g., being mentally healthy or sane) in the sense of being an addition to something complete when the first term in the binary opposition can be supplemented by "having a lack that could be fulfilled." Balkin, *supra* note 10, at 759. What is missing in the binary value of mental health? Mental health is not an objective state made present to society; rather, it is but one condition of representing (and masquerading around as) the objective state of existence. Mental health appears to possess Derridean presence; however, similar to mental illness, it is a sham. Both are modes of being. Both are mediations of authentic existence, not absolute ways of comportment. The latter is delayed through the representation of mental health, mental illness and their sundry variations.

IV. Executing the Incompetent Death-Row Prisoner: Contributions from Structural Legal Semiotics and Legal Deconstructionism

The previous section identified two non-traditional models of legal inquiry. We contend that both structural legal semiotics and legal deconstructionism, as distinct methods for engaging in discourse analysis, inform our prior case law assessment of treatment refusal for prisoners with mental disorders awaiting execution. In order to demonstrate the utility of each model's analytical tools, we first present an assessment of the signs "treatment" and "competency" from a structural legal semiotic perspective. We then examine these signs from the standpoint of legal deconstructionism.

A. Structural Legal Semiotics and the Sign of Treatment

Diagram 2: The Sign of Treatment and the Semiotic Square

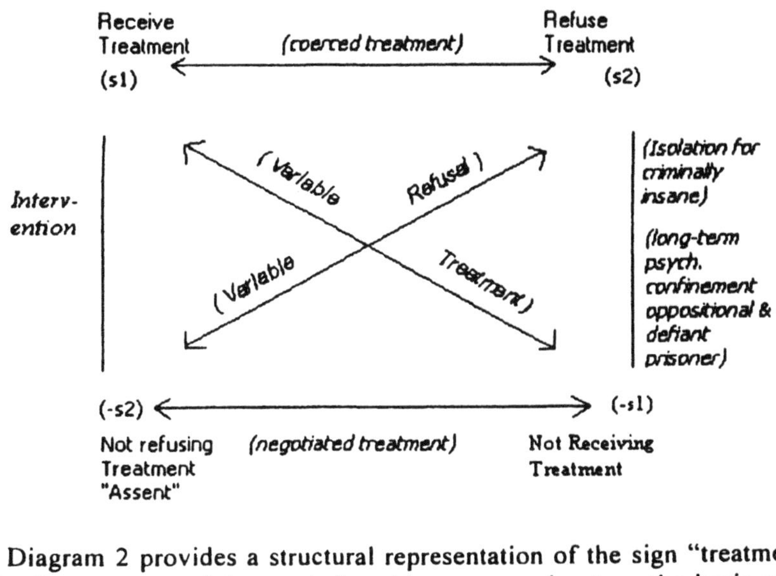

Diagram 2 provides a structural representation of the sign "treatment." The four corners of the semiotic grid are mapped out on the basis of binary oppositions consistent with the model's emphasis on contraries and contradictions. The "s1" term is "receiving treatment."

Its opposite value (the "s2" term) is "refusing treatment." The negation of refusing treatment is "not refusing treatment." This is the "-s2" value.

The negation of receiving treatment is "not receiving treatment." This is the "-s1" term.

We also note that Diagram 2 includes the semantical relationships generated from the contraries and contradictions. The sum of these various associations constitutes the deep structure of meaning[98] at work in the U.S. Supreme Court's evaluation of treatment refusal for mentally disordered prisoners on death row. The individual relationships formed by the interplay of particular binary terms are also revealing. They tell us more about the Court's preference for certain juridical meanings at the expense of certain others. Thus, we are able to comment on those hidden assumptions and implicit values endorsed by the U.S. Supreme Court and those that are not.

In the analysis that follows, we begin with the more obvious associations and move on to those that are less conspicuous. The connection between "receiving treatment" and "refusing treatment" is receiving coerced treatment. In this relationship, we understand that the effect of resisting that which one would otherwise receive can only produce some form of unwanted and forced intervention. The right to forcibly medicate mentally disordered prisoners was precisely the constitutional question at issue in the *Harper* case.[99] Recall, however, that while *Harper* acknowledged the use of coercion under certain circumstances, it did not address forced treatment for incompetent death row inmates. This matter was subsequently examined in the case of *State v. Perry*.[100]

In addition, it is worth noting that while the Court's constitutional analysis in *Harper* and *Perry* hinged on the Eighth Amendment's prohibition of cruel and unusual punishment, the semiotic square and the semantical tension of receiving and refusing treatment enables us to locate this same meaning (i.e., coerced treatment as punishment) without expressed reliance on the Constitution. This is an example of how non-legal language (i.e., the jargon of treatment) is translated into legal discourse.[101]

98. The terms are not chosen randomly. They logically arise from the operation of contraries and contradictions signifying the binary oppositions. Thus, the terms or values themselves are not only an expression of the semiotic square but an accurate representation of how non-legal discourse informs and translates the events of a given case into legal discourse. *See* JACKSON, *supra* note 50, at 102, 86-99; *see also* MILOVANOVIC, *supra* note 8, at 115-17.

99. Washington v. Harper, 494 U.S. 210 (1990) (concluding that coerced treatment was permissible provided it was in the best medical interest of the inmate and secured the safety of correctional personnel and/or other prisoners). *See also supra* notes 32-38 and accompanying text.

100. 610 So.2d 746 (La. 1992). *See also supra* notes 39-45 and accompanying text.

101. For a more general application of this point in law and legal decision making, *see* LAW, *supra* note 65, at 80-86. This point cannot be overemphasized.

The relationship between "receiving treatment" and "not refusing treatment" (i.e., "assent") is "intervention." Treatment assent or, in the less extreme semantical form, treatment allowance is not equivalent to receiving treatment. The former value (assent) is a more active signifier connoting some meaningful participation in or agreement with the decision making process. The latter value (allowance) is a more passive signifier, connoting general acquiescence to, perhaps submissiveness with, medical intervention. In the context of an incompetent prisoner awaiting execution, the tension that is drawn out by the interplay of binary values is the administration of drug therapy (i.e., "intervention") where the result is capital punishment. Similar to our previous semiotic inquiry, doctrinal legal analysis of constitutional law is largely unnecessary for arriving at this stated meaning. We note, though, that the intervention (legally constituted as "medicate to execute") was precisely what the Court rejected in *Perry*.[102] In this ruling, the Louisiana Supreme Court found unconstitutional the termination of a mentally ill prisoner's life where the state's interest was made clear: treat to punish. Thus, we see once again how the grammar of treatment (i.e., "intervention") is transformed into legal discourse (i.e., medicate to execute), consistent with the U.S. Supreme Court's concern for weighty constitutional matters (i.e., the cruel and unusual punishment clause of the Eighth Amendment).

The remaining relationships found among the various contraries and contradictions are not so easily discernible. Given that the space limitations of this Article render our task essentially provisional and exploratory,[103] we focus on only two of the remaining four semantical interplays in binary opposition.

The discursive connection between "refusing treatment" and "not receiving treatment" is twofold. In both instances, the association requires a

---

What it demonstrates is how the events of a case unconsciously become codified by jurists into legal language. This transformation is the result of placing non-legal language on the semiotic square along with legal discourse where the former grammar makes possible the translation of the latter grammar. *See id.* at 84; *see also supra* note 98 and accompanying text.

102. Perry v. Louisiana, 498 U.S. 38 (1990).

103. Our exploration specifically requires that we unpack the underlying structure of meaning formed through unconscious semiotic production. Although certainly useful in their own right, the semantical value of "variable treatment" contained between the binary oppositions "receiving treatment" and "not receiving treatment," as well as the semantical value of "variable refusal" located between the binary tension "receiving treatment" and "not receiving treatment" will not be systematically investigated. The semiotic terms "treatment assent" and "not receiving treatment" are, however, germane to other binary oppositions and, accordingly, will be examined in our structural legal semiotic analysis elsewhere. *See infra* notes 104-110 and accompanying text.

judicial outcome (a meaning) that is less than affirming one's constitutional right to treatment refusal but more than not receiving any treatment at all. On the one hand, the product of the oppositional values suggests isolation for the criminally insane. This is not the same as endorsing treatment refusal and it is more than not receiving treatment. Indeed, it is a "type" of treatment in which medication refusal is acknowledged. On the other hand, the effect of the oppositional terms implies long-term psychiatric confinement for the oppositional and defiant prisoner. Again, this is less than constitutionally upholding one's right to refuse treatment, and it is more than not receiving any medicolegal response. Validating this form of confinement is not as extreme as the semantic option of isolation.[104]

Both semiotic results suggest a number of things regarding the unconscious intent of the Court. Most especially, as a constitutional safeguard, treatment refusal is identified as such a fundamental freedom that any possible judicial recommendation or ruling short of endorsing it completely or requiring compulsory drug treatment (provided *Harper* justifications are in place) are not constitutionally enforceable. In other words, "middle ground" solutions generated from the semiotic square and the binary terms at issue are not within the scope of discursive possibility in law. In addition, the semantical tension underscores an ongoing polemic in mental health law circles. In short, this polarized tension pits the psychiatric community's need for patient treatment[105] against the legal profession's demand for individual liberty.[106] Finally, given the ostensible division between psychiatry and law on such matters,[107] the more essential value at

104. Long-term institutionalization in a mental health unit of a prison, pending the results of a competency determination to exercise one's right to refuse treatment, is precisely the result envisioned by this possibility. Indeed, this was the placement in which Walter Harper was housed. Recall that he was detained in a Special Offender Center under the Washington State Department of Corrections. *See supra* note 33 and accompanying text.

105. On the matter of necessary psychiatric treatment, *see generally* Paul Chadoff, *The Case for Involuntary Hospitalization of the Mentally Ill*, 133 AM. J. PSYCHIATRY 496, 496-501 (1976). On the question of treatment for persons who are obviously ill, *see generally* Darold Treffert, *The Obviously Ill Patient in Need of Treatment: A Fourth Standard for Civil Commitment*, 36 HOSP. & COMMUNITY PSYCHIATRY 259, 259-64 (1985). On the issue of needing to control mentally ill patients, *see, e.g.*, Jack Zusman, *The Need for Intervention: The Reasons for State Control of the Mentally Disordered*, *in* THE COURT OF LAST RESORT: MENTAL ILLNESS AND THE LAW 110-33 (Carol A. B. Warren ed. 1982).

106. *See, e.g.*, Stephen J Morse, *A Preference for Liberty: The Case Against Involuntary Commitment of the Mentally Disordered*, 70 CAL. L. REV. 54, 106 (1982).

107. For a more detailed assessment of these medicolegal tensions within the

stake in treatment refusal deliberations is the configuration of paternalism in psychiatric justice.[108]

The relationship between "not refusing treatment" and "not receiving treatment" is also worth noting. The semantical possibilities at this intersection include "contemplated treatment" or more likely "negotiated treatment." The latter option is more probable given that the binary value "assent" implies some active engagement with the process of drug therapy intervention. Identifying negotiated treatment as the meaning between the two values in binary opposition is based on locating a value that is less than assenting to treatment, but more than not receiving any treatment at all.

Similar to our previous analysis, what is striking about the oppositional terms and the deeper structure of signification embedded at their semantic intersection is that the logic of negotiation conveys a certain positive appreciation for the parties involved. To negotiate with someone is to accept to his/her competency or, at the very least, to recognize his/her capacity for the self-representation of interests. The absence of such an acknowledgment is to convey, implicitly, that the party in question is not able to bargain or arbitrate on one's own behalf.

As the holdings in *Washington v. Harper*[109] and *Perry v. Louisiana*[110] reflect, competency is an important marker for adjudicating the rights of mentally ill prisoners, including their possible execution.[111] What we underscore, however, is that by teasing out the deeper structure of meaning in the "not refusing treatment" and "not receiving treatment" binary opposition, we can locate the conspicuous disappearance of this significant matter. Indeed, what we notice is that, while the U.S. Supreme Court contemplates one's constitutional right to exercise treatment, there appears on an unconscious level a conviction that the prisoner's competency does not exist and that, therefore, one's capacity to negotiate treatment is not even a justifiable possibility. Again, the proof of this statement stems from the absence of "negotiated treatment" as a viable consideration in right to refuse treatment deliberations.[112]

---

contemporary history of institutionalization, *see* ARRIGO, *supra* note 6, at 8-23.

108. *See* CONTOURS, *supra* note 7, at 129-174. For a detailed application in the related civil commitment arena, *see* Bruce A. Arrigo, *Paternalism, Civil Commitment, and Illness Politics: Assessing the Current Debate and Outlining a Future Direction*, 7 J. L. & HEALTH 131, 131-67 (1992/1993) [hereinafter *Paternalism*].

109. 494 U.S. 210 (1990).

110. 498 U.S. 38 (1990).

111. We examine this notion much more systematically in our structural legal semiotic examination of the sign of competency. *See infra* notes 112-122 and accompanying text.

112. The history of this perspective in diverse mental health contexts is substan-

B. Structural Legal Semiotics and the Sign of Competency

DIAGRAM 3: THE SIGN OF COMPETENCY AND THE SEMIOTIC SQUARE

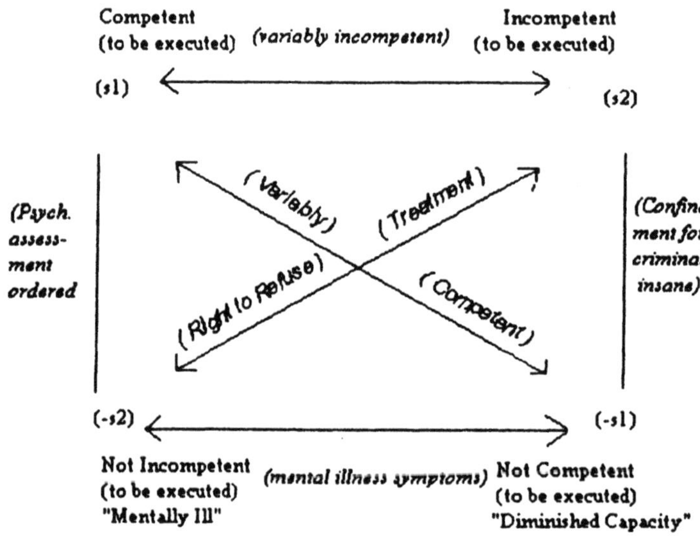

Diagram 3 provides a structural representation of the sign "competency." We note that the four corners of the semiotic square include specific values in binary opposition as contraries or contradictions. Starting with the upper-left hand corner, the "s1" value is "competent." The opposite of competent is "incompetent," identified in the upper-right hand corner as "s2." The negation of incompetent (the "-s2" term) is "not incom-

tial. *See generally* ANDREW SCULL, SOCIAL ORDER/MENTAL DISORDER: ANGLO-AMERICAN PSYCHIATRY IN HISTORICAL PERSPECTIVE (1989); GERALD N. GROB, MENTAL INSTITUTIONS IN AMERICA: SOCIAL POLICY TO 1875 (1973); GERALD N. GROB, MENTAL ILLNESS AND AMERICAN SOCIETY, 1875-1940 (1983);, DAVID ROTHMAN, THE DISCOVERY OF THE ASYLUM (1971); DAVID ROTHMAN, CONSCIENCE AND CONVENIENCE: THE ASYLUM AND ITS ALTERNATIVES IN PROGRESSIVE AMERICA (1980). For a more medicolegal analysis, *see generally* Insanity, *supra* note 95; *see also* John E. Myers, *Involuntary Civil Commitment of the Mentally Ill: A System in Need of Change*, 29 VILLANOVA L. REV. 367, 367-433 (1993/1994). For public policy orientation, *see generally* JOHN LAFOND & MARY DURHAM, BACK TO THE ASYLUM: THE FUTURE OF MENTAL HEALTH POLICY IN THE UNITED STATES (1992); RAEL JEAN ISAAC & VIRGINIA C. ARMAT, MADNESS IN THE STREETS: HOW PSYCHIATRY AND THE LAW ABANDONED THE MENTALLY ILL (1990) [hereinafter MADNESS]. For a philosophical and psycholegal evaluation, *see supra* notes 6-7 and accompanying text.

petent," located in the lower left-hand corner. One who is not incompetent is still less than competent to be executed. The person is simply mentally ill. The negation of "competent" is "not competent," situated in the lower right-hand corner as the "-s1" value. One who is not competent is less than incompetent; the person's capacity is merely diminished. There are a series of semantical relationships produced from the interaction of the contraries and contradictions. Similar to our structural legal semiotic investigation of the sign "treatment," we consider the more evident associations and then address those connections that are less apparent.[113]

The effects of joining the term "not incompetent" (i.e., mentally ill) with the value "incompetent," generate the "right to refuse treatment" outcome. In this binary relationship, we understand that something more than mental illness and something less than incompetency is required to fill the semantic chain of meaning. In the context of mentally disordered death row prisoners who might be found incompetent, the only plausible outcome is the invocation of treatment refusal. This semantical meaning is consistent with the holding in *Ford*,[114] where the Court concluded that mentally disordered prisoners had a right to refuse drug therapy (i.e. treatment) given the Eighth Amendment's prohibition on cruel and unusual punishment.

The association between the value "competent" and "not incompetent" provides additional information regarding the Court's understanding of mentally disordered prisons on death row. The identified semantic possibility must reflect something more than mental illness while not aligning

113. We do not, however, address the less noteworthy relationships. For example, the oppositional terms "competent" and "not competent" yield the meaning "variably competent." The oppositional values "competent" and "incompetent" produce the semantic meaning "variably incompetent." What these relationships suggest is that the Court esteems more totalizing understandings for the sign of competency. In other words, precisely because the Court does not recognize shades of competency or degrees of incompetency in its decision making capacity, it can only interpret and validate behavior that falls into this "either or" context. *See* CONTOURS, *supra* note 7, at 177-80. The result is that an assortment of differences (within the competency and incompetency constructs) remains concealed, glossed over, and repressed as outside the juridical sphere. Thus, the possibility for promoting and codifying alternative readings of the law and psychiatric justice are denied. For an analysis of this very issue in the context of community-based treatment for the mentally disabled, *see Logic*, *supra* note 38, at 23-29. We note further that the Court's inability to recognize how competency and incompetency occur on different continua parallels our previous semiotic assessment on the relationship between the binary oppositions "treatment assent" and "not receiving treatment." *See supra* notes 109-110 and accompanying text.

114. Ford v. Wainwright, 477 U.S. 399 (1986). *See also supra* notes 20-34 and accompanying text.

itself entirely with the competency to be executed term. One plausible interpretation is the request for a psychological assessment to review competency. Again, we see how the semiotic grid produces meanings that naturally follow from the play of language contained within the semiotic square. In this particular instance, we see how the "unconscious rationality" in law is made manifest by returning to the logical play of oppositional values. The deep structure of clinical intervention (i.e., psychological assessment) materializes in the manifest structure of legal discourse (i.e., a competency evaluation).[115]

The relationship between the oppositional terms "not incompetent" and "not competent" produces some interesting results as well. The exchange of values here indicates that the semantical interpretation must generate something less than full blown mental illness and something more than diminished capacity. Given that the context for utilizing the semiotic square focuses on the potential death row execution of mentally disordered prisoners, one possibility is mental illness symptoms. This meaning obtains because characteristics of illness are not synonymous with a diagnosable disorder. Further, what is typically subsumed under the legal construct diminished capacity is a specified cataloging of clinical traits.

The hidden assumption at the crossroads of this binary opposition is the esteem afforded clinical judgements by legal decision brokers. Indeed, although in recent times the U.S. Supreme Court has demonstrated ongoing deference to the wisdom of psychiatry and mental health practitioners in matters related to criminal and civil mental health law,[116] such consideration comes at an appreciable price for prisoners and patients.[117] In

115. What is identified in the semiotic square as a clinical matter (psychological discourse) becomes a juridical matter (legal discourse) when the semantic meaning of assessment is translated into the grammar of competency. *See* LAW, *supra* note 65, at 110-11.

116. *See supra* note 38 and accompanying text.

117. The logic of legal deference implies an acceptance of psychiatry's understanding of mental illness. Psychiatry generally endorses a disease model; that is, people with diagnoses are identified as "ill" and not "well." This logic is consistent with the medical imperative in which sickness is presumed, regardless of intervening anomalies. *See* INSANITY, *supra* note 112, at 45-103. Moreover, psychiatry argues that treatment, in the form of anti-psychotic medication, can produce efficacious results. *See Logic*, *supra* note 38, at 10-11. In response to these clinical observations, the Court system and/or legal tribunals assign a presumption of validity to these diagnostic statements. *See id.*, at 37 n.10; *see, e.g.*, Youngberg v. Romeo, 457 U.S. 307 (1982), in which Justice Powell concluded that there is no reason to believe that the wisdom of judges and juries is any more accurate in such matters than the wisdom of mental health experts. *See id.* at 322-23. Regrettably, however, "[t]he best available evidence shows . . . that, at a very general level, providing [drug] therap[y] to mentally ill individuals is better than doing nothing

short, many persons cycle in and out of institutional settings without appropriate care,[118] receive inadequate placements in the community,[119] or succumb to bouts of chronic and persistent homelessness,[120] resulting, on occasion, in death.[121]

We note once again that this deep structure of meaning is brought to the fore by working within the parameters of the semiotic grid. Psychological discourse (i.e., symptoms of mental illness) gives rise to legal discourse (i.e., the jargon of clinical judgement as presumptively valid).[122] Further,

---

at all." Mary L. Durham & John Q. LaFond, *A Search for the Missing Premise of Involuntary Therapeutic Commitment: Effective Treatment of the Mentally Ill*, 40 RUTGERS L. REV. 303, 356 (1988).

118. This phenomenon is known as "revolving door" institutionalization. The nature of involuntary civil commitment laws are such that one can only be confined as long as the person poses a threat of danger to oneself and/or to others. Once those symptoms giving rise to psychiatric hospitalization dissipate, mental health law requires that the person be released from confinement. Although release typically includes a discharge plan with outpatient therapy and medication, if the plan is not followed it can lead to the re-appearance of those very symptoms that precipitated involuntary hospitalization. This process repeats itself such that the cycle of care is revolving. *See Logic*, *supra* note 38, at 14; *see generally* ISAAC & ARMAT, *supra* note 112.

119. The question here is twofold: (1) is the locus of care least intrusive *see e.g.*, Lake v. Cameron, 364 F. 2d 657, 660 (D.C. Cir 1966), *cert. denied*, 382 U.S. 863 (1966); and (2) is the locus of care least confining, *see, e.g.*, Donald H. J. Hermann, *Autonomy, Self-Determination, the Right of Involuntarily Committed Persons to Refuse Treatment, and the Use of Substituted Judgement in Medication Decisions Involving Incompetent Persons*, 13 INT'L J. L. & PSYCHIATRY 361, 382-84 (1990). As Arrigo contends, "[t]hese matters challenge clinical judgements regarding what constitutes the most effective psychiatric intervention, and medical and legal decisions about where that intervention can best be administered." *Paternalism*, *supra* note 108, at 151-52. As a practical matter, however, "some psychiatrically disabled persons wind up in welfare hotels [and] poorly maintained personal care and boarding homes." CONTOURS, *supra* note 7 at 13.

120. *See, e.g.*, H. RICHARD LAMB, THE HOMELESS MENTALLY ILL: A TASK FORCE REPORT OF THE AMERICAN PSYCHIATRIC ASSOCIATION (1984); CONTOURS, *supra* note 7, at 102-04. As Isaac and Armat contend, "[m]any of our modern institutions for the mentally ill exist in the open air: parks, alleys, vacant lots, and steam grates on our city pavements." ISAAC & ARMAT, *supra* note 112, at 1.

121. There are various types of psychiatric confinement "casualties." *See* CONTOURS, *supra* note 7, at 104-15. The most extreme is the loss of life suffered at the hands of ineffective and inefficient medicolegal decision making and policy. For a representative illustration of this particular casualty phenomenon, *see id.* at 105-08.

122. *See supra* note 115 and accompany text. A related issue, especially in the context of treatment refusal cases, is the legal doctrine of "substituted judgement." *See In re* Richard Roe III, 421 NE.2d 40 (Mass. 1982), for an application to an actively psychotic and dangerous mentally ill person. *See, e.g.*, *In re* Quinlan, 355

as we indicated, the practical effect of this unconscious semiotic activity has been the spawning of a panopoly of civil and criminal dilemmas in mental health law and policy.[123]

C. Legal Deconstructionism and the Sign of Treatment

While the structuralist approach employs binary oppositions to understand how meaning is *generated* from within non-referential parameters of discourse, legal deconstructionism exposes the free play of differences and dependencies within hierarchical oppositions. Similar to our structural legal semiotic inquiry, we address the sign of treatment and competency independently. Along the way, we comment on where and how legal deconstructionism offers insight not contained in a more doctrinaire analysis of (mental health) law.

1. Reversal of Hierarchies

In the context of incompetent prisoners on death row, the sign of treatment includes the binary values "receiving treatment" and "refusing treatment." To "treat" someone or something means to look upon another in a particular manner. It is to hold oneself out to another in a specified way. To receive treatment, then, implies that the one who confers such an offering does so from within a unique perspective. But to treat someone is also to consign a reward; it is to regard the recipient as special or worthy of some gift. We convey this sentiment in such expressions as, "*How about I treat you to lunch.*" In medical discourse, however, the one who receives attention is regarded as ill.[124] Thus, the treater comports him or herself as a manager of illness; that is, as the one who treats the sick party to relief, to comfort, and to cure. It follows, then, that the dominant value ("receiving treatment") assumes its position because medical intervention is understood to give the gift of reparation: repairing, remedying, correcting illness and disease.

In the instance of psychiatric treatment, the same logic applies. The person who receives medical care and drug therapy is regarded as diseased

---

A. 2d 647 (N.J. 1976), *cert. denied sub. nom.*; *In re* Storar, 420 N.E.2d 63 (N.Y. 1981), *cert. denied*, 454 U.S. 858 (1981), for the relationship of substituted judgement in "right to die" cases. "Substituted judgement allows decision makers (the courts or state agents) to substitute their own psychiatric theories or preferences for those of an incompetent person [and c]ourts depend on this doctrine." *Logic*, *supra* 38, at 11.

123. *See* CONTOURS, *supra* note 7, at 47-94.

124. *See supra* note 115 and accompanying text; *see also supra* note 112 and accompanying text; SCHEFF, *supra* note 96 and accompanying text.

(and dangerous) and in need of special care.[125] The gift of treatment intends the elimination of suffering and pain. But here the treater makes an erroneous leap on two fronts. First, the logic of the gift is built around the discourse of reciprocity.[126] Second, the one who bestows treatment does so on the basis of presuming to know what gift is in the recipient's best interest.[127]

What is troubling about the first misstep is that the treat or award of drug therapy creates, intended or not, a debt of gratitude or reciprocation in the recipient. We convey this sentiment in such expressions as: "*Since you treated me to lunch yesterday, let me treat you to lunch today.*"[128] In addition, the giver of the gift is heartened by the bestowal of the treat; "consciously and explicitly" pleased for her or his display of generosity.[129]

---

125. *Logic*, *supra* note 38, at 11-12.

126. The notion of gift giving and the theme of reciprocity are traceable to the work of Emerson. *See* RALPH WALDO EMERSON, ESSAYS & LECTURES (Joel Porte ed. 1983). Emerson indicates that the problem with the gift is that it: (1) holds itself out as a threat to one's independence; (2) leads to a real or implied contractual debt; and (3) produces unwanted feelings of inferiority in the receiver and dependence in the giver. *See id.* In short, the logic of the gift represents a system of exchange. *See generally* THE SOCIOLOGY OF GEORG SIMMEL (Kurt H. Wolff ed., trans. 1950). For additional commentary of the concept of the gift and gift giving, *see generally* FREDERICK W. NIETZSCHE, THUS SPOKE ZARATHUSTRA: A BOOK FOR ALL AND NONE (Walter Kaufmann trans. 1995); MARCEL MAUSS, THE GIFT: THE FORM AND REASON FOR EXCHANGE IN ARCHAIC SOCIETIES (W. D. Halls trans. 1990); GEORGE BATAILLE, THE ACCURSED SHARE: AS ESSAY ON GENERAL ECONOMY, VOLUME 1: CONSUMPTION (Robert Hurley trans. (1988); DECONSTRUCTION IN A NUTSHELL: A CONVERSATION WITH JACQUES DERRIDA (John Caputo ed. 1997) [hereinafter DECONSTRUCTION].

127. We also note a third fallacy embedded in the gift of treatment. The decision to intervene, forcibly or otherwise, in the form of drug therapy is based on the recipient's overt speech-thought-behavior and not on the basis of identifiable contagion. There are a myriad of problems associated with this approach, and the literature is replete with opponents commenting upon them. *See* Scheff, *supra* note 96, at 163-74; SZASZ, *supra* note 96; *see also supra* note 6-7 and accompanying text. What is observed is then typically catalogued and traced to specific mental disorders through the use of psychometric tests and other clinical instruments producing a "treatable" diagnosis. *See generally* AMERICAN PSYCHIATRIC ASSOCIATION, DIAGNOSTIC AND STATISTIC MANUAL OF MENTAL DISORDERS (4th ed. 1994).

128. The question arises whether it is ever possible to offer a "pure" gift; that is, whether one can treat without expecting to receive. According to Caputo, this gift-giving "could take place only if everything happened below the level of conscious intentionality, where no one intends to give anything to anyone and no one is intentionally conscious of receiving anything." DECONSTRUCTION, *supra* note 126, at 147.

129. *See id.* at 141.

Indeed, although offered without expectation of explicit gratitude,[130] the gift of treatment simply fortifies and nourishes the narcissism of the giver.[131] Thus, we come to the first paradox of conferring and receiving treatment: the one who treats, instead of giving, receives, and the one who is treated, instead of receiving, is in debt.

What this exchange produces is the circular economy of reappropriation and reciprocation. Treatment, as a gift, serves a purpose. It signifies narcissism disguised by the pretense of generosity ("*let me treat you!*"), or it represents the anticipation of exchange masked by the facade of beneficence ("*I can treat you if you let me*"). In both instances, the implication is the same. The person who gives believes he or she has something of currency: an award the other desires. Indeed, the consignor harbors the conviction, implicitly or otherwise, that the offering, much like any present, is a gift worth possessing.[132]

This conviction gives rise to the other mistaken, or at least questionable, belief. When the justification for the gift of treatment is that the recipient's interests are best served by the award, the one who gives exercises power.[133] The presumption is that the receiver of the award will be treated

130. The theme of gift giving appears in the work of Nietzsche, including the context of "gratitude and revenge." FREDERICK NIETZSCHE, HUMAN, ALL TOO HUMAN 46 (Marian Farber & Stephen Lehmann trans. 1996).

131. For an historical overview of the gift, including a Derridean account of the economy of narcissism in the circle of exchange and reciprocation, *see generally* THE LOGIC OF THE GIFT: TOWARD AN ETHIC OF GENEROSITY (Allan Schrift ed.1997).

132. We recognize that there are those mentally confined or treated persons who welcome the gift of treatment or, retrospectively, come to appreciate it. In some mental health circles this has been coined "thank you" therapy. *See generally* ALAN A. STONE, MENTAL HEALTH AND LAW: A SYSTEM IN TRANSITION (1975). But there are also those who do not welcome the gift of treatment. *See* James C. Beck & Edward A. Golowka, *A Study of Enforced Treatment in Relation to Stone's "Thank You" Theory*, 6 BEHAV. SCI. & L. 559, 565 (1988) (no evidence of the "thank you" thesis in 62% of the cases where patients were committed against their will). For general commentary on assent notwithstanding initial refusal, *see* Kane et al., *Attitudinal Changes of Involuntarily Committed Patients Following Treatment*, 40 ARCHIVES GEN. PSYCHIATRY 374, 374-77 (1983); *see also* Schwartz et al., *Autonomy and the Right to Refuse Treatment: Patients' Attitudes After Involuntary Medication* 39 HOSP. & COMMUNITY PSYCHIATRY 1049, 1049-54 (1988).

133. Power is also implied when the treat involves reciprocity. Once you bestow your gift, I can never completely repay you. Even if I return to you many more gifts, your initial act of generosity creates a chasm of reciprocation that can never be filled. Even though it may remain unspoken or repressed, this is because we both know that it was you who treated me first. *See* DECONSTRUCTION, *supra* note 126 and accompanying text.

to mental health pain relief and to the reparation of psychiatric illness.[134] Under these conditions, refusing the gift of treatment ostensibly makes no sense.

Rejecting the gift of treatment, however, is not so much a constitutional exercise of one's right,[135] as much as an existential statement about the will to forfeit receipt of an unwanted gift. This waiver of the award not only destabilizes the exercise of the giver's power over the receiver, it relinquishes the would-be gift recipient from the possibility of indebtedness and reciprocity. Thus, the giver's treat is returned not because it fails (potentially) to serve the best interests of the individual, but because even if it did, it still fails to have the same currency for the receiver that it does for the giver. This, then, is the second paradox of receiving and refusing treatment: the giver, instead of offering something of benefit for which the receiver is obliged, gives something that is unwanted for which the re-

---

134. Following the state court decision in *Riggins*, the government's assertion of the necessity for involuntary treatment of a criminal pre-trial and trial defendant must be based on two factors: (1) a compelling state interest; and (2) the means used to achieve the state's objective are necessary. Failing to meet these conditions requires the government to pursue a "less intrusive means" for maintaining its interests. *See* State v. Riggings, 808 P.2d 535, 540 (Nev. 1991). *See also* Bruce Winick, *Psychotropic Medication and Competency to Stand Trial*, 3 AM. B. FOUND. RES. J. 769, 813-14 (1977) [hereinafter *Psychotropic*]. We note further, however, that a "less intrusive means" does not imply the cessation of drug therapy altogether.

> [T]he 'less intrusive means' standard should be read to require that medication be discontinued for a reasonable period of time in order to allow a determination to be made concerning whether the defendant's competency can be maintained in the absence of medication . . . . If the defendant reverts to an incompetent state during a trial period without medication, the 'less intrusive means' standard then would require that other less intrusive treatment approaches be considered before medication is resumed.

WINICK, *supra* note 1, at 320-21. In the case of some patients, the Court has even considered "drug-free holidays" as a way to assess medication necessity. *See, e.g.*, Rogers v. Omin, 634 F.2d 650, 656 (1st Cir. 1980); Rennie v. Klein, 462 F. Supp. 11131, 1146 (D.N.J. 1978). The literature is replete with clinical studies questioning the efficacy of the "cure" of drug treatment. *See, e.g.*, George Gardos & Jonathon D. Cole, *Maintenance Antipsychotic Therapy: Is the Cure Worse than the Disease*, 133 AM. J. PSYCHIATRY 32, 34-36 (1976).

135. For some examples of the constitutional argument, *see* Bruce Winick, *The Right to Refuse Mental Health Treatment: A First Amendment Perspective*, 34 U. MIAMI L. REV. 1 (1979-80) [hereinafter *Perspective*]; Bruce Winick, *New Directions in the Right to Refuse Mental Health Treatment: The Implications of Riggins v. Nevada*, 2 WM. & MARY BILL RTS. J. 205, 205-37 (1993) [hereinafter *New Directions*]; Bruce Winick, *Legal Limitations on Correctional Therapy and Research*, 65 MINN. L. REV. 331, 331-420 (1981) [hereinafter *Legal Limits*]; Alexander D. Brooks, *The Right to Refuse Antipsychotic Medications: Law and Policy*, 39 RUTGERS L. REV. 339, 339-76 (1987).

ceiver is defiled.[136] In short, according to the gift recipient, treatment is not a gift worth possessing. Behind the presentation of the treat is an absence which the receiver recognizes and, therefore, rejects.

2. Differance and Trace

The deconstructive interplay of the signs "*receiving treatment*" and "*refusing treatment*" demonstrates how mutually interdependent these values in hierarchical opposition truly are. The gift of drug therapy depends on its refusal in order for the award to convey its value. Conversely, the rejection of the offering takes on meaning only in relation to what the oppositional term signifies. Thus, neither value position can be foundational or privileged; rather, the terms can only express thought and action through the co-emergence of meaning situated in their intrinsic mutuality. It is this mutuality which gives the terms their identity, and it is through this mutuality that one meaning of Derrida's notion of "differance" appears. Put simply, each value defers to the other in the sense of being fundamentally dependent on the other.[137]

The inversion of hierarchies, then, deconstructs the metaphysics of presence (i.e., *receiving treatment* as the dominant value). What is given is devoid of substance for the receiver and, thus, rendered an absence. But here, too, we note that this activity of de-centering the gift of treatment does not elevate its refusal to a position of status. Indeed, while the two terms are differentiated from each other (a second meaning of Derrida's "differance"), precisely because we articulate one of the values in hierarchical opposition, we announce the other. That is to say, when we speak of refusing treatment we always and already speak of receiving it and vice versa. In deferring the unspoken term, we still, unconsciously and prethematically, make its absence present.[138] This is the third meaning of Derrida's concept of "differance."

We note further, however, the relationship between "differance" and the trace at work in the sign of treatment. Through the performative depend-

136. For example, in some instances, the death row prisoner is characterized as not making a competent, knowledgeable, voluntary choice to exercise treatment refusal. For a consideration of these matters, *see* WINICK, *supra* note 1, at 347-65.

137. Balkin, *supra* note 10, at 764-67; *see also supra* note 89 and accompanying text.

138. This is exactly the constitutional and policy debate, implicit or not, in mental health law circles when the right to refuse treatment doctrine is invoked. For example, when medication refusal was invoked in *Harper*, the limits of exercising this right were expressly ascertained. The Court reasoned that the prisoner's protection against bodily intrusiveness could not be sustained when the forced treatment was in his best medical interest and when it protected others from a risk of danger he posed while not medicated. *See supra* note 37 and accompanying text.

encies and differences contained within the sign, each term not only contains the trace of the other within it, but the remnant of the other is that which makes possible the deconstruction of the hierarchical oppositions.[139] As previously explored, the concealed, though lingering, trace of "receiving treatment" in "refusing treatment" and of "refusing treatment" in "receiving treatment" demonstrates the undecidability of meaning in legal discourse and decision making.[140]

3. Arguments That Undo Themselves

Supporting the dominant value of "receiving treatment" is an argument that undoes itself on two fronts. First, the value specified for this sign (i.e., the receipt of psychiatric illness reparation as a gift worth possessing) is really not a reward at all. If anything, it is an encumbrance for the one who rejects it. Moreover, that which does not benefit the recipient, even if it is believed to do so by the giver, is really not a gift worth giving. At best, it can only narcissistically satisfy the one who does the giving. Indeed, the receiver of treatment is indebted and must give, and the giver of treatment is aggrandized and must receive. Thus, the justification of treatment (as a gift of pain management or relief) is undone because it can never convey or accomplish what it intends. Forcibly medicating, as a gift, becomes an act of refutation. The giver refuses to accept the other's right to reject treatment. As an act of resistance, we see, then, that the limitations of giving treatment are much like the limitations of refusing treatment. Both are expressions of non-acceptance: neither party welcomes the other's point of view.

The second logic of justification that is ungrounded with the sign of "receiving treatment" is that it is better to refuse that to receive. By refusing unwanted drug therapy one is not indebted to the giver. By resisting uninvited medical intervention the economy of exchange, of reciprocation and re-appropriation, is not mobilized. By averting the obligation of gratitude, one destabilizes the power the giver would otherwise have over the course of the recipient's future. Exercising treatment refusal, then, is a gift waiting to be received. The refuser longs for it to be embraced by all those willing to acknowledge the refutation. In particular, the treater is invited to accept the refuter's gift of autonomy and self-

139. *See supra* note 92 and accompanying text.

140. *See* SPEECH, *supra* note 74, at 157-62. "Each sign in the chain of meaning is somehow scored over or traced through with all the others, to form a complex tissue which is never exhaustible." MICHAEL SARUP, AN INTRODUCTORY GUIDE TO POST-STRUCTURALISM AND POSTMODERNISM 36 (1989). For an application in the realm of feminist jurisprudence, *see* Drucilla Cornell, *The Philosophy of the Limit: System Theory and Feminist Legal Reform*, *in* DECONSTRUCTION AND THE POSSIBILITY OF JUSTICE 68-91 (D. Cornell et al., ed. 1992).

determination. Of course, like all gifts, it is better to refuse than to receive. This activity once again returns us to Derrida's notion of "differance," trace, and the inversion of hierarchies.

D. Legal Deconstructionism and the Sign of Competency

1. Reversal of Hierarchies

In the context of right to refuse treatment matters for death row prisoners, the sign of competency includes the values "competent to be executed" and "incompetent to be executed." The dominant term assumes its position because it endorses and generally implies that one makes a choice knowingly,[141] rationally,[142] and reasonably.[143] We note, however, that the mechanisms or standards by which competency is defined and/or operationalized vary enormously.[144] Thus, to be competent, under the law, is to be qualified or to be fit. It is the capacity to make one's own decisions, regardless of how ridiculous the choices appear.[145]

But such competency is itself undecided;[146] that is, there is no guarantee when one objects to medical intervention that the refusal itself might not get interpreted as a display of incapacity or unfitness.[147] Indeed, although the medicolegal community may classify a particular request as "grossly incompetent," the plea can be deemed permissible in other mental health treatment contexts.[148] Competency, then, is already, and to some extent, incompetency. It is, in part, the absence of qualification and authorization to make knowing, reasonable, rational decisions. Interestingly, this is

141. PAUL APPELBAUM ET AL., INFORMED CONSENT: LEGAL THEORY AND CLINICAL PRACTICE (1987).

142. *See also* Alan Meisel & Loren H. Roth, *Toward an Informed Discussion of Informed Consent: A Review and Critique of the Empirical Studies*, 25 ARIZ. L. REV. 265, 284 (1983).

143. *See, e.g.*, THOMAS GRISSO, EVALUATING COMPETENCIES: FORENSIC ASSESSMENTS AND INSTRUMENTS 314 (1986); Paul Appelbaum & Loren Roth, *Competency to Consent to Research*, 39 ARCHIVES GEN. PSYCHIATRY 951, 951-53 (1982); Harold I. Schwartz & Loren H. Roth, *Informed Consent and Competency in Psychiatric Practice*, 8 PSYCHIATRY AND THE L. 409, 415 (1989).

144. *See* WINICK, *supra* note 1, at 349 (exploring several tests for competency).

145. "If patients are competent, their treatment decisions must be respected, even if they refuse treatment, no matter how foolish their decisions appear to be." *Id.* at 348.

146. *See supra* note 140 and accompanying text.

147. To be clear, "[o]bjecting patients retain a qualified right to refuse the intervention in question." WINICK, *supra* note 1, at 351.

148. *See id.* at 352. *But see* Zinermon v. Burch 494 U.S. 113, 118 (1990) (request for psychiatric treatment was denied a patient who thought that such hospitalization amounted to being in heaven).

what gives incompetency its specialized and differentiated meaning.

Similarly, however, the binary value "incompetent to be executed" is not a privileged term, given the limits of its hierarchical opposition. To be incompetent does not preclude the articulation of certain desires (e.g., the refusal of unwanted or forced drug therapy). The resistance is, presumably, a comment on the invasiveness of the medical intervention. Moreover, it is clear that some mentally disordered people exercise this right, receive forced treatment over objection, and, once restored to "competency," still adamantly profess disapproval with the coerced medication in the first place.[149] This returns us to the fuzzy logic distinguishing competency and incompetency in treatment refusal matters for death row prisoners. In short, when a person says no to forced treatment both before and after competency restoration, can it be said that the individual was ever really incompetent? The interpretation most favorable to coerced treatment proponents is that the person was, to some extent, competent and incompetent simultaneously. Indeed, the patient was at least sufficiently fit and qualified to make a choice about refusing treatment.

In addition, we note that the refutation, if truly made incompetently, can only proceed from some measure of competence.[150] Here, then, we see the discursive feedback loop embedded in the "competent to be executed" and "incompetent to be executed" values. In law, the significations we assign to one term mutually depend on the meanings we specify for the other term. What we take to be a dominant value (i.e., "competence") is itself dependent on the concept it was privileged over (i.e., "incompetence"). But this value ("incompetence") can only take on social use and value if based on its binary opposite ("competence"). Neither term is foundational. The mutuality of both values is what makes thought and action pertaining to death row execution matters possible.

2. Differance and the Trace

Given the mutuality of reliances situated within the binary terms for the sign of competence, we see how Derrida's notion of "differance" demarcates the oppositional relations. "Competent to be executed" and "incompetent to be executed" defer to one another in that the presence of one

149. *See* Alan Miesel, *The Exceptions to the Informed Consent Doctrine: Striking a Balance Between Competing Values in Medical Decisionmaking*, 1979 WIS. L. REV. 413, 425 (1979).

150. One general standard balances the value of the individual's freedom to choose, albeit potentially wrong, against society's interest in ensuring that such choices are not harmful to others, albeit largely paternalistic. "The justification presumably is that the injury caused by denying such [mentally ill patients] autonomy would be exceeded by the harm produced by honoring the choices of incompetent people." WINICK, *supra* note 1, at 348.

value makes the absence of the other manifest, and vice versa. This represents one meaning of "differance." In addition, the force of the terms in the mental health law arena signals their differentiation. For example, an incompetent individual who asserts a right to treatment refusal given impending execution can, under certain circumstances, still be sentenced to death.[151] This is the second reading of "differance." Finally, the two values retain identity only because of the performative nature of differences and dependencies unconsciously activated through a deconstructive critique. Again, situated within each term is the trace of the other. In other words, given that each value contains the remains of the other within it, the logic of "differance" and the deconstruction of hierarchical oppositions is discoverable. This is the third interpretation of "differance."

3. Arguments That Undo Themselves

Ungrounding the justification for the dominant value "competency to be executed" is not difficult to discern. Indeed, arguments for endorsing the privileged term really amount to supporting, albeit temporarily and incompletely, the value that is absent. As we have already indicated, to be competent is also to be incompetent; that is, to not act knowingly, rationally, and reasonably in all instances. We come to this conclusion because: (1) the standards by which competency is defined remain somewhat inconsistent and variable; (2) there are times when the courts endorse requests that border on or may be acts of incompetence;[152] and (3) there are times when restoration of competence through forced treatment over refusal, does not alter the patient's desire to be free from unwanted medication in the first instance.[153] In each instance, the presence of "competent to be executed" as the dominant value is eroded by what it directs us to; namely, the value of "incompetent to be executed." Once again, though, the logic of deconstruction in relation to arguments that undo themselves is not to privilege that which heretofore was absent. Indeed, the inversion of the hierarchy is possible only because incompetence is a value that can be measured against, although momentarily and provisionally, its binary opposite. Thus, we have the play of differences and dependencies at work revealing mutual interdependence.

V. CRIMINAL MENTAL HEALTH CONFINEMENT: FUTURE THEORY, POLICY, AND PRACTICE

The preceding application exposed the principles of structural legal

151. State v. Perry, 610 So.2d 746, 751-52 (La. 1992).
152. *See supra* note 148 and accompanying text.
153. *See supra* note 149 and accompanying text.

semiotics and legal deconstructionism to the matter of treatment refusal for incompetent prisoners awaiting execution. The results of our assessment point to a number of implications for theory, policy, and practice. The comments that follow are limited. They merely reflect our overall concern for the plight of mentally disordered prisoners awaiting execution and, therefore, should not be interpreted beyond this scope in mental health law.

The observations described below are also provisional. Our analysis theoretically addressed only two dimension of treatment refusal for mentally ill death row inmates: the sign of treatment and the sign of competency. In order to present a more detailed evaluation of implications, other signs (e.g., mental illness, dangerous, informed consent) would require a careful and systematic exploration. Here, too, we would need to utilize the techniques of critical legal inquiry as previously described.

Of primary importance in our assessment of criminal mental health law is the power of language to shape both thought and action. It would be easy to dismiss the manner in which language modifies, regulates, obfuscates, or transforms decision making. After all, discourse is merely about words and, short of hate speech, words, in and of themselves, do not give rise to harm. We disagree. Language structures thought in ways that are not neutral.[154] Words are value- laden and they privilege certain perspectives at the expense of others. Whether written or spoken, there is always something more that "insists" in discourse. At times, the insistence is a subtle, but forceful, realization that we have failed people, intentionally or not, because their lives remain deeply marred; caught in the crossfire of illness politics.[155] On many fronts, the dilemmas that plague criminal (and civil) mental health systems users are a constant and vivid reminder of how we have abandoned or forgotten them. But words are all we have – incomplete and unsatisfying as they are or can be.

Although philosophically based on different presuppositions, both structural semiotics and deconstructionism return us to the power of words. In the context of treatment refusal for prisoners on death row, the pain experienced through the text of mental health law is real and the harm is equally deep. This is not to imply that there is a concerted institutional effort to undermine constitutional safeguards; rather, it is an observation about the insidious nature of language which often speaks through the one who communicates from within the preconfigured con-

154. *See supra* notes 6-7 and accompanying text; *see also Political History, supra* note 10, at 1517; Tiefenbrun, *supra* note 50, at 91-93.

155. *See* CONTOURS, *supra* note 7, at 148-57 (exploring several civil and criminal contexts in which law and medicine struggle to address adequately the needs and interests of psychiatric patients). *See generally* ISAAC & ARMAT, *supra* note 112.

fines of a specialized grammar like the law.[156]

Incompetent persons suffering from mental illness asserting their treatment refusal right can be executed under specified provisions. This very sentence alone is both illuminating and frightening. What is provocative about the statement is that the United States Supreme Court has, in its unique way, attempted to fashion a public policy that balances competing institutional and individual interests. What is troubling about the assertion is that the Court's response to date has been anything less than satisfying. This is not a knee-jerk response built around a healthy dose of liberal outrage. Rather, it comes from understanding that signs such as "mental illness," incompetence," and "execution," are saturated and cloaked within a multitude of complex and nuanced meanings that ultimately, when decoded, reveal the vast array of hidden contradictions, ambiguities, inconsistencies, dependencies, and differences contained within their usage. As a result, we wonder why the rush to end life through the public policy initiative of capital punishment?

We note, too, that when addressing questions of treatment refusal for incompetent death row inmates, mental health law is considerably informed by ideology.[157] This is a specific reference to unconscious values and unstated assumptions concerning the Court's regard for mentally ill prisoners, their imminent executions, and the systems of which they are a part. Both our structural semiotic and our legal deconstructionist investigations demonstrated where and how the line between law and politics (i.e., ideological viewpoints) is not so clearly demarcated. For example, we witnessed the role of ideology in our structural semiotic exploration of how the Court dismisses degrees of meaning for the binary tension "not refusing treatment" and "not receiving treatment." Embedded within the semantical play of differences, given the discursive constraints of the semiotic square, was the Court's inability to locate "middle ground" solu-

156. This is a reference to the combinatory effects of discourse and subjectivity to mobilize one's desire and to produce, at best, a circumscribed form of knowledge that represents limited understanding of human behavior and social phenomena. *See* LACAN, *supra* note 8, at 25-29. For applications to law and psychiatry, *see generally* Bruce Arrigo, *Transcarceration: Notes on a Psychoanalytically-Informed Theory of Social Practice in the Criminal Justice and Mental Health Systems*, 27 CRIME L. & SOC. CHANGE (1997); Bruce Arrigo, *The Behavior of Law and Psychiatry: Rethinking Knowledge Construction and the Guilty-But-Mentally-Ill Verdict*, 23 CRIM. JUST. & BEHAV. 572, 572-92 (1996).

157. Commenting on the ideological nature of law when informed by deconstruction, Balkin states that "[l]egal doctrines both reflect and regulate social life. The choice of protected rights and of enforcement techniques reflect views, whether obvious or obscure, about social relations. Law tells a story about what people are and should be." Balkin, *supra* note 10, at 761-62. *See also* MILOVANOVIC, *supra* note 8, at 101.

tions (e.g., "negotiated treatment" or "contemplated treatment"). Indeed, the one core value we located was paternalism.[158] While we recognize that identifying this value is certainly not new; the degree to which it is situated as such first and foremost through language, is relatively underdeveloped.[159]

A similar argument about ideological decision making is traceable to how the Court interprets the sign of treatment. The gift of coerced intervention is anything but a precious reward or esteemed value for the recipient. Indeed, the gift of treatment creates an economy of reciprocity. If not derailed by the receiver, it renders the presenter a glorified recipient and the receiver an indebted giver.

Given the structural and performative power of language to unearth concealed meanings and given the ideological core of mental health law on matters of treatment refusal for incompetent prisoners awaiting execution, we recognize the need for new and alternative vistas of meaning to impact medicolegal practices in ways that more fully affirm all those constituencies involved. For example, the operative disease model of psychiatry continues to signify that people are understood most especially on the basis of their identifiable symptoms. The whole of one's treatable identity, then, is reducible to the sum of the dysfunctional parts. This is a deficit model of intervention.[160] In addition, given the deference the legal community bestows upon medicine on matters of psychiatric import, the medicolegal establishment endorses, tacitly or otherwise, a similar approach.

One strategy for overcoming such reductionism comes from discourse analysis. We suggest that persons with mental illness could be described as "psychiatric citizens," "mental health consumers," "users of clinical services," "differently abled," and the like.[161] Remember, if language structures thought in ways that can never be neutral, there are values implied in these signs as well.[162] The question, of course, is how would such a seemingly minor change impact the policy and practice of psychiatric justice?[163]

158. *See supra* notes 106-110 and accompanying text.

159. *But see supra* notes 6-7 and accompanying text (describing various contexts in which language structures both civil and criminal mental health law).

160. *See supra* notes 6-7 and accompanying text.

161. For a more detailed chronicling of observations along these lines, *see* CONTOURS, *supra* note 7, at 175-202.

162. For example, following these descriptions, one interpretation is that persons with psychiatric disorders are active participants in the choices that they make, and in the world around them. This logic (potentially) dispels the myth that they are "sick," "passive," and "incapacitated." CONTOURS, *supra* note 7, at 175-202.

163. Consider how the semiotic square would be recast when using such terms

Terminating the life of a person while on death row is a contentious and vexing social issue. Terminating the life of a person who resists treatment, is found incompetent, and who is then forcibly medicated over objection, is even more disagreeable and complex. Clearly, our project focused less on what mental health confinement law actually says on such matters, and more on what it does not say but potentially means. Therefore, our response did not consider changing or amending the constitutional law as much as it recommended reevaluating the assumptions behind the law's selection of language. This is a necessary first step before criminal confinement decisions in mental health law can be enacted, and, regrettably, it is one that is sorely and repeatedly overlooked. We owe this much to those whose lives hang in the balance. We owe this much to those who seek an end to illness politics. In the final analysis, we owe this much to the future of psychiatric justice.

through the binary oppositions of contradictions and contraries. Consider, as well, what alternative hierarchical oppositions would present themselves when deconstructing the play of differences and dependencies in the newly constituted dominant and repressed values.

Acknowledgments

Dusky v. United States, 362 U.S. 402 (1960): 402-403.
Pate v. Robinson, 383 U.S. 375 (1966): 375-391.
Drope v. Missouri, 420 U.S. 162 (1975): 162-183.
Ford v. Wainwright, 477 U.S. 399 (1986): 399-435.
Penry v. Lynaugh, 492 U.S. 302 (1989): 302-360.
Washington v. Harper, 494 U.S. 210 (1990): 210-258.
Riggins v. Nevada, 504 U.S. 127 (1992): 127-157.
Louisiana v. Perry, 610 So.2d 746 (La. 1992): 746-782.
Godinez v. Moran, 504 U.S. 389 (1993): 389-417.
Cooper v. Oklahoma, 517 U.S. 348 (1996): 348-369.
Wexler, David B. and Winick, Bruce J. "Therapeutic Jurisprudence and Criminal Justice Mental Health Issues." *Mental and Physical Disability Law Reporter* 16 (1992): 225-231. Reprinted with the permission of the American Bar Association, Commission on Mental and Physical Disability Law.
Arrigo, Bruce A. and Williams, Christopher R. "Law, Ideology, and Critical Inquiry: the Case of Treatment Refusal for Incompetent Prisoners Awaiting Execution." *New England Journal on Criminal and Civil Confinement* 25 (1999): 367-412. Reprinted with the permission of the New England School of Law.

For Product Safety Concerns and Information please contact our EU
representative GPSR@taylorandfrancis.com
Taylor & Francis Verlag GmbH, Kaufingerstraße 24, 80331 München, Germany

www.ingramcontent.com/pod-product-compliance
Ingram Content Group UK Ltd.
Pitfield, Milton Keynes, MK11 3LW, UK
UKHW022207190926
475702UK00003B/237
9780815340645